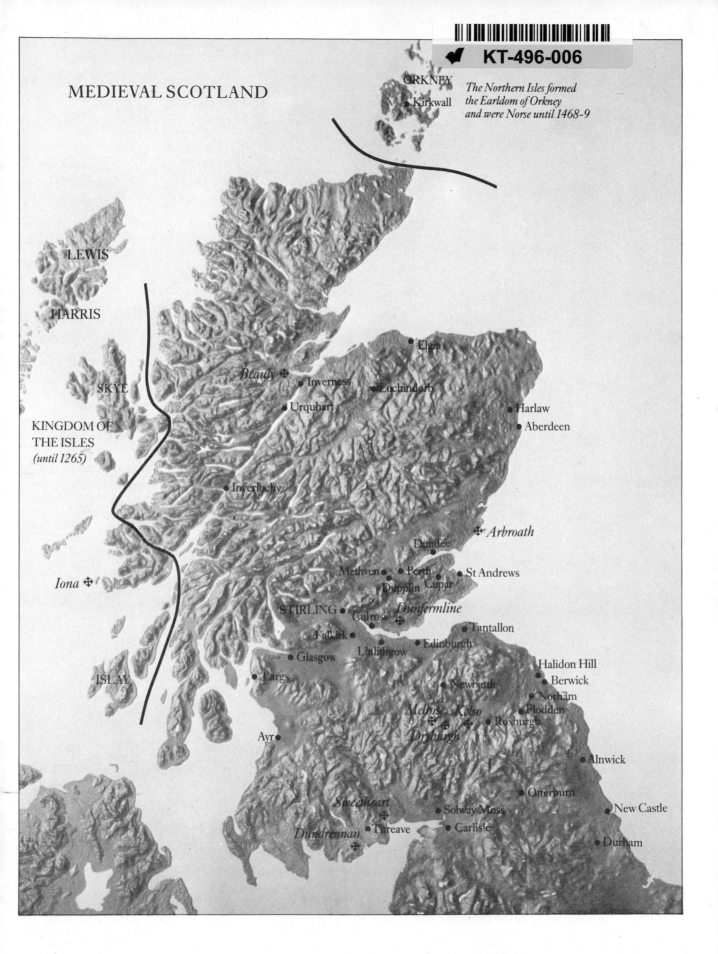

MEDIEVAL SCOTLAND

KT-496-006

The Northern Isles formed the Earldom of Orkney and were Norse until 1468-9

ORKNEY
Kirkwall

LEWIS

HARRIS

SKYE

KINGDOM OF
THE ISLES
(until 1265)

Iona ✠

ISLAY

Elgin

Beauly ✠
Inverness
Lochindorb
Urquhart
Harlaw
Aberdeen

Inverlochy

✠ *Arbroath*

Dundee

Methven Perth
Dupplin Cupar St Andrews
Dunfermline
STIRLING Culross
Tantallon
Falkirk Linlithgow Edinburgh
Glasgow
Halidon Hill
Largs Newbattle Berwick
Norham
Melrose *Kelso* Flodden
Dryburgh Roxburgh
Ayr
Alnwick

Otterburn

Sweetheart New Castle
Solway Moss
Dundrennan Threave Carlisle
Durham

SCOTLAND'S STORY

Six designs for uniting the Scottish and English flags,
commissioned by the monarchy in 1603 when James VI, King of Scotland,
became James I, King of England. (*NLS*)

SCOTLAND'S STORY

A New Perspective

TOM STEEL

COLLINS
8 Grafton Street, London W1

in association with
Channel Four Television Company Limited
and Scottish Television Limited

1984

By the same author

THE LIFE AND DEATH OF ST KILDA

William Collins Sons and Co. Ltd
London · Glasgow · Sydney · Auckland
Toronto · Johannesburg

Steel, Tom
Scotland's story.
1. Scotland – History
I. Title
941.1   DA760

ISBN 0 00 216351 9

First published in Great Britain 1984
© Tom Steel 1984

Photoset in Linotron Ehrhardt by
Rowland Phototypesetting Ltd, Bury St Edmunds, Suffolk
Illustration origination by Gilchrist Bros. Ltd, Leeds
Printed and bound in Great Britain
by William Collins Sons and Co. Ltd, Glasgow.

To Jackie with love and thanks

David, Happy Christmas 1984

with love Anne

Contents

Acknowledgements

Most books are the result of an obsession and *Scotland's Story* is no exception. I have to thank colleagues and friends for helping make mine a reality. William Brown, Deputy Chairman and Managing Director of Scottish Television and his Director of Programmes, David Johnstone, must be thanked for committing resources to make both book and television series as encompassing as they are. Thanks must be given to Scottish Television for allowing me to make use of some hundred and sixty interviews I conducted for the series and for making available the vast collection of photographic reproductions created by the series. The maps in the book are based upon the three-dimensional map commissioned by Scottish Television. I must also thank Jeremy Isaacs for suggesting that I should put, both on screen and paper, the history of the country that is the birthplace of both of us.

The source material of the book has been extensive and varied. Apart from calling upon the published works of modern historians, many of whom are English and have thrown much-needed light on Scottish history, I have also made use of the works of many Canadian, Australian and New Zealand historians, many of whose published works are not readily available in Britain. Some of my sources have been unusual. I must thank my father, who not only brought me up to be proud of my native land but also interested in it, and as editor of *Scotland's Magazine* published many excellent articles about Scotland upon which I have drawn freely.

To put flesh on the bones of historical fact, I have quoted liberally from the works of Scotsmen long since passed. I must thank those publishers who over the centuries have reprinted their works in full or shortened form and thus made their view of the Scotland in which they lived still accessible. I must equally thank the editors of *The Scotsman* and the *Glasgow Herald* who have kept an emigré author informed of his native land for two decades.

I must also thank Caroline Bingham for reading through the manuscript and making many valuable suggestions, in particular, with regard to the earlier chapters. Douglas Matthews is also to be thanked for the hours of work that have provided the book with a comprehensive and intelligent index.

Last and certainly not least I must thank my wife Jackie, who has been a tower of strength these past five years. She has given encouragement when interest waned and put in much hard work to make this book a reality. She has typed, checked, and re-typed the manuscript and ensured that the facts, if not the opinions, in this book are correct.

Introduction

ON 1 MARCH 1979, the Scots voted in a referendum to decide whether they wanted a greater say in how they were ruled. For centuries the people of the north had complained they had been misgoverned from Westminster and although few thought the Labour government's plan for a Scottish Assembly a perfect one, at least it was a chance for the Scots to have some degree of independence.

On a bleak and cold Thursday less than 33 per cent of the Scottish electorate voted Yes. Against the proposed Assembly were 31 per cent. Saddest of all, however, given the history of the Scottish people after the parliamentary union with England in 1707, over 36 per cent did not bother to vote at all. Under pressure from some Scottish MPs, the government had previously agreed that the Assembly would only go ahead if 40 per cent of the electorate were in favour. Devolution was not so much voted out by the Scots, but rather, by a legislative sleight of hand, not voted in. The Scots were to remain North Britons – for the time being.

Perhaps why Scots did what they did in March 1979 is not so remarkable. They have long been made to feel the underdog by the more powerful and numerous English. A severe lack of confidence – some would say inferiority complex – undermines the Scottish nation. The two countries have been rivals for centuries and the English are still wary of their northern neighbours. The prospect of several thousand Scottish football fans invading London creates much the same response now as the news in 1745 that Prince Charles Edward Stewart and his Jacobite army had reached Derby. True the Bank of England today does not panic and there are no rumours that the Royal family plans to quit the country; but tube and train drivers threaten to strike and shopkeepers and publicans in London board up their windows and bolt their doors. Who then are these men of the north who can still put fear into their southern neighbours? For a start, the Scots are not as homogeneous as they would lead you to believe.

Scotland is a country of many peoples. The Lowland Scot is of Anglo-Saxon stock and there is little to distinguish him from his English neighbour apart from his different history. To the north and west, there is the Scotland of the Gaelic Highlander. In the Orkneys and Shetlands, yet another society, more akin to Scandinavia. For centuries Lowland, Highland and Norse Scots were wary of each other. There were bloody battles, yet in time Scots did come to regard themselves as one.

What, then, united them? It was certainly not language. In the Highlands and much of the Western Isles they spoke Gaelic. In Orkney and Shetland they spoke a dialect akin to the language of Norway. The Welsh take pride in their old language, the Scots do not. Lowlanders feel little sense of guilt that they cannot speak Gaelic – the language which even in the early Middle Ages was spoken by at least three-quarters of Scotland's population.

Nor were the Scots united by the clan system. Scotland is not a nation of 'Macs', walking around in kilts as many English and other foreigners imagine. Among the most common surnames in Scotland are Smith, Brown and Wilson – hardly names to indicate that the Scots are a marauding Highland Host. Yet, curiously, the culture of the Celt in bastard form came to symbolize Scotland.

The nation is nostalgic and at times woolly about its past. Since the days of Sir Walter Scott the psyche has been drowned in romance. The heroic figures of Scott's novels – Rob Roy, Montrose and Young Lochinvar – stir the blood of Scots at home or abroad. Although the reality of Scotland's worthies has been overshadowed by folktale and song, the myth of history genuinely reflects the nation's soul. Modern Scots see themselves in their heroes: men up against it, winning through against untold odds. The struggle is for individual recognition whether in battle, on the sportsfield or in the bank. Part of the myth is that the English get blamed for much they were never responsible for. True, the English were hardly hospitable neighbours; but most of Scotland's paragons were done down by fellow Scots. William Wallace was betrayed to the English by a Scotsman and the Stewart monarchs as Kings of England or in exile can hardly be said to have done any favours for the country that nurtured their Royal House. Historically, the Scot has often been his own worst enemy.

The Scots have only themselves to blame for their image. Sir Walter Scott's historical novels enriched the world of literature but did the Scottish people a great harm. Glasgow's music halls from the end of the nineteenth century created the bizarre Scots comic, with his Lowland accent and Highland dress. The image of the Scot created by entertainers like Sir Harry Lauder and Will Fyffe – the man of a dram and a song, dressed in a kilt with a Lowland shepherd's stick, dour and canny to the point of meanness – has stuck. In truth the Scots loved Lauder as much as the rest of the world: like the Jews, the Scots invent the best jokes about themselves and one needs only to look at the current success of Billy Connolly to see that old habits die hard.

In the Edwardian era, picture postcards were another exuberant image. When the boom peaked in 1903, some six million comic postcards of Scotland and her people were posted in Britain alone. The images produced by the Scottish postcard makers of Dundee were innocent enough but to modern Scots they seem awful. Edwardian Scotland, however, was more confident, devoid of the soul-searching that permeates the country now.

In the twentieth century the stereotype found new vehicles to perpetuate it. One of the earliest British feature films, *MacNab's Visit to London*, made in 1905, brought tears of laughter to cinema-goers' eyes as it told of the Scots bumpkin on a visit to his cousins in London, practising golf in the living room, frightening the maid when his kilt falls off and having to be told to go home.

Radio and television, despite their strong Scottish connections, have done little to correct the image. John Logie Baird from Helensburgh invented the first television system in 1929, and the BBC, under Lord Reith went on the air with the world's first television service seven years later. To promote the new medium there was a joke about the Scotsman who accidentally breaks a bottle of iodine and then cuts his finger so as not to waste it. Television programmes like the *White Heather Club* have brought the image into the living-room. Scottish country dancing, accompanied by the accordion band – both late inventions – have reduced the once proud reels of Highland men to the level of the barn dance. The culture is debased but it is still strong enough to stir the blood, to be the stuff of which nations are made.

Although a British citizen, the Scot sees himself as different from the inhabitants of other parts of the United Kingdom, as indeed he is. Scotland has different institutions, the old fought-for threads that, woven together, have helped make the Scots Scottish. The Church of the Scot is Calvinist, staunchly democratic: there are no appointed bishops in the Kirk which has moulded the nation's mind and soul for 300 years. Even those of other faiths or no faith at all hold it in high esteem. From the beginning the Kirk had a social conscience and it is still the largest social work agency in Scotland, caring for the nation's alcoholics, law-breakers and old people.

With the Kirk came Scotland's system of education, more democratic in concept than that of England. Since the sixteenth century, the Scot has been better educated than his southern cousins. While Oxford and Cambridge were the only two universities in England, Scotland could boast four. As late as the end of the nineteenth century only one English child in every 1300 received a secondary education, while in Scotland the proportion was one in 200. The English have since caught up.

Scotland's legal system is also different from that of England. Deeply rooted in Roman and Germanic customary law, the Scottish system is regarded by many as more logical than the legal system of England, based as it is on common law. Despite the fact that Scotland has had a legal system without a legislature (a distinction it shares with the American District of Columbia) her lawyers have been in the van of preserving the nation's inheritance.

Brought up to *think* differently, Scots also *feel* unique. Supporters follow the national football team round the world like a tartan army and even at Murrayfield the normally more dignified supporters of rugby have whistled when the British National Anthem is played. During the Edinburgh International Festival, busloads arrive to cheer and honour their own. On the esplanade of Edinburgh Castle the pipes and drums of Scotland's regiments have paraded before the world since 1948. At the Tattoo, the Scots sing 'Scotland the Brave', a patriotic hymn written by Cliff Hanley for a pantomime, that has only one Scots word in it – 'hame'. But the swaggering sentiments of the song are real enough.

From the Scots, the English have drawn much. Scots are proud that Scotland gave the Royal House of Stewart to rule over both countries when Elizabeth I of England died without an heir, yet still resent a little the fact that, in 1603, it was a delighted James VI of Scotland who left Edinburgh for the greater wealth of London. As James I of England, he rarely set foot in Scotland again.

When the independent parliaments of both Scotland and England were dissolved in 1707 in order to create a new parliament of Great Britain, the position of the Scots as poor relations was further exacerbated. The English then, as now, believed they had absorbed Scotland politically. Legally they did not, although the numerical strength of English representation in the new parliament meant that the voice of the Scots from the start was smothered by the demands of English squires. To this day, despite having produced a number of British Prime Ministers in the last century – William Gladstone, Ramsay MacDonald, Harold Macmillan and Alec Douglas-Home among them – the Scot at home feels *his* country has benefited little.

Yet since the Union of 1707, the contribution of the Scots to the well-being of Britain has been disproportionately large. Most Scots gave themselves wholeheartedly to the new nation and called themselves North Britons. Unfortunately the English have never seen themselves as South Britons. A Scotsman, quite rightly, still objects when foreigners refer to him as English. When Scottish sportsmen do well, newspapers and television usually refer to a 'British success'. When the English do well, there is no attempt at disguise.

The Union with England has lasted less than 300 years. The Scots have fought the English for longer and have an independent history that goes back to the Stone Age. This Union that is seen as permanent and sacrosanct is still a new thing and should be treated with care. A body of Scots opinion was critical of Union before the ink on the treaties was dry and in recent time was strong enough to frighten Britain's major political parties into considering radical changes in the constitution that could have created the federated Britain that some in Scotland hoped for in the early eighteenth century. Scottish nationalism may now be a relatively dormant force, but voices are still raised to question the validity and fairness of the present system.

The Scots find it easy to pat themselves on the back. The 'here's tae us, wha's like us', syndrome is alive in the land and after a football victory over England can manifest itself in vulgar form. Where in the world save Wembley Stadium could you witness anything approaching that tartan clad army, waving banners with the slogan 'Remember Prestonpans' – to remind the English of Prince Charles Edward Stewart's famous victory over the Hanoverian army in 1745?

But there is truth in the Scottish boast. A poor and inhospitable land has bred people of remarkable talent. The world would have been a poorer place without Alexander Graham Bell, James Watt, Thomas Telford, Sir Walter Scott, Robert Burns, Adam Smith and David Hume, and the Scots also played a disproportionate part in creating an empire called British but in reality more Scottish than English. The English are thought of by the world as imperialists; yet the Scots founded and ran the colonies without incurring the wrath of those they ruled over, perhaps because they too knew what it was like to be dominated by English interest.

Through that empire, Scotland gave the world remarkable men. In Australia, it was a Scot, John McDouall Stuart, who first crossed the continent and another, John Macarthur, who had a vision of Australian agriculture that helps Australia prosper today. Had it not been for Lachlan MacQuarie, the once penal colony of Botany Bay may never have become the gracious Victorian city of Sydney. The same could be said about the

Scots who went to Canada, New Zealand and Africa. In Canada the Scots are the third largest ethnic group and the list of important names in Canadian history reads like the Jacobite roll-call at Culloden. In New Zealand the Scots have equally contributed in the fields of politics, science and education. To Africa they brought Christianity, education and medicine.

In 1979, the United States Census Bureau looked at the characteristics of Americans of Scottish, English, French, German, Irish, Italian, Polish and Spanish origin. The Scots emerged superior. Of all European immigrants they were the best educated and the best paid. Twenty-five of seventy-three Americans honoured in the nation's Hall of Fame claimed some Scots ancestry. So too have eleven United States Presidents, a half of all Secretaries of the US Treasury and a third of the country's Secretaries of State.

To Scots at home, much of their national pride rests in the land itself – a country more beautiful than bountiful. Geography conspired to make the creation of a nation impossible and hence the struggle to overcome the barriers of nature made Scottish unity and nationhood once achieved the more precious. Throughout Scottish history there is one word constantly on the lips of her people – freedom. A rugged land moulded a rugged people. Scotland consists of some twenty million acres of land, but less than a quarter of it is good enough to support man. A million acres are taken up with fresh water and foreshore, another million covered in forest. On eleven million acres nothing can grow. Everywhere in Scotland are barriers to people communicating. The spine of Scotland, the watershed between the Atlantic Ocean and the North Sea, forces people apart. Communities from the beginning hugged the fertile coastal areas and for centuries the only way to make contact was by sea. As a result the land is still a patchwork of dialects and customs. The people of Ayrshire can still find it hard to converse with Aberdonians. The citizens of Scotland's ancient capital, Edinburgh, regard themselves as different from those of Glasgow only forty-five miles away, and in many important ways they are. What united people in the past was a common cause, the desire to be independent, and the history of that desire is proudly upheld by Scots today.

From birth the Kirk and the school drum Scotland's rich and remarkable history into her children. In England, the average schoolchild is taught nothing about Scotland and her past: in Scotland, children learn the history of both countries, before and after they were united, and every year there are dozens of events, many going back hundreds of years, that celebrate the nation's history like the Common Ridings of the Border towns with their roots in the days when villages were never safe from English attack. To the Scot, history remains real. Past struggle and success are honoured by a people who have rarely had reason to be optimistic about the future. Scotland's story has been for the most part a bloody one, always lively and never dull.

1

Few and Far Between

EARTHQUAKES and volcanic eruptions shaped Scotland forty million years ago. Four Ice Ages followed and the land was split and eroded. As the last ice melted, straths and glens were formed and ground for the first time became sheltered and fertile. As vegetation slowly spread, Scotland's native wildlife arrived – grouse, ptarmigan, the golden eagle and the owl. Voles and mice were the first animals, followed by red deer, the wolf and the wildcat. The last to arrive was man himself. The people of Scotland were to come from Europe, from Spain, France, Germany, the Low Countries and Scandinavia.

Scotland's earliest human visitors were nomads, hunters in search of mammals, birds and fish. For 2000 years, from 6000 BC, men from the south travelled up by boat to places like Morton, in north Fife. They stayed in Scotland but a few weeks at a time, living off the flesh of deer, wild boar, whelks and fish. Then they took to their primitive vessels of hollowed-out tree trunks and, hugging the shore, returned south. Visitors also crossed from Ireland, less than twenty miles from Scotland's western seaboard, to fish and beachcomb. While they foraged, Scotland's early visitors often lived in caves, like those at Wemyss in Fife. The remains of Scotland's first house, built over 7000 years ago, have recently been excavated at Crathes, near Banchory. The circular stone structure was about twenty-five feet across and probably housed no more than eight or nine people.

From about 4500 BC came the farmers from the continent of Europe. The raising of plants and breeding of stock was first developed in the east, thousands of years before, while most of Britain lay under a blanket of ice. The newcomers were responsible for the introduction of wheat, barley, rye and domesticated livestock. For 2000 years these Stone Age farmers cut down forests, set fire to them and unwittingly enriched the soil with potash. As the first crops were harvested, people gave up a purely nomadic existence and, with better supplies of food, the population grew.

The farmers settled near the sea and on Scotland's islands. Around 3000 BC, settlers came from Baltic Europe to Oban and the island of Tiree. Others from the Mediterranean made their way by boat to the Stirling area, in an age when the town was at the head of a sea estuary. Men also came to live on Orkney: Skara Brae, preserved by a freak sandstorm, is a near perfect example of a Stone Age village. Each of the ten houses has a central hearth

Dun Carloway on Lewis is one of the best preserved Iron Age brochs in the Western Isles. The double wall, which still rises to thirty feet, is eleven feet thick, evidence of the remarkable architectural talents of Scotland's earliest inhabitants. (*STB*)

and furniture – beds and cupboards – made of stone. The village housed probably no more than thirty people who lived with their domesticated cattle and sheep. They ate vast quantities of marine shellfish, especially limpets. They also ate birds, such as the gannet, and used their bones and beaks to make awls to help fashion clothing. These early settlers dressed in hides and the women made pottery, baked in peat fires.

Water was then the only safe means of communication. Land travel meant forest or swamp and wild animals. Boats and boatmen brought colonists, the seed of new crops and domesticated animals like oxen. The people lived near the shore and coastal and inter-island trade was continuous and far-reaching. Stone quarried on the Western Islands of Rum and Arran found its way, by sea, to the eastern seaboard. Axes made at Tievebullaigh in northern Ireland were exported to Aberdeenshire, Lewis and Shetland. They were also imported from Langdale in the English Lake District and from Craig Llwyd in north Wales. Communities were small and scattered, but not without knowledge of each other's existence.

Papa Westray, in the north of the Orkneys, is an island with rich and fertile soil which was first inhabited 5000 years ago. Its first people made fine pottery, mallets out of whalebone, borers and grinders and bone awls to make holes in leather to fashion clothes. From the year 2000 BC, the first people settled Jarlshof. Like those of Skara Brae, these first Orcadians ate shellfish and reared livestock, such as the primitive Soay sheep and short-horn cattle. At Jarlshof, they grew barley and wheat and flax for linen clothing, and their diet also included veal and mutton and a little pork. They were not primitive by contemporary standards: their homes were similar to those found in Minoan Crete.

Stone Age man became religious. Chambered cairns, like Maes Howe in Orkney, were built to honour the dead, many long before the Pyramids of Egypt. Since the cairns were erected by people who had no trees their builders had no logs to use as levers or rollers to move the huge stones into

Skara Brae, built between 2500 and 2000 BC, consists of ten one-roomed houses. A sandstorm forced its inhabitants to live elsewhere, but preserved the village intact. Many tools from Skara Brae are now in the Scottish National Museum of Antiquities in Edinburgh. (*STB*)

place. At Maes Howe the stone slabs, some weighing three tons, are so closely fitted together that a knife blade cannot be inserted between them. Collective tombs, the resting-place of generations of a family or clan, are found all over Orkney. Life for the early people of Scotland was hard, brutish and short; but a struggle religiously honoured in death.

The hunters and farmers were followed by the Beaker people, so called because they laid beakers in the tombs of their dead. They may have come from the Rhine, by way of the Low Countries and across the North Sea. They may have brought bronze to Scotland; they were subsequently joined by other metalsmiths from central Europe and Spain. The Beaker people were skilled engineers and surveyors, and may have built the vast stone circles like the Stones of Stenness and the Ring of Brodgar in Orkney. These were erected not for the family but for the community and acted as religious centres for the Orkney islands as a whole. Thirty stone circles and henges have been found in Scotland. Their purpose remains a mystery; but their construction is uniform, and they were designed and laid out using the 'Megalithic Yard', a near exact common measurement. Such monuments took years to build, the stones carried many miles. The most famous are the stones at Callanish in the Isle of Lewis. This avenue of nineteen monoliths leads to a circle of thirteen stones and was completed at least 1500 years before the birth of Christ. The Callanish circle was probably linked to astronomy: the coming of the seasons and equinoxes would have been of vital importance to these early farmers, and the stones at Callanish are well

The Standing Stones at Callanish on Lewis date from between 2000 and 1500 BC. No one knows how the Stones were transported and set up without mechanical aid. The chambered cairn in the centre of the circle may have been an altar for human sacrifice. Sir James Matheson, who owned Lewis in the nineteenth century, had the area surrounding the Stones cleared of peat.   (*STB*)

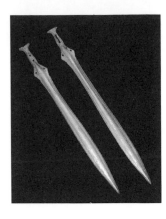

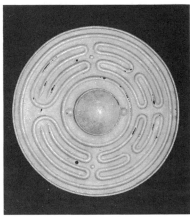

Two bronze swords dating from the late eighth century BC, found in 1846 at Arthur's Seat, Edinburgh. A bronze shield from the same period, found in Aberdeenshire, was probably used for ceremonial purposes, and was a forerunner of the Highland targe. (*NMAS*)

sighted for observing the movements of the moon. The early inhabitants of Lewis, though remotely placed, were not alone. Their culture and their stone circle were mirrored at Stonehenge in England and at Mycenae in Greece.

With the introduction of metal came weapons and war. Around 1000 BC came two inventions – the sword and the shield. Areas of Europe rich in copper and tin became important and battles were fought to protect them. In Europe, throughout the millennium before the birth of Christ, warfare was endemic. The copper and bronze goods found in Scotland were mostly got by trading with Irish smiths. Scotland was on the main trade route from Ireland to Scandinavia and her early inhabitants became tireless seamen, travelling to Ireland, Scandinavia and Europe. They bartered food and animal hides for bronze implements. Only the most powerful could afford bronze weapons: they became chiefs, leaders of bodies of warriors and their families.

In the last thousand years before Christ the Celts came to Scotland. A combative people, of fine physique and fair hair, the Celtic tribes had a strongly matriarchal society. Their economy was based upon agriculture – farming in the fertile areas of Scotland and the raising of livestock in the Highlands. The society of these late Bronze Age Celtic settlers was similar to that of the people of Hallstatt in Austria. They arrived in Scotland before the sixth century BC and were followed in the fifth century by Celtic people who may have come from Switzerland. With the arrival of the Celts, the existing population of Scotland felt a need to fortify their settlements. They were widely scattered and chiefs of groups or clans had to protect what they had from raiding neighbours. For defence, men dug ditches and threw up ramparts, such as those found at Traprain Law in East Lothian. New strongholds, including hilltop forts, were constructed all over Scotland. Attack and defence became a part of life.

The reason was simple: land was becoming precious. The weather deteriorated during the centuries before Christ and wetter conditions caused peat to form in the uplands of Scotland and forced hill farmers down to the coast. Well-established colonies, jealous of their land, livestock and store of metals, built forts like that at Finavon, near Forfar, which could shelter 400 people in an attack.

Around 2500 years ago, some of Scotland's people lived in crannogs, timber-framed buildings built in lochs, weighed down with branches and bracken and surrounded by boulders. The crannog offered its occupants safety from wild animals and from raiders while the loch supplied them with food when under attack.

Between 100 BC and AD 100, an age when commercial sea raiders were looking for slaves for the Roman Empire, over 500 dry-stone brochs were built in Scotland on the islands of the north and west and in Caithness and Sutherland. Dry-stone building came to Scotland between 800 and 500 BC. The practice originated in the Alps and was introduced by way of France, Spain and Ireland. The firebrand or spear was the weapon of the day and the broch's great height could adequately defend those within it while the positioning of the brochs was strategically so good that during the Second World War lookout posts were built near them.

In AD 80 Gnaeus Julius Agricola, Governor of the province of Britannia,

An artist's impression of a Bronze Age crannog. These artificial islands, based upon a raft of logs with layers of stone, earth and brushwood, were built for defence. One of the best examples is on Loch Kinord in Aberdeenshire.   (*S*)

decided to invade the north. It was less than forty years since the Romans had first set foot on British soil and their presence was already Romanizing conquered people in England. In order to secure a strong northern frontier, Agricola decided to subdue the tribes of Scotland. He reached the River Tay with an army of 20,000. By the following year, AD 81, a chain of twenty Roman forts had been built across the stretch of land that divided the Forth and the Clyde. Two years later Agricola came north again and this time turned west to secure Galloway. He then struck north into Morayshire by land, his navy supplying him by sea. This route was later followed by Edward I, Cromwell and the Duke of Cumberland in their campaigns to conquer Scotland. The Roman general advanced without much incident. He built ten more forts and consolidated his victories by building over 1300 miles of road north of the River Tyne.

Possibly at the Pass of Grange, near Huntly, was fought the Battle of Mons Graupius around about the year AD 84. Agricola, with over 5000 men, faced a united force of tribes under Calgacus, in command of some 30,000 Caledonii, Tacitus's name for the inhabitants of Northern Scotland. Tacitus, Agricola's son-in-law, wrote an account of the campaign and imagined the speech Calgacus might have made to his men:

> Battles against Rome have been lost and won before, but hope was never abandoned, since we were always here in reserve. We, the choicest flower of Britain's manhood, were hidden away in her most secret places. Out of sight of subject shores, we kept even our eyes free from the defilement of tyranny. We the most distant dwellers upon earth, the last of the free, have been shielded till today by our very remoteness and by the obscurity in which it has shrouded our name. Now, the farthest bounds of Britain lie open to our enemies; and what men know nothing about they always assume to be a valuable prize . . .
>
> A rich enemy excites their cupidity; a poor one, their lust for power. East and West alike have failed to satisfy them. They are the only people on earth to whose covetousness both riches and poverty are equally

James Proudfoot's impression of the hill fort of Edinburgh, *c* AD 100, which eventually became the site of the town's Castle.   (*SE*)

tempting. To robbery, butchery and rapine, they give the lying name of 'government'; they create a desolation and call it peace . . .

Agricola launched an uphill attack and defeated the Caledonii, who with their wounded retired into the hills. At Mons Graupius, according to Tacitus, Calgacus lost 10,000 killed or wounded, whereas the Roman casualties were just 360 men. The Romans, however, did not follow up their victory. Agricola's campaign had one lasting achievement; his fleet sailed round the north of Scotland and proved for the first time that Britain was an island. His term as Governor over, he returned to Rome.

Agricola's Scottish campaign was a costly fiasco. His fort at Inchtuthill on the Tay, which was to be a base for over 5000 men, was abandoned before it was completed. Occupying over fifty acres, it was to have held sixty-four large barracks, six granaries, a hospital and a large workshop. Retreating in haste, the Romans never fired the kitchen ovens and the hot water system for their baths was never installed. Pottery and glassware were smashed and nearly a million nails were buried so that the local tribes could not use the metal to make arms.

Walls were Rome's solution to the problem of protecting their part of Britain from the northern tribes. In AD 118 it is said the men of the north of England and Scotland had wiped out a whole legion based at York, and five years later the Emperor Hadrian built a wall from the Tyne to the Solway. About twenty years later, the Antonine Wall was built from the Clyde to the Forth, by legionnaires from Germany, Gaul, Spain, Egypt and the Middle East, to keep the most northerly tribes at bay. Often they married local girls and founded families. Lollius Urbicus, who built Antonine's Wall, had been sent to Britain to conduct another campaign to subdue the north. He reoccupied most of the land taken by Agricola and built numerous small forts to control the activities of the local population. But he was never able to re-man Agricola's old Highland forts.

The Antonine Wall, begun about AD 142 ran from Bo'ness to Old Kilpatrick and was nearly forty miles long. The turfed stone wall and the forts like Rough Castle every two miles along it took three years to build. Again, however, after just fifteen years of occupation, the Romans in the face of renewed attacks, were forced to retreat south. They finally abandoned the Antonine Wall in AD 185. Thereafter Scotland was looked after by troops

stationed on Hadrian's Wall. Less hostile tribes, in receipt of judicious bribes, were given the task of keeping the Roman peace. In AD 208, however, Septimius Severus was forced to conduct two more Scottish campaigns. Like Agricola, he got as far as the Moray Firth, but won no battles and on his death his son, Caracalla, made a sort of peace with the Scottish tribes and quit the country.

The Romans left little in their wake. True the network of roads they constructed probably did much to stimulate trade and social contact between tribes. Their abandoned forts gave homeless folk shelter. But their most important achievement had been that their attempts to conquer Scotland brought tribes together. When the Romans first came they estimated there were seventeen distinct tribes in the north. Less than two centuries after they left there were only four main peoples inhabiting Scotland. The most enigmatic were the Picts.

The Picts, about whom we know little, were a fusion of some of the original Celtic tribes who had settled much of the east coast. They are identifiable with the Caledonii whom the Romans encountered in the first century AD; but the origin of the Picts is uncertain. They grew in strength ultimately to control the country from the Pentland, or Pictland, Hills in the south to the Pentland Firth and beyond in the north. By the time of the Romans they had established thriving communities in the valleys of the Earn and the Tay, with Dunkeld a centre of importance. They were probably not very thick on the ground and were combined by a sort of federation. It is interesting to note that the Pictish kingdom, Fife, is still thought of as independent. Many Picts lived in 'wheelhouses', circular buildings divided into ten or so dwellings by stone piers, like that found at Jarlshof. According to the twelfth-century *Historia Norvegiae*, the Picts . . .

> . . . did marvels in the morning and in the evening building walled towns, but at mid-day, they entirely lost strength and lurked, through fear, in little underground houses.

The inhabitants worked their fields systematically and introduced the quern for grinding corn, still used, this century, in the remote Highlands.

The Picts tattooed their bodies. The reason is unknown; but it was probably to keep off sickness, or indicate caste and rank, or perhaps purely for decoration. Their society was probably polyandrous, their women taking not only a legal husband but other sexual partners as well. Descent through

The Romans associated with Scottish history and Calgacus are commemorated on a frieze in the Scottish National Portrait Gallery in Edinburgh. (*SNPG*)

A section of the Bridgeness Distance Slab found at Bo'ness, West Lothian; it marked the completion by the Second Legion of part of the Antonine Wall. (*NMAS*)

the female line in families like the Hays, with Pictish roots, is still practised. The Picts waged guerrilla war on the Romans for over a century; but they were not the barbarians the Romans claimed. Their ornately engraved symbol stones, found in many places in eastern Scotland, are proof of a cultured people.

The second of the four peoples the Romans called Britons. They inhabited western Scotland, around Strathclyde, and their lands stretched south down into Cumbria and Wales. In Scotland their main fortress was the rock at Dumbarton. The Britons, however, do not seem to have organized themselves into a unified political force and were therefore to become the least important of Scotland's four main races, although their stock produced one of Scotland's heroes, William Wallace, whose family came originally from Wales.

The Angles, the third people, occupied lands that stretched north from the River Humber in England to the Firth of Forth. They had colonized by sea and established themselves at Bamburgh, St Abb's Head and Dunbar. Driving inland, the warlike, land-hungry Angles ousted the Britons on the east coast and carved out the kingdom of Northumbria.

The fourth group were the Scots. About AD 500, Fergus Mor, son of Eric, moved the seat of the kingdom of Dalriada from his palace at Dunsererick in County Antrim to Dunadd near Lochgilphead. When they first settled, only about 150 made the crossing from County Antrim, but the numbers quickly grew. The Scots were a Celtic warrior aristocracy, their power was sea-based as well as land-based. Every twenty houses were obliged to provide two seven-benched boats. They also brought the sport of shinty to Scotland. They pushed into Kintyre and settled the fertile shores of Loch Fyne and Loch Long. They took the Western Isles as their own. An expansive people, they looked eastward for more and better land. Scotland's eastern seaboard, then, as now, was drier and therefore better suited to farming. As the Scots

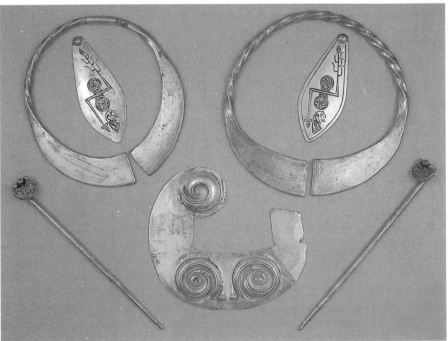

Seventh-century Pictish silver found at Norrie's Law in Fife.   (*NMAS*)

took to agriculture, their expansion became a matter of conquest rather than infiltration. They swept across Scotland, taking with them their Gaelic speech and culture, alien to the indigenous peoples of the east and north. But the Scots of Dalriada were not a single united people. By the seventh century there were at least seven distinct families lording it over independent territories.

The Scots brought their ancient rights of kingship from Ireland. Footmark stones, like that found at Southend in Argyll, were associated with early ceremonies of inauguration of chiefs. Among early Indo-European people shoes played an important part of the inauguration of a king, a practice which survives in the folk tale of Cinderella.

Christianity helped to fuse the four main peoples of Scotland into a nation. St Ninian is said to have brought Christianity to Scotland; but it is likely there were Christian communities in the country before him. Ninian, born about the year AD 350, was a Briton. His parents were probably influenced by Christian Roman soldiers and he travelled to Rome for religious instruction. At Whithorn in Kirkcudbrightshire he built his *Candida Casa*, his 'white house', which served as a church and was probably situated in the grounds of the present kirk. He went on to establish a group of monastic cells on the Isle of Whithorn and from there began his missionary work among the Britons of Strathclyde and the Picts of Fife and Angus. He or some of his disciples may have travelled north as far as Orkney and Shetland and established monastic colonies on Birsay and St Ninian's Isle, although the latter may have been founded after Ninian's death.

The British were the source of Scottish Christianity. St Patrick, born in Strathclyde, was captured by an Irish king during a raid and taken to Ireland. He returned to preach the gospel among the Britons of Strathclyde until AD 432, when he left Scotland to continue his missionary work in Ireland. From St Patrick, however, came saints that were to take the gospel into Argyll and convert the east coast Picts and push south into Northumbria. Little is now known about Scotland's other saints, partly because it was not in the interest of imperialist Scots to write about any other saints than their own. St Serf is said to have worked among the people of Fife from a base at Loch Leven and at Culross may have educated St Kentigern. Of Welsh or Cumbrian stock, Kentigern was brought up by monks, and changing his name to Mungo founded a monastery round which the town of Glasgow was to grow.

The Scots of Dalriada had their own missionaries, like St Oran, who is said to have established monastic communities on the islands of Iona, Mull and Tiree. Then, when Columba, known in Gaelic as *Colm Cille*, 'Dove of the Church', came from Moville in Ireland, they had among them the missionary who was to make them Scotland's dominant tribe.

Columba may not have come to Scotland through choice. An ardent copier of manuscripts, he secretly transcribed a rare Gospel which belonged to his Irish teacher. The dispute over ownership became a public scandal in Ireland and led to war. Columba was excommunicated and advised to leave the country. In AD 563, at the age of forty-two, he arrived at the island of Iona by coracle, accompanied by twelve followers. Who gave Iona to Columba is a matter of controversy. There is some suggestion that the matter could have been agreed by the rulers of the Picts and the Scots.

A Pictish sculptured stone, one of three that stand by the roadside at Aberlemno in Angus, once the heartland of a Pictish kingdom. (*Author*)

St Ninian, the first missionary to Scotland whose name is known.   (*BL*)

Every year Scots make a pilgrimage to St Ninian's Cave near Whithorn in Kirkcudbrightshire, said to have served as the saint's oratory. On the wall and on the rocks outside are votive crosses dating from the eighth century. (*Author*)

Columba and St Aidan, the monk of Iona who evangelized Northumbria from Lindisfarne. Later Bishop of the Angles, Aidan died in AD 651. (*SNPG*)

Iona quickly became a centre of knowledge and religious learning. Where now stands a stone church, Columba and his disciples lived in cells of turf and stone similar to those still found in more remote parts of Ireland. But he was a skilful politician as well as a preacher and was determined to establish a Scots monarchy. He persuaded his people to choose his third cousin, the Scots sub-king of the Argyll Dalriada, as their ruler. Aidan the False was inaugurated *c* AD 574. Columba laid hands upon him with the words,

> Believe firmly, O Aidan, that none of your enemies will be able to resist you unless you first deal falsely against me and my successors.

Christianity combined with conquest, murder and marriage to unify Scotland. The new king helped turn the military tide in favour of his people in their campaigns to wrest new lands from other settlers.

The early Celtic Church was monastic. It demanded obedience and poverty from its clergy, who were monks, not priests. It was a Church without much organization and lacking in wealth. Religious buildings were small, designed only to shelter the altar while Mass was celebrated. The worshippers stood in the open. Unlike the Church of Rome, which revered St Peter, the Celtic Church preferred to follow the example of the disciple St John, a Christianity founded upon love not law.

Columba helped convert the Picts to Christianity, and by the middle of the eighth century there was an abbot established in the heart of Pictland – St Andrews, or Kilrymond as it was then called. The King of the southern Picts, Nechtan, was committed to the new faith and there followed a remarkable flowering of Pictish stones linked to the Christian faith. But conversion was slow, the work of many decades. The Picts of the south became Christian in the seventh century but it was a hundred years before those of the north took to the faith. In AD 565 the Pictish King Bridei is said to have been visited at Craig Phadrig by Columba, who wanted safe conduct for the missionary Cormac to go and work among the Orkney islands. Aidan,

A mural by William Hole (1846–1917), one of several he painted to decorate the Scottish National Portrait Gallery, depicts the mission of Columba to the Picts.   (*SNPG*)

one of Columba's disciples, took Christianity from Iona to Northumbria. An Angle prince fled to Iona for refuge and returned to become King Oswald of Northumbria. It was he who invited Aidan and other monks from Iona to set up a monastery at Lindisfarne.

The Celtic Church, however, calculated the date of Easter by an antiquated method and so celebrated the Resurrection earlier in the year than the followers of Rome. King Oswald's wife, however, was an Anglo-Saxon Christian so that the Northumbria Court was celebrating two Easters a year. As Bede pointed out,

> When the king, having ended his fasting, was keeping the Paschal Feast, the queen and her retainers would be fasting and celebrating Palm Sunday.

To resolve the matter the King was forced to call a Synod at Whitby in Yorkshire in AD 663. At Whitby, Wilfrid of Ripon voiced the superiority that those of South Britain even then felt they had over those of the North. He told the Columbans:

> Even if your fathers were true saints, surely a small company on a corner of a remote island is not to be preferred to the Universal Church of Christ.

The Queen won the day, and the Celtic Church of Iona was to wane in importance as a result. Slowly Celtic monasticism was replaced by Roman Catholic orthodoxy. About AD 710 King Nechtan was persuaded by Abbot Ceolfrith of Northumbria to adopt the Roman Church, and the monks of Iona accepted the Easter ruling in AD 716.

Christianity was a new and powerful magic. Springs and wells blessed by Columba and his disciples became objects to be venerated. So too were relics. In AD 732, a refugee Angle from the south brought the relics of the disciple St Andrew, the elder brother of St Peter, from Hexham to St Andrews. House-shaped shrines, like the Monymusk Reliquary which

A stained glass window at Whitby commemorates the famous Synod in AD 663 when King Oswald of Northumbria decided to adopt the Roman ruling on the date of Easter. The Celtic monks under St Colman, Bishop of Lindisfarne, retired to Iona. Oswald's decision led to the unification of the English church under the rule of Rome. (*STV*)

A cast of the ninth-century cross found at Kildalton, Islay. (*NMAS*)

contained Columba's bones, were constructed for the memorials of the new religion.

But the main struggle, by the seventh century, was for land. On Saturday, 20 May 685, the Picts at Dunnichen, near Forfar, crushed the Angles in the Battle of Nechtansmere. Bridei, King of the Picts, confronted an army commanded by Egfrith of Northumbria. Egfrith was killed and the Angles withdrew to Lothian and the Tweed Valley. Had Nechtansmere gone the other way, there might have been no Scottish state. The Scots, meanwhile, extended their kingdom north beyond Oban and as far east as Atholl, whilst the Picts of the north and south were having to fend off a new enemy, the Norsemen.

The Vikings had come before to plunder. They raided Lindisfarne in 793 AD and sacked Iona two years later. Now they came to make a home for themselves. In the late ninth century, according to the *Laxdaela Saga*, Ketil Flatnose . . .

> . . . decided to go west across the sea to Scotland because . . .
> he thought it would be good living there. He knew the country well for
> he had raided there extensively.

Overpopulation in Norway forced them to seek land elsewhere and the Orkney islands were only two days' sail. Jarlshof became a Viking settlement around 800 AD, and soon the Norsemen arrived in enough numbers to make the northern isles of Orkney and Shetland part of Scandinavia.

The Norsemen were not simply warriors. They settled their new-won islands and sowed oats and barley, kept lambs and cattle and produced quantities of wool. Nor were they fiercely anti-Christian. Although between AD 795 and 806 Iona was laid waste three times, and on the last occasion, at Martyr's Bay, every member of the monastic community was murdered, the sacking of Iona was an exception rather than the rule. Norsemen rarely killed priests or razed their places of worship to the ground. But they spread west

Dunnichen Hill, near Forfar in Angus, was the site of the Battle of Nechtansmere fought in AD 685. Had the Northumbrian army been victorious the Pictish kingdom of King Bridei might have been absorbed by King Egfrith.   (*Author*)

and settled in Skye and Lewis, where to this day four-fifths of the island's 126 villages have names that are Norse in origin. Later the Vikings moved north to settle the Faroes and Iceland.

Norse communities flourished. Their longships, a new style of boat, and adopted by the local inhabitants of the northern and western isles, gave the chiefs a new mastery of the seas. They also embraced the new religion. In 995 King Olav Tryggvason of Norway visited the Orkneys and ordered the Earl and his people to adopt Christianity under pain of death. The Brough of Birsay became the seat of the Viking Earldom of Orkney and the first cathedral was built on the island.

The Norsemen, however, had nibbled away at the Pictish empire. By the middle of the eighth century they had forced the Picts to move their capital south, possibly to Scone in Perthshire, and the threat of the Norsemen was indirectly responsible for the collapse of the Pictish kingdom. In the west of Scotland, the Norsemen used their island bases to attack Dalriada. The capital of the Scots, Dunstaffnage, near Oban, was threatened, and under the leadership of Kenneth MacAlpin, the Scots were forced to seek refuge east. MacAlpin may have had a claim to the Pictish throne through the marriage of his father to a Pictish princess, since Pictish inheritance was matrilinear. From AD 843 MacAlpin was subduing the southern Picts and had created a kingdom the Irish Scots called Alba. On Moot Hill at Scone, he was made King.

For the ceremony MacAlpin was seated upon the famous Stone of Scone. Its origins are obscure, but it was probably brought from Antrim to Argyll. To the Scots of Dalriada, the making of their monarch was a marriage to the land and the people he ruled and sitting on a stone was a token of that marriage. The tradition has continued. In 1953 Queen Elizabeth II of England and I of Scotland was also crowned upon the Stone of Scone.

By the middle of the ninth century, there existed a precocious kingdom, Alba, that was slowly unifying the tribes of northern Britain. The Scots, however, did not obliterate the Picts. Both were Celtic and they had

A replica of a Norse longship, off Largs in Ayrshire. At a pageant to commemorate the Scottish defeat of King Haakon a group from Shetland brought the ship south. (*Author*)

Kenneth MacAlpin succeeded his father as King of Scots in AD 841 and later became King of Picts. He invaded the rich Lothians six times in an attempt to enlarge Alba at the expense of the King of Northumbria. Kenneth I moved the headquarters of the Church from Iona to Dunkeld in Perthshire. (*SNPG*)

much in common; but over the decades the Scots exploited and settled the Pictish lands. By the twelfth century, Scots Gaelic had replaced the Pictish Celtic language. People by custom took the language of their king. Since the dominant Scots had little interest in Pictish records they were never copied and ultimately disappeared. The royal families of the Picts and Irish, moreover, probably inter-married until the Pictish system of government was peacefully bred out of existence.

By AD 960 the King of Alba, as the Scots kingdom was called, ruled over Edinburgh. Norsemen had helped destroy the northern English kingdoms, and therefore played a part in helping the peoples of Scotland unite. Attacks on England by the Danes in the tenth and eleventh centuries also enabled the Scots to extend their power south. When Cnut seized the English throne, Malcolm II, around 1018, won a famous victory at Carham, south of the River Tweed. Sixteen years later, Strathclyde became part of the Scottish kingdom.

When, later, the Scots wrote a history of these remote centuries they created some seventy Pictish kings to lend authority to their own rule. Monks like Adamnan, Columba's biographer, justified Scots ascendancy by manufacturing history. But, in truth, the Scotland of the tenth and eleventh centuries was a Celtic state. The country's monarchs and aristocracy spoke Gaelic, as did the majority of the people. Scots had given the country its name and sense of national identity. Their culture was akin to that of Ireland's people and the two continued to be linked well into the seventeenth century. Their language, Gaelic, spawned Europe's oldest vernacular literature, and their music, played on the harp, Europe's most advanced. Manuscript illumination was the finest flower of Celtic art.

And yet, curiously, when Kenneth MacAlpin was made King, the Dalriada Scots probably accounted for less than ten per cent of the population of Alba – Scotland. Their power and influence spread through sub-kings. Relatives of Kenneth MacAlpin became Kings of the Picts, and in AD 908 a grandson of Kenneth became sub-king of Strathclyde. By the middle of the tenth century something resembling a Scottish nation was emerging. Its society was the forerunner of the clan system that later

Macbeth (*c* 1005–57), his wife Gruoch, grand-daughter of Kenneth III, and Duncan I (*c* 1010–40). Duncan I, killed in battle by Macbeth, was not the old man portrayed here and in Shakespeare's play, nor were Macbeth and his Queen the evil couple of the English dramatist's imagination. (*SNPG*)

dominated Scotland. Kings were appointed by tanistry: a 'tanist', or successor to the king or chief was designated from among a kindred group. Chosen during the lifetime of the reigning king, he was usually a brother, a nephew or a cousin. Always, the 'tanist' was thought to be the best man for the job, of the right age and sound in mind and body. Tanistry meant conflict and murder. Of the fourteen kings who reigned between AD 943 and 1097, ten were murdered.

The first king to appear out of the mists of history was Malcolm II, the son of Kenneth II. Malcolm ruled for nearly thirty years and in that time killed off as many 'tanist' claimants to his throne as he could so that his grandson, Duncan, could succeed. Malcolm was determined to establish a Royal House, a family claim to the succession.

Macbeth, and his wife, Gruoch, however, were both of royal blood and had a just claim to the throne. Macbeth was getting old and, given King Duncan's youth, could see his chance of becoming king slipping away. In 1040, therefore, Macbeth killed Duncan in battle and exiled his two sons, Malcolm and Donald Bane. These events were not unusual in the history of the Scottish monarch. Macbeth did what was then expected of any 'tanist' who wanted to exercise his right to the throne and Shakespeare's *Macbeth* made a villain of a man who had every right to rule Scotland.

For seventeen years, Macbeth ruled wisely. Under him, probably, the north and south of Scotland were united for the first time. Macbeth was generous to the Church and made a pilgrimage to Rome in 1050. He was defeated by Duncan's son, in 1054 at Dunkeld, and in 1057 Malcolm III, with the help of the English King, Edward the Confessor, invaded Scotland and killed Macbeth in battle at Lumphanan north-west of Aberdeen. With that battle any hopes of a purely Celtic Scotland died. Malcolm slaughtered Macbeth's family so that his own kingship would not be threatened, and, more important, took an English wife. Kingship was to be enhanced at the expense of Celtic culture, and never again were the emerging English kings to leave the north alone.

2

The Auld Enemy

BY THE BEGINNING of the Middle Ages, the boundary between what became Scotland and England was a fluid one. There were 'English' living in what is now Scotland and 'Scots' living in England. Exactly where the line should be between the two emerging monarchies preoccupied Scottish history for 500 years.

After his father, King Duncan, had been killed by Macbeth, Malcolm, aged nine, had been sent by his uncle to the English Court of Edward the Confessor. In 1058, with the help of Siward, Earl of Northumbria, he became King of Scotland. In his late twenties, Malcolm III, called *Cean Mòr*, Gaelic for 'Great Chief', married Ingibjorg, the daughter of the Norse Earl of the Orkneys, in the hope, perhaps, that the marriage would ultimately bring him Norse-held lands in the north. The couple had three children; then Ingibjorg died and Malcolm took a second wife, Margaret. She had been brought up in Hungary before her family came to take their place at the Court of Edward the Confessor in 1057. When he died nine years later, they decided to return to the Continent and tradition has it that their boat was driven by storms north into the Firth of Forth, where Malcolm offered them shelter and hospitality.

The young widowed King fell in love and married Margaret in 1069. Encouraged by his new wife, he invited the Normans to take lands in Scotland, where they could introduce their ideas and influence. Unlike England, Norman overlords did not conquer the Scots by military means. Many Norman families had interests both north and south of the border. The two de Brus brothers, for example, came from Brix in Normandy in 1060 to give advice to Malcolm, King of the Scots, and were granted some land near Kelso – the lands of Bulden. Then, when William the Conqueror became King of England in 1066, the de Brus brothers were given English estates in Sussex and Yorkshire.

William the Conqueror realized that geography made a conquest of Scotland impossible. A show of strength, however, would help put the Scottish King in his place. In 1072, William took an army and navy to the Firth of Tay, and at Abernethy Malcolm III became the English King's 'man'. To make sure of peace Malcolm's eldest son was taken off to be brought up in England.

The sprawling no-man's land of Cumberland and Northumberland, however, saw little peace. Cattle and slaves were regularly rounded up by

St Margaret (*c* 1046–93), married Malcolm III *c* 1069, according to her biographer Turgot, the Prior of Durham. Malcolm III (*c* 1031–93) remained illiterate throughout his life and Margaret's influence on him was immense. (*DDC*)

marauders on both sides, and the Scottish King himself led a raid into
Northumbria in 1070. He was to lead another three, and Robert, William of
England's eldest son, saw fit to establish a New Castle on the Tyne to mark
the northern limits of his father's kingdom. When Rufus, William's second
son, became King he built a castle at Carlisle in 1092 to keep the Scots at bay.
It seemed at the time that the English monarch was content to draw the
northern border of his kingdom on a line between Newcastle and Carlisle.
Rufus, however, suggested that Malcolm should travel south to discuss the
matter, then changed his mind and refused to see the Scottish King.
Insulted, Malcolm invaded England for the fifth time at the head of a large
army. At Alnwick, however, he was ambushed and killed by an English
Norman knight he thought to be a friend. Shocked by the news of her
husband's death, Queen Margaret died three days later.

Margaret was devout. She had spent her life attempting to bring worship
in Scotland in line with orthodox Roman Catholic practice and her children
continued this work. The first two to rule, Edgar and Alexander, had a real

William the Conqueror (1028–87), the
first Norman King of England, was
promised the English throne in 1051
by Edward the Confessor; he invaded
England in 1066. He introduced
Norman lords and social organization
as well as administrative and legal
practices, which were in turn adopted
by the Scottish monarchy.   (*BL*)

A romantic portrayal by William Hole
of Margaret's landing in Scotland. She
may have been born in Hungary while
her father Edward was in exile. When
William the Conqueror excluded her
brother Edgar the Atheling from the
throne it is said a storm drove her to
Scotland.   (*SNPG*)

David I (c 1084–1153) was the youngest son of Malcolm III and Margaret. He spent his youth in England and did much to reorganize his kingdom on Norman lines. (*SNPG*)

hold over the Scots kingdom, which comprised little more than the lands that lay between the Forth and the Spey. Elsewhere was either in the hands of the Norse Earls or too remote to administer. But the Royal House took a secure hold on the kingdom of Scotland in the reign of David I. He too had been brought up in the English court and had been much impressed by Norman society and government. Accordingly on his return to Scotland he brought Anglo-Normans north, among them the de Balliol and Lindsay families. Also his marriage to the widow of a Norman and daughter of a Saxon was of great dynastic importance – a Celt marrying into the Anglo-Norman aristocracy. With this beginning of Scotland's 'Golden Age' came the introduction of the feudal system whereby the king owned all the land and his barons owed him allegiance for their areas in return and which gradually replaced old communal Celtic laws. These new Anglo-Norman overlords built their motte and bailey castles in Scotland, the symbol of their authority and power. Into them they put their officials and artisans – clerks, bailies, falconers, fletchers, foresters, lorimers, tailors and taverners: men with functions that were to become family surnames. The old landowners still held their lands but as tenants of Norman overlords, and gradually the new men established themselves, not only with their long swords and chain armour but as people who were respected for a certain sense of justice and for the improvements they carried out.

David I continued to develop the administration of the royal household. New offices were created, those of Constable, Chancellor, Chamberlain, Marshal and Steward to supervise the running of the kingdom. Royal revenues, henceforth, were efficiently administered and account books kept and inspected. Justiciars, judges who were also barons, travelled the country administering the king's law. Sheriffs, appointed by the king, looked after his castles, collected his taxes and organized the defence of his realm. Under David I there were the first signs of the Scottish monarchy attempting to achieve the impossible – a national system of justice and administration.

The King and his court were constantly on the move. Royal rents were paid in kind and had to be eaten before they rotted. The constant perambulations of the court also fulfilled another function – the King could be seen to rule. The most powerful instrument he had to help him was the Church. Nine Anglo-Norman bishops were appointed and Church and State in feudal Scotland, as elsewhere, became indivisible.

David was also responsible for bringing monasticism back to much of Scotland. The Cistercians were given lands at Melrose and Newbattle in the Borders. Their vast abbeys became centres of religious inspiration and of enlightened agriculture, for David gave the Church large amounts of the country's best land. His piousness impoverished his successors: later kings were forced to rely upon unpopular taxation to keep the monarchy going. Fine parish churches were also built, like those at Leuchars in Fife and Dalmeny outside Edinburgh. Piousness brought craftmanship to Scotland. The great abbey at Dunfermline, endowed by David I, was built by Norman craftsmen whose skills were imitated by native Scots. Royal piety was to be rewarded in 1192, when the Pope in Rome declared the Scottish Church to be directly responsible to the Holy See rather than via the mediation of Canterbury or York.

Fourteen small towns, among them Stirling, Perth, Dunfermline and

A Pictish brooch made in Scotland or Ireland, c AD 700, which was found at Hunterston in Ayrshire in the 1830s. Pictish silver metalwork, some of twenty-eight pieces dating from the eighth century, which were found buried at St Ninian's Isle, Shetland in July 1958.
On the island of Birsay in the Orkneys, a Pictish symbol stone was uncovered dating from the same period.
A Pictish silver casket, dating from the mid-seventh century, called the Monymusk Reliquary, is said to have contained at one time a relic of St Columba, the Scots religious leader.   (*NMAS*)

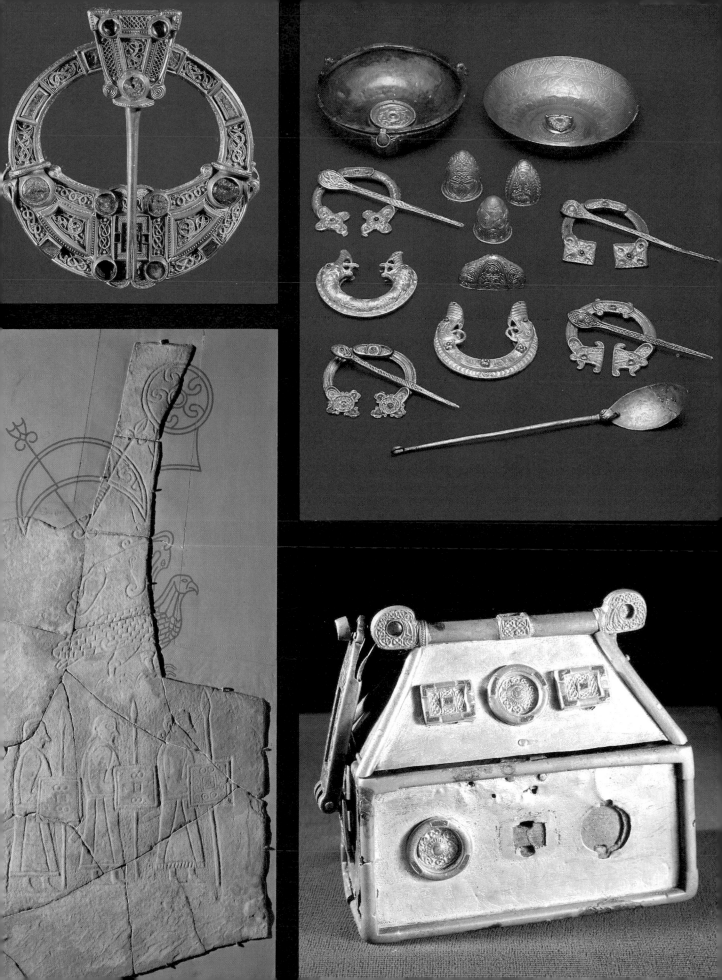

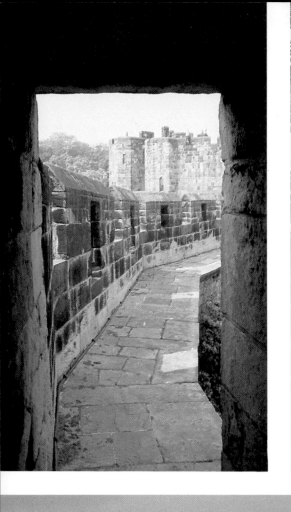

David I was outstanding in his generosity to the Church and founded several monasteries. Edinburgh, Berwick, Roxburgh and Stirling were founded as burghs during his reign and he encouraged Normans, English and Flemings to settle in Scotland. Celtic resentment at his Anglo-Norman policies led to rebellions in the north, but these were crushed. (*SNPG*)

Alnwick Castle in Northumberland, the most formidable of England's northern castles, originally built by the Normans. A cross marks the spot where, it is said, King Malcolm III of Scotland was killed in 1093, and a stone the place where King William I was captured in 1174. The castle became the home of the Percy family from 1309, who ruled the north like kings.

Threave Castle (*right*), built in the fourteenth century on an island in the River Dee in Kirkcudbrightshire, was the stronghold of the Percy family's deadliest rivals, the Douglases. When the Douglas family threatened James II in 1455, the Scots King forced them to yield after bombarding Threave with Mons Meg.

Flodden Field in Northumberland (*below*): a monument honours the dead of both Scotland and England who fell in battle on 9 September 1513. Every year at the battle site there is a service of commemoration, and wreaths are laid. (*Author*)

Edinburgh, were given the status of Royal Burgh with special trading privileges. To encourage trade, David introduced a standard system of weights and measures and established at Berwick and Roxburgh mints to make silver pennies, Scotland's first proper metal currency. Trading with the Continent slowly increased and Flemish wool merchants began to settle on the east coast at Berwick and Aberdeen.

Life for the ordinary people of Scotland, however, changed little. There was still little sense of a united nation. Government meant the king in person, not the office, and David still addressed his charters to his faithful subjects, naming them by race – French, English, Scots, Welsh and Galwegians, the independent dwellers of Galloway. Scotland's new nobility spoke French. The Church, the literate class, conversed in Latin, and 'Inglis' – English – was slowly becoming the language of Southern Scotland. In time, the Scots of Dalriada went the same way as the Picts. Gaelic ceased to produce literature, and the driving-force of the emerging nation came from the new Anglo-Norman overlords.

The Great Seal of Alexander I
(c 1077–1124). (*NMAS*)

Alexander III (1241–86). (*NMAS*)

But the problem of the Anglo-Scottish border remained unsolved and the King of Scotland found himself drawn into war to help neighbouring Northumbria. In 1138, David I assembled a vast army which confronted the English at Cowton Moor in Yorkshire. The Battle of the Standard, as it became known, brought about a defeat of the Scots by the superior knights of England that included in their number both Robert de Brus, an ancestor of King Robert the Bruce, and de Balliol. Cowton demonstrated the clash of loyalties that bedevilled Scotland for centuries: many of those powerful owned land in England as well and paid homage to two kings. Yet although David was defeated he managed, by skilful diplomacy, to have Northumbria ceded as a fief to Scotland; the Scottish boundary was extended south to the River Tees.

In 1153 David I was succeeded by his grandson, Malcolm IV. He, in turn was succeeded by his brother, William. During the sixty years that these two brothers ruled, Scotland was a land of peace and promise. A colony of Flemish settlers were asked to come to upper Clydesdale, where the land was rich for farming, and their rearing of sheep contributed greatly to the development of trade with the burghs. Berwick, on the east coast, became Scotland's most important town. Growing exports to the Baltic and northern Europe of wool, furs and salted fish made Berwick rich. Scots, in increasing numbers, could afford to import wine, woven materials and spices.

Increased prosperity showed itself in building. In nine years between 1240 and 1249 the Bishop of St Andrews consecrated no fewer than 140 churches. Monasteries were built at Pluscarden, Deer, Culross, Beauly and Sweetheart. By the end of the thirteenth century there were thirty-eight monastic houses in Scotland – richly endowed abbeys of the Augustinian, Cistercian and Benedictine orders.

Henry II, King of England, insisted that Northumbria be restored to him. King William, known as 'The Lion of Justice', resented the English demands and organized an invasion of England in 1174. Outside Alnwick

New Abbey or Sweetheart, one of the most beautiful monastic ruins in Scotland, was founded in the thirteenth century by Devorguila, wife of John Balliol of Barnard Castle. Built in 1273, the Abbey was the last pre-Reformation Cistercian foundation in Scotland. Devorguila was buried in front of the high altar with the embalmed heart of her husband, which for years before her own death had been her 'sweet, silent companion', worn round her neck. (*Author*)

Castle, William was captured and taken off to Falaise Castle in Normandy, where he was forced to accept the King of England as his feudal overlord. In addition, the Scots Church was placed under the English Church and castles in southern Scotland were garrisoned by English troops. They were to remain in English hands until Richard Coeur-de-Lion, desperate for funds to finance his Crusade, sold William's castles back to him and renounced his feudal superiority. Between 1174 and 1292, the two kingdoms were at peace.

William died in 1214. His son, Alexander II, and grandson, Alexander III, ruled for over seventy years. Both were capable rulers; but for the majority of Scots who scraped a living off the land, life was narrow. The population of less than 300,000 did not travel and had little in the way of material possessions. Their homes were of stone and turf, shared with precious livestock and little different from the dwellings of the Highlands. In much of the Lowlands 'fermtouns' were slowly emerging – villages with arable land around them. The land was divided into 'ploughgates', an area that could be worked by a team of oxen. Those who owned the beasts began to live in a compact group of dwellings. But to own an ox was the mark of wealth. Most Scots owned nothing, and by the thirteenth century there was a growing class of peasants who held no land by title and paid heavy rents in kind and in labour. Their diet was fair if limited. South of the River Forth, wheat, peas and beans were eaten most. Cheese was already a staple food and meat and fish were in good supply. Ale was the drink of the common man. Lords and bishops could afford imported wine from France.

When Alexander III died, St Andrew replaced the monarch during the Interregnum on Scotland's Great Seal. (*NMAS*)

The twelfth century, all over Europe, was an age of towns. Scotland's Kings made sure their nation was no exception. It was in their financial interest to create them. Royal Burghs paid rent to the king in cash, not kind, and monarchs needed money to develop their government and enrich the prestige of their rule. By the end of the thirteenth century, the burghs of Scotland were providing the monarchy with an eighth of its income. Abbeys, cathedrals and lords were also allowed to found burghs. The King gave the Bishop of St Andrews the right to create a burgh with trading privileges, and some of the new towns, like Aberdeen, were granted exclusive rights to fish the waters around the coast. From the beginning Scotland's burghs were full of foreigners. Many of the people of Aberdeen spoke French, many of Berwick's inhabitants, Flemish. The Scots were taught to trade and manufacture goods by Europeans. By 1286 there were thirty-five Royal Burghs and thirteen which were the creations of the Church and the nobility. Yet Berwick, the most prosperous, had a population of little over 1000 and most of Scotland's emerging towns had only a few hundred living within their walls. The total population of all forty-eight burghs was less than 30,000, a tenth of Scotland's population.

Robert I (1274–1329), grandson of Robert Bruce, a Competitor in 1290. (*NMAS*)

The ordinary people not only paid rent but had to provide their lord and their king with military service. From the time of William the Lion, everyone who possessed land had to keep at least one horse. Although the Scots fought on foot, they were carried to the place of battle on shaggy horses bred in the Highlands. Twice a year the lord would have a Wappinschaw – a show of weapons when ordinary men presented themselves with a bow and quiver. Others, farther up the social scale, like foresters, had to own a crossbow and a spear. Those with land valued at over a hundred Scots shillings a year had to come armed with a dagger and sword as well as bow and arrows. It was wise to accept feudal obligations. The law of the land was harsh. The gallows stood ready outside every burgh and castle and many had a pit, like the bottle dungeon at St Andrews Castle, where miscreants were left to rot in an airless hole.

The Scots monarchs, however, could do little to bring law and firm government to those who lived north of the Highland line. There were no roads to link isolated glens. All the king could do was put his trust in local lords and clan chiefs in the hope that they would carry out his will. By threats of death and the confiscation of lands parts of the Highlands were slowly tamed.

Much of Northern Scotland, of course, and the Western Isles belonged to the men of Norway. Thorfinn the Mighty was not only Earl of Orkney, Lord of the Hebrides and Lord of the Isle of Man, but also held nine Scottish Earldoms and ruled over extensive lands in Ireland. Converted to Christianity, he made a pilgrimage to Rome and subsequently built a church on Birsay. However piety did little to halt the struggle for power. The Norse Earl, Magnus, was brutally murdered by his cousin, Earl Hakon, who wanted overall control of the islands. St Magnus Cathedral, founded in 1137, honours Orkney's first saint. The Earls of Orkney were for ever versatile, interesting and violent; but under their rule the islands enjoyed a rugged prosperity.

In the Western Isles politics were more complex. The Norse King of Dublin, the King of Man and the Earl of Orkney in turn laid claim to overlordship. Under Norse rule, the Hebrides, that lay on the trade route from Dublin to Norway, were prosperous and well populated and they had an importance in early medieval Scotland they were never again to enjoy.

William the Lion made three attempts to extend his rule north; but he got no further than building two castles, Dunskaith in the Cromarty Firth and Redcastle in the Beauly Firth. Even the west of Scotland proved hard to control. It was not until 1221 that Alexander managed to subjugate part of Argyll and Kintyre and secure some allegiance from the mainland chiefs. The people of Galloway, like the Norsemen, also exploited any weakness shown by Scotland's royal house. Fergus, Lord of Galloway, rebelled three times against the crown. When he died in 1161, his sons again rose and forced William the Lion to build castles at Ayr, Lanark and Dumfries to pacify the south-west. It was not until 1234, when the last of the old Celtic lords of Galloway died, that the area stopped trying to divorce itself from the rest of Scotland.

In 1263 the ageing King Haakon of Norway brought a large fleet south in an attempt to halt Scottish imperialism in the Western Isles. He unfortunately delayed too long in the Orkneys and Skye and October storms wrecked most of his ships. Haakon himself stumbled ashore at Largs to face the Scottish army and a so-called battle took place which consisted of no more than a clumsy charge of horse along the beach, and a counter-charge. The Scots then fell back and allowed the Norwegians, short of food and supplies, to sail away. In 1266, by the Treaty of Perth, Haakon's successor, King Erik, sold the Western Isles for little over £2500 an annual rent of £60, and a bride. Alexander III's daughter, Margaret, became Queen of Norway.

By the last quarter of the thirteenth century Scotland had enjoyed a long

Edward I (1239–1307), justly known as 'The Hammer' of the Scots. (*BL*)

period of relative peace but a riding accident near Kinghorn in Fife brought about a dynastic crisis which proved to be a national disaster. In 1286, Alexander III was killed when he was thrown from his horse. His golden reign had been marred by personal tragedy. His wife had died in 1275 and six years later he lost a younger son. His daughter, Margaret Queen of Norway, also died, and, more important, his eldest son. The next in line was the three-year-old daughter of the Norwegian king, the Maid of Norway. Guardians of the realm were chosen from among the Scottish nobility to carry on the government of Scotland on her behalf.

Edward I of England was quick to exploit the crisis. He immediately suggested a marriage between the Maid and his own son, and in 1290, a treaty was agreed between the English King and the Scottish nobility. The Scots, however, were well aware of the risks involved and demanded that Scotland remain independent, with its own parliament and laws. No Scot, according to the treaty, was to do homage to the English King and they also refused Edward's request to garrison Scotland's southern castles.

The little Maid of Norway was sent for, only to die on the stormy voyage. Scotland was without a monarch and immediately thirteen Scottish lords laid claim to the throne, including John Balliol and Robert Bruce. Both were powerful men, with large estates on both sides of the border. Both had sound claims and were prepared to fight to become king. Fearing civil war, the Bishop of St Andrews invited Edward I to arbitrate on the matter, and in

John Balliol (c 1250–1313) was selected by Edward I of England from among the thirteen Competitors for the Scottish throne in 1292 and is seen here paying homage to the English King. In Scotland he was known as 'Toom Tabbard', or empty coat, when he resigned in 1296.   (BL)

Norham Castle by the River Tweed. In 1291 in the church nearby, Edward I, it is said, opened the Convention that gave the Scottish throne to Balliol. (*Author*)

Caerlaverock castle in Dumfriesshire, one of the Scots castles besieged by Edward I of England in 1300. (*Author*)

The Auld Alliance of 1295 was renewed at the Château de Vincennes outside Paris in 1326 and did not come to an end until the Reformation in 1560. (*Author*)

1291, at Norham on Tweed, Edward presided over a convention at which the rival claims were put forward. Twenty-four bishops and barons from England, together with eighty Scottish representatives, spent six months scrutinizing the evidence. Edward awarded the throne to John Balliol.

The Bruce family refused to accept the decision. Old Robert Bruce called upon his son, the Earl of Carrick, to pursue the family claim.

Edward I meanwhile demanded that Balliol pay homage to him, claimed the right to hear appeals from Scots barons, and demanded they help pay for his military exploits. Edward made clear his intention to reduce Scotland to the status of an English shire. He had just completed his bloody conquest of Wales and, corrupted by power, wanted Scotland too.

By 1295, even Balliol had had enough. He renounced his allegiance to Edward and negotiated an alliance with France. The initiative was a desperate one. By signing the Auld Alliance, as it came to be called, Balliol allied Scotland with England's fiercest enemy. The following spring, Balliol crossed into England at the head of an army. Bent on revenge, Edward I retaliated, and at Wark Castle met with a confused band of eighty Scots nobles, all of whom held lands on both sides of the border. Among those present at Wark was the seventh Robert Bruce who, together with his son, later to become King of Scotland, paid homage to Edward. Balliol was furious. He confiscated all the Bruce lands in Scotland and gave them to his brother-in-law, John Comyn. The struggle for the mastery of Scotland thus became three-cornered, between Balliol, Bruce and the Comyn family. The issue of the succession affected ordinary folk little; but it divided the nobility and the Church.

After the conference at Wark, Edward took Berwick-upon-Tweed and razed it to the ground. English troops slaughtered hundreds, and the hard-working colony of Flemish craftsmen and traders were killed to a man. Every building was sacked. The Scots were horrified by the brutality. The town was never to recover its commercial status, and the seeds were sown in Scotland for a hatred of the English that was to last 300 years. Berwick was subsequently rebuilt as an English garrison, the citizens of London being asked to design the new town. Next Edward, with the help of soldiers supplied by Robert Bruce, slaughtered Balliol's army. The Scottish King may have relinquished his crown in the churchyard at Strathcathro and was imprisoned in the Tower of London for three years. He subsequently retired to his family's estates in France and died in 1313, a broken, forgotten failure.

Edward was bent on making his conquest of Scotland complete. He took every castle from Roxburgh in the south to Elgin in the north and stuffed them with English troops. In August 1296, he staged a mammoth act of Scottish allegiance at Berwick and some nobles were thereafter ordered to serve in his wars against France. Those who remained in Scotland were forbidden to leave the country without Edward's consent. The official records of Scotland were confiscated and burnt or else taken to London. The Stone of Scone, Scotland's symbolic Coronation Stone, was taken to Westminster Abbey, to lie beneath the throne of England. The Scots were to be humiliated, although the present inhabitant of Scone Palace, Lady Mansfield, maintains that, according to local legend, the bishop deliberately gave Edward the wrong Stone. The Yorkshire chronicler, Walter of Guisborough, moreover, states that the Stone of Scone was large, concave and made in the shape of a round chair. Other authorities claim the stone was made of black basalt, not the sandstone slab that now rests in Westminster Abbey.

English officials now governed Scotland. English garrisons manned every strategic castle and their barbarity bred and hardened Scottish national feeling.

William Wallace, the second son of Sir Malcolm Wallace, was born at Paisley around the year 1270. His father was chief vassal of the Steward of Scotland and was one of those who had refused to pay homage to Edward in 1296. At the age of twenty-six, William savagely murdered the English Sheriff of Lanark and, it is said, chopped him into little pieces. The murder sparked off Wallace's campaign to rid Scotland of the English. He conducted guerrilla warfare on the English forces from the forests of southern Scotland, fighting in the name of Balliol.

Wallace's army made many of their weapons themselves. They fought with twelve-foot-long spears, axes and knives in tunics of rough hide or homespun cloth; only a few wore plate or helmets. The rebellion quickly became a national one, fuelled by bitter resentment. In the north, Andrew de Moray captured the castles of Aberdeen, Inverness, Montrose, Brechin, Forfar and Urquhart and he like Wallace was supported by the local burgesses while the Scottish barons and earls stood aside, refusing either to harry or help the English. Moray and Wallace joined up and became, in their own words, 'leaders of the army of Scotland'.

By 11 September 1297 Wallace and his army commanded the slopes of Abbey Craig overlooking Stirling and its vital castle. His army included men from all over Scotland, from Galloway, Aberdeen and the Highlands as well as central Scotland. Edward I's Governor of Scotland, John de Warenne, the Earl of Surrey, had at his command a formidable army of cavalry, archers and foot soldiers. Hugh de Cressingham, England's Treasurer, was concerned about money. Fearing a long-drawn-out siege that would put a strain on Edward's coffers he persuaded Surrey to take the English army across the wooden bridge at Stirling and engage the Scots.

From Abbey Craig, Wallace and his men rushed to meet them as they stumbled on the marshy ground on the Scottish side of the little bridge. The battle lasted an hour. The Earl of Surrey was stranded, unable to cross with his foot soldiers because of the dead and wounded that

Sir William Wallace (c 1270–1305), one of Scotland's most heroic figures, a man of relatively humble origins, who led the opposition to English rule and was subsequently knighted and appointed Guardian of Scotland in the name of the King John Balliol. (*SNPG*)

William Hole's dramatic depiction of the fate of the English at Stirling Bridge on 11 September 1297, when William Wallace and Andrew Moray launched their attack on Stirling Castle. (*SNPG*)

cluttered the bridge. He fled the field and Stirling Castle surrendered.

The day had been won by Scotland's lesser knights, freeholders and peasants, who had rallied to Wallace's side because the aristocracy were not prepared to defend them or the nation. Many at Stirling feared that Edward I would soon call upon their services to fight his wars against the French, and they were also aware that it was only a matter of time before the English King would sequester their cash crop and main export – wool – to help finance his expansionist policies. The nobility of Scotland had looked on. Both the Earl of Lennox and James, the Steward of Scotland, had tried to intervene on behalf of Surrey, in an attempt to stop the battle taking place. Only when Surrey fled the field did they feel safe enough to join in and plunder the broken English army. The skin of the great carcass of Cressingham was flayed, and Wallace, according to the far from reliable writings of the English chroniclers, had some of it made into a belt for his sword. Other southern rumours claimed that Cressingham's flesh was cut up into bits and taken in triumph throughout Scotland.

William Wallace had shown the Scottish people that the English were not invincible. But as Guardian of Scotland, he was to rule for less than a year. Hero though he was, he lacked royal authority; and the Scottish nobles, torn two ways by greed and feudal ties, refused to lend him support. Nevertheless Wallace ruled with confidence. He restored Scots to offices in the land previously held by Englishmen, and he wrote to the Hanseatic towns of Lubeck and Hamburg claiming that trading links could be restored now that the Scots had been 'recovered by war, from the power of the English'.

Edward I was eager for revenge. Having made peace with France, he moved his seat of government from London to York and prepared for war. He crossed the Tweed at the head of a massive army, 12,500 foot soldiers and over 2000 cavalry. At Falkirk on 22 July 1298, Edward faced Wallace. The English won the day, but the battle was no rout. The Scots spearmen stood their ground and Edward had to concede that Scotland was not yet conquered. Above all, Wallace was still alive.

The years that followed the Battle of Falkirk were grim. The south of Scotland endured Edward's harsh campaigns and the great strongholds of Roxburgh, Caerlaverock and Bothwell paid heavily for Wallace's success. Resistance was followed by fresh outbursts of English savagery. At one stage, Edward brought north a fleet of sixty ships and 1500 men to quell the stubborn inhabitants of Galloway. By the spring of 1303, Edward was embarking on his sixth invasion of Scotland and within a year was besieging Stirling Castle, the last to hold out against him.

The scale of Edward's attack was immense. Thirteen siege engines were constructed on site. Lead was stripped from the roofs of local churches. Sulphur, saltpetre and cotton thread, the materials for Greek fire, were brought north from York. The assault began on 21 April 1304 and it was three months before the Scots garrison of just thirty men led by Sir William Oliphant, finally surrendered. It remained in English hands for a decade. By occupying Stirling, the Cockpit of Scotland, Edward was able to reimpose his rule. The Scottish nobles once again submitted to him and in return were given back some of their English lands.

Wallace was hunted down and ultimately betrayed by a Scot, Sir John Menteith, on 5 August 1305. In Westminster's Great Hall, he stood trial, accused of treason by a king he had never acknowledged. Condemned to death, he suffered the most barbarous of sentences meted out in the Middle Ages. He was dragged on a tumbril from Westminster to the Tower of London, then taken to Smithfield, where he was hanged, drawn and emasculated. His head was cut off and piked above London Bridge. His severed limbs were sent to Newcastle, Berwick, Perth and Aberdeen and placed by the open sewers of the towns for all to see. The author of the Lanercost Chronicle commented:

> Butcher of thousands, threefold death be thine. So shall the English
> from thee gain relief, Scotland be wise and choose a nobler chief.

Robert Bruce, the eighth in the family to bear the name, became restless. Governor of Carlisle and Sheriff of Lanark in the service of Edward I, he was in secret league with the Bishop of St Andrews and others, waiting for the time he could assume the crown of Scotland which he believed was rightly his. In February 1306 Bruce killed John Comyn, his nearest rival, in the church at Dumfries, when a quarrel broke out at a meeting which had been arranged to attempt a reconciliation between the two claimants. Bruce then went to Scone, where the strangest coronation in Scottish history took place. On 25 March, Isabella, Countess of Buchan, crowned Bruce King. Robert's four brothers were in attendance, as was his wife. Apart from the family, only two abbots and the Earls of Atholl and Menteith witnessed Bruce's coronation. The Countess of Buchan was the only available representative of the family of the Earls of Fife, who possessed the immemorial right of seating the King of the Scots on the stone of inauguration. Down to Alexander III, Scottish Kings, like the Lords of the Isles, had been made, not crowned. Robert I, it seems, was crowned by Isabella as a means of enhancing the quality of his kingship in the eyes of his enemies and foreign princes. He later secured Papal consent to the official crowning and anointing of his son, David II.

On hearing of the coronation Edward I took swift revenge. A petition was sent to the Pope asking that Scone Abbey be razed to the ground. Three of Bruce's brothers were executed along with the Earl of Atholl. Bruce's wife and the Countess of Buchan were imprisoned. Bruce's rule collapsed. He was excommunicated for killing Comyn and at Methven in Perthshire, on 19 June 1306, Bruce was defeated by an English army under the leadership of the Earl of Pembroke and forced to take refuge in the hills of Kintail and Kintyre.

Robert Bruce and Isabella, Countess of Buchan, sister of the Earl of Fife. She was imprisoned by Edward I of England at Berwick Castle, but not in a cage, as popularly claimed.   (*SNPG*)

In April 1307 the tide turned. At Glentrool in Dumfriesshire an English army of Yorkshiremen and Borderers was slaughtered by Bruce's men. On 10 May the same year Bruce won another resounding victory at Loudoun Hill when he defeated a large English force under the Earl of Pembroke. Ironically, money from his English estates probably helped finance the campaign, for although King Edward removed his lands in and around London he still continued to write to his land agent in Essex for rent.

History was in Bruce's favour. Edward I, a sick man, died at Lanercost Priory, near the Solway on 7 July 1307. The English were dealt a bad card, Edward II, a young fop with none of his father's flair for war. The new King took little interest in holding Scotland; the English garrisons were left to their own devices and the guerrilla attacks of Robert Bruce.

Bruce took his campaign north of the Forth and Clyde, capturing castles when he could and destroying them so that the English could not use them again. By the summer of 1309 Dundee and Banff were the only strongholds north of the Tay still in English hands. Comyn's old supporters, the Earls of Buchan and Ross, hindered Bruce's progress. Ruthlessly, Bruce destroyed these families and laid waste their estates. Robert Bruce was an inspirer of men. Those who remembered him when Archdeacon Barbour came to write his life recalled him as 'debonair'.

By 1311 Bruce had finally pushed the English out of Galloway and Lothian. He had subdued the Scottish nobility, who hated him more than they hated the English. In 1313 Bruce took Perth, Roxburgh and Edinburgh; he was now the acknowledged King throughout northern Scotland and the south-west. He held parliaments, issued charters and through loyal bishops opened up diplomatic relations with Europe.

Only Stirling Castle, the most strategic of all, held out against him, and without Stirling, Bruce could never hold the nation. As he besieged the castle, Edward II stirred himself to come to the aid of the beleaguered English garrison, with an army of 20,000 men and 3000 cavalry. Bruce's brother Edward, meanwhile, had agreed with the English commander of Stirling that if Edward's army did not show itself by midsummer 1314, the English would surrender Stirling to the Scottish King. Edward Bruce thus committed King Robert to a full-scale confrontation which he would have preferred to avoid. As a brilliant guerrilla leader, Robert I shunned pitched battles against a numerically superior enemy and it is odd that his popular fame was to rest on a military 'set-piece'.

Edward II almost arrived too late. It was Sunday 23 June before he led his army up the old Roman road from Falkirk. The Scots had taken up positions in the Torwood ahead of them. The English knights, anxious for the fight, pushed ahead of Edward's main force and engaged the Scots that evening. Bruce broke his battleaxe cleaving the skull of Henry de Bohun and by nightfall, Scots morale was high. At dawn the following day, the English found themselves caught between the branches of the Bannock burn. They would have to fight, hemmed in by boggy ground. The Scots, on the other hand, were drawn upon dry ground and unlike the English troops were seasoned fighters. They had fought hard for six years to win this day.

The Battle of Bannockburn, 23–24 June 1314: the greatest victory the Scots were ever to have in their history. (*SNPG*)

The English were amazed to see the Scots boldly attack. Bruce's spearmen pushed back the Earl of Gloucester while his knights and the English bowmen, usually deadly in battle, could not fan out and do damage. When they tried to, Sir Robert Keith's light cavalry dispersed them and the English were forced to retreat into their own ranks. Crowded together, the English were confused and in disarray. The rout began. The Bannock burn filled up with the corpses of horses and men and the English in flight used their dead and wounded as a bridge. Edward II fled the field and made for Dunbar, where his fleet lay at anchor. The victory was the culmination of a most remarkable military campaign. In the age of the great armoured horse and the castle, both had been destroyed by guerrilla tactics. The battle was important too because the Scottish army was drawn from the four quarters of Scotland, remaining in the field as a disciplined body. For the first time the Scottish nation had acted as one.

The spoils of victory were enormous. Henceforth the Scottish army would be better armed than it had ever been. Huge ransoms were exacted for the English barons who had been captured. Scotland became rich in a single day. The battle should have marked an end to the long war with England; but the greatest danger of the victory was over-confidence that the Scots would now feel able to invade the south. First, however, they had to wrest the burgh of Berwick from the English. It was only in April 1318, when an English burgess opened the gates of the town after a three-month siege, that the castle surrendered. Carlisle, the other gateway to Scotland, remained firm in English hands.

Bruce held a parliament at Cambuskenneth and confiscated the lands of the Balliols, the Comyns and the Earl of Atholl who had deserted him on the eve of Bannockburn. Those like Gilbert Hay, Earl of Erroll, who had stood by him, profited. Hay was given Comyn land and made Lord High Constable. The Gordons, a Lowland family, were also given other Comyn lands in Aberdeenshire.

After the Battle of Bannockburn, some, like Sir Walter Fitzgilbert de

Hamilton, who had supported Edward II, thought it wise to switch sides. He was Governor of Bothwell Castle, one of the strongest castles in Scotland. After Bannockburn various people took refuge there, among them the Earl of Hereford, who was considered a very important prize. De Hamilton surrendered castle and refugees to Bruce.

Bruce was King of Scotland; but was still excommunicated and unrecognized by Europe as an independent monarch. At a meeting of his Council at Newbattle Abbey it was agreed to send letters to the Pope to have him accepted. The Abbot of Arbroath Abbey, the Scottish Chancellor, drafted three letters, one of which was a Declaration of Independence to which fifty nobles added their seals. In high-flown language it petitioned the Pope to write to Edward II telling him to leave Scotland in peace. The language was purposely florid because any papal letter to the King of England would repeat word for word the sentiments expressed by the Scots. The Declaration was sent to the Pope at Avignon in 1320 and he sent the Scots a favourable reply on 29 July. As an act of diplomacy, the Declaration of Independence had worked. With papal support, European allies were won over.

The Declaration, however, gave birth to an historical myth. The Scots, it was claimed, were an ancient people of Celtic Iberian stock, who had travelled from Egypt, by way of Spain and Ireland. The petition made much of the Gaelic tradition of the Scots and little mention, for obvious reasons, of the Anglo-Norman presence in Scotland. To have done so would have given credence to the King of England's claim to overlordship. In many respects, however, the sentiments of the Declaration were correct. It was in fact the middle folk of Scotland who had made their mark in the struggle for independence. But the 'democratic' aspect of the Declaration of Arbroath is often overstressed. After all, the signatories were nobles and Robert I would not have ruled without them, and in that sense, the Declaration was truly national.

When King Robert the Bruce held a parliament at Cambuskenneth in 1326 he summoned not only barons and representatives of the clergy, but also representatives from Scotland's burghs. It was the first time that their presence had been officially requested and the reason was made obvious by the agenda. The two main topics of discussion were the succession and money. The parliament agreed that henceforth a tenth of all rents were to be paid directly to the King to help defray the expense of government. The Estates, as the Scots parliament was called, also swore loyalty to Bruce's little son, David and, more important as events were later to show, to the son of Bruce's daughter Marjory, who had married the hereditary Steward of Scotland.

The office of Steward was held by the Fitzalan family, who had come from Brittany in the middle of the twelfth century. The family's surname became corrupted to Stewart, and by the oath of allegiance to Marjory's son the Scottish succession was made safe to the present day, when Prince Charles, the heir apparent, is the twenty-ninth 'Prince and High Steward of Scotland'.

By 1326 Bruce, it was said by the English, had leprosy. His son and heir was two years old. The heady aftermath of victory at Bannockburn masked the urgency of the impending crisis. Scotland's troubles with the 'Auld Enemy' were about to start all over again.

3

Fame then Flodden

KING ROBERT THE BRUCE died in 1329 and was laid to rest in Dunfermline Abbey. He left a new kingdom in a proud but sorry state. The peace treaty with England signed at Northampton in 1328 had brought an uneasy end to war. Bruce's son was just five years old and many in Scotland were troubled by the crowning of the boy as King David II. The claim of the former Royal House of Balliol was still a valid one, and few doubted that Edward Balliol would pursue it.

South of the Border, Edward II was also dead. He had been deposed by his unloving wife and her lover Mortimer to make way for his son. Imprisoned in Berkeley Castle in Gloucestershire, he had been murdered with a red hot poker thrust up his anus in 1327. Edward III was fifteen years old, and the Border between the kingdoms was still in dispute. Family feuding made the wars more bloody but the main reason was one of political geography.

The Border lands were rich: the Scots could not afford to lose them if they were to have a nation at all. To the English, on the other hand, the region south of Carter Bar in Northumberland, was the least prosperous part of their nation and would only be politically viable if the kingdom extended northwards to include the Scottish Borders. The struggle for control was lengthy, and vicious. Dryburgh Abbey was destroyed twice by the English, in 1322 and again in 1385. The Cistercian abbey at Melrose suffered the same fate, as did the greatest Border abbey of them all, Kelso. Castles were of course centres of the struggle. Lochmaben near Dumfries was captured, lost and re-captured twelve times. Six long sieges were waged in the process. Roxburgh Castle was also of major strategic importance. In 1460, King James II of Scotland died besieging it. His widowed Queen ordered that the castle and the town be razed to the ground so that the English would have nothing to fight for.

These centuries of Border warfare nurtured the Scottish military tradition, but in human terms were disastrous for Scotland, depriving the poor nation of some of its finest young men. The boundary was also the scene of civil war. While the Scottish nation endured the rule of ten princes who were mere children between the death of King Robert I and the accession of James IV, Regents ruled. Great barons like the Douglas family carved out empires for themselves.

David II (1324–71). Although married from the age of five to Joanna, sister of Edward III of England, he had to fight off English invasion for much of his reign. (*NMAS*)

Edward Balliol (*c* 1283–1364) was the elder son of King John. From 1324 the English used him to threaten Robert I and he was crowned King of Scots. Despite Edward's Seal, Scots regarded David II as their rightful King. (*NMAS*)

David II, seen here with Edward III, was a prisoner of the English King for eleven years. He was freed in 1357 after promising a huge ransom; but he died childless. (*BL*)

David II was crowned at Scone in 1331. A new English invasion was inevitable. Led by Edward Balliol, the son of Bruce's rival, the Scottish barons who had been disinherited by King Robert plotted to regain their lands. Henry Beaumont, through his wife, Alice, claimed the Earldom of Buchan. David of Strathbogie, his son-in-law, believed the Earldom of Atholl to be rightfully his. Gilbert Umfraville demanded the Earldom of Angus and the lands that went with it. All were among those who sailed north from the Humber in 1332.

The Scottish army, under the leadership of the Regent, the Earl of Mar, faced the invaders at Dupplin Moor, near the River Earn in Perthshire. The Scots were brutally defeated. An English chronicler noted with bloodthirsty glee that the pile of Scottish dead stood more than a spear's length high. After Dupplin, Edward Balliol was crowned King of the Scots. The ceremony was attended by many nobles and clergy who eighteen years before had been glad to fight alongside Robert Bruce at Bannockburn.

Scots barons loyal to King David took to the guerrilla warfare perfected by Bruce. Slowly they pushed Balliol's family south and ultimately forced its leader to flee the border in his underpants.

Edward III decided the time was ripe to take over Scotland in person. He marched north to meet the Scots at Halidon Hill, two miles from the town of Berwick. On 19 July 1333 the English defeated the Scots army under the leadership of Sir Archibald Douglas. The English archers, with their six-foot bows of yew, ash and elm, slaughtered the Scots in their thousands.

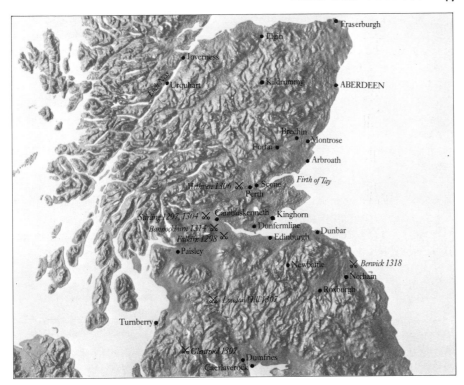

Douglas, the Regent, was mortally wounded and six Scottish earls, seventy barons and nearly 500 Scottish knights were killed. More Scottish spearmen lay dead on the ground than could be counted. The English lost fourteen soldiers. Bannockburn had been revenged.

Edward Balliol was restored to the throne of Scotland, prepared to pay homage to the English King who had won the day so decisively at Halidon Hill. The southern counties of Scotland from Dumfries to Haddington were now under direct English rule. All Scotland's Border castles were stuffed with Englishmen. David II and his young Queen were sent to France for safe keeping. King Philip VI offered the couple asylum at Château Gaillard. Only Scottish children, it was said, dared call David Bruce King of the Scots.

The Battle of Halidon Hill should have put an end to an independent Scotland once and for all. It did not. Strategically placed castles like Dumbarton, Loch Leven, Kildrummy and Castle Doon in Galloway held out. Scotland's geography helped the Scots slowly to fight back. It was money, however, that forced Edward III to abandon Scotland. He could not afford to patrol the Border lands. Castles cost up to £10,000 to build and the troops to garrison them had to be paid. It cost the King of England wages of £10,000 a year to fortify his new-won lands, and he received but a fifth of that sum in taxes from the Border people. His ambitions in France were also to prove costly. At Crecy, Edward III defeated the French but was drawn into a long struggle, a Hundred Years' War.

David II returned to Scotland. The French held him to the terms of the Auld Alliance, which had been renewed by King Robert, and the King of France demanded the Scots invade England to divert Edward III. Rashly the young Scots King and Robert the Steward led an army into England. They

Souden Kirk on the border of England and Scotland. Here James II, Earl of Douglas, and his supporters planned the campaign which led to the Battle of Otterburn in August 1388. The Scots returned to the churchyard after their victory to bury their dead.   (*Author*)

met at Neville's Cross, near Durham on 17 October 1346. English archers again won the day. King David fought with personal courage before being taken prisoner. Robert the Steward, according to English accounts, fled the field before the battle started. More impartially, Robert the Steward withdrew in good order and did not do as much as he might have done to support the King. At all events, David II disliked him thereafter, and did what he could to block the Stewart succession. The victorious English laid the Standard of Scotland at St Cuthbert's shrine in Durham Cathedral. David was taken prisoner. It was to be eleven years before he returned to Scotland. In 1356 Edward III ravaged the south-eastern counties with a brutality not seen since the days of Edward I, in what came to be known as Burnt Candlemas.

The Scots magnates could not look to France to rescue their monarch. Defeated at the Battle of Poitiers the same year, the French King John was himself a prisoner of the English. On 3 October 1357, the Scots were forced to sign a treaty at Berwick. King David's ransom was put at £160,000 and was to be paid in ten yearly instalments. Scotland's Great Customs, the taxes on exports of wool and hides, were increased dramatically to raise the ransom money. But only two instalments of the ransom were ever paid. King David II used the additional revenue to restore the authority of his government and relied on diplomacy to keep Edward III at bay. When the Scots King died in 1371, he left a monarchy richer than it had ever been; but he died without an heir. The great line of Bruce came to an end.

The Scots looked to the Steward's house and David's cousin for a king. With the approval of the Estates, Robert the Steward was crowned. In his fifties, he was an old man to take on such an onerous job. Like many of the Stewart kings who succeeded him, Robert II was a mediocre man and found it difficult to keep his own family in check let alone rule the Scottish nation. Only a handful of King Robert's family were legitimate; but all of them were troublesome. Before long most of the noble families of Scotland had married a Stewart; but this distribution of royal blood did little to keep the peace.

Scotland disintegrated into a lawless shambles. Border baron vied with Border baron, and in the Highlands, clan chief fought clan chief. The rule of law was forgotten.

King Robert II's main handicap was that he could not ride a horse. Being immobile, he was unable to travel round his kingdom to maintain and dispense royal justice. So serious was this weakness that the Estates invited his son John, Earl of Carrick, to take over the administration. On the death of Robert II, John of Carrick succeeded and took the name of Robert III, as John was considered by the Scots an ill-omened name for a king.

Robert III succeeded his father in 1390. In his own epitaph, he described himself as the most miserable of men, and nobody then or since has seen need to question his judgement. He too was in his fifties when he became King, like his father had problems managing a horse, and was forced to rely on his older brother, Robert, whom he made Duke of Albany. The duke's idea of justice was well illustrated at North Inch in Perth in 1396. Two clans, probably Clan Chattan and Clan Key, were in dispute. With Albany's blessing, they fought it out to the death, thirty men a side. King Robert III viewed the proceedings with his courtiers. The bloodletting went on until there were but a dozen men standing.

In the north, Robert III's youngest brother went on the rampage. From Lochindorb Castle, his stronghold, the Wolf of Badenoch, as Alexander Stewart was called, took revenge on the Bishops of Moray and Ross who had excommunicated him in 1389 for deserting his wife. He burned to the ground the town of Forres and the magnificent cathedral of Elgin. He subsequently did penance, but his sons proved equally rebellious.

Robert III sent his younger son, James, to safety in France. With the luck that was so often to bedevil the Stewart house James was captured en route by the English and for eighteen years was a 'guest' of the English court. When he heard of his son's capture, Robert III died. As he was laid to rest in Paisley Abbey, there was something approaching civil war in Scotland. But it was not anarchy. The Scots were bound together by ties of kinship that were not purely feudal, but uniquely Scottish.

For thirty of the hundred years that followed Robert the Bruce, two of Scotland's kings were prisoners in England. With the monarch out of the country, the nobles who were Guardians of the Realm did their best; but they found it difficult to control others of their class. When weak kings like Robert II and Robert III were on the throne the nobles were able to build their own empires and royal feudalism collapsed. Ordinary folk looked to their nearest baron for security and justice, not their king. The most famous noble family to emerge during this period was the house of Douglas.

The Douglases, descended from Robert the Bruce's faithful supporter, had been granted wardenship of the Border Marches and made lords of Galloway by David II. The family thrived on chivalry, athleticism, military skill and unadulterated greed. Their wealth lay in arms not in their land. When Scotland was at peace with England, the Douglases found battles of their own to fight.

In 1388 James 2nd Earl of Douglas led an army into the neighbouring Percy earldom of Northumberland. He laid waste villages and looted what he could. Having captured the standard of Henry Percy – Shakespeare's Hotspur – he retired to Scotland in triumph. Revenge was swift. On

Sir James Douglas (c 1286–1330), 'the Good Sir James', who was active in all Bruce's campaigns and received extensive estates. When he went to Spain to fight against the infidels he took Bruce's embalmed heart with him, as Bruce had wished to go on a Crusade. (*SNPG*)

5 August 1388 the two families again met at Otterburn, where a hand-to-hand battle went on all through the night. Douglas was killed, but the Scots went on to win the battle, and captured Hotspur.

The barons of Scotland had much the same problems as their King. Castles cost a great deal of money to build and maintain. The great Douglas stronghold, Tantallon in East Lothian, was manned by mercenaries. War became a business in medieval Scotland. Booty made war a profitable occupation; ransoms were the occasional jackpot. To avoid bankruptcy, Scots barons hired out their private armies to the kings of Europe, where the armed men of Scotland had won a proud reputation. In 1424, the 4th Earl of Douglas had at least 7000 men fighting in France and earned himself a French dukedom.

The Scottish kings frequently paid for the services of their barons and their armies by awarding lands and titles. Royal patronage thus created monsters. By the end of the fifteenth century, the Douglas family controlled Galloway, Douglasdale, Annandale, Clydesdale, Lothian, Stirlingshire and Moray. With such power, they were able to threaten the monarchy and dictate their own terms. James I, James II and James III made strenuous efforts during their short, violent reigns to put the magnates of Scotland in their place and finally brought about the demise of the House of Douglas.

At first glance, the reigns of the early Stewarts seem marked by constant struggle between the Crown and the nobility. In each reign the Stewart monarch had problems with a family or group of families; but if the Crown had not enjoyed a significant proportion of support from the nobility it would not have remained in the Stewart family, and certainly it would not have survived a series of royal minorities. The fact that it did so suggests rather that the nobility of Scotland had an exaggerated respect for the monarchy: they might manipulate Scotland's boy-kings to further their own ambitions or enhance the power of their families, but no boy-king was murdered or set aside.

So far as the reigns of adult monarchs were concerned, since Scotland's kings did not have the resources to rule by compulsion, they were necessarily obliged to rule with a measure of the consent of their powerful subjects and in general they had sufficient consent to enable them to deal with the recalcitrant. Significantly, it was to be the would-be absolutists, James I and James III, who were assassinated.

In 1424 James I rode north from London a free man. His youth had been a restless one. He had fretted over his captivity and was angered by the lack of enthusiasm that the first Duke of Albany, the Guardian of Scotland, had shown to bring about his release. James I was also penniless. He had complained bitterly while captive in England about his poor wardrobe and now, a free man, he had to raise a ransom of £40,000 in six years. But he had learnt much at the English court. Monarchy, he had observed, had to be seen to assert itself. The second Duke of Albany, who had succeeded to the Governorship on the death of his father, was swiftly arrested and tried for treason. Along with many of his family, Albany was executed. James's own family, the Stewarts, legitimate and illegitimate, were the main focus of the young King's vendetta. They held many of Scotland's earldoms at the time of his return to Scotland. Within a few years they held none.

James saw no reason to tame the ambitious barons of Scotland, and

James I (1394–1437), second son of Robert III, was born in Dunfermline and spent nearly half his life as a 'guest' of the English.   (SNPG)

resolved simply to annihilate them. Scotland had fifteen earldoms when he took over; when he died there were eight, only four of which were still held by the same families. But he lacked the means to follow through his ruthless policy. In 1437 some of the nobility took fright and James I was brutally murdered in his bedroom. The Queen, who witnessed her husband's death, wrought a terrible vengeance. Atholl, Robert Stewart, Graham and their murderous accomplices were made to suffer long and appalling torture before being executed.

James I showed the way. Succeeding Stewart monarchs would have to raise sufficient funds by taxation to be able to assert their authority and control a nobility loyal to the monarchy as an institution but not necessarily to individual Kings. But the King's premature death left a six-year-old on Scotland's throne. The 5th Earl of Douglas, so far unaffected by the attempt to weaken the power of the barons, was made Governor. When he died two years later, in 1439, Sir William Crichton, later created Lord Crichton, succeeded to the Governorship. Jealous of the house of Douglas, Crichton had the new young Earl of Douglas and his brother murdered at a dinner party in Edinburgh Castle in front of James II. He then had the Douglas estates commandeered; but the family skilfully won their lands back.

James II (1430–60), was born in Holyrood; he married Mary, daughter of Arnold, Duke of Gueldres, who acted as Regent during the minority of her son. (*SNPG*)

In 1452 James II, aged twenty-three, murdered the 8th Earl of Douglas; but again the house of Douglas reasserted itself and within four years had formed an alliance with the rising Yorkist party in England which threatened the Scottish crown. In 1455 James II besieged Threave Castle, the Douglas stronghold in Kirkcudbrightshire. The King's cannon won the day and the Earl of Douglas was forced to flee south to England. James II set about creating a new nobility. The lands of old barons were confiscated and given to new nobles. The Gordons, the Campbells and the Earl of Huntly were given lands and authority in exchange for loyalty.

Anglo-Scottish relations, meanwhile, became strained. James II decided in 1460 that the time had come to drive the English out of the Royal Burghs of Berwick and Roxburgh. He took a personal interest in the campaign and fell victim to the ill-luck that beset the Royal House of Stewart. A new type of cannon exploded and killed him outright. He was twenty-nine years old.

Again Scotland endured a Governor of the Realm, and even when James III took power himself, he proved a lazy man, not fond of the business of government. Rarely did he reward his nobles, who therefore looked to his brothers, Alexander, the Duke of Albany, and John, the Earl of Mar, for firm government. In 1479 James III imprisoned both and Mar died at Craigmillar Castle. The Duke of Albany escaped to England, where he plotted to seize the Scottish throne with the help of the Duke of Gloucester. James reluctantly prepared for war and called his nobles to meet him at Lauder Fort. Negotiations took place and, without a fight, James was forced to return to Edinburgh, where it was agreed that the Duke of Albany, who was besieging Edinburgh Castle, should again become Regent. Richard of Gloucester was persuaded to return to England in exchange for the town of Berwick. What was once Scotland's leading Royal Burgh thus became part of England for ever. When Albany restored James III to the throne he was himself again forced to take refuge in England and, eventually, France.

James III (1452–88), born at St Andrews; he married Margaret, daughter of Christian I of Denmark and Norway. Personally acquisitive, he was challenged by some of his nobles and murdered by them after the Battle of Sauchieburn in June 1488. (*SNPG*)

Some of the nobility again challenged the Stewart monarch. At Blackness, in the Firth of Forth, James III faced a band of rebellious nobles led by

When his father was killed during the siege of Roxburgh in August 1460, James III became King at the age of eight. He is seen here in William Hole's painting being presented to the nobility by his mother while the body of his father lies in state in the background. (*SNPG*)

the Home family but settled by negotiation. Matters came to a head on 11 June 1488, when the King faced his nobles at Sauchieburn near Stirling. This time fighting took place and James III was wounded and subsequently murdered. His son, another James, had led the rebel lords. The nobility of Scotland wanted a monarch willing to play the feudal game, and reward their loyalty. James III had collected taxes too efficiently, and famine, plague and bad harvests had made many nobles feel exasperated and squeezed. In James IV they found a king to their liking.

The struggles of the early Stewart monarchs to assert themselves in Lowland Scotland were but half their problem. To the north and west there was another Scotland, which comprised at least half the nation. Lowlanders, like John Major of St Andrews University, despised the uncouth north:

One-half of Scotland speaks Irish, and all these as well as the Islanders
we reckon to belong to the Wild Scots. In dress, in the manner of their
outward life, and in good morals, for example, these come behind the
householding Scots.

They live upon others, and follow their own worthless and savage chief
in all evil courses sooner than they will pursue an honest industry. They
are full of mutual dissensions, and war rather than peace is their normal
condition.

Highland and island society was based on the extended family, to which the
bards often lent credibility by the invention of common ancestors. Ancient,
often mythical history strengthened and justified ties. The extended family
was not yet called a clan, but the foundations of the clan system were firmly
laid. Unconscious of class, the Highlanders lived in a society apart, owing
allegiance to nobody. It is said that when early Highland chiefs took their
oath on the Stone of Scone they filled their boots with earth, whereby they
could argue they had never left their own land.

Most Highlanders made a living by hunting, stealing and fighting. What
little agriculture they attempted was usually doomed to fail. The soil north of
the Highland Line was sour, thin and waterlogged. Autumn gales ruined one
harvest in four. Good harvests of barley and oats in one glen were commonly
plundered by neighbours who had not been so lucky, or burned in retribu-
tion for some wrong. Cattle rearing was the backbone of what little economy
existed, and the scraggy cattle were also plundered by neighbours. By the
fourteenth century Highland cattle were being sent south to market, along
the natural routes that became the drove roads of later centuries. The
Highlanders kept few sheep, but goats, often wild, were raised for food.

Life was often miserable. The ordinary home was a long, low hovel of
stone and pebble, held together by mud and roofed with heather thatch.
Similar in construction to the more modern Black House, they had neither
windows nor chimney. Smoke, damp and filth were unavoidable. The
holding of the chief to whom they owed allegiance was feudal, based on a
Royal Charter. But there was no tradition of land ownership. Chiefs thought
nothing of moving their people from one glen to another; and many, like the
chiefs of the Camerons, the Macnabs and the MacGregors, owned no land
at all, their people scattered as tenants of other chiefs over half the
Highlands.

Highlanders were not necessarily of Celtic origin. Flemish and Norman
families, like the Frasers and the Grants, invented a history to justify the
binding of those of their name together. The idea that the eldest son of the
chief automatically succeeded his father was also a feudal invention. In
ancient times a Celtic family or group chose the best and most able among
them to lead. The chief's authority was absolute. He practised his own law in
his own court. Criminal and civil cases were tried without any reference to
the Royal Sheriff. Punishment was harsh and normally swift. The chiefs
frequently called upon their followers to fight vendettas. Often these were
prolonged and bloody wars. They were frequently the consequence of the
theft of wives or cattle; and murder and pillage were commonplace.

In the Borders of Scotland, the lands of families like the Douglases and
the Hamiltons, the 'name' played a similar role to that of the 'clan' in the
Highlands. It was culture, not social organization, that separated Highland

and Lowland Scotland. The Gaelic language was a potent force in the north. In the Middle Ages, schools of Gaelic poetry flourished and most chiefs employed a bard to compose poems for great occasions. A tradition of formal artistic composition existed in the Highlands before anywhere else in Europe. Gaelic life was rich in song: everyday life was celebrated; there were songs about sowing, spinning, weaving, rowing, and laments for meagre harvests. The sound of bagpipes was not yet to be heard; the harp was the favoured instrument. The kilt and whisky had also not yet been invented.

Norse influence waned when James III retrieved Orkney and Shetland from Denmark. Through his marriage to Margaret, daughter of Christian I of Denmark, Norway and Sweden, in 1469, James III received a pledge of the Norwegian crown's estates in the Northern Isles, against the non-payment of his bride's dowry. As the pledge was not redeemed, the estates, and hence the Isles, fell to the Scottish crown.

The Lord of the Isles was monarch of the Highlands. At Loch Finlaggan, on the island of Islay, he was inaugurated with ritual akin to that of the ancient kings of Dalriada. Clad in white, he placed his foot in a hollowed-out footstep and received a white rod and sword to symbolize power. Bishops and priests attended and Mass was heard. The power of the Lord of the Isles was shrouded in Celtic mysticism, which made the task of controlling the isles more difficult for Lowland Scottish kings.

On 24 July 1411 at Harlaw in Aberdeenshire, Donald, 2nd Lord of the Isles and his retainers faced the might of the Scottish monarchy for the first time. Donald claimed the Earldom of Ross, in right of his wife, and the battle was not just a Highland versus Lowland confrontation. The battle was the bloodiest ever fought between Scots. Nine hundred of the clan Donald and nearly as many Lowlanders were killed. The Lord of the Isles was defeated, but not vanquished. Donald subsequently called himself Earl of Ross, as did his son and grandson.

Seventeen years later James I summoned over forty Highland chiefs to meet him and his parliament at Inverness. Alexander MacDonald, 3rd Lord of the Isles, was among those who attended. Each chief appeared before the King, only to find himself seized and thrown into a dungeon. Three were ultimately hanged. An embittered Lord of the Isles sacked Inverness when the King and his parliament took their leave. James quickly retaliated and marched his troops into Lochaber, where he demanded the Lord pay him homage in Edinburgh. Wearing a shirt and drawers only, with his claymore held by the blade, MacDonald knelt before the High Altar at Holyrood and offered James his weapon. The title, however, lived on until 1497, when it fell forfeit to James IV; it is now vested in the monarch's eldest son, the Prince of Wales.

James IV, who succeeded to the throne in 1488, was popular and generous. He could leap on a horse without the aid of stirrups and ride, it was said, a hundred miles a day. He was Scotland's most energetic monarch since Robert the Bruce. James loved many women, a failing shared by other Stewart monarchs, and begat a vast number of children, most of them illegitimate. Scotland had not known such a fertile monarch since the days of Robert II. One of his mistresses was Margaret Drummond, and the nobles, disapproving, poisoned her and her two sisters with a bowl of porridge.

James IV (1473–1513) was the figurehead of the rebellion which overthrew his father. As he was fifteen no Regency was necessary and he assumed power in person. (*MS*)

Margaret Tudor (1489–1541), daughter of Henry VII, married James IV in 1503. The marriage contract included a treaty of 'perpetual peace' with England. (*CAC*)

James for political reasons married Henry VII's daughter, Margaret Tudor, a marriage which was to change the history of Scotland and England for ever.

Like the three short-lived Jameses before him, James IV realized that authority had to be visible in order to keep ambitious barons in check and, following the example of his Tudor counterparts in England, he invested monarchy with awe. Impressed by the princes of the Italian city states, he tried to imitate them. He had one of his children educated by Erasmus and personally dabbled in medicine, music and alchemy, but much of what he tried to do failed. In 1507, James gave Walter Chapman and Andrew Myllar permission to set up a printing shop in Edinburgh. It was intended that they publish law books, Acts of the Scottish Parliament, religious books and chronicles to extol the nation's achievements. But all the Royal Printers published before they died were Bishop Elphinstone's *Breviary* and a handful of ballads. After their deaths the press was silent. Scots had to import books from England and elsewhere as before.

Education, however, did make advances during James IV's reign. In 1496 he commanded that the children of barons and freeholders learn perfect Latin and study the arts and the law. The King could do little to ensure compliance with his wishes; but there is evidence that by this time there was a school in many of Scotland's burghs, often linked to the local church.

Higher learning, however, was in the doldrums. In an attempt to revitalize St Andrews University, founded in 1412 when Scots because of war and religious differences could not be educated in England, James IV endowed St Leonard's College in 1512. Aberdeen University, which he founded in 1495, was the first in Scotland to teach medicine. Ten years later, the Royal College of Surgeons had its tentative beginnings, when the barbers, also the surgeons of Edinburgh, petitioned the Burgh Council to legislate that those wishing to practise must first pass an examination in anatomy. As a result the body of an executed criminal was thereafter made available every year to students for dissection.

The bold, outward-thinking spirit of the Italian Renaissance was absent from the universities of Scotland. Pure logic, the discipline of the Middle

James IV was one of Scotland's most popular Stewart monarchs. A prince of the Renaissance, he patronized men of science and literature, and encouraged education.   (*SNPG*)

The King also encouraged printing. Walter Chapman (*c* 1473–*c* 1538), a clerk in the office of the King's Secretary, supplied money for the establishment of Scotland's first printing press directed by Andrew Myllar, an Edinburgh bookseller who before his association with Chapman brought into Scotland books printed abroad. The book plates of the two men were used when they set up their printing press in 1507.   (*NLS*)

Ages, continued to be the main subject taught. John Major, the Provost of St Salvator's College, St Andrews, was the most famous scholar of his day. A man of massive learning, he indulged in the logical fruitless disputations of former years and stamped the mind of a generation with his pedantry.

The King's great passion was architecture. James IV began Falkland Palace in Fife as a royal hunting lodge and made the stronghold of Stirling Castle more gracious. A south side was added to the palace at Linlithgow. Imposing buildings were symbols of royal authority and prestige: immortality in stone.

To lessen the power of his barons James IV set up new courts in the Borders to mete out swift and deadly justice to feuding families. He learnt to speak Gaelic and visited the Highlands six times in the first seven years of his reign. Hoping to extend his authority beyond the Highland Line, he continued his predecessors' policy of granting land to non-royal families. In 1509, Huntly and Argyll were made Heritable Sheriffs and the west of Scotland was divided between the two of them. In time they were to prove as loyal as they were distant from the court.

In the Lowlands kinship, as in the Highlands, was the mainstay of society. Scotland, north and south, was never a strictly feudal society, and slavery was never strong. Like the Highlander, the Lowlander was a fighter first and a farmer second. His diet was simple. Most ate two meals a day that consisted of porridge, bannocks and cheese. Chickens, eggs and salmon were usually plentiful. In the nearby forests, there were deer, rabbits and game to supplement meals. Most paid their rents in kind, usually foodstuffs, and had to work the laird's lands. Unlike English farmers, few in Scotland had legal rights. Tenants could be evicted at short notice, and often were. There was no common land, no free pasture as in England.

The Royal Burghs of Scotland were growing in size and importance. All belonged to the monarch and were built on his land. Royal Charters granted their tradesmen, or burgesses rights in exchange for revenue. Only they were allowed to hold markets and fairs or to trade in skins, hides and wool with foreign merchants. A few, like Dunfermline and Glasgow, belonged to the Church and were later given the same privileges as the Royal Burghs. Towns, however, were still small. They consisted usually of a single street, the High Gait or Street, with lanes off, called wynds. Once a week a market was held around the Mercat Cross. All goods had to be weighed at the Tron, a public weighing centre, and rules about trade were made and maintained from an early date.

Glasgow was a small village with one main street and a church. Traders waited at an approach road outside the town, called Argyle Gait, until it suited Glasgow burgesses to admit them and their wares. Trade privileges were guarded jealously and as the Scottish Crown became more dependent upon the Great Customs levied on the Royal Burghs, burgesses protected their status even more. A Convention of Royal Burghs was set up to resolve disputes and lay down rules about trading between burghs. Glasgow and Dumbarton argued over who controlled trade on the River Clyde: Dundee and Perth were often at loggerheads over the River Tay. The Convention did not formally come into existence until the middle of the sixteenth century but there is evidence that the burghs were having regular discussions well before then.

Yet the Scottish merchant at the end of the fifteenth century was rarely a rich man. He probably lived with his family in a single room, called a 'solar', above his shop or place of business. Material possessions were few. Furniture normally comprised a trestle table, a tablecloth, a towel, basin and laver or jug. Every burgess owned at least one cup, a stool, a bed with sheets and a feather bed, together with a bench for seating family and guests. He usually made his own beer and had a kitchen furnished with a kettle, a gridiron, a pitcher for water, a basin, a cauldron, a roasting iron, a mazer – wooden drinking vessel – a platter for serving food, a crock for pots, a pan, pestle and mortar and spoons. If burgesses were short of material wealth, they made up for it in their growing influence on Scottish affairs. By the reign of James IV they had firmly established themselves as the Third Estate of the Scottish parliament, which was regularly meeting in Edinburgh.

Edinburgh was Scotland's capital, although it was made up of little more than 400 dwellings. The inhabitants already practised the unsavoury custom of throwing their garbage out into the street and Edinburgh was a stinking filthy town. It also had a reputation for violence. In 1494, the Town Council saw fit to instruct all merchants and tradesmen in the High Street to have a sword and axe to hand to help break up street fights. It was here, often reluctantly, that the Estates, the Scottish parliament, met.

Both Scots barons and the burgesses resented being summoned to parliament. Neither could afford the time nor the expense. It was found necessary, from early times, to delegate parliamentary authority to committees. The details of legislation were passed to a small select group of senior barons and clerics vested with the authority of the full Scottish parliament. David II twice in 1367, and again in 1369, appointed commissioners to finish the business that parliaments had begun. By 1370 he had founded on a regular basis the body that became the Lords of the Articles, a business committee which looked after the drafting of legislation. Much of the business of the Estates, of course, was legislation about money.

James I had needed to raise the money to pay his ransom, and within a

James Proudfoot's impression of Edinburgh in 1400. The town grew up at the foot of the Castle and its inhabitants lived in crowded squalor until well into the eighteenth century. (*SE*)

year of his return to Scotland put before the Estates legislative proposals designed to improve the nation's economy by increasing taxes. Salmon fishing, in the close season, was forbidden. Rooks and wolves were to be hunted down and killed. The cultivation of peas and beans was to be encouraged and the export of gold and silver banned. Prices of goods in the market were to be fixed and regulations about dress were introduced to cut down extravagant imports. Even football, a game seemingly well established by that time, was banned as a frivolous waste of energy and time. Such royal authoritarianism was anathema to James's subjects and in fact he lacked the ability to enforce his will.

Parliament was also a court, and since the time of King David II the monarchy had been disturbed by the amount of time it devoted to suits. Judicial committees to oversee the administration of the law were set up by both James I and James II. James IV formalized the committee, the forerunner of the Scottish Court of Session, and strengthened it by appointing nine representatives from the Estates who in future were to sit under the Chancellor, supposedly three times a year. But Scottish common law was weak. Unlike in England, the law in Scotland applied only to certain parts of the country and covered only some aspects of life. Until the *Institutions* of James Dalrymple first presented Scottish law as a coherent system in 1681, Scottish kings had to content themselves with legal institutions which had no strong base.

Medieval monarchy worked properly only through the support of the nobility and strength. If law was lacking and difficult to enforce, cannons were the answer. Artillery was too expensive for barons and kings therefore could dominate. James II took a keen interest in the use the English monarchy made of artillery, and at Ravenscraig in Fife designed and built the

Mons Meg, now restored to its former glory at Edinburgh Castle, was probably imported from Flanders by James III in 1455 for the siege of Threave Castle, the Douglas stronghold. The gun subsequently had a chequered career: it burst when firing a salute for James VII, was taken to London in 1754, and only returned to the Scots in 1829.   (*SDD*)

first castle in Britain that could be defended by firearms. Scots, however, did not know how to cast cannon and Mons Meg, the most prestigious weapon to be found in Europe, was imported by James III from Flanders. Expensive to make, Mons Meg cost a fortune to use. Her gunners and gunpowder had to be imported, and a host of beasts and people were needed to move the monster around. When James IV laid siege to Norham Castle in Berwick-shire in 1497, it took over 220 men and 90 carthorses to drag Mons Meg there.

Royal strength also needed a navy. Trade had to be protected and a war fleet helped to discourage invaders. James IV commissioned *The Great Michael*, one of the greatest medieval examples of megalomania. Launched in 1511, she was 240 feet long and could carry 420 gunners and sailors and 1,000 soldiers. Her iron came from France and the Low Countries, and much of her timber from the Baltic, as the forests of Fife could not provide enough. Even her compass was imported. At Newhaven, outside Edinburgh, a new dockyard and ropeworks were built for her construction.

In 1512, Henry VIII of England attacked France. In all likelihood James IV did not want war; he was married to Henry's sister Margaret and peace had brought prosperity. But when the French invoked the Auld Alliance – that albatross of Scotland's diplomatic history – James felt forced to accede to their request for the loan of his fleet, including *The Great Michael* and grudgingly took an army south to distract Henry from France. He crossed the Tweed at Coldstream and set up camp on Branxton Hill overlooking Flodden Field at the head of the largest and best-equipped army ever to have invaded England – at least 35,000 men. Over 7,500 Highlanders were by his side as his ability to speak Gaelic had made him genuinely popular, and he had also mustered the flower of his nobility, including fifteen Lowland earls, twenty barons and hundreds of knights.

Thomas Howard, Earl of Surrey at the age of seventy commanded the smaller English army of some 25,000 men. He asked James, with whom he had been friendly since his marriage to Margaret Tudor, to leave Branxton Hill and join battle on Flodden Field. James refused, remarked that 'it ill befits an earl to tell a king what to do'. Surrey's son then suggested a ruse of war to counter the Scottish military advantage. The way to get the Scots off the hill, he argued, was to march round to the north so that James would think that his lines of communication were being cut. This worked perfectly. On 9 September 1513 James impetuously ordered his men to charge. The Scots attack came to a muddy halt at the foot of Flodden Edge and the fifteen-foot spears of the Scots were chopped by the English bills. Eight feet long, with axe-like blades, these bills scythed through the Scottish troops. In two hours of battle, 10,000 Scots were killed; James IV, at the age of forty, was hacked to pieces with his men, his body so mutilated that it was not recognized until the following day. The Howard family were rewarded by a grateful Henry VIII; the Dukedom of Norfolk was restored and in acknowledgement of the part the family had played in the victory an augmentation was put upon their arms depicting the top half of the Scottish lion with an arrow down its throat.

Flodden was not a unique battle. The Scots had been defeated before by the English and more Scots were probably killed at Halidon Hill. The tragedy of Flodden lay in the loss of the Scottish King and the ruling nobility.

The Coat of Arms of the Duke of Norfolk. The Howard family had ceased to be Dukes of Norfolk after the Battle of Bosworth in 1485, when they were on the opposite side to Henry VII of England. His son, however, owed the Howard family a debt of gratitude. (*DN*)

Flodden Field in Northumberland, 9 September 1513. The military artist, Richard Scollins, depicts the horror of the battle which, in English popular history, more than made amends for defeat at Bannockburn. (*RS*)

As a result of the battle some families almost ceased to exist. The head of the Fleming family of Barochan and six of his seven sons were killed in what was meant to be merely a diversionary action.

After almost five centuries, Scots still feel a deep hurt. In the Borders each year the people of Coldstream make a pilgrimage to lay wreaths at the memorial at the foot of Branxton Hill. At the Border town of Selkirk they share this sense of patriotic outrage. Each year, eighty horsemen ride in the Common Riding, the same number that the town gave up to fight for James. In 1513 only one came back, proudly bearing a captured English banner, and every year they parade a replica and cast the flag to the music of a traditional tune, 'The Liltin''.

Perhaps Flodden showed the Scottish nation that they could never again expect to defeat their mightier neighbour. Flodden was the climax of two centuries of war with England. The tragic loss of the King and much of the nation's manhood should have meant an end to battle. Unbelievably, even after two centuries of war, the fight was far from over.

4

Knox and the Reformation

THE IMMEDIATE CONCERN OF SCOTS after Flodden was that the English would follow up their crushing victory. The citizens of Edinburgh began constructing a third wall round their town to fend off invaders. The other major worry was to find someone to govern Scotland. The heir, James V, was one year old.

James IV's young widow, Queen Margaret, married again with almost indecent haste. Archibald Douglas, 6th Earl of Angus, was her choice. Angus was an Anglophile, out to further his own ambitions, and his enemies looked elsewhere for a Regent to govern Scotland during the infant King's minority. A group of nobles sent a letter to John, Duke of Albany, a cousin of James IV, inviting him to act. The choice was hardly wise. Albany was the son of Alexander Stewart, who had plotted with the Duke of Gloucester against his brother James III. Besides, he was virtually a Frenchman; Scottish chronicles and state papers had to be translated into French for him, and he was totally under the sway of François I of France. In any case, after a couple of years Albany returned to Rouen to renew the Auld Alliance, and stayed four years. Although Albany was honest and able, the Scots clearly had to find another way of coping with the royal minority.

William Hole's evocative study, 'News of Flodden'. (*CAC*)

In July 1525, the Estates decided that James should remain, 'in company', as they put it, with certain lords and prelates, who would ensure his safety and advise him on a three-month rota basis. The Earl of Angus and Gavin Dunbar, together with the Archbishop of Glasgow, were nominated to take charge of the young King for the first quarter. But once the boy was in his clutches the Earl of Angus refused to part with him. The King was held captive in Edinburgh Castle and from 1526 Scotland virtually became a Douglas kingdom. At thirty-five the Earl of Angus was the most powerful man in Scotland and he packed all prominent and lucrative posts with his family and allies. He had James V crowned surrounded by 200 Englishmen sent north by James's uncle, Henry VIII.

It was not until 1528 that James V escaped from Edinburgh to Stirling, where a small army, led by Angus's enemies, gathered round him. Angus had little choice but to quit Scotland for England, and James, aged sixteen, took over direct rule. Like his father, James longed to be a true prince of the Renaissance. For this he needed money, and money became his obsession. His policy at home and abroad, and his relationship with the Church, were all linked to his insatiable thirst for funds. He had the Estates pass an act that allowed him to feu out crown lands for a greater return. He made an expedition to the Western Isles in an attempt personally to make sure his taxes were better paid. He even kept a flock of 10,000 sheep on his royal estate in Ettrick so that money could be made from their wool. By the end of his reign he had increased his royal revenue by half.

In order to save himself money, James persuaded the Pope to pay for the setting up of a College of Justice. In 1541, the Scottish parliament ratified the College, which consisted of fourteen judges, seven nominated by the Church and an equal number of lay members, sitting under an ecclesiastical President. After hard bargaining the bishops made a payment of £72,000 towards the running costs of Scotland's first paid judicial bench. By the middle of the century this Court of Session was split to provide an 'inner' and an 'outer' house, equipped to act as both a court of first instance and a court of appeal.

James's best source of revenue was to be marriage. The Holy Roman Emperor, Charles V, and the monarchs of both France and England sought to provide him with a bride. In 1536 he went to France, where François I offered James Marie de Vendôme. The Scots King refused the ugly woman and reluctantly the French King was persuaded to agree to the marriage of his daughter Madeleine to James V, who invoked the terms of the Treaty of Rouen of 1521, negotiated by Albany, which provided for his marriage to a Daughter of France. James married Madeleine on 1 January 1537, and took her back to cold windswept Scotland, where the climate killed her that July at the age of sixteen. In the same year, the French King sent Mary, daughter of the Duke of Guise. She had married the Duke of Longueville, and at twenty-two was a recent widow like the unfortunate James. The offer was an attractive one: Mary of Guise came with a dowry of 150,000 livres.

James and his new Queen lived in style. In fourteen years he lavished

James V (1512–42) was born at Linlithgow. At the age of twenty-five he married Mary of Guise (1515–60), a daughter of one of the most powerful families in France. (A)

£50,000 on his royal palaces – as much as his four predecessors had spent altogether. At Holyrood he built a new tower and completed a quadrangle. At Stirling Castle he built a courtyard palace and a royal presence chamber richly decorated with elaborate carvings. Outside the palace, more decoration – a fine set of statues, including, of course, one of himself.

Surrounding himself with the trappings of a Renaissance prince, James also used the printing press to enhance his reputation. Hector Boece, the Principal of King's College, Aberdeen, wrote a history of Scotland up to 1437. He produced a fictitious account that stretched back to the dark days of Dalriada in order to underline James V's claim to kingship. European scholars and princes alike had to be made aware of the antiquity and even imperial character of Scotland's throne.

During James's minority, some of the lords of the north and the west had done what they pleased. The Earl of Argyll had raised rents in the name of the crown and kept them for himself. The Earl of Huntly had also quietly pocketed the King's money. Both had to be reminded of the monarch's power. James V refused to grant the 4th Earl of Argyll the Lieutenancy of the Isles, giving it instead to Macdonald of Islay, Argyll's enemy.

The rule of law was also brought to the Borders. In 1530 James ordered the hanging of Johnnie Armstrong, the infamous raider who operated from Gilnockie Tower in Liddesdale. James took the offices of Warden of the Marches away from their powerful traditional owners and gave them to lesser men who would be more dependent upon him. But peace in the Borders also depended on peace between Scotland and England, and by 1542 war again looked likely. A meeting between James and Henry VIII had been arranged at York but the Scots nobility refused to let their King leave the country, fearing that, as in the past, he might be taken prisoner. In August English troops under Sir Robert Bowes crossed the border, followed by the Duke of Norfolk. Roxburgh and Kelso were both burned. James called his army to meet him at Fala Muir, outside Edinburgh, but many lairds did not bother to come. Since Flodden, which the Scots rightly felt was fought on behalf of France, many had lost the taste for war. Those who did present themselves refused to advance towards the English border and at the town of Lauder they disbanded and went home, fearing they might lose another King and one who had no child to succeed him. Undaunted James set about raising another army. On 24 November 1542, at Solway Moss, 10,000 Scots under the command of Sir Oliver Sinclair were routed and over 1000 taken prisoner by the English. Three weeks later, on 14 December, James, aged just thirty, died at Falkland Palace a broken man. But at least Mary of Guise had borne an heir a week before the King's death. 'It cam wi' a lass and it'll pass wi' a lass' was the ailing James's remark. The child was baptized Mary.

The Stewart family had won the throne of Scotland through Robert the Bruce's daughter, Marjory. Now the Stewarts seemed about to lose it through the marriage of a female heir. Mary was James V's only legitimate child; but he had sired six illegitimate sons and two illegitimate daughters. All but one of these bastard children died before they were forty and only Robert of Holyrood had any children. Mary Queen of Scots was of a Royal House that seemed spent. She was James V's only surviving legitimate child. Mary of Guise had borne him two sons, both of whom had died in infancy.

Hector Boece (*c* 1465–1536) wrote his *History of Scotland* in 1527. A former Professor at Montaigu, Boece was Principal of King's College, Aberdeen which had been founded in 1495 with the help of James IV.   (*NLS*)

Mary Queen of Scots as a young Queen, a coloured aquatint in the collection of the Duke of Atholl. (*A*) At Lennoxlove in East Lothian the Duke of Hamilton has the silver box said to have contained the infamous 'Casket Letters'. (*H*)   Copies of Mary's supposed correspondence with Bothwell were said to incriminate the Scottish Queen in Lord Darnley's murder. A fragment (*middle right*) of one of the letters from the library at Hatfield House in Hertfordshire. (*HHL*) A detail (*bottom left*) from the Memorial portrait to Mary Queen of Scots at Blair's College, Aberdeen. After her execution portraits of Scotland's hapless Queen continued to be painted (*bottom right*).   (*SNPG*)

William Elphinstone (1431–1514), made Bishop of Aberdeen in 1483, was the author of the *Aberdeen Breviary* and founded King's College. (*NMAS*)

Scotland's future, however, was not only to be determined by the quality of her monarchs, but by the condition of her Church.

By the late Middle Ages Catholicism in Scotland was in decline. Few Scots attended church regularly. The nation could boast only three saints, St Margaret, Malcolm Canmore's wife, St Magnus of Orkney and Bishop Gilbert of Caithness who had founded the cathedral at Dornoch. Only the last of these was a Scot. Monastic communities were small. Only twenty-three monks lived in the vast abbey at Melrose in the Borders, and the abbot, their spiritual leader, was little more than an administrator. The rules of celibacy were often ignored. Cardinal Beaton of St Andrews had eight illegitimate children and Bishop Hepburn of Moray had nine. The monks at Inchcolm in Fife had kept women in their monastery. Even Iona, the home of Scottish Christianity, had degenerated. By the 1420s, one of the nuns was the daughter of one of the monks. A few monasteries, like the Charterhouse at Perth, still commanded respect. Built in 1429, it housed the country's only colony of the pious Carthusians. Pope and Bishops, like the monarchy itself, conspired to rob the Church of its wealth, selling much of the Church's lands to the nobility and the gentry. Parish churches had their wealth appropriated by abbeys and cathedrals. The Church in Scotland had become top-heavy – grand cathedrals meant impoverished parishes.

Tithes, or teinds as they were called in Scotland, were supposed to maintain the priesthood. One tenth of the value of all produce was supposed to be made over to the priests. By the sixteenth century, however, most teinds were being used to keep cathedrals and abbeys in the grand state to which they had become accustomed. The poorly-paid priesthood attracted men of little talent. Many were debauched illiterates and some parishes were left without a priest at all. Most priests had to live off about £14 a year, whilst professional men by the sixteenth century could expect to earn up to £100. Meanwhile friars roamed the country as preachers. Some had become professional beggars, with a reputation for unlicensed greed.

Lack of funds, or misappropriation of them, meant that some church buildings were in dire need of repair. Wars had destroyed many and others crumbled in the cause of greed, not economy. By 1512 the little church at Lismore in Argyll, for example, was in such poor condition that the king had suggested that the Episcopal See of Argyll should move its base elsewhere. Churches were collapsing long before the zealous Protestants attacked them.

The ordinary folk of Scotland were in need of spiritual help. In the Middle Ages the Day of Judgement loomed large. Doom was portrayed alongside Heaven, and seemed just as real. Men genuinely sought a meaning for death, and many were conscious of the abuse that was bringing the Catholic religion into disrepute. Bishop Elphinstone of Aberdeen had printed his *Breviary* in an attempt to bring new meaning to the lives of the saints. In a late but deliberate attempt to save souls the Church tried to explain salvation to the burgesses and rising gentry. Lairds put money into collegiate churches, and by 1500 a dozen of these were to be found in the Lothians alone. Burgesses in the growing towns paid for altars and enhanced cathedrals. St Giles in Edinburgh was given its stone crown by Edinburgh's wealthy laymen and more aisles were added and more altars consecrated in order to multiply the saying of Mass.

me troucres bo ce que faires touchant luy, il
m'a presché que cestoit vne folle entrepri
qu'auecques mon honneur Ie ne peus pourreu
is, espouser Don qu'estant marié Dois m'am
o que ses gens ne l'endurergient pas. o que
neurs o dedroient. Somme il est tout contra
luy ay dist qu'estant venue sy auant sy vous n
en retires de vous mesmes que persuasion
mort mesmes ne me furoient faillir o ma pro

AVLA FODRINGH

REGINAM·SERENISS·Mᴬ REGVM FILL
VXOREM·ET MATREM, ASTANTIB
OMMISSARIIS ET MINISTRIS R

MARIA
D   G
SCOTIÆ
PIISSIMA REGINA
FRANCIÆ DOTARIA
ANNO
ÆTATIS REGNIQ
36
ANGLICÆ CAPTIVIT
10
S   H
1578

Yet despite the efforts of the pious, anti-clericalism became widespread. The Augustinian and Carmelite orders came in for the greatest contempt. By the sixteenth century two-fifths of all legitimations of bastards in Scotland were for the offspring of the clergy. Books and broadsheets denounced corruption. Morality plays, like Sir David Lyndesay's *Ane Satire of the Three Estates*, quickened public contempt. The play was first performed before James V in Cupar, Fife in 1540. James V and his court are said to have laughed out loud at the cruel portrayal of the Church. James subsequently ordered the clergy to reform themselves; but did not set an example since he secured rich benefices for his bastard children. The King's ambiguous attitude did much to set the scene for the Reformation.

But although there were movements of dissent in James V's reign the Protestant Reformation did not come suddenly. As Scotland still lacked a printing press of its own, Protestant literature was smuggled in from England and the Low Countries. In July 1525 the Scots parliament felt it necessary to pass an act prohibiting the import into the country of Lutheran books and tracts; but it did little to stop the spread of Protestantism. In the search for the true meaning of life and death, many turned to the Bible. The Testaments, both Old and New, had only been studied by a few. From England, a copy of Wycliffe's fourteenth-century translation of the Bible was brought to Scotland and some of it secretly translated into Scots by Murdoch Nisbet. From 1525, William Tyndale's translation of the New Testament, secretly printed at Worms in Germany, was smuggled in and avidly read. But it was not until 1983, in fact, that a New Testament in Scots was finally published.

Martin Luther gave religion a new meaning. 'If a Christian has faith he has everything,' he claimed. 'Faith unites Man to God.' Patrick Hamilton studied under Luther at Wittenberg and returned to Scotland to become the first Reformer of note. Hamilton, a nephew of the Earl of Arran and a great-grandson of James II, had been made abbot of Fearn in Ross-shire whilst still a boy. His appointment was purely a financial one and he performed no spiritual duties. At fifteen he took a masters degree at Paris and went on to study under Erasmus at Louvain. While at Marburg

'The Covenanter's Baptism' (*top left*) by Sir George Harvey (1806–76) (*AAG*), and his 'Covenanter's Communion' (*NGS*), illustrate how the period of religious upheaval has been a source of inspiration to Scottish artists. Although relatively few Scots were executed for their faith, the cause of the Covenanters is deeply rooted in the nation's psyche: 'Condemned Covenanters on their way to execution in the West Bow, Edinburgh', (*below*) by an unknown artist. (*CAC*)

Patrick Hamilton (1504–28) learnt Lutheran doctrines as a student on the Continent. When he advocated reformed ideas in Scotland he was burned to death at St Andrews. His *Patrick's Places*, theses advocating religious reform, angered Scotland's Roman Catholic church. (*HAG*) (*NLS, left*)

> **Major**
> **Deu. 6**
> **Mat. 22**
>
> ¶ He that louyth god and his neyghboure kepeth all the commaundementes of god
> Loue thy lorde god with all thyne harte, with all thy soule and with all thy mynde. This is þ first and greate commaundement.' The seconde is like vn to this: that is / loue thy neyghboure as thy silfe. In these two commaundementes hange all the lawe and the prophetes.
>
> **Minor**
> **1. Joa. 4**
>
> ¶ He that loueth god / loueth his neyghboure. If a man saye / I loue god / and yet hateth his brother / he is a lyar.
> He that loueth not his brother whom he hath sene / how can he loue god who he hath not sene
>
> **Coclusion**
> ¶ He that loueth his neyghboure as him selfe kepeth all the commaundementes of god

University Hamilton wrote *Patrick's Places*, which he hoped would stimulate religious debate. The book became an immediate bestseller. In 1527, Hamilton returned home to Linlithgow, where he began to preach the Lutheran word. He was quickly summoned to St Andrews to answer charges of heresy before Alexander Alesius, who had been ordered by Archbishop Beaton to reclaim Hamilton's soul. Instead Hamilton converted him.

It was hoped that, once set free, Hamilton would sensibly quit the country, but he continued to preach. The abuses and scandals that beset the Church interested him little. He was more concerned with doctrine. He was dangerous because he openly preached justification by faith alone; and Archbishop Beaton of St Andrews was determined to make an example of him. Hamilton was arrested and ordered to recant. When he refused, Beaton had Hamilton burned to death. The Reformation in Scotland was given its first martyr, and Hamilton, at the stake, was aware of the importance of his sacrifice. He told onlookers:

> As to my confession I will not deny it for awe of your fire, for my confession and belief is in Jesus Christ . . . I will rather be content that my body burn in this fire for confession of my faith in Christ than my soul should burn in the fire of Hell for denying the same.

It took six hours before Hamilton was dead: the bonfire had not been built properly and it was raining. While Hamilton publicly suffered an onlooker advised the Archbishop:

> My Lord if ye burn any more, except ye follow my counsel, ye will utterly destroy yourselves. If ye burn them, let them be burned in deep cellars, for the reek of Master Hamilton has infected as many as it blew upon.

Relations with England were to fuel the fire of the Reformation. After the death of James V, James, the 2nd Earl of Arran, returned to Scotland to become Governor. A Protestant, Arran ruled Scotland during the Catholic Mary's minority and Henry VIII decided to exploit the confusion. Henry wanted the Scots to betroth their young Queen Mary, aged one, to his son Edward, aged five. Mary would then, according to Henry, be brought up in England, and the Scots would be forced to accept the King of England as Lord Superior.

Henry handled the matter clumsily. He used bribery to help win over the Scottish nobility, offering the hand of his daughter, Elizabeth, to the Earl of Arran, together with 5000 English troops who could be used to put down Scottish opposition to Mary and Edward's marriage. Arran, next in line to the Scottish throne after Mary, was offered the kingdom of Scotland should Henry find it necessary to march north and conquer the Scots. The nobles who had been taken prisoner at the Battle of Solway Moss in 1542 were allowed their freedom on condition they promoted Henry's cause, and in 1543, the Scottish nobility were offered money in the hope that they would agree to the English scheme. Mary of Guise, the infant Queen's mother, made counterbids, paying the Earls Angus and Bothwell pensions of £1000 each to oppose the match.

The Earl of Arran, however, persuaded a corrupted and divided parliament to agree to the English marriage. The terms were finally settled in two treaties drawn up at Greenwich on 1 July 1543. When Mary reached her eleventh year she would marry Edward, Henry VIII's son, and there would

During the minority of her daughter, Mary of Guise took an active part in the struggle for power, supporting the French cause against those Scottish nobles in favour of association with England; when she became Governor in 1554 she pursued a policy of French domination. She was lenient to the Scottish Reformers until 1559 when she provoked a rebellion which brought Scotland's long political connection with France to an end. (*SNPG*)

be peace between Scotland and England until the marriage took place. Both treaties were solemnly ratified by the Scots at Holyrood on 25 August 1543.

Within a week, the Earl of Arran suddenly re-embraced the Catholic faith and made Cardinal Beaton, the nephew of Archbishop Beaton who had burned Hamilton, and Mary of Guise members of a new Council that would govern Scotland. Beaton, made Chancellor of Scotland, immediately had the infant Mary crowned Queen of the Scots on 9 September 1543, the thirtieth anniversary of Flodden.

Henry VIII reacted swiftly to Arran's *volte-face*. One Sunday in May 1544, the people of Edinburgh woke up to see a vast English fleet lying off Newhaven. Under the Earl of Hertford, English troops had been sent to take Edinburgh. Cardinal Beaton, unable to hold the town, fled to Linlithgow. Although Edinburgh ultimately fell into English hands, the castle held. In anger, Hertford set fire to Holyrood Palace and the town. It is said the city burned for three days.

James Beaton (*c* 1480–1539) acted as Chancellor of Scotland for thirteen years and was a staunch supporter of the French connection.   (*BCA*)

The following year another English army, led by Sir Ralph Eure and Sir Brian Layton, was cleverly defeated by the Earl of Angus at Ancrum Moor. Not only men, but women and children took part in the battle, as an inscription on a local grave illustrates:

> Fair Maiden Lilliard lies under this stane,
> Little was her stature but muckle was her fame,
> Upon the English loons she laid many thumps, And
> when her legs were cuttit off,
> She fought upon her stumps.

In 1545 Hertford crossed the border again, determined to force the Scots into fulfilling the terms of the Greenwich treaties. The Scots called Hertford's invasion the 'Rough Wooing' as the English ravished the countryside. Five Scottish market towns were destroyed, seven border monasteries burned and 243 villages plundered. Hertford razed four abbeys, Kelso, Melrose, Dryburgh and Eccles. Sixteen keeps and castles were taken and garrisoned by English troops. Throughout southern Scotland, fields of crops, barns and windmills blazed. Hertford's campaign did much to sour relations between the Scots and the English and pushed the former into the hands of the French.

The Protestant Reformer, George Wishart, meanwhile, had returned to Scotland in 1543 as a political activist, an agent of Henry VIII. Two years later Cardinal Beaton had Wishart arrested. He was burned, like Hamilton, at St Andrews, while Beaton looked on. In fact most who were burnt to death by the Church of Rome died in Beaton's diocese, where the Archbishop seemed more concerned about an ideology than a faith.

In the early hours of the morning of 29 May 1546 Beaton was murdered at St Andrews Castle. His assassination was planned by Henry VIII and carried out by a group of Fife Protestants who opposed his pro-French policy. Led by William Kirkcaldy of Grange, who was in collusion with a Scot in London, the sixteen conspirators broke into the castle and threw Beaton's servants out. Having hung his body from the window from which he had watched Wishart burn, the assassins fortified the castle and appealed to England for help. The Earl of Arran retaliated by besieging the castle and called upon the French to send troops. The Castilians, as the Protestants at

George Wishart (*c* 1513–46), a teacher in the Grammar School at Montrose, went first to Germany and Switzerland when charged with heresy. After studying at Cambridge he returned to Scotland in 1543 and was burned to death three years later by Cardinal Beaton at St Andrews. (*SNPG*)

A contemporary view of the Battle of Pinkie where supporters of the Scottish Catholic cause were heavily defeated in September 1547. (*NGS*)

St Andrews came to be called, held out until July and were joined by sympathizers, including John Knox.

John Knox was born in Haddington about the year 1512. He started his working life as a teacher and family tutor and in 1536 was ordained as a priest. It was not until 1545 that he showed any interest in the Reformation. Now imprisoned in St Andrews Castle, Knox, like the other 150 Castilians waited for English troops to relieve them. Unfortunately, the French arrived first. After a month, the Castilians were forced to capitulate, and Knox was among those sent to France to work as galley slaves. Scottish Protestantism seemed crushed and Mary of Guise was jubilant.

Henry VIII, meanwhile, had died. Hertford, now Duke of Somerset, ruled England in the name of Henry's boy heir, Edward, and was as determined as England's old King had been to compel the Scots to give up their alliance with France. In 1547 he invaded Scotland once again and the Earl of Arran raised another Scottish army to meet him. The two faced each other at Pinkie, near Musselburgh. Somerset had 16,000 men; but Arran's army was larger. The River Esk lay between the two, and instead of waiting for the English to attack, the Scots boldly crossed the river to meet the invaders. Fifteen hundred Scots were taken prisoner and over 1000 killed. English losses were slight. The Scots called the day of the battle, 10 September 1547, Black Friday.

Again the English moved to occupy eastern Scotland. Dundee was savagely sacked and strongholds like Broughty Castle were manned by

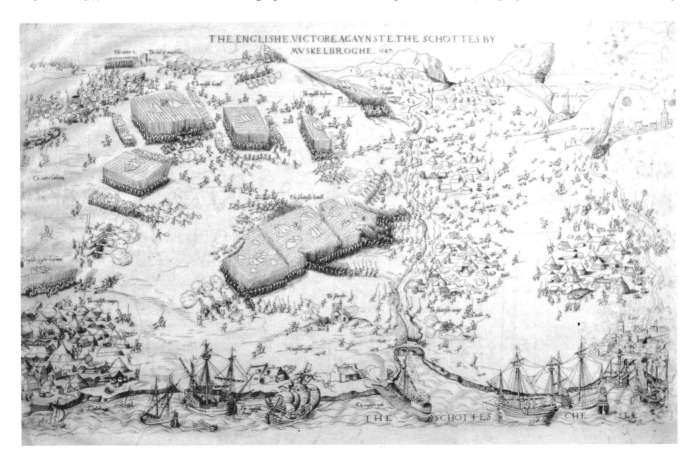

English troops. The town of Haddington was chosen by Somerset as the English headquarters and, realizing they could not push the English out by themselves, the Scots appealed to the French for help.

In July 1548, 7000 French troops, veterans of campaigns in Italy and Germany, arrived. The French, however, refused to let them fight until the Scots agreed to their child Queen Mary marrying the Dauphin, the future King of France. She would be sent to France immediately and Scottish castles, once cleared of the English, would be handed over to the French. Scotland it seemed was to be free of the English only to be dominated by the French. By the Treaty of Boulogne, signed in 1549, the English reluctantly agreed to withdraw. French troops occupied Scotland for eight years and were hated and distrusted by the ordinary folk on whom they were billeted. But with this strong French presence, Scottish Catholics held on to power.

Although content with its political victory, the Church was aware of its need for spiritual reform. In August 1552 Archbishop Hamilton's *Catechism* was distributed. Written in simple, moving language, the *Catechism* was a genuine attempt to meet some of the points raised by the Reformers. John Hamilton, who was Archbishop of St Andrews, tried in a series of councils to put the worse abuses right:

Mary Queen of Scots left Dumbarton on 29 July 1548.   (*CAC*)

> This synod exhorts that neither prelates nor their subordinate clergy keep their offspring born of concubinage in their company, nor suffer them directly or indirectly to be promoted in their churches, nor under colour of any pretext to marry their daughters to barons or make their sons barons out of the patrimony of Christ.
>
> Likewise it is statute that no cleric having the means of an honourable livelihood according to his own calling engage in secular pursuits, especially by trading, . . . or by leasing farms from others allow himself to be withdrawn by farm work from spiritual exercises to the neglect of his proper cure of souls.

Little, however, was done to improve the quality of the priesthood, or make bishops visit parishes and personally root out abuse. The Church failed to answer the Reformers' principal argument that it did not preach the Word of God.

In 1549 a Council demanded that Bishops preach in person four times a year. Ten years later, in 1559, another Council asked Bishops to preach frequently and called on them to explain the meaning of the Sacraments to their congregations; but Scottish bishops were loath to take to the pulpit. Parishes remained neglected. The vast income of the Church, some £300,000, could have endowed each parish in Scotland with £300 a year and attracted better men; but there was not the will to reform.

Mary of Guise realized that, to be secure, she would have to win over the Scots nobility, many of whom were declared Protestants. In 1550 she took a group of nobles to France where the Earl of Glencairn, the Lords Home and Maxwell and the Master of Ruthven were granted pensions by the French King. In Scotland, meanwhile, Frenchmen ruled.

In England the young Edward VI died on 6 July 1553 and his Catholic sister, Mary, became Queen. The Protestant party in Scotland could no longer rely on England to help them. Mary of Guise now felt strong enough to remove the Earl of Arran, who in 1550 had been created Duc de Châtelherault with a yearly income of 30,000 livres. In 1554, by a mixture of

John Knox (c1512–72). A supporter of George Wishart, he was involved with the murderers of Cardinal Beaton, and when St Andrews fell to Mary of Guise he was sent to the French galleys. (*NLS*)

John Calvin (1509–64), a French Reformer in Geneva, was John Knox's mentor. (*SNPG*)

The Temple de l'Auditoire, Geneva, in which Calvin and Knox preached. It is now used by Scottish, Dutch, Italian and Spanish Protestants. (*Author*)

threats and bribes, he was forced to relinquish his office and members of his family were also deprived of power. She, however, continued to recognize the family's claim to the Scottish throne, should her daughter Mary bear no children. Skilfully, Mary of Guise, now Scotland's official Regent, used patronage to neutralize the Scottish nobility. The Earl of Argyll was weaned from supporting the cause of the Reformation by making a Campbell Bishop of Brechin. The Earl of Glencairn was kept inactive by a further pension, this time the annual sum of £900 from Kelso Abbey.

After serving his sentence in the French galleys, John Knox lived in England. During his five-year stay he met all the leading English Reformers, including Thomas Cranmer, and the English thought highly of him. But when the Catholic Mary became Queen of England in 1553, Knox fled to Frankfurt and then to Switzerland. In Geneva, he met John Calvin, whose Protestantism was an uncompromising fighting faith. Calvin preached the total powerlessness of man; man was predestined: only God's elect would be saved. The Church, argued Calvin, was the company and multitude of men chosen of God, and the Bible, the Old Testament as well as the New, could not err. The Bible was the source of truth, although the truth was often difficult to find. In Scotland, Calvinism spread rapidly, and became the dominant spirit of the Reformation.

In 1557, five noblemen, the 'Lords of the Congregation' as they called themselves, made a band or covenant to quit the Roman Church and work to make Scotland Protestant. The Covenant or First Bond, signed in December, was designed to promote faithful ministers and defend them and their congregations from interference. Within a year, burgesses and gentry throughout Scotland had subscribed to it, and the nobility rather than Knox and his religious colleagues took over leadership of the Reformation.

Meanwhile Mary of Guise was planning her daughter's future. On 14 December 1557 Scottish commissioners had been sent to Paris to conclude the marriage treaty between their young Queen Mary and the future King of France. Four out of the eight commissioners died before leaving France. They had learnt too much, it was rumoured, and the French had poisoned them. During the discussions the Scots had been pressed to send the crown of Scotland to France and had stubbornly refused. They would not allow the Dauphin, François, to be crowned with it. The Crown Matrimonial was to be allowed the French prince but not the Scottish succession. The marriage contract would be a personal union of the crowns of France and Scotland without any loss of Scottish sovereignty.

On 24 April 1558, in Notre Dame Cathedral, Mary of Scotland, fifteen and vivacious, married François, Dauphin of France, a sickly, feeble and physically stunted boy. Unknown to the Scots, Mary had signed three documents less than three weeks before the marriage that gave away her Scottish kingdom. The French House of Valois was to succeed to the throne of Scotland on her death. In France, the Dauphin openly boasted that he was King of Scotland.

In 1558 Mary Tudor of England died. Elizabeth I, the Protestant, succeeded her and now it was the turn of Catholics to burn at the stake. England under Elizabeth would be a Protestant country, by force if necessary. In Scotland, Mary of Guise was bent on suppressing the Lords of the Congregation's Covenant. She demanded that Protestant preachers appear

The Monument de la Réformation erected in Geneva in 1917. The figures from left to right are John Calvin, Guillaume Farel, Théodore de Beza and John Knox.   (*Author*)

before her in obedience to the Church of Rome. When none saw fit to show themselves, the French Regent outlawed them all. Then on 1 January 1559 one of the most curious documents of the Scottish Reformation appeared. On the doors of friaries and hospitals in all the major Scottish burghs was pinned what came to be known as the Beggars' Summons. It demanded that friars quit their houses by 'flitting Friday', 12 May, so that the poor of the town could take possession of them. For a long time, the Church had ceased to support those in distress, and the houses and hospitals, it was claimed, belonged to the poor by right. The Summons was drawn up and distributed by men of substance in a deliberate attempt to rouse the mob into action.

As a result of the Summons, many burghs, including Dundee and Perth, publicly embraced the reformed faith, and the Protestant nobility recalled John Knox to Scotland. He landed at Leith on 2 May 1559, to a reception that astonished him. In Edinburgh he was surrounded by an adoring regiment of women. Knox, however, was not the father of the Scottish Reformation; nor was he to be its most important disciple, although he himself thought he was. His contribution was that he could stir men's minds. An Englishman said of him that in an hour of preaching Knox could put more heart into his congregation than 500 trumpets continually blustering. He was the Reformation's rabble-rouser.

On 11 May 1559 Knox preached at St John's Church in Perth, where he denounced the Roman Church as idolatry. As he spoke, a priest approached the altar to say Mass. A boy threw a stone at him and the congregation rioted. Images were wrecked along with sacred pictures. Perth rioted for two days. Two monasteries and an abbey in the town were gutted – stripped of their gold and silver, their lead, meat, wine, linen and furniture. The mob even pulled up trees in monastery gardens and threatened the inmates with death. They went on to raze the abbey at Scone and the Regent Mary realized she had to act swiftly. She summoned her forces under Argyll, Lord James Stewart and the Hamiltons and marched towards Perth on 22 May. In reply,

John Knox preaching before the Lords
of the Congregation on 10 June 1559;
by the celebrated Scottish artist,
Sir David Wilkie (1785–1841).
(*NGS*)

'Sacking a Church at the time of John
Knox' by John Prescott Knight
(1803–81). In fact, less damage was
done to ecclesiastical property in
Scotland than in England.   (*TG*)

the Lords of the Congregation assembled their own army, occupied St Andrews and sacked the town's magnificent cathedral. Within weeks the French faction lost the support of much of the nobility it had so carefully and expensively bought. Argyll and Stewart drew their forces back from Perth and then deserted them. 'You cannot tell friend from enemy, and he who is with us in the morning is on the other side after dinner,' Henri Cleutin, Sieur d'Oysel, the French Ambassador and chief adviser to Mary of Guise, was moved to remark. Mary of Guise was forced to retreat to Edinburgh and thence to Dunbar. The Lords of the Congregation entered the capital in triumph, while she waited for French troops to arrive. By late August, 2000 arrived from France, and Mary, with an army of 4000 was bent on revenge. She took Leith and fortified the port. Outnumbered, the Protestant forces left Edinburgh and realized that only the English, disinterested until now in Scotland's religious squabbles, could save the day. And the English for an incredible unforeseen reason, chose to intervene.

In France, Henri II died in July 1559, and his son, Mary Queen of Scots' husband, became François II. Arrogantly he added the royal emblems of Scotland and England to his coat of arms. Like all of Catholic Europe, the new French monarch regarded Elizabeth I of England as illegitimate and believed that his wife, Mary Queen of Scots, was the rightful heir to England's throne through her descent from Henry VII. Elizabeth desperately needed allies, and the Protestant Scots were the closest available.

In August 1559, Elizabeth sent money north to assist the cause of Protestantism. In January 1560, although she could not afford it, she sent the English fleet to blockade the French and lay siege to the French garrison heavily fortified at Leith. The French held out and fought bravely. On May Day alone, they slaughtered 1000 English troops. The Scots meanwhile stood back and let the English do their fighting for them. Then on 11 June Mary of Guise died of dropsy in Edinburgh Castle. On hearing the news, the French garrison at Leith surrendered. On 6 July 1560, by the Treaty of Edinburgh, the French agreed to withdraw their troops from Scotland and recognize Elizabeth Tudor as Queen of England. The Scots were not party to the Treaty; but a series of 'concessions to the Scots' were made. No foreigners were henceforth to be appointed to office in Scotland, and the government of the country was to be entrusted to a council of twelve, seven nominated by Mary Queen of Scots, who was still in France, and five by the Scots parliament which was to meet on 1 August 1560. Both the French and the English agreed that the question of religion was a matter to be settled by Mary and her husband.

When the Estates met in accordance with the Treaty of Edinburgh a large number of earls and Roman Catholic Bishops, including those of St Andrews, Dunblane and Dunkeld, attended. Twenty-two burghs also sent representatives; but what proved of greatest importance was that the new parliament contained 110 lesser barons. For a week they debated whether they were a legal assembly or not. Mary Queen of Scots, after all, had not ratified the Treaty of Edinburgh, a prerequisite to the Estates assembling. By a majority vote, it was decided that they were legally constituted despite their Queen's reluctance to sign. The Estates business committee, the Lords of the Articles, was appointed from the ranks of those in favour of the Protestant faith and the Reformers grasped the chance to

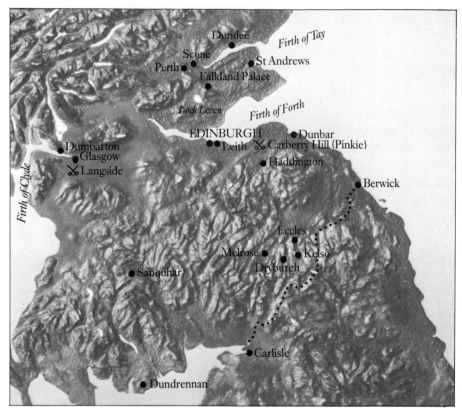

turn a political victory into a religious one. The authority of the Pope in Scotland was formally abolished and the celebration of Mass forbidden. Knox was asked to produce a definition of the new faith and in four days of prodigious effort came up with the twenty-five *Articles of Confession of Faith*. The 'Scots Confession', as it was otherwise known, remained the basis of the reformed faith of Scotland for over eighty years.

In return for confirming the new faith in the Estates the nobles of Scotland grabbed two-thirds of the old Church lands. By Act of parliament, they gave themselves legal right to the Roman wealth they were already collecting; and the Roman clergy, whose ranks had dwindled to 3000, were either pensioned off or subsequently chose to join the new reformed Kirk.

But the parliament that met in Edinburgh in August 1560 was illegal, despite its own thoughts on the matter. Mary Queen of Scots had refused to ratify the Treaty of Edinburgh because by doing so she would deny all claim to the English throne. Tragic events in France brought about her return to Scotland. A Catholic, she would come back to a kingdom in which Protestantism was now the ascendant force.

5

Mary and an End to the French Connection

MARY QUEEN OF SCOTS had been sent to France at the age of five. At the châteaux of Fontainebleu, Blois and Chambord in the Loire Valley, the young Scots Queen grew up. Cocooned by life on a lavish scale, with a huge royal household to service every need, Mary was taught how to draw and dance and become an accomplished musician on the lute and virginals. Her education had been broad: she learnt Italian and Spanish and understood a little Latin. Under the supervision of her four uncles, especially the Cardinal of Lorraine, Mary had become a devout Catholic. In 1560, her happy life was shattered. She mourned the passing of her boy husband, François II, King of France, at Christmas as the result of a septic ear. The English Ambassador, Sir Nicholas Throckmorton, commented that the dead king had left, 'as dolorous a wife as she had good cause to be'. At the age of seventeen, Mary now had little place in the new Court of François's young brother, Charles, and his formidable mother, Catherine de Medici, Regent of France.

The widowed Mary could have graced any Court of Europe. Charles IX, King of Navarre, thought of divorcing his Queen in order to be free to marry Mary, and the Duke of Finland and King Frederick of Denmark also had designs on her. The insane Don Carlos of Spain, son of Philip II, was put forward as a suitor; but when the Spanish King could no longer conceal his son's madness, Scotland was considered by Mary's avuncular advisers more attractive.

In the twelve months before her return on 19 August 1561, the Protestant Reformers continued to be busy. The Estates, having adopted Knox's *Confession of Faith*, went on to commission a 'Book of Reformation' to lay down the organizational structure of the new Kirk. *The First Book of Discipline*, as it was called, proposed that the Kirk should take over the old structure of Roman Catholic bishoprics. Superintendents with status and function similar to Bishops were appointed over districts of Scotland to preside over Kirk courts. What, however, made the new Church revolutionary was that laymen, Elders, were to be given responsibility in religious matters. Each parish was to appoint a Kirk Session to assist the minister. The Kirk, moreover, was to hold a regular General Assembly, attended by laymen as well as superintendents.

The Bible was the basis of the Scottish Confession of Faith. People had to know and understand the Scriptures, and preaching was therefore to be an

John Knox was one of the committee commissioned by the Estates to organize the structure of the new Kirk. *The First Book of Discipline* was published in 1560. (*CAC*) (*NLS, below*)

intrinsic part of worship. Ministers were instructed to speak in Scots and in a loud, clear voice so that everybody could hear. The seven Sacraments of Roman Catholicism were reduced to two, Baptism and Communion. The Reformers believed that Communion was the principal means of grace for the Christian. All the faithful were to share in the celebration and worshippers were to be seated at long tables in keeping with the original Lord's Supper. Nobody was to kneel: to do so before bread and wine smacked of idolatry. The emphasis was to be not on what is in the bread or what happens to it but on what happens when God comes to a community of people sitting together, praying, and experiencing His grace. This was a rather evangelical and dynamic view; in a sense the Church itself became the body of Christ.

Roman Church festivals were banned. To Calvinists, Christmas was the 'heathen feast of Christ's Mass'; Christ's birth, like his death, was to be remembered throughout this year, not just on one day. With Christmas banned, the old midwinter festival of the Norsemen took over: Hogmanay, with no Christian associations whatsoever, became Scotland's main celebration.

The Book of Discipline also laid down that the new ministry was not to live humbly. Ministers were to have manses and glebes – land on which to grow crops and raise a cow – and be paid adequately. Their sons were to be eligible for bursaries to enable them to go to school and university and dowries were to be made available for their daughters. Ministers' wives, if widowed, would be provided for by the Kirk. Sensible attention was paid to social needs. Relief was planned for the poor and great stress put upon the need and duty to educate the laity. The Reformers felt it was their moral duty to train men's minds and wished every congregation to have a school. A national system of free, compulsory education was advocated, but the noble ideal could not be put into practice. In January 1561, the majority of nobles refused to ratify clauses in *The First Book of Discipline* concerning tithes which alone could have provided sufficient funds to finance the education plans. In the previous thirty years the Lords of the Congregation had grabbed a considerable amount of land from the old Church. To give up those revenues would not only reduce their financial prestige but also create a vigorous, well-endowed Kirk that could pose a real threat politically.

Most of the existing Church buildings continued to be used by the Reformers. St Giles in Edinburgh was whitewashed and some forty altars, once maintained by the Trade Guilds, were removed. Seventeen booth-like side chapels, stuffed with idolatrous relics, were also thrown out. The new religion was harsh for the simple adherents of the old faith. The crusading zeal of the Reformers forced folk to throw out all objects of piety. Scots were to be pulled together under the Law of God. Discipline, Calvin had said, was 'the very sinews of religion'.

But the appeal of the Reformed religion was Lowland: the Kirk's numbers as small as its aspirations large. Even as late as 1565 there were still more Catholics than Protestants in Edinburgh and a third of Scotland's nobility by 1600 were still of the old Church. This tenuous hold of the Kirk on the minds of the people gave grounds for the English obsession that a revival of French Catholic influence in Scotland, fostered by Mary, was imminent.

On her first Sunday in Edinburgh, Mary Queen of Scots attended Mass.

The mob of Edinburgh rioted and Lord James Stewart, her half-brother, had to hold closed the door of her chapel to stop the people breaking in. Knox, a master of stirring violent passions, declaimed in St Giles against Mary's act of worship:

> That one Mass was more fearful than if ten thousand armed enemies were landed in any part of the realm, of purpose to suppress the whole religion.

But Mary was no fanatic. Her French friends had advised her 'to serve the time, to accommodate herself discreetly and gently to her own subjects . . . and, in effect, to repose most upon those of the reformed religion'. She took as her advisers Lord James Stewart and the diplomat William Maitland of Lethington, both Protestants, and she gave little encouragement to the Jesuit, de Gouda, when he was sent to Scotland as the Pope's representative in 1562, declining to send a Scottish representative to the last Session of the Council of Trent which met to counter the Reformation. Her administration went about its work as if the Acts of 1560 were law.

Indeed for Mary, reversal of the 1560 legislation was out of the question. A part of the Thirds, levied on old Church property now in the hands of the Scottish nobility, was being used by the Crown to help pay the expenses of government, including the cost of the Queen's bodyguard, and Roman Catholics in Scotland had little to offer. They had no leadership. The two clerics who might have provided it, Archbishop James Beaton of Glasgow and William Chisholm of Dunblane, had gone abroad.

Meanwhile Mary had to make do with a poor kingdom, whose population was a fraction that of France. Fond of masques, music, cards and dancing, she brought gaiety to the Scottish Court. In her quieter moments she indulged her love of literature and poetry in the company of George Buchanan and embroidered fine tapestry with her four 'Maries', ladies-in-waiting who had accompanied her from France. From 1562 to 1566 she spent the clear-aired months of spring at Falkland Palace in Fife. There she pursued her love of archery, hunting, hawking and golf. She was tall, nearly six feet, and had learnt her charm at the French Court. But she was also a tomboy, who liked wearing men's clothes and mixing with her soldiers. In Inverness in 1562, she amazed the English Ambassador by claiming when the soldiers came back from sentry duty, that 'she was sorry she was not a man to be all night on the fields and to walk the causeway with buff coat, steel helmet, buckler and broadsword'.

For the first four years of her reign in Scotland, Mary was a conscientious Queen. She presided regularly over her Council, attended the opening of the Estates and, above all, dispensed justice, a vital duty of Scottish monarchs. She travelled extensively throughout her kingdom, and her 'progresses', as they were called, enabled her to get to know Scotland and her nobility, and her subjects to get to know their youthful Queen. For all her charm and vivacity, she was a political animal. In the eyes of Catholic Europe, Mary Queen of Scots had justly asserted her right to the throne of England, and throughout her life her policy was designed to maximize that claim. Mary realized that politically she needed the support of the Scottish Reformers.

The leaders of the Kirk, however, were anxious: the monarch was supposed to be the magistrate who would purify and control their Calvinist

William Hole's painting of Mary Queen of Scots' arrival in Edinburgh is a somewhat romantic portrayal: in fact it was pouring with rain when she arrived in August 1561 to rule Scotland. (*CAC*)

John Knox became minister of St Giles Kirk in Edinburgh after the Reformation. He immediately set about writing his memoirs, his *History of the Reformation*, which contains many documents of historical importance but gives his own role in the religious upheaval more prominence than he was entitled to claim. (*NLS*)

Church. Knox was deeply shocked by Mary's attending Mass regularly and her gay court parties were seen as pagan rites. Her interest in the works of Boccaccio and Rabelais – banned by Reformers and Catholics alike – smacked of Old Testament decadence. In contrast, Mary saw Knox as a renegade priest. He had been sentenced to death by a Church court and legally did not exist. Knox, on the other hand, regarded himself as 'The Joshua of the Scots'. It was an opinion not shared by his contemporaries; but he truly believed he had been given the duty to lead the Scots to the Promised Land.

Knox and Mary met four times. At the first and most important of their confrontations, which took place in her apartments at Holyrood Palace on Thursday, 4 September 1561, Knox took pains to lecture the Queen on the power of princes and in his *History of the Reformation* gives his own version of what he said, or perhaps would have liked to have said:

> My travail is that both princes and subjects obey God. And think not, Madam, that wrong is done unto you when ye are willed to be subject unto God: for it is He that subjects people under princes, and causes obedience to be given unto them; yea God craves of Kings That they be as it were foster-fathers to his Church, and commands queens to be nurses unto his people.

Mary saw society as a hierarchy. In France the doctrine of divine right was gaining ground; kings were gods among men and a law unto themselves.

Such ideas, of course, were alien to the Scots, who believed that their King was by and large one of their own number, elevated to rule.

To Knox Kirk and State could be twin pillars of God's house on earth, complementary governments of God's people. Mary would have to be converted if she was to take her place in his new Commonwealth of Israel. But Mary remained unconvinced. She was as well aware as her adversary of the 'democratic' implications of the Reformation. Calvinism, by advocating a form of 'nation state', would undermine monarchy. Instead of kings ruling directly under God, the Reformers were claiming that a contract existed between the monarch and the people, and moreover, between the monarch, the people and God.

So Knox and Mary remained implacable enemies. When Mary was captive in England, Knox wrote to William Cecil, later Lord Burghley, advocating her death.

> If ye strike not at the root the branches that appear to be broken will bud again.

Despite Knox's tirades, Mary was to cling to her Catholicism for the rest of her life; but it was the men in her life and her marriage that made her a Jezebel in the eyes of the Scots.

Marriage was the major problem facing any ruling queen in the sixteenth century. Elizabeth I of England chose not to marry: but used the prospect of marriage as a political and diplomatic carrot. Mary, however, needed a husband to provide heirs that would improve her claim to the English throne. In an attempt to isolate Mary from Catholic Europe, in 1564 Elizabeth suggested Mary marry her own lover, Robert Dudley. Negotiations went on for a year: but while they dragged on another scheme was being hatched.

Henry Stewart, Lord Darnley, was born in 1545 at Temple Newsam, five miles east of Leeds. His mother, Margaret Douglas, Countess of Lennox, was the daughter of Margaret Tudor by her second marriage, to the 6th Earl of Angus, so that Henry was Mary's own first cousin. Politically marriage to Darnley would enable Mary to score against Elizabeth I by uniting two claims to her throne. So amidst great celebrations and festivities the couple were married at the Chapel Royal of Holyrood Palace on 29 July 1565. The bells had barely ceased ringing before Mary realized her mistake. Darnley was an arrogant playboy, lacking sense and principle. The Catholic marriage did not impress the Scots. Elizabeth of England was also angry: Darnley had married without her consent. She promptly sent Lady Lennox to the Tower and made it clear to Mary that her marriage had done nothing to improve her position as heir to the English throne.

Soon jealousies began to grow, particularly with Lord James Stewart, Earl of Moray, who withdrew in May 1565 from Mary's Council and in August raised a rebellion. Mary pawned her jewels to raise an army to fight her half-brother. Moray gave her forces the slip and no battles were fought in what came to be known as the Chaseabout Raid. The escapade ended on 6 October, when Moray fled to England for safety.

Realizing the worthlessness of her husband, and having lost her most able adviser, Mary turned her back on the Scottish nobility and leant heavily on her household staff. She began to bring foreigners into her Court and relied on non-aristocratic advisers, like Sir James Balfour, who became Clerk-Register.

Mary Queen of Scots
(1542–87). (*AAG*)

Henry Stewart, Lord Darnley
(1546–67). (*SNPG*)

William Maitland of Lethington
(*c* 1525–73), son of Sir Richard
Maitland, was a Lord of Session and a
devotee of Anglo-Scottish amity.
(*SNPG*)

Soon Mary and Darnley fell out. The Queen was pregnant and could no longer ride or hunt; Darnley pursued these pleasures on his own. Upon their marriage, Mary had agreed to give Darnley the title of King, but not the authority that went with it. Darnley became petulant.

Within ten months of their marriage, the Queen was seeking solace from David Rizzio, an Italian singer and musician who arrived in Scotland with the Ambassador of Savoy. Attracted first by his musical skills and a mutual love of cards, Mary made him a secretary on the establishment she maintained as Queen Dowager of France. Believing that Rizzio was the father of Mary's unborn child, Darnley plotted with the Earls Argyll, Glencairn, Rothes, Ochiltree, Boyd and Kirkcaldy of Grange to kill the Italian in such a way as to terrorize his wife. On the evening of 9 March 1566, Darnley and the others broke into Mary's supper room in Holyrood, where she was dining with Rizzio and her half-sister, Janet, Countess of Argyll. Rizzio was dragged out screaming and killed with fifty-six dagger strokes. Mary was deliberately jostled and held at gunpoint in the hope that she would miscarry. The next day she was locked in her bedroom while Darnley, acting as king, suspended parliament. She was never to forgive Darnley for endangering her own life and remarked to Lord Ruthven, 'it is within my belly that one day will avenge these cruelties and affronts'.

At nine o'clock in the morning on 19 June 1566, the future James VI was born in Edinburgh Castle. Darnley did not stir himself to see the child until the afternoon. Before witnesses, Mary made clear to him who was the father of the child:

> My Lord God has given you and me a son, begotten by none but you.
> This is the son whom I hope shall first unite the two kingdoms of Scotland and England.

James's birth, however, only weakened Mary's own position. The Scots now had an heir, and Mary, who was seriously ill after her confinement, was desperate to find men of assured loyalty. She began, skilfully, to detach Darnley from his allies. On 20 June she pardoned her half-brother Moray and looked to the thirty-year-old Earl of Bothwell. A Protestant, patriotic and loyal, Bothwell held five castles in south-east Scotland and could, if required, muster men to defend the Queen. Mary was vulnerable and frightened. In the Earl of Bothwell, however, she found security from a notorious womanizer. For generations his family had had the reputation of being more than just kind to widowed Scottish Queens. In 1543 Earl Patrick Bothwell had procured a divorce with a view to marrying Mary of Guise; his son now consoled her daughter.

In both private and public life, Darnley continued to behave abominably; even those with whom he had conspired to murder Rizzio considered that he had betrayed them. The estrangement of the Royal couple presented a major problem of state, and at Craigmillar Castle, outside Edinburgh, Mary met with some of her nobles in November 1566. She made it clear she was against divorce from Darnley because it might make the baby James illegitimate. Maitland of Lethington suggested there might be 'other means': violence was the only option open to the Queen.

Darnley meanwhile fell ill with syphilis in Glasgow, and Mary went to visit him. At the end of January 1567 she had him brought to Edinburgh and placed him in a house at Kirk o'Field on the outskirts of the town known as the 'Old Provost's Lodging'. On Sunday, 9 February, Mary left a wedding masque at Holyrood to go and visit him. Accompanied by the Earls Bothwell, Argyll, Huntly and Cassillis, she spent a few hours consoling her husband while the lords played dice. Then Mary reminded the group that they must return to the ball, and gave Darnley a ring as a token of her affection. Darnley, sulking, was left alone with his two valets.

At two o'clock in the morning there was an explosion. The bodies of Darnley and his servant Taylor were found some distance away from the smoking ruins. They had obviously left in a hurry: Darnley was dressed only in his nightshirt. It looked as though they had been woken by the noise of the conspirators and tried to escape. Neither was marked by the force of the explosion and their murder remains Scotland's greatest unsolved mystery.

The amount of gunpowder used suggests that some of the plotters may well have wished to kill not only Darnley but the Queen as well. But for the masque, she had intended staying with him on the night of 9 February. The murder appears to have involved many, each of whom played a different role. There was Sir James Balfour, the unscrupulous brother of the man who had suggested the lodgings. He was reported to have bought gunpowder a few days before. The Earl of Moray curiously quit Edinburgh for St Andrews the day before the explosion and made his way to France. He returned later to be the chief beneficiary of Darnley's death, when he assumed the Regency for James VI in 1567. There was also the Hamilton family, dynastic rivals of the House of Lennox. Châtelherault, their leader, owned a house on the north

James Hepburn, 4th Earl of Bothwell (c 1535–78). Although a Reformer, he had supported Mary of Guise and was out of favour with Mary Queen of Scots until 1565. (SNPG)

James Stewart, Earl of Moray (1531–70), a son of James V by Margaret Erskine, joined the Reformers in 1559. He was created Earl of Mar in 1562 and Earl of Moray the following year. When he raised a rebellion against Mary's marriage to Darnley he was forced into England, but was involved in Darnley's plot to murder Rizzio. (SNPG)

'The murder of Rizzio' by William Allan. David Rizzio (c 1533–66) was born in Turin. A plaque at Holyrood marks the spot where he was murdered on 9 March 1566. (NGS)

side of the Kirk o'Field quadrangle, and was there that night. The Earl of Bothwell, however, was the prime suspect. According to four witnesses gunpowder in large quantities had been delivered to his home and then taken by packhorses to the fatal house at Kirk o'Field.

Few facts are known. The powder that blew up the house was certainly stored in an adjoining building and transferred through communicating vaults shortly before the explosion; but by whom is not certain. From all contemporary accounts, Archibald Douglas and his men were given the task of surrounding the house, and it was probably he who smothered Darnley as he fled. Douglas had been involved in Rizzio's murder in 1566 and was later to be a staunch supporter of Mary after she was deposed. After the murder, cartoons and placards appeared in Edinburgh accusing Mary as well as Bothwell. In an attempt to scotch rumour, the Queen offered a reward of £2000 for information. The Scottish people were convinced that the Earl of Bothwell was responsible for the murder, and he was brought to trial on 12 April. However, when Mary's Privy Councillors met to discuss the form of the trial, Bothwell sat in with them, and on the day of the hearing he packed the city of Edinburgh with armed men. Lennox, the chief prosecutor, was stopped on the road from Linlithgow, and no one, therefore, came forward to support the charge. The jurors were forced to acquit.

A week later, at Ainslie's Tavern in the Canongate, twenty-eight lords and prelates took supper with Bothwell. Although they signed a document supporting his marriage to Mary, she refused Bothwell's proposal and left Edinburgh to join her son, James, at Stirling. On 24 April as Mary was returning to the capital, Bothwell with 800 men persuaded her to accompany him to Dunbar Castle, claiming that there was a risk of a rebellion against her in Edinburgh. At Dunbar, Bothwell raped Mary so that she would have to marry him. Mary's claim, however, that she had been raped was not widely believed as she had accompanied him to Dunbar without any show of resistance. On 7 May 1567, fearing pregnancy, Mary authorized Bothwell's divorce from his new wife, Lady Jean Gordon, and a week later married him herself.

The newlyweds quickly fell out. It is likely that Bothwell on their honeymoon disclosed an indiscreet relationship between his father and her mother which shocked her. The scandal may, in fact, have concerned Mary's own birth. The marriage, although Protestant, outraged the Scottish Reformers, and brought about an immediate rebellion. Bothwell and Mary, besieged at Borthwick Castle, escaped and raised an army for their defence. The two armies met in June 1567, at Carberry Hill, the rebel Scottish nobles blatantly two-faced. They carried a banner showing the infant James VI praying for revenge beside his father's corpse with the words 'Judge and revenge my case, O Lord'. But there was no fighting; the warm summer's day went by with challenges to duels being thrown out and not accepted, and the tragi-comedy ended as the Queen's army drifted away. Bothwell himself fled the field and made for Orkney. From there he went to Norway, where he was arrested by the King of Denmark and died, a madman, in a Danish prison in 1578. His mummified body used to lie in Faarevejle church near Dragsholm and has recently been buried.

Mary was taken by the Lords of the Congregation to Edinburgh where the mob demanded she be burnt. Knox branded her the 'Scottish whore'

Bothwell's mummified remains. (*Politikens*)

William Hole's painting, 'Mary taken captive to Edinburgh', depicts accurately the anger of the mob: they felt she had disgraced the monarchy by her association with Bothwell.   (*CAC*)

who, by her very presence, had become the instrument of intrigue, murder and suspicion. From the pulpit of St Giles he called for her overthrow. She was imprisoned at Loch Leven Castle on 16 June 1567 and formally renounced her throne on 24 July. Five days later at the church of the Holy Rude in Stirling, James, aged thirteen months, was crowned James VI of Scotland. John Knox preached the sermon at the first Protestant coronation in Scotland's history; but only five earls and eight lords thought it prudent to attend. Mary's Protestant half-brother, James Stewart, the Earl of Moray became Regent, and in December had parliament re-enact all the Reformist religious legislation and make the *Confession of Faith* a test for every holder of crown office. The Revolution of 1567 was as swift as it was unprecedented. The sovereign had actually been deposed and imprisoned by her own subjects.

On 2 May 1568, the eighteen-year-old 'Willie' Douglas daringly rescued Mary from Loch Leven Castle and the Queen joined up with a group of loyal nobles led by Hamilton, the fifth Lord Seton and Argyll. Eleven days after her escape, Mary's army of 6000 men faced a force three-quarters that strength under the Earl of Moray at Langside, outside Glasgow. For Mary the battle was a disaster. The Queen lost over 300 men.

5th Lord Seton (*c* 1530–85), pictured above with his family, was Provost of Edinburgh in 1557 and 1559. A strong supporter of Mary Queen of Scots, he was captured at Langside on 13 May 1568.   (*SNPG*)

Defeated at Langside, Mary and her escort made for the wilds of the south-west and reached Dundrennan Abbey on 15 May. After dinner, she penned a fateful letter to the Queen of England.

> You are not ignorant, my dearest sister, of great part of my misfortune, but these which induce me to write at present, have happened too recently yet to have reached your ear . . . I am now forced out of my kingdom, and driven to such straits that, next to God, I have no hope but in your goodness. I beseech you, therefore, my dearest sister, that I may be conducted to your presence, that I may acquaint you with all my affairs.

In the company of some twenty attendants, including Lords Herries, Fleming and Claud Hamilton, Mary crossed the Solway on Sunday 16 May

At the Cistercian Abbey of
Dundrennan in Dumfriesshire,
founded by David I in 1142, Mary
Queen of Scots spent her last night
on Scottish soil.   (*Author*)

Elizabeth I (1533–1603) spent a lonely
childhood and was rigorously
educated. When she became Queen in
1558 England was deeply divided by
religious strife, but within ten years she
had restored some stability. The arrival
of her cousin Mary Queen of Scots and
a claimant to her own throne was, to
say the least, an embarrassment.
(*NMM*)

and was brought on the 18th to Carlisle Castle. Only twenty-five years old,
she would never see Scotland again.

Elizabeth did not know what to do. Mary was a potent figure in European
politics and heir-presumptive to the English throne. But, it was claimed, she
had married the man who had murdered her husband. To make matters
more complex, Mary was Elizabeth's cousin. At the grim fortress of Carlisle
every comfort was afforded. Officially Mary Queen of Scots was a royal
guest: privately she was to be watched and guarded.

Mary's support in Scotland was still considerable. Elizabeth knew that
she could not easily acknowledge the Earl of Moray's administration as the
legal government and proposed an inquiry, ostensibly to investigate Moray
and the others who had rebelled against their Queen, but in reality to give
them a chance to state their case.

Mary was not allowed to speak in person at the inquiry, which opened at
York on 4 October 1568, but was represented by seven commissioners.
Moray attempted to justify his rebellion by blaming Mary for not prosecuting
Bothwell for Darnley's murder. Mary's defence was that Bothwell had been
formally acquitted and that her marriage to him had been approved by a large
number of Scottish lords. She pointed out that less than a tenth of the
Scottish nobility had taken part in James's coronation. Mary was so far
winning; as proof of that, Elizabeth ordered the inquiry move to Westminster
on 3 November so that Moray would have direct access to the English Queen
and her ministers.

The new tribunal was larger and more impressive; but Mary was again
refused permission to present her case in person. In protest, her representatives walked out. A full-scale indictment of Mary could now begin, and for
the first time the infamous Casket Letters were introduced. These had been
discovered in Edinburgh on 20 July 1567. Inside a silver box had been found
eight letters, allegedly from Mary to Bothwell, a sequence of rather bad
French sonnets and two contracts of the marriage between them. The

content of the letters seemed to indicate that Bothwell had ravished Mary while she was still in love with Darnley and that she became party to the plot to kill him. Six months, however, had elapsed since the letters had been found, and they had never been used in Scotland to justify the deposition of Mary. No one has ever found the originals, and, as evidence, the copies were questionable.

On 16 December 1567, the conference was moved to Hampton Court; but Mary, at this stage, was still safe. The tribunal was private and not a court of law. Mary, after all, was Queen of Scotland and could not be tried, especially by an English court. In January 1569, Elizabeth was forced to declare that her inquiry had proved nothing 'whereby the Queen of England should conceive an evil opinion of her good sister'.

In the middle of winter, Mary was moved with her retinue to Tutbury Castle in Staffordshire. Her custodian, the 6th Earl of Shrewsbury, was to guard her for 16 years. The castle was damp and cold and Mary developed the rheumatism that was to bedevil her the rest of her life. She also caught a fever, and the Earl, fearful of his charge dying on him, asked Elizabeth if he could move Mary to his more hospitable home, Wingfield Manor. There she exchanged love letters and gifts with Thomas Howard, 4th Duke of Norfolk, but when Elizabeth discovered their marriage scheme the Duke was sent to the Tower. He was only released when he renounced all thought of such a marriage; but he was still in love.

Mary became an inveterate plotter. Using her revenues as Queen Dowager of France, she attempted to build up a group of English Roman Catholics who might win her the two kingdoms. In November 1569 the northern Catholic Earls of Northumberland and Westmorland began an uprising that was doomed to failure from the start. The plan was to take Mary to Scotland where troops would be raised to put her back on the throne. She was swiftly removed to Ashby-de-la-Zouch Castle and then on to Coventry where she was lodged in a house in the town. The Earl of Northumberland crossed the Scottish border only to be taken prisoner by the Earl of Moray, and the rebellion petered out.

Mary was returned to the custody of the Earl of Shrewsbury, who obtained permission to move his ward to Chatsworth, where she enjoyed riding, hunting, hawking and indulging in fine needlework in the sunshine of the Bower.

But on 28 November 1570, Mary left Chatsworth for Sheffield Castle, where she was to spend almost a third of her life. Conspiracies continued unabated. The Duke of Norfolk had become involved with a plot inspired by Roberto Ridolfi, an Italian banker, who was already consulting with Mary's official envoy, Leslie, Bishop of Ross. Ridolfi's scheme was to bring about an invasion of England from the Netherlands led by the Duke of Alva. This, in turn, would be supported by a Catholic uprising in England which would free Mary and take Elizabeth prisoner. Walsingham got wind of the plot and had Norfolk swiftly arrested and taken back to the Tower. At the end of January 1572 he was tried for high treason and he was executed in the following June. On the scaffold, Norfolk still professed his innocence:

> I take God to witness I am not nor never was a Papist, since I knew what religion meant.

Tutbury Castle.   (*Author*)

Thomas Howard, 4th Duke of Norfolk (1536–72) was Queen Elizabeth's lieutenant in the north between 1559 and 1560. His desire to marry Mary Queen of Scots was seen by Maitland of Lethington as furthering the cause of Anglo-Scottish relations, but Elizabeth of England disagreed, especially when the Duke was involved in the northern rebellion of 1569. (*SNPG*)

Mary would only admit that she had written letters to the King of France and Spain and to the Pope asking for help to restore her to the Scottish throne.

The English Parliament called for Mary's trial. Elizabeth refused, but allowed a Bill to be passed depriving Mary of all claim to the English throne and making her liable to stand trial if she was found involved in further plots. More damning, Elizabeth allowed the evidence against Mary to be published; the Queen of Scots stood publicly indicted as a murderess. Then, advised by her ministers, Lord Burghley and Francis Walsingham, that while Mary was alive there would always be a Catholic threat to the throne, Elizabeth agreed to their setting a trap for her Scottish cousin.

In 1586, Anthony Babington was persuaded to play the leading role in a conspiracy which, again supported by Spanish arms, was supposed to procure the murder of Elizabeth and Mary's release. Gilbert Gifford, once a Catholic supporter but now persuaded by Walsingham to act as an English spy, was sent to try and communicate with Mary, who it was believed must be in the thick of the plot. Messages in code to and from Mary, now imprisoned at Chartley Manor in Staffordshire, were carried inside beer barrels and, unknown to Mary, were intercepted and read.

Once Walsingham was in possession of the facts the conspirators were hunted down and arrested. Babington and his friends were found guilty and executed at Lincoln in September 1586. News of the discovery and betrayal was cleverly kept from Mary. Walsingham could now move on the Queen of Scots. Arrangements were made to take her on a hunt in Chartley Park, during which she was confronted by a party of horsemen and challenged by Elizabeth's emissary Sir Thomas Gorges. He spoke of Mary's conspiracy and declared that she had been guilty of encouraging Catholics to overthrow the English Queen. Mary was taken to Tixall Hall, near Stafford, and her two secretaries were arrested and taken to London for questioning. Walsingham's agents, meanwhile, searched her chambers at Chartley for correspondence and notebooks. After the papers were examined, it was decided that Mary should stand trial under the Act of Association of 1585 and a warrant was issued for her arrest. On 21 September Mary left Chartley for Fotheringhay Castle in Northamptonshire.

The trial began on 15 October. Mary was brought before thirty-six peers, privy councillors and judges on charges of having plotted to harm the life of Elizabeth. Mary insisted on defending herself and did so with dignity and skill, maintaining, correctly, that she was not answerable to any court but to God alone:

> As an absolute Queen I cannot submit to orders, nor can I submit to the laws of the land without injury to myself, the King my son and all other sovereign princes.

Accused of having assumed the name and arms of England while in France Mary replied that it was at the insistence of her French father-in-law. She did not refute that she had a rightful claim to the English throne, but vehemently denied that she had ever plotted for the death of Elizabeth. Despite her brilliant defence, the verdict was a foregone conclusion. The court at Fotheringhay, however, had no power to pass sentence, which was a matter for Queen Elizabeth alone. Realizing the implications to monarchy, Elizabeth hesitated.

In Scotland, James VI was goaded by Scottish public opinion to attempt to save his mother's life and in some very stiff letters to Elizabeth made a better effort to do so than is usually credited to him. His emissaries, however, got short shrift from the English Queen:

> Tell your King what good I have done for him in holding the crown on his head since he was born; and that I mind to keep the league that stands now between us, and if he break, it shall be a double fault.

Under great pressure from her own ministers, Elizabeth agreed to sign the death warrant on 1 February 1587, five months after Mary's trial. She insisted that it be placed among other papers of state requiring her signature so that it could appear she signed it by mistake. The deed done, it is said she jested about it. Mary's old gaoler, Lord Shrewsbury, was given the awful task of informing the Queen of her sentence on 7 February 1587.

Mary spent her last hours writing letters. At two o'clock in the morning of 8 February 1587, she wrote to her brother-in-law the King of France:

> The Catholic faith and the assertion of my God-given right to the English crown are the two issues on which I am condemned, and yet I am not allowed to say that it is for the Catholic religion that I die, but for fear of interference with theirs. The proof of this is that they have taken away my chaplain, and, although he is in the building, I have not been able to get permission for him to come and hear my confession and give me the last Sacrament, while they have been most insistent that I receive the consolation and instruction of their minister, brought here for that purpose.

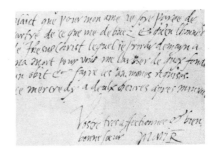

Mary's last letter to Henri III, King of France. (*NLS*)

Yet Mary contrived to die a Catholic martyr. As she approached the block, she spurned the Protestant Dean of Peterborough with the remark, 'I am settled in the ancient Catholic Roman religion and mind spend my blood in defence of it.' Dressed in a gown of black satin and a petticoat of crimson velvet, she was led to the platform that had been erected in the Great Hall of Fotheringhay. The death warrant was read and her gown was then removed. Beneath she wore a shirt of deep maroon, the Catholic colour of martyrdom. She handed her rosary and prayer book to her attendant ladies and, blindfolded by one, placed her head on the block. With outstretched hands she murmured in Latin, 'Into Thy hands, O Lord, I commend my spirit'. The first blow of the executioner's axe did not sever the neck; another was needed, with a sawing action to cut the sinews. Simon Bulle, the executioner, then attempted to hold the head high, but as he grabbed the auburn tresses a head with grey hair fell to the ground. The Dean of Peterborough called out to the assembled witnesses, 'So perish all the Queen's enemies.' Mary Queen of Scots was forty-four years old.

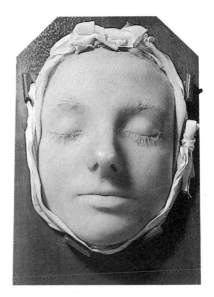

Mary's death mask, now at Lennoxlove. (*H*)

On the instructions of Elizabeth, Mary's clothes were burned and her body and head encased in a casket of heavy lead. Every drop of blood was scrubbed from Fotheringhay that day, lest some be found by her followers and become a relic of her martyrdom. The casket was taken to nearby Peterborough Cathedral. Later, in 1612, James, her son, built a magnificent monument to Mary at Westminster Abbey. When he got to know of his mother's treatment in captivity, James ordered the castle at Fotheringhay to be razed to the ground. Now only a mound where thistles grow remains as evidence of the deed done by the River Nene on that cold February morning.

Elizabeth of England was solely responsible for Mary's death. She tried to blame Burghley and Walsingham, however, protesting she had never intended to kill her cousin. On 14 February 1587 she wrote to James VI professing innocence. The Scots King in his turn banished the Master of Gray, one of the emissaries who had sought his mother's reprieve. Mary's death haunted both monarchs for the rest of their lives. And yet, curiously, Elizabeth had never met her, and James from the age of thirteen months had no memories of his mother.

Mary made three errors of judgement. In an attempt to enhance her claim to England's throne, she married Darnley. Politically the marriage made sense: personally the worthlessness of Darnley cancelled out its benefit. In Scotland, the match disgraced the young Queen. And then by marrying the Earl of Bothwell, after Darnley's mysterious death, Mary ruined her international reputation. Her fatal mistake was to flee to England. By doing so she not only gave some credence to the claims made against her, but left at a disadvantage the considerable number of Scottish lords prepared to support her. Her tragic life made Protestantism in Scotland permanent, the last and possibly most successful Reformation in Europe.

Mary Queen of Scots was no martyr; nor was she naïve. She was, like many Stewart monarchs, a political loser.

6

James and Crowns United

AFTER JAMES VI'S CORONATION in 1567 Scotland was plunged into civil war for nearly twenty years, and it was not until the year of his mother's execution that James could rightly claim that he ruled in deed and name. His minority was the last in Scotland's history; but during it the nation was done great harm.

A portrait of the young James VI in Falkland Palace. (*NTS*)

After Mary fled, the Protestant nobles resolved to educate their young ruler in their own way. When James was four years old, George Buchanan, aged sixty-three, was designated his teacher. Born in Killearn in Stirlingshire, Buchanan had studied in Paris and became the greatest of the Scottish humanists, famed for his Latin poems and dramas. He had befriended Mary on her return to Scotland but had turned viciously against her after Darnley's murder. In 1568 he had given evidence against Mary at Elizabeth's enquiry, and during her years of captivity, Buchanan was an avid pamphleteer against the deposed Queen. His *History of Scotland* was a vehicle for anti-Catholic propaganda.

Under the strict guidance of Buchanan, the young James quickly mastered Latin and Greek. He committed long passages of the Bible to memory and with a personal library of over 6000 books became the best educated prince of his day. Sir Henry Killigrew, when James was just eight, remarked:

> He speaketh the French tongue marvellous well, and that which seemed strange to me, he was able extempore to read a chapter of the Bible out of Latin into French, and out of French after into English, so well as few men could have added anything to his translation.

The King's education was gruelling. His day began with prayers, followed by lessons in Greek. After a breakfast of meat or game washed down with ale or wine, he studied Latin, then Scottish or classical history. Dinner was taken at midday and the afternoon was given over to composition, arithmetic, geography, with astronomy and rhetoric before supper. By the age of sixteen James was the author of respectable poetry. But he led a lonely, abnormal childhood, brought up in the company of staunch old Presbyterians. His love of learning, although natural, was precocious.

George Buchanan (1506–82). (*SNPG*)

Buchanan drummed into his young pupil the Calvinist concept of kingship. Kings derived their authority from the people, and could be got rid

James VI was nineteen before he began to direct the nation's policy. The Earl of Moray was the first of four Regents, followed by the King's grandfather, Matthew Stewart, 4th Earl of Lennox (1516–71). (*SNPG*)

John Erskine, Earl of Mar (*c* 1510–72) succeeded Lennox as Regent on 5 September 1571; he died the following year. (*SNPG*)

of if they failed in their duty. 'He must believe that as king,' claimed Buchanan, 'he exists for his subjects and not for himself.' John Knox had unsuccessfully tried to persuade Mary equally.

Meanwhile Scotland outside the classroom of Stirling Castle became a nation of lawless aristocrats, governed by four Regents, all ambitious men. Two were soon to be murdered and one beheaded by his noble enemies. In his youth, James VI was subject to nine kidnapping attempts and lived in constant fear of his own life. The number of heads of state and other prominent persons assassinated during his lifetime gave him good cause for fear. From childhood he disliked all shows of violence. According to Sir John Oglander, an Englishman who met James only twice:

> King James was the most cowardly man that I ever knew. He could not endure a soldier; to hear of war was death to him and how he tormented himself with fear of some sudden mischief may be proved by his great doublets, pistol-proof; as also his strange eyeing of strangers.

Political, rather than religious differences divided Scotland. Catholic and Protestant lords alike were wrestling with the aftermath of having deposed Mary. In 1567 the nobles had agreed that the Earl of Moray, Mary's half-brother, should be Regent, but on 23 January 1570 he was shot by James Hamilton of Bothwellhaugh, who, hidden by a line of washing, aimed his musket from an upper window as the Earl rode through Linlithgow. Moray was remembered as the 'good regent'. The house in Linlithgow where the assassin had hidden belonged to the Archbishop of St Andrews, John Hamilton. Moray's friends hanged the old cleric at Stirling in 1571 without the troublesome formality of a trial.

The Earl of Lennox, Darnley's father, was then appointed Regent under pressure from Elizabeth. His rule was short. The Protestant party in Scotland had divided into King's and Queen's men, with the leading nobles mostly on the side of Mary: James and his Regent had to fall back on the support of the ministry and the gentry of Lowland Scotland, who, above all else, wanted a Protestant monarch. By August 1571, therefore, Scotland virtually had two parliaments. Maitland of Lethington and Kirkcaldy of Grange held Edinburgh Castle for Queen Mary and had their own parliament. The Regent Lennox held the more valid one, at Stirling, if only because of the King's presence. James was forced to make appearances there in a makeshift crown, as the real one was beyond his reach in Edinburgh.

On 4 September, Lennox was shot in the back in an incompetent attempt by Grange and Lethington to capture the King's lords at Stirling; John Erskine, the Earl of Mar, succeeded him as Regent. In little over twelve months, on 28 October 1572, he too was replaced. As Sir James Melville noted in his *Memoirs*:

> He was nobly treated and banqueted by the Lord of Morton; shortly after which he took a vehement sickness which caused him to ride suddenly to Stirling where he died.

Strangely, James Douglas, Earl of Morton, became the next Regent, appointed just before John Knox, already paralysed, was finally silenced and went to meet the God he so confidently knew. He died in Edinburgh on 24 November 1572.

Morton's Regency, the last great showing in Scotland's history of

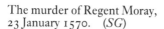

The murder of Regent Moray, 23 January 1570.   (*SG*)

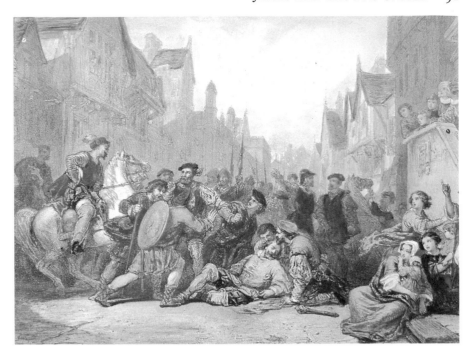

Douglas blood, lasted six years. A competent man, he strove to bring order to the land. He laid siege to the supporters of Mary with English help and to help James hold his capital in the future rebuilt the destroyed Edinburgh Castle in the form it is today, with its great half-moon battery. Morton was outspoken, arrogant, shrewd and ambitious, a typical product of an age when the aristocracy of Scotland had to be tough to succeed.

Morton's greatest achievement as Regent was that he made a genuine effort to solve the problems of establishing the Protestant Kirk. The Kirk relied on the state for money and since there had been an increase in the number of ministers the Church's share of 'The Thirds' was not enough. In 1572, by the Concordat of Leith, Morton got an agreement which bound the bishoprics into the new Church. The Crown was to nominate the bishops, the chapter of ministers to approve them and the superintendents to consecrate them. The nominated bishops were Morton's personal choice, and folk called them 'tulchans', the name given to calfskins stuffed with straw which countrymen used to induce their cows to yield. The old bishoprics were indeed to be milked of their wealth, most of which found its way into private pockets; and under Morton, Scotland, it seemed, would have an established Episcopal Church similar to that found in England. Presbyterians like Andrew Melville prevented this from happening.

James Douglas, 4th Earl of Morton (*c* 1516–81) succeeded Mar as Regent. Morton was involved in Rizzio's murder and was executed as an accessory to Darnley's murder. (*SNPG*)

Presbyterianism stemmed from Geneva, where John Calvin had been succeeded by Théodore de Beza. The Bible, argued de Beza, made no mention of bishops, and he concluded that they should therefore be replaced by Presbyteries composed of elders appointed for life. His reasoning was not wholly spiritual: bishops were expensive and the new Church needed to expand its parish activity.

Andrew Melville returned to Scotland in the summer of 1574, after a decade of study in Switzerland and France. He had been a teacher of Humanity at Calvin's Academy and was to make his name bringing Scot-

Andrew Melville (1545–1622) spent ten years on the Continent, largely at Geneva. He was exiled by the King from 1584 to 1585, summoned to London in 1606 and not allowed to return to Scotland. He ended his career at Sedan.   (*SAU*)

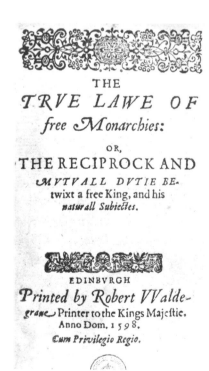

THE

TRVE LAWE OF

free Monarchies:

OR,

THE RECIPROCK AND

MVTVALL DVTIE BE-
twixt a free King, and his
naturall Subiectes.

EDINBVRGH

Printed by Robert VValde-
grave Printer to the Kings Majestie.
Anno Dom. 1 5 9 8.

Cum Privilegio Regio.

James VI was the most educated prince of his day and could argue about politics and theology with any scholar in Europe.   (*NLS*)

land's education system into line with Genevan teaching. In two years, Melville transformed the curricula at Glasgow University and introduced specialized teachers. His new charter remained the basis of the university's teaching for 300 years.

Melville was one of thirty ministers who now began to formulate *The Second Book of Discipline*. In many respects this reaffirmed much of what the original generation of Reformers had claimed – the theory of two kingdoms, the rejection of Royal supremacy over the Church and the insistence upon the General Assembly. Melville's personal contribution was that he restated these tenets forcibly at a time when the Scottish monarchy was trying to reassert its control in religious matters. As Morton told Melville, 'There will never be quietness in this country till half a dozen of you be hanged or banished.'

The 'reforms' laid out in *The Second Book* were not benevolent. Scotland was to be ruled by a dictatorship of the Presbytery. Ministers of the Kirk were henceforth to wear hodden-grey on weekdays and blue serge on Sundays. Their wives were forbidden to wear bright coloured clothes or jewellery. The Sabbath day was to be strictly Calvinist, beginning at six o'clock on Saturday evening and lasting twenty-four hours; during that time no work was to be done. Nothing was to be bought or sold on a Sunday, alehouses were to close, dancing, gaming and music were banned. Frequent attendance at communion was now regarded as a public renunciation of Popery and was, therefore, compulsory. By 1574, eighty gallons of wine were consumed at St Giles alone during the celebration of the sacrament.

The Kirk inflicted harsh punishment upon those who broke its strict rules. 'Jougs', a form of handcuffs, appeared outside many a parish kirk and the 'brank', a padlocked helmet of iron that thrust a triangular tongue into the victim's mouth was an effective way of silencing evil talk. Wives who had dirty hands or who nagged their husbands could be banished. Fornicators were also to be sent away and if they dared to return to the same parish could be burnt to death. Witches and sorcerers were condemned to die at the stake or suffer an equally slow and painful death.

Melville reasserted the division between Church and State when he told James at Falkland Palace:

> There is twa kings and twa kingdoms in Scotland, there is Christ Jesus and His kingdom the Kirk whose subject King James the sixth is, and of whose kingdom not a king, nor a head, nor a lord, but a member.

James was furious at this threat to his authority, and in May 1584 he passed the so-called 'Black Acts' which reaffirmed Episcopal Church government, the rule of bishops and the supremacy of the King, parliament and the council over all estates, temporal and spiritual. Melville and some of his followers were forced into exile.

The King reacted as vehemently to the political theories of his teacher Buchanan. He had become impressed by the ideas of the French philosopher Jean Bodin, who argued that the law was the command of the king and that sovereignty, therefore, was the right to make that law. In his *Trew Law of the Free Monarchies* James the Protestant Reformation King, explained his theory of the Divine Right of kingship, claiming that under God he had the sole right to rule. The theory of Divine Right was a direct consequence of

Jesuit doctrine; if the Counter-Reformation was ever to succeed Protestant kings would have to be deposed. Three methods were thought valid by the Counter-Reformers. Kings could be brought back into the fold by invasion from outside, by resistance and revolution, or, ultimately by tyrannicide.

While in Scotland, James could do little to put his theories into practice. He was so poor that he frequently could not pay the bills of his tradesmen. To rule, he had to hope that his choice of advisers found favour among his nobility. Usually his choice was greeted with revolt.

In 1579, James's cousin the thirty-year-old Esmé Stewart, Seigneur d'Aubigny, arrived in Scotland from France. James first met Esmé on 15 September in the Great Hall of Stirling Castle, and fell in love with him immediately. He had been Gentleman of the Bedchamber to Henri III of France, the most perverted of all the French monarchs, and was probably well versed in homosexual encounters. It was reported that James was 'in such love with him as in the open sight of the people, oftentimes he will clasp him about the neck with his arms and kiss him'. In 1581 Esmé was made Duke of Lennox and a Privy Councillor. James's nobles became anxious and suspected the new Lennox of being a Catholic agent. Their Popish scare resulted in the King making the Negative Confession in 1581, which denounced all forms of Papistry and was in later years to form the first part of the National Covenant. But many nobles remained unconvinced of James's loyalty to Protestantism.

On 31 December 1581, at Lennox's instigation, Captain James Stewart dramatically interrupted a session of the Privy Council. Stewart fell to his knees before the King and accused Regent Morton of having helped murder his father, Darnley. Morton was immediately arrested, and although Elizabeth tried desperately to secure his release, on 2 June 1581 met his grisly end in Edinburgh, embracing his own mistress, 'The Maiden', the refined form of guillotine he had invented.

Protestant nobles realized they would have to get rid of Esmé Stewart, Duke of Lennox. In August 1582, while he stayed in Edinburgh, James went hunting in Atholl. He was met by the Earl of Gowrie who offered him hospitality at Ruthven. The following morning he refused to let the King go until James signed a proclamation declaring himself a free King and ordered Lennox to leave Scotland. Lennox sadly took his farewell on 21 December and wrote to James; 'I desire to die rather than to live, fearing that in your disdain you have found a cause for loving me no more.' He was to die in France on 26 May 1583 and in his will bequeathed James his embalmed heart. It was not until June 1583 that the King managed to escape Gowrie's grasp. On 3 May 1584, the Earl was executed; but the so-called Raid of Ruthven was a severe blow to James's sovereignty.

On 5 July 1586, the year before Queen Mary's execution, James VI and Elizabeth of England agreed a pact to keep the peace. James was given a small but much-needed subsidy of £4000 a year, and this alliance with England, whose throne he hoped soon to inherit, henceforth dominated his reign.

In October 1589 James married Anne of Denmark. Her large dowry helped finance his reign, which was to be marked by the emergence of professional administrators like Sir John Maitland of Thirlestane. The Scottish King began to feel more secure, but his northern lords were in open revolt.

Esmé Stewart, 1st Duke of Lennox (c 1542–83). (*SNPG*)

Anne of Denmark (1574–1619), daughter of Frederick II, married James VI in Oslo on 24 November 1589. (*NTS*)

Henry (1594–1612), eldest son of James VI; he was created Prince of Wales in 1610. (*NTS*)

The Catholic Earls, Huntly, Errol and Angus plotted with Philip II of Spain to land troops in Scotland and from there mount an invasion of England. James VI, who liked to back both sides, in order to scare Elizabeth of England into naming him her successor, was involved.

On 3 October 1594 the Earl of Huntly defeated the government forces under King James and the Earl of Argyll at Glenlivet; but the victory could not be followed up politically.

James tried to resolve the age-long feud between Huntly and Moray, and commanded both to come south to Donibristle and submit to his arbitration. But on 7 February 1592 Huntly fired the house. Moray died with the remark, 'You have spilt a better face than your own.' Despite a public outcry, James merely confined Huntly to Edinburgh Castle for a week as punishment.

Challenges to James's authority came from the Lowlands as well. The Earl of Bothwell, the Protestant nephew of Queen Mary's third husband, was a disreputable, deranged man who hated Catholics with passion. He made four separate attacks on James, in his own palaces, each time managing to escape arrest. It was not until the Battle of Glenlivet, when Bothwell was forced to flee the field to die ultimately in Naples, that James could feel at ease.

James came to rely on a group of lesser nobles – 'new men'. Ecclesiastical properties that were in the monarch's hands were erected into hereditary temporal lordships, and the majority of these Lords of Erection, as they were called, came from families of lairds. In an age that saw the beginnings of modern bureaucracy, these creations of 'new men' were an attempt to control the magnates.

At this time of Reformation and Jesuit Counter-Reformation, a great debate was taking place about the nature of government. In 1598, James wrote *Basilikon Doron* as advice for his young son Prince Henry. He told the four-year-old:

> First of all things learn to know and love that God, whom to ye have a double obligation; first, for that He made you a man; and next, for that He made you a little God to sit on his throne, and rule over other men.

James argued that Kings were answerable to God, who would be their judge. James genuinely feared the Day of Judgment and *Basilikon Doron* stressed upon Prince Henry his obligation to rule well and to be a just king.

The Scottish nobility, *Basilikon Doron* informed the young prince, had a 'feckless, arrogant conceit of their greatness and power', while Scottish merchants suffered from the mistaken belief that the monarch existed purely to ensure they made a profit.

James and Elizabeth of England played cat and mouse politics. She continued to dangle her throne before the canny and crafty King of the Scots: he in turn consorted with Spain and flirted with Catholic peers and their plots to try and force the old Queen to name him as her successor. When the Spanish Armada sailed to defeat in 1588, he was careful to ensure that over 400 Spanish sailors shipwrecked off Scotland's shores were humanely treated and helped to return home. James's succession to the throne of England remained uncertain, although in secret correspondence, Sir Robert Cecil, the Queen's secretary, assured him:

> Your ship shall be steered into the right harbour, without cross of wave or tide that shall be able to turn over a cockboat.

On 5 August 1600, as James rode out of Falkland Palace he was met by Alexander Ruthven, the nineteen-year-old brother of the second Earl of Gowrie, who told the King that he had found a man about to bury a horde of gold coin in the fields outside Perth. James paid a visit to Gowrie House to investigate what looked like a chance to claim some treasure. On his arrival he went upstairs with Alexander Ruthven, supposedly to interview the man discovered with the treasure. The King, who was later to make great play of the incident, claimed that Ruthven locked the doors behind them as they ascended the stairs. The courtiers next saw James at a turret window shouting, 'I am murdered! Treason! My Lord Mar, help! help!' Led by a youth named John Ramsay, the nobles rushed into the house to find James struggling with the Master of Ruthven. Ramsay stabbed Ruthven in the neck, and the nobles then slashed him to death as he reeled down the stairs. The Earl of Gowrie was also killed by Ramsay.

At the end of August the bodies of Gowrie and the Master of Ruthven were brought to Edinburgh, and in a macabre session of parliament were found guilty of treason. Their name, memory and dignity were formally extinguished and their property devolved upon the King. The dead bodies were then hanged, drawn and quartered at the Mercat Cross and fixed to public places in Edinburgh, Perth, Dundee and Stirling.

James's official account was thought then, as now, a clumsy fabrication. It may be that the King was attempting to seduce the young Ruthven; but if so, why not in the privacy of his own palace? It could be that James saw in the Ruthven family the makings of a Protestant coup. Perhaps the whole ghastly affair came about by accident; but James continued to persecute the family for over twenty years. The Gowries were, after all, his hereditary enemies. The first Earl of Gowrie's father had stabbed Rizzio to death in front of his mother, Mary Queen of Scots and the first Earl had abducted James when he

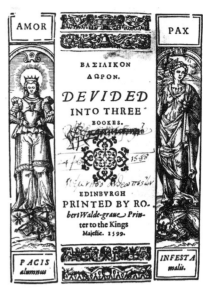

Basilikon Doron was first printed privately in 1599; a revised edition was published four years later. (*NLS*)

The Gowrie Conspiracy, 5 August 1600. (*SNPG*)

James VI of Scotland hearing news that he had become King of England. (*CAC*)

was a boy of sixteen in the Raid of Ruthven. At the time of the so-called Gowrie Conspiracy James owed the family some £80,000 and the Conspiracy certainly enabled James to avenge one of the wrongs suffered by his mother.

In the small hours of the morning of Thursday, 24 March 1603, Elizabeth died at Richmond Palace. Sir Robert Carey, who had been sent previously to James with Elizabeth's poor excuses for Mary's execution, set off for Edinburgh, before the official messenger, in a bid for the King's favour. As he wrote in his *Memoirs*:

> The King was newly gone to bed by the time that I knocked at the gate. I was quickly let in and carried up to the King's chamber. I kneeled by him, and saluted him by his title, King of England, Scotland, France and Ireland. He gave me his hand to kiss and bade me welcome.

Wasting no time, James bid farewell to his subjects at St Giles early in April and left with his court for London.

James's accession to the throne of England came at a significant moment in Scotland's history. In the sixteenth century, the Scots were an outward looking nation, justly proud of their contribution to Europe. England's interests would now take precedence: and Scotland's freedom would be circumscribed. Many Scots viewed the union of the two crowns cautiously, for their poor nation was about to be linked to a rich and powerful one. But James himself basked in England's opulence, and although he talked in broad Scots all his life, was never homesick. He called his two kingdoms by a new name, Great Britain, which he had to force an unwilling English Parliament to use.

When he left Scotland, James was bankrupt. On his way south, he had to stop at York and wait until money was sent up from London before he could complete his journey. Yet he was to prove a wasteful King who grossly overestimated the wealth of the English throne. Elizabeth of England had managed to get by on about £220,000 a year. James VI's expenditure in 1607 alone was in excess of half a million pounds. His poverty and that of his son, Charles I, meant that they had to rely on parliament for subsidies. As a result the English Parliament met frequently, and gained in stature and importance.

North Britain – Scotland – James VI and I claimed, was ruled by remote control:

> This I must say for Scotland, here I sit and govern it with my pen, I write and it is done, and by a Clerk of the Council I govern Scotland now, which others could not do by the sword.

Hundreds of Scots followed James south and settled in London. They profited greatly and in so doing gave birth to the Scottish dilemma. Tam Dalyell, the present MP for West Lothian, lives in the gracious country house his ancestor Thomas Dalyell built on profit made in London from James becoming King of England.

Scots born before his accession to the British throne were debarred from holding government office and not allowed to sit in the English Parliament. They became so much lumber at Whitehall, recipients of patronage without doing anything in return. The most notorious was James's favourite Robert Carr of Ferniehurst, who was knighted in 1607 and later became Earl of Somerset. James soon after his accession banished Anne, his queen, to

Denmark House, preferring the company of young homosexuals like Carr, as Francis Osborne pointed out:

> The king's kissing them after so lascivious a mode in public and upon the theatre, as it were, of the world, prompted many to imagine some things done in the retiring-house, that exceed my expressions no less than they do my experience.

The union of the crowns was a severe blow to the Scots. Their King was 400 miles away. The burgesses of Scotland felt, rightly or wrongly, that trade began to suffer. By controlling the Scottish Privy Council and the Lords of the Articles, James also drew the teeth of the Estates. The Stewart ambition to be rulers of England once realized, brought little benefit to Scotland.

James used the power of England to extend his rule to the Highlands, where clan feuds still raged. The MacGregor clan, which occupied extensive lands from Glenorchy through Argyll to Perthshire, was perfectly placed for swift raids on the rich Lowlands around Stirling and the fertile valley of the Clyde. In 1602, they stole 300 head of cattle from the Colquhouns, together with 100 horses, 400 sheep and an equal number of goats. James swiftly outlawed the MacGregors; but, unperturbed, Alastair MacGregor of Glenstrae clashed with an army led by Alexander Colquhoun at Glenfruin in 1603 and slaughtered over two hundred of the Colquhoun clan. James had the MacGregors hunted down like animals. Proscribed for 173 years in all, the clan took to the hills and survived only as 'children of the mist'. Most Highlanders, however, made a living by raiding and running protection rackets. Meal, for food, was regularly levied from Lowlanders whose estates bordered on the Highlands in exchange for a promise not to steal livestock or harvests. Blackmail, the exaction of black meal, began in the Highlands of Scotland.

In 1609, James ordered Andrew Knox, Bishop of the Isles, to meet with several West Highland chiefs at Iona and try and persuade them to accept the more peaceful lifestyle of the Lowlands, to abandon their Catholicism and accept the reformed religion. In future, the eldest son or daughter of the clan chief was to be sent south to learn to speak, read and write English. The bards, who it was thought helped nurture feuds with their poetry, were banned and the chiefs grudgingly agreed to reduce the size of their retinues, which were little less than private armies. James VI and his successors continued to see it as a mission to civilize the Highlander and stamp out his general intransigence and Papist ways.

But Iona made little difference. In 1612, some of the Neish clan raided the Macnabs as they were about to sit down to Christmas dinner. In revenge, Macnab of Macnab's four eldest sons, urged on by their mother, swooped on the Neishes and killed almost the whole family.

When James made the first formal invitation to Scots to participate in the plantation of Ulster in 1609, there were already several hundred Scots settled along the coasts of Antrim and Down. More than seventy nobles, burgesses, lairds and merchants took up holdings and settled tenants on them. Not all were Protestants. Sir George Hamilton of Greenlaw, for instance, who planted Strabane, was a Catholic and he brought up his wards in his own faith. The motives for the Scots plantation of Ulster were political, strategic, financial and religious.

A Victorian impression of a Border Raid.   (*NGS*)

In 1611 James VI remarked of his Ulster plantation:

> the settling of religion, the introducing civility, order and government amongst a barbarous and unsubdued people, to be acts of piety and glory, and worthy always of a Christian price to endeavour.

Ireland was to be made part of Protestant Europe and James approached the project with missionary zeal. By the end of his reign over 8000 Scots capable of bearing arms had settled there.

The scheme to colonize Ulster had an earlier Scottish precedent. In 1597 an Act had been passed by the Estates designed to encourage 'civility and policy' in the Western Isles and the more remote parts of the Highlands by the establishment of townships. The Duke of Lennox and others agreed to plant 'the hitherto most barbarous Isle of Lewis' and 'develop the extraordinary rich resources of the same for the public good and the King's profit'. In 1599, a group of over 500 settlers set sail for Lewis; but the harsh conditions killed many soon after they had arrived and others were massacred three years later by the local inhabitants, and some say eaten. Undeterred, James in 1605 urged further plantation of the Isles as well as the Mull of Kintyre, which he granted to the Earl of Argyll in the hope that he would encourage Lowlanders to settle what was then wilderness.

Borderers were thought the best settlers because Lowland Scotland had a surplus of population, and the English were worried by the numbers who flooded south. In 1605, the English Council wrote to its Scottish counterpart urging that Scots who were entering service with foreign armies, like that of Gustavus Adolphus, should leave from ports nearer home than London; and such was the northern exodus that the Scottish Council issued proclamations repeatedly to try and stem the flow. Other Scots were making for France, Holland or Poland as students, merchants and soldiers. By 1616, William Lithgow estimated some 30,000 Scots were settled in Poland. By 1621, Scots looking for land had turned their attention to North America. Sir William Alexander was granted a charter to found a colony in Nova Scotia, but met with little success.

James VI's other main Scottish concern was his determination to break the power of the Kirk. He fell in love with the orderly, manageable established Church of England and wished the reformed Church in Scotland to be the same. In 1606, he invited eight leading Scottish ministers to come and talk with him in London. They duly obeyed only to find themselves and their faith abused before the English Court. Their leader, Andrew Melville, was sent to the Tower of London for three years and forbidden to set foot in Scotland again.

But James could argue with reason that the religion of Scotland was not yet set. Protestantism had only just reached the northern county of Caithness and the Isles of Orkney and Shetland. The western seaboard of the country and the Western Isles knew little of it, except in those parts where the Earl of Argyll held sway. It was not until the early seventeenth century, when Irish priests began missions to the Western Isles, that the Word of God in any interpreted form was found in the remote Hebrides. In the north-east Catholicism was still a vital force, and the Gordon family still practised their religion undisturbed. Cut off from Lowland religious and political squabbles, Aberdeen nurtured Episcopacy.

Sir William Alexander, Earl of Stirling (*c* 1567–1640), born at Menstrie Castle in Clackmannanshire. He was a poet and as a courtier was given Nova Scotia as a gift by James VI in 1621. (*SNPG*)

James had made clear his view of Scottish Presbyterianism at the Hampton Court Conference in 1604. 'A Scottish Presbytery . . .' he declared, 'agreeth as well with a monarch as God and the Devil.' He is said to have yelled at one Scottish delegation, 'I give not a turd for your preaching.' Accordingly he set about anglicizing the Kirk. By 1610, he had increased the number of Scottish bishops to eleven and created two archbishoprics. Two Courts of High Commission were also erected to help the bishops enforce ecclesiastical law on the English model. His reforms had little effect although some of the bishops, like Bishop Forbes of Aberdeen, were wise and tolerant men who won respect. And so far James had done little to tamper with ordinary congregational worship. The Sabbath was still Calvinist. Trouble, however, resulted from James's visit to Scotland in 1617, his first since becoming King of England. The visit had to be postponed again and again until the English Treasury could be persuaded to finance it. At the Royal Chapel of Holyrood, the King introduced an organ and a choir into the service and Edinburgh folk were angry and deeply suspicious. He was resolved to impose on the Kirk four major reforms. Scots, like the English, he believed should receive communion kneeling. Easter and Christmas were to be celebrated as religious festivals. Confirmations were to be performed by bishops, not ministers, and private communion and private baptism were in future to be allowed. At a General Assembly of the Church of Scotland at Perth in 1618 the ministers were bullied into accepting what came to be known as the Five Articles of Perth, but many refused to put them into practice. In anger, James banned the General Assembly and it was not to meet again for twenty years.

James VI died in 1625. Scots mourned his passing but felt they had gained little by giving Great Britain its first monarch. The only lasting monument to his interest in the nation's religion was to be the Authorized Version of the Bible which he commissioned in 1604.

Britain's new King, Charles I, was incapable of understanding the feeling with which Scots clung to their faith. 'Baby Charles', as James VI always called him, had, like his father, endured a lonely and unhappy

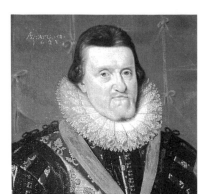

A portrait of James VI painted shortly before his death at the age of fifty-eight. (*NTS*)

Charles I (1600–49), second son of James VI, who although born at Dunfermline spent most of his life in England. (*SNPG*)

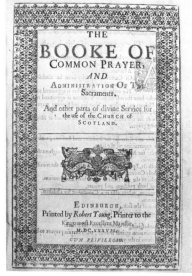

King Charles I's Revised Prayer Book. (*NLS*)

childhood. Never intended as heir to the throne, he had always been overshadowed by the brilliant and likeable Prince Henry, until Henry died of typhoid in 1612. Charles had gone to London with his father at the age of three and knew nothing but English ways. As he grew up, he made few friends, and now he chose to live in a cultured, artistic, aloof world of his own.

Like his father, Charles believed in Divine Right. His disdain for democratic assemblies was obvious, and by 1628 he had deeply offended the English Parliament. A year later he was to prorogue it and to rule for the next eleven years with decreasing funds without the advice of England's elected representatives. Charles I was devout. His brand of Protestantism was that of William Laud, then Bishop of London and later Archbishop of Canterbury, a man who loved ritual and religious orthodoxy. English Puritans repulsed by Laud and his King were tortured and thrown into prison. Political loyalty, Charles believed, could only flourish if his subjects were united under a single Church. The Kirk would have to be brought into line.

In 1625, Charles compelled the Scottish nobles to give up the ecclesiastical property they had taken at the Reformation. By his Act of Revocation, he gave back to the Church the landed wealth that could make it self-supporting. In so doing, of course, he helped solve his own financial problems; land and taxes could now maintain his bishops. Eight years later he visited Edinburgh for the first time. At St Giles, he was crowned King of Scotland, the service conducted with full Anglican rites. Church music, choirs and surplices, Charles thought, would reveal to the Scots his concept of religion. The Scots were not over-impressed. At Charles I's coronation an observer noted:

> There was a four-cornered table in the manner of an altar standing within the kirk having thereupon two books, with two waxed chandeliers and two wax candles which were unlighted, and a basin wherein there was nothing. At the back of this altar there was a rich tapestry wherein the crucifix was curiously wrought; and as these bishops who were in service passed by this crucifix, they were seen to bow their knee and beck, which bred great fear on in-bringing of popery!

In the same year, Archbishop Laud attempted to plant 'the beauty of holiness' in Scotland. The Scottish clergy were required to wear gowns or surplices. In 1634 nine bishops were installed in the Scottish Privy Council and the two High Commission Courts introduced by James VI were amalgamated and the new Court for Scotland given sweeping powers.

Determined to follow through his belief that the Church should in many respects be the government of the land, Charles made Archbishop Spottiswoode of St Andrews Chancellor of Scotland. The General Assembly, however, was not part of the King's plans and was still not allowed to meet, and the Presbyteries, the other democratic element of Kirk government, were abolished. The Scots, Charles believed, should have a new prayer book and, realizing that the *English Book of Common Prayer* would be unacceptable, he set up a commission to prepare a *Revised Prayer Book* for use in his northern kingdom. On 23 July 1637, the new liturgy was read for the first time in St Giles. The Dean, Dr Hanna, had hardly begun the service before there was an uproar. Armed guards had to be brought in to force the rioters out. In Edinburgh and other towns there were violent public demonstrations, and the Scottish Privy Council, fearing its safety, locked itself in Holyrood

Palace. Robert Baillie, the minister for Kilwinning, wrote in his *Letters and Journals*, 'almost all our nobility and gentry of both sexes counts that Book little better than the Mass'.

By the end of 1637, opposition to Charles had become organized. A committee known as the Tables, consisting of four members from each Estate, was set up in Edinburgh under the leadership of John Leslie, the 6th Earl of Rothes, and James Graham, the 5th Earl of Montrose. Charles replied in February the following year by sending north a Proclamation demanding that all the Scottish nobles who had resisted the *Prayer Book* were to submit to his will and conform. On 28 February 1638 a group of Scottish nobles met at Greyfriars kirk and signed a bond, a National Covenant. The Scots, no longer with their King in their midst, felt politically impotent and the Covenant was a means of expressing national as well as religious resistance to the despotic aims of Charles I.

The National Covenant was the work of Alexander Henderson, minister of the Kirk at Leuchars in Fife, and Johnston of Wariston, once described as a 'lynx-eyed lawyer full of fire and energy and gloom'. It incorporated the Confession of Faith signed in 1581 by James VI and detailed the Acts of Parliament that had established the Calvinist religion and the liberty of the Kirk. The National Covenant pledged those who signed it, 'to labour by all means lawful to recover the purity and liberty of the Gospel as it was established and professed'. The Covenanters declared that King Charles's ecclesiastical reforms, 'do sensibly tend to the re-establishing of the Popish religion and tyranny, and to the subversion and ruin of the true reformed religion, and of our liberties, laws and estates.' The Marquis of Montrose was the first to sign the National Covenant. Over 150 noblemen signed the

Alexander Henderson (1583–1646), minister of Leuchars, was one of the authors of the National Covenant, and Moderator of the Glasgow General Assembly in 1638.   (*SNPG*)

William Hole's impression of the signing of the National Covenant in Greyfriars Churchyard in 1638. (*CAC*)

original copy of the document between four o'clock in the afternoon and eight o'clock in the evening on 28 February. The following day, further copies were made available in the Tailor's Hall in Edinburgh's Cowgate and were signed by more nobles, members of the Kirk and the Commissioners of the Royal Burghs. The congregation of the capital signed a month later. Lord Wariston remarked that the Covenant represented 'the great marriage day of this nation with God'.

King Charles had brought about exactly the sort of crisis which would unite the Scottish people against him. He told his English Council that he would have to use force against 'this small cloud in the North'. Growing discontent in England indicated that if he wished to raise an army there might be opposition, as the Duke of Northumberland pointed out:

> I think there is reason to fear that a great part of them will be readier to join with the Scots than to draw their swords in the King's service . . . God send us a good end of this troublesome business, for to my apprehension no foreign enemies could threaten so much danger to this kingdom as doth now this beggarly nation.

Charles's small cloud was to cause a storm which would help engulf all Britain in civil war.

7

Kirk and Covenant

COPIES OF THE NATIONAL COVENANT that was signed in Edinburgh on 28 February 1638 were taken throughout the country by mounted messengers. Most of those who signed it felt deeply that King Charles had been wrongly advised. Scots became engrossed by a sense of national purpose, infected by the enthusiasm shown by one of the unappointed leaders of the movement James Graham, the Earl of Montrose.

Born in 1612, the fifth Earl of Montrose had spent much of his youth in Perthshire and in Angus on his family's estates. Handsome and talented, James Graham could count mathematics, archery and golf among his accomplished pursuits. A sincere but tolerant Calvinist, Montrose got signatures on the National Covenant even in Aberdeenshire, the heartland of Scottish Episcopacy. Charles I, meanwhile, played for time. As he had no standing army, he could do little to enforce his threat of putting the rebellious Scots down by military means, and had to allow a General Assembly of the Church of Scotland to meet in Glasgow. Charles sent north a London Scot, his cousin the 3rd Marquis of Hamilton, as his Commissioner to the Assembly with the instructions to 'flatter them with hopes until I be ready to suppress them'. Covenanting nobles arrived in the town in November 1638 accompanied by bands of armed retainers.

As the debates became violent Hamilton tried to dissolve the Assembly. The delegates ignored him. After three weeks of deliberations, they had passed Acts deposing and excommunicating bishops, banned the new *Service Book* and appointed a Commission to inquire into ecclesiastical abuses that had grown up in the attempt by the Stewart kings to make Scotland's Church at one with that of England. Charles replied by declaring that the Assembly's legislation was null and void and prepared for war.

The King made two attempts to reduce the Covenanters by force and both were humiliating disasters. Alexander Leslie, who as a Field-Marshal in Gustavus Adolphus's army had fought for Sweden in Germany, was put in command of the Covenanter army. The Covenanters could call upon experienced soldiers, men who had served in Europe's great religious and political struggle – the Thirty Years War.

Throughout Scotland, ministers called upon their congregations to 'shake out their purses' to arm troops in defence of their religion. The strategic castles of Edinburgh, Stirling and Dumbarton were seized by the

James, 3rd Marquis, 1st Duke of Hamilton (1606–49) had led a force to support the Protestant cause in the Thirty Years' War. After the General Assembly in Glasgow he opposed Scottish intervention in the English Civil War. (*SNPG*)

Covenanters and a constant watch put over the Firth of Clyde for the army the King intended to send from Ireland.

The Marquis of Hamilton meanwhile sailed north with an army bound for Aberdeen, where it was hoped he could link up with the loyal Marquis of Huntly. His mother was waiting for him. She had two pistols and, it is said, specially cast silver balls. If her son set foot on Scottish soil against the Covenanters she would shoot him herself. An epidemic of smallpox decimated Hamilton's men and he was forced to try and make peace with the Covenanters. The Earl of Montrose led an army up from his estates in Angus and scattered Huntly's Royalists. Aberdeen, however, changed hands twice before Montrose finally routed Huntly's men at the Battle of the Brig o'Dee in the summer of 1639.

The main Covenanting army under General Leslie had taken up positions on Duns Law overlooking the River Tweed, where the General was joined by Highland troops under the Earl of Argyll. It was truly a Church army, as Robert Baillie, one of the army's chaplains, wrote:

> Every company had flying at the captain's door a brave new colour stamped with the Scottish arms and this motto, 'For Christ's Crown and Covenant' . . . had you lent your ear in the morning or especially at even and heard in the tents the sound of singing psalms, some praying and some reading scripture, you would have been refreshed.

King Charles's ill-paid army finally arrived hungry and downhearted, but neither side wanted to fight and a truce was arranged at Berwick in June 1639. The Covenanters promised to disband and hand back the Royal castles on condition that the King allowed the Estates and the General Assembly to meet and discuss how the Kirk should be organized. When both met in Edinburgh they re-enacted the legislation passed in Glasgow the previous year, but Charles, determined not to give the Royal assent, ordered the Estates to adjourn until June 1640 and set about raising another army.

The Covenanting army had never disbanded and began to re-muster at Kelso and Dunbar in May 1640. The following month the King refused to reassemble the Estates and in defiance the Scottish parliament met and again enacted the legislation they had passed the year before. In an attempt to force the King to accept the legislation, the Covenanters invaded England. Leslie's army, led by Montrose, waded across the Tweed at Coldstream and marched in triumph to take Newcastle. Charles, still unable to raise an army sufficient to defeat the Scots, was forced to agree to another truce, and signed a Treaty with the Covenanters at Ripon in June 1641.

But in Scotland, however, the Covenanters began to fall foul of each other. Archibald Campbell, the 8th Earl of Argyll, a staunch Calvinist, was eager to exploit the situation and extend his personal power. Argyll spoke of deposing the King. The nobility of Scotland, he claimed, had the overriding duty to protect the nation's people. The more moderate Montrose met at Cumbernauld House in Dumbartonshire with eighteen other nobles who agreed to act together in support of the King. The Cumbernauld Bond was an expression of alarm at the *political* extremism of the Covenanters. The great national movement was divided.

The Covenanters under Argyll and others ruled Scotland for eleven years. During that time they attempted to create a theocracy, a nation

Archibald Campbell, 8th Earl and 1st Marquis of Argyll (1607–61), known as Cross-eyed Archibald. (*SNPG*)

governed in God's name by the Committee of Estates. The Kirk was given more power than ever before: Scotland was ruled by Presbyteries and the General Assembly which now dictated to the Estates. Laws were passed for the care of the poor and the sick and every parish was to have a school, paid for by the local landowners. Merchants were forbidden to trade with Roman Catholic countries, lest they be subject to 'religious contagion'. Church attendance was again made compulsory.

Under the Covenanters those suspected of witchcraft suffered most. The Bible demanded, 'Thou shalt not suffer a witch to live', and in 1640 the General Assembly ordered ministers 'carefully to take notice of witches, charmers and all such abusers of the people'. In 1643, in Fife alone, thirty witches were burned.

Charles's war against the Covenanters had forced him to summon his English Parliament. But the King's intransigence over religion and his autocratic, arrogant view of government drove the English parliament to take up arms to defend its rights. When Charles raised his standard at Nottingham in 1642, the English Parliament looked to the Covenanting Scots for help; and under Argyll a Solemn League and Covenant was signed with the English parliamentarians in 1643. The Scots agreed to attack Royalist positions from the north in return for their expenses which, it was estimated, would be some £30,000 a month. The agreement was 'solemn'; the English Parliament bound itself to bring English worship and ecclesiastical polity into line with those of Scotland. It was agreed that an assembly would meet at Westminster to make the faith of both nations the same. The English ultimately reneged on the Solemn League and Covenant but the Scots, by accepting the Westminster confession of faith, stood by the conclusions of the assembly. By the League and Covenant, the Scots hoped that the English might bring their Puritan Church into line with that of Scotland. Montrose rightly sensed that the English were cynically using a Presbyterian crusade for political ends; that their prime concern was to make sure the Scots were on their side in the Civil War.

The portrait of Charles I that hangs in Drum Castle in Aberdeenshire. (*NTS*)

The army of the English Parliament was reorganized under Oliver Cromwell. From 1644 it was clear that Charles I was doomed. In July that year, Charles I was defeated at Marston Moor and in 1645 was humiliated at the Battle of Naseby. Only Montrose's campaign in Scotland gave heart to Royalists on both sides of the Border. Under Montrose, Lieutenant-General of the King's forces in Scotland, there had been one of the most remarkable campaigns in British, let alone in Scottish history.

Montrose had penetrated the Covenanting lines and joined up with Alastair MacDonald, the son of MacDonald of Colonsay who was given the same nickname as his father, Colkitto, Coll 'ciotach' or 'left-handed'. Colkitto, from Ireland, was well versed in hill fighting. With Montrose, a military leader who could inspire men to feats of daring and bravery, the two men between 1644 and 1645 achieved the near-impossible.

In February 1644, Montrose, now created a Marquis, captured Dumfries and, with the help of six cannons from the Duke of Newcastle's army, went on to take Morpeth in Northumberland in May. At that time his forces only numbered 2200 men, but they were seasoned fighters. On 1 September his army, stronger by the addition of 500 bowmen, faced the Covenanting army under the leadership of Lord Elcho west of Perth, at Tibbermore.

Oliver Cromwell (1559–1658), an unfinished portrait of the architect of England's New Model Army of which he was appointed General of Horse and second-in-command to General Fairfax. He played a major role in the decisive Royalist defeat at Naseby. (*BQ*)

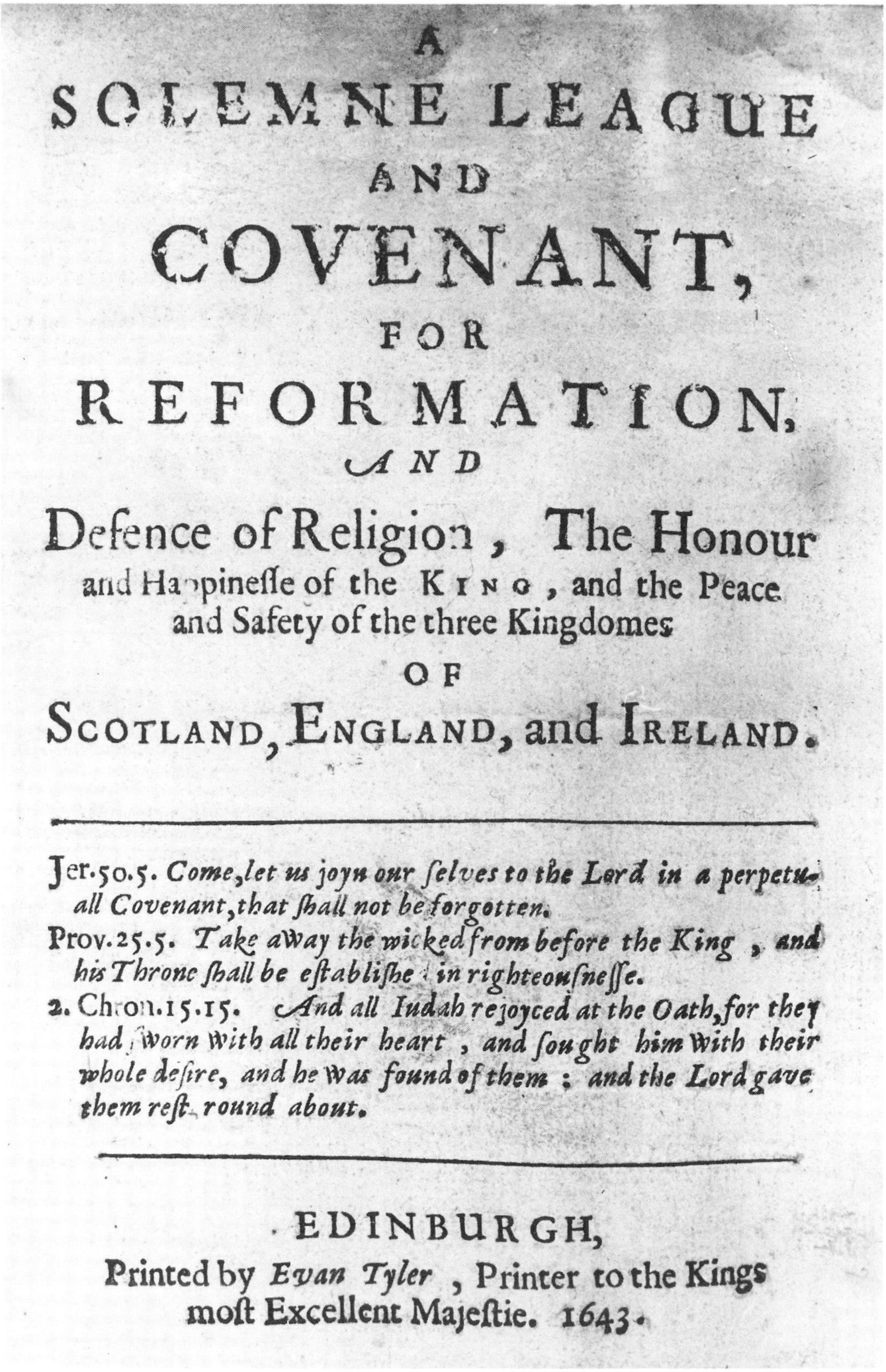

A SOLEMNE LEAGUE

AND

COVENANT,

FOR

REFORMATION,

AND

Defence of Religion, The Honour
and Happinesse of the KING, and the Peace
and Safety of the three Kingdomes

OF

SCOTLAND, ENGLAND, and IRELAND.

Jer.50.5. *Come, let us joyn our selves to the Lord in a perpetu-*
all Covenant, that shall not be forgotten.
Prov.25.5. *Take away the wicked from before the King, and*
his Throne shall be establishe in righteousnesse.
2. Chron.15.15. *And all Iudah rejoyced at the Oath, for they*
had sworn with all their heart, and sought him with their
whole desire, and he was found of them: and the Lord gave
them rest round about.

EDINBURGH,

Printed by *Evan Tyler*, Printer to the Kings
most Excellent Majestie. 1643.

(NLS)

Montrose won a dazzling victory. Elcho's army numbered some 7000, with 700 cavalry and nine cannon. But the Covenanters' battle cry of 'Jesus and no quarter' failed them and Elcho's losses were great. Montrose entered Perth in triumph. His Highland troops, however, after looting the town, drifted off to their mountainous homes, and by the end of September he was campaigning outside Aberdeen with only 1500 men. The Covenanters, now under the leadership of Lord Balfour of Burleigh, numbered a thousand more. Yet Montrose again routed them and took Aberdeen, where he received reinforcements and decided to attack the heart of the Campbell kingdom.

In the depth of winter, Montrose crossed the mountains to attack Argyll's base at Inveraray, by way of Loch Tay, through Crianlarich to Glen Orchy and Loch Awe. Argyll, realizing the Marquis's intent, hastened his army to

The passage of Montrose's army through Glencoe. *(AAG)*

his stronghold, confident, given the severe cold, that he could pick off the starving and frozen Royalists at his leisure. After all, the Campbells' proud boast, 'It's a far cry to Loch Awe', had been justified until then. Surrounded on all sides by mountains and the sea, they felt no one could attack them at Inveraray. Yet when Argyll got there he learnt that the army of Montrose was advancing down Glen Shira. Argyll took fright and escaped by way of Loch Fyne, leaving several hundred of his clansmen to die at the hands of Montrose's Highland troops. After the plundering, one of the MacDonalds wrote, 'We left neither house nor hold unburned, nor corn nor cattle that belonged to the whole name of Campbell.' But Montrose was again plagued by desertion, and at Kilcumin found himself left with his original force of 1500.

He was in a dangerous position. To the north, at Inverness, was the Earl of Seaforth with an army of 5000. Behind him, at Inverlochy, was Argyll's army of 3000 men. But he escaped by way of a prompt cross-country detour and by 1 February 1645 was bearing down again on Argyll at Inverlochy. The following day as the sun was rising the MacDonalds charged down the slopes of Ben Nevis on to the unsuspecting Campbells encamped below. Argyll, injured, left by boat, as his men faced Montrose. The Covenanters lost nearly 1500 men while only ten Royalists were killed.

In despair, the Covenanters asked the English to help, while Montrose took his men on to Elgin. There the ranks of his army were swelled to about 2000 men. He then moved south to Aberdeen, burning the town of Brechin on the way, and captured Dundee. General William Baillie of Letham, who, like Leslie, had served under Gustavus Adolphus, and General Hurry, were bent on retaking the town for the Covenanters with an army of some 4000 men; but as they approached Dundee Montrose withdrew his forces back to Brechin, drawing the enemy with him. At Auldearn on 9 May 1645, Montrose and the military genius of Colkitto defeated General Hurry and inflicted some 2000 casualties. During the battle, both leaders used cavalry provided by the Gordons and the Grants for the first time. They kept them in reserve until the battle was in full flight, then unleashed them on their unsuspecting enemy. At Alford on 2 July the Royalists went on to defeat General Baillie's army and the General, together with Argyll, just managed to escape capture. His battle for control of the Highlands now complete, Montrose decided to retire to Dunkeld and await reinforcements. Then on 15 August 1645, at Kilsyth, the Marquis inflicted a further swingeing defeat on the Covenanting forces of General Baillie by cutting his army in half with a brilliant cavalry charge. Argyll, as at Inverlochy, took to the water to escape. With the whole of Scotland now defenceless before him, Montrose took Edinburgh.

The campaign had been brilliant; but whenever Montrose crossed the Highland Line his clan troops ultimately deserted him. When he entered Glasgow, his Highlanders, after looting, retired to the hills with their booty, and Colkitto, his able commander, took leave of the city to let more Campbell blood. He then retired to Ireland, where he died in 1647. Montrose had needed Colkitto to hold the Irish to his cause. In the end, Alastair Mac-Donald's war had not been Montrose's war, as the former's chief aim was the recovery of the fortunes of the MacDonalds, not of Charles I. By the summer of 1645, half his army had left him, but Montrose was determined to try and join up with King Charles in England. In an attempt to break out of Scotland he came face to face with the Covenanter army under David Leslie, Lord Newark, who had fought with Cromwell at Marston Moor. Montrose had encamped at Philiphaugh, near Selkirk, when he was surprised by Leslie on 13 September. The ensuing battle was a bloodbath that put paid to the Royalists' 'Glorious Year'. For his own safety, Montrose was persuaded to quit the field. He lost able soldiers and friends. Lord Ogilvie and Sir William Rollo were among those taken prisoner. Lord Ogilvie managed to escape the night before his execution but many died on the scaffold. Among them were three eighteen-year-old boys. When the last of them was beheaded, an attendant Covenanting minister is said to have rubbed his hands and remarked, 'The work gangs bonnily on.' One officer, O'Cahan, who had come with the troops from Ireland, was hanged over the Castle wall at Edinburgh.

The Covenanters wrought vengeance on those who had supported Montrose. When Leslie later besieged Dunaverty Fort, its 300 defenders came out to surrender. They were hacked to pieces. Others in Kintyre were

James Graham, 1st Marquis of Montrose (1612–50). (*SNPG*)

David Leslie, 1st Lord Newark (*d.* 1682) served under Gustavus Adolphus and joined the Covenanting army in 1643. He fought at Marston Moor before facing Montrose at Philiphaugh. (*SNPG*)

smoked out of caves and handed over to the Scottish regiment serving in France; they would not see Scotland again for fifteen years. In June 1646 the Lamonts, who had supported Colkitto and fought at Philiphaugh, were massacred by the Campbells. Sir James Lamont's castles of Toward and Ascog were besieged and forced to capitulate. Two hundred prisoners were taken by boat to Dunoon, where thirty-six were hanged from a single tree and the rest slaughtered or buried alive.

At Newark, in May 1646, Charles I surrendered to the Scottish army. He stubbornly refused to accept the Covenant, although by doing so he might have saved his Crown, and the Scots – owed nearly half a million pounds under the terms of the Solemn League and Covenant – when offered part payment handed Charles over to the English. His Scottish subjects had sold him, the King bitterly claimed. Argyll and his party objected to the accusation. They had merely agreed to evacuate Newcastle, their English headquarters, in return for the payment of their troops by the parliamentarians. The 'blood money', however, did not all go to the troops. Argyll personally received £30,000, as did the Duke of Hamilton, who argued it was compensation for the damage done to his estates.

In Scotland, reaction to the King's arrest was strong. The 2nd Earl of Lauderdale, who had helped frame the Solemn League and Covenant, visited the King in England. He promised Charles Scottish military support if he agreed to make England Presbyterian for a trial period of three years. The King slyly agreed to the proposal and a Treaty called The Engagement was signed on 27 December 1647. But this attempt to play one side of Scotland off against the other failed when, in August 1648, the Engagers, led by the Duke of Hamilton, were badly beaten at Preston in Lancashire and dispersed in a series of running battles.

In 1648, the Parliament of England tried King Charles and executed him outside Whitehall on 30 January 1649. Montrose, who was in Brussels, is said to have fainted at the news of his King's death. He retired from the world for two days, then emerged in black armour bent on singing Charles's 'obsequies with trumpet sounds' and writing his epitaph 'in blood and wounds'.

John Maitland, 1st Duke of Lauderdale (1616–82). (*SNPG*)

In Scotland, the Earl of Argyll was also moved by the execution, and sent a delegation to The Hague to treat with the dead King's eighteen-year-old son, offering the young Charles the Scottish throne if he agreed to sign the Covenant. But Montrose advised him against signing such a Treaty and promised to win the new King his throne by conquest instead. Charles II, like his father, was a double-dealer. He continued to talk with Argyll while allowing Montrose to return to Scotland and to his death.

Montrose published an appeal to the loyal people of Scotland:

> All those who have any duty left them to God, their King, Country, Friends, Homes, Wives and Children, or would change, now at the last, the tyranny, violence and oppression of these rebels with the mild and innocent government of the just prince; or revenge the horrid and execrable murder of their sacred King, redeem their nation from infamy, themselves from slavery, restore the present and oblige the ages to come, let them as Christians, subjects, patriots, friends, husbands and fathers join themselves forth with us. Dead or alive, the world will give them thanks.

For his execution Charles I wore a double shirt; it was winter and he was afraid any trembling might be interpreted as fear. (*SNPG*)

The Marquis of Montrose on the way to his execution. (*NGS*)

With 500 Danish and German mercenaries, he crossed over to Orkney. Then, his army more than doubled by Orcadian recruits, Montrose crossed the Pentland Firth. His campaign proved short-lived. At Carbisdale on the River Oykell, his army was cut to pieces on 27 April 1650. Montrose managed to flee the field to spend two days in the wilderness of Sutherland before being captured at Ardvreck Castle. His host, McLeod of Assynt, handed him over for the princely sum of £25,000.

As he had already been declared a traitor in 1644, Montrose was not tried. He was to be hanged at the Mercat Cross in Edinburgh on a gibbet thirty feet high, and only after three hours would he be cut down and quartered. His head was to be set on the Tolbooth, his limbs on the town gates of Stirling, Glasgow, Perth and Aberdeen. It was the fate of a criminal, not a nobleman whose only crime had been loyalty to a deceitful House of Stewart. All the officers captured at Carbisdale suffered death by the axe, or the Maiden. The rank and file Orcadians, herded into Edinburgh, were sent to work as slaves in the coalmines of Fife.

On 21 May 1650, the Marquis of Montrose was taken down the High Street of Edinburgh to the Mercat Cross and the gallows. The mob, primed to throw stones, could only shed tears. Before paying his executioner, Montrose made a short speech.

I do but follow the light of my own conscience, which is kindled to the working of the good spirit of God that is within me . . . I leave my soul to God, my service to my prince, my good will to my friends, and my name and charity to you all.

Montrose cried for God's mercy on an afflicted Scotland as he was pushed off the scaffold. An English witness remarked:

It is absolutely certain that he hath overcome more men by his death in Scotland than he would have done if he had lived.

Eleven years after his death, the Kirk and government in Scotland allowed Montrose a state burial. His friends had held on to his whitened bones and his son had guarded the silver box that contained his heart since it was removed from his body the night after the execution. The body lay in state for a week at Holyrood before it was borne by fourteen Scots lords up the Canongate to St Giles, where a white marble statue now shields his remains.

Unknown to Montrose, the future Charles II had disowned him before his execution. The King had no alternative but to put his faith in Argyll, and returned to Scotland in 1650. In Edinburgh, Charles played the farcical role of a Covenanted King. He was harangued by worthy Presbyterians and forced to renounce his parents. The Earl of Argyll arranged a coronation in the little church at Scone, and placed the Crown of Scotland on Charles's head himself on New Year's Day 1651.

But any hope of Charles II being able to rule effectively came to an end at the Battle of Dunbar on 3 September 1650. Until then David Leslie had effectively outgeneralled Oliver Cromwell; but at Dunbar the ministers of the Covenanted Kirk demanded the Scottish troops become a 'Gideon's Army' and saw to it that the ranks were purged of all but the faithful. Leslie should

Charles II (1630–85) was proclaimed King at Edinburgh on news of his father's execution. He was eighteen when he sat for this portrait.   (*MK*)

'The Scots holding their young King's nose to the grindstone', 1651.   (*BM*)

have won the day. The Scots army had over 22,000 troops compared with Cromwell's 11,000. His defeat was due to the Kirk's meddling in military matters and urging that the Scots forsake their high position on Doon Hill. Some 3000 Scots were killed or wounded and twice that number taken prisoner.

King Charles was forced into exile in 1651, after his humiliating defeat at Worcester on 3 September. Argyll, unlike David Leslie, refused to march south and fight for the King. Leslie was taken prisoner at Worcester and spent nine years in the Tower, whilst in Scotland the Earl of Argyll had accepted the rule of Oliver Cromwell by 1652. General Monck, Cromwell's Commander-in-Chief in Scotland, undertook a short sharp campaign to subdue the Highlands. Sir Ewan Cameron of Lochiel, a staunch Episcopalian, held out for a time, and is said to have killed an English officer by biting out his throat, 'the sweetest bite', Sir Ewan claimed, he had ever tasted.

Sir Ewan Cameron of Lochiel (1629–1719), 17th Chief of clan Cameron, who fought with Montrose and later with Claverhouse.   (*CL*)

Under Cromwell, Scotland was united with England: thirty Scots were selected to represent the nation in the parliament at Westminster. Seven commissioners, four English and three Scottish, administered justice in Scotland, and new sheriffs were appointed for all the Scottish counties. But the cost of the enforced union was great and Scotland was severely taxed to pay for her unwelcome new rulers. General Monck was given the thankless task of trying to raise £10,000 a month. Even so, Cromwell was responsible for the most efficient and just government Scotland had witnessed in centuries.

In 1660, General Monck, helped by Cameron of Lochiel, set out from Coldstream in the Borders and restored Charles II to the thrones of England and Scotland. Scots rejoiced at the Restoration in the hope that the years of warring and poverty would come to an end. They were to be terribly disillusioned.

King Charles II was personally neither vindictive nor a religious zealot, but the twenty-five years of his reign were years of revenge and fanaticism in Scotland. Argyll, who had been made a Marquis by the new King in 1649, hastened south on his accession. He was refused an audience. Charles's advisers had Argyll sent back to Scotland to stand trial for treason. Ably defended by George Mackenzie, Argyll was acquitted of having played a part in the execution of Charles I; but Monck, who acted as Prosecutor, produced ample evidence that Argyll had worked alongside the Cromwellians. Although he rightly pointed out that to condemn him on that charge was to condemn him on 'the epidemical fault of the whole nation', Argyll was found guilty. He was allowed a quicker death than Montrose, execution by the Maiden. On the day he took dinner, waited upon by his own servants, and then slept until two hours before his execution. On the scaffold, he noted that the block was not level, produced a ruler to check it and demanded a carpenter correct it before he would place his head on it. His head was placed on a spike outside the Edinburgh Tolbooth, recently vacated by the head of Montrose. Both men were martyrs to the House of Stewart they had sought to serve. Both died for ideals, like Charles I, even if he pursued them by devious, insensitive means.

General George Monck (1608–70) came north with Cromwell in 1650 and acted as Commander-in-Chief in Scotland in 1651 and from 1654 to 1660.   (*BQ*)

Once restored to the throne, Charles II never visited Scotland. Like his father, he appointed a Scottish Privy Council to do his work in Edinburgh, through a Secretary based in London. The Earl of Lauderdale, a London

'The last Sleep of Argyll' before his execution in 1661. (*CAC*)

Scot who, like Leslie, had been imprisoned after the Battle of Worcester, was made Secretary of State for Scotland in 1661. The Earl, who held the office for nineteen years, was hardly an appealing man. According to one contemporary:

> He made a very ill appearance, he was very big; his hair was red, hanging loosely about him; his tongue was too big for his mouth, which made him bedew all that he talked to; and his whole manner was rough and boisterous, and very unfit for court.

Lauderdale recalled the Scottish Estates, which, planted with Royalists, met in January 1661. All legislation that had been passed by the Covenanters in the years following 1633 was cancelled.

Like his father and grandfather, Charles II wanted Scottish bishops. Charles, however, like his ancestors, failed to realize that the ministers of the Kirk were different from English parsons. The Scottish ministry was a professional one, and after eleven years of Covenanter rule had a place in the political as well as social fabric of the land. It was a body with its own discipline and sense of purpose. Charles, however, through Secretary Lauderdale demanded that ministers who had taken over congregations since 1649 were to seek out their lay patrons and be formally presented to take their charges from the bishop of the diocese. Over three hundred ministers, a third of the Scottish ministry, refused to comply and were forced to abandon their churches and manses. This substantial number came to form a nucleus of political and ultimately military resistance to the monarch's ill-conceived wishes.

By 1665, illegal services held in the open air, called Conventicles, were numerous and popular. The meetings had armed piquets stationed to protect them and the Covenanting ministers became the focus of Scottish dissent. The government made severe efforts to crush them by force,

Sir Thomas Dalyell (c 1599–1685).
After service in Russia he acted as
Commander of the King's forces in
Scotland from 1666 to 1685. He raised
the Royal Scots Greys in 1681.
(SNPG)

John Graham of Claverhouse
(1648–89) was active against the
Covenanters in the south-west
between 1682 and 1685. Created
Viscount Dundee by James VII, he
withdrew from the Convention in 1689
when it repudiated the Stewart
monarch.   (SNPG)

goading the Covenanters into open armed rebellion. In November 1666, a group of Covenanters captured Sir James Turner, the Commander of the government's troops in the south-west of Scotland. They marched him, in his nightshirt, through Ayrshire and Lanarkshire heading for Edinburgh. All the way, they were shadowed by the troops of General Tam Dalyell, Commander of the King's army in Scotland.

On 28 November 1666, at Rullion Green outside Edinburgh, 900 Covenanters were hopelessly defeated by Dalyell. Fifteen of their leaders were hanged in Edinburgh and others suffered a similar fate in Glasgow and Ayr. Many were imprisoned and tortured. Some thirty women and children who had followed the Covenanting forces were also put to the sword despite the fact that Dalyell had given them quarter. In disgust General Tam resigned his commission.

Lauderdale came north in 1669 as the King's Commissioner and adopted a new policy, offering parish appointments on less stringent conditions than before. With the help of Robert Leighton, Bishop of Dunblane, Lauderdale persuaded about a hundred 'outed' ministers to accept indulgences and return to their parishes. Those who still chose to dissent were rounded up, together with their lay supporters. Special prisons, like that on the Bass Rock in the Firth of Forth, were constructed to house them. Sandy Peden, one of the most famous Conventicle preachers, described his imprisonment there:

> We are close shut up in our chambers, not permitted to converse, diet, worship together, but conducted out by two at once in the day to breathe in the open air, envying with reverence the birds their freedom. Again we are close shut up, day and night, to hear only the sighs and moans of our fellow prisoners.

After four years he was released but, caught preaching illegally, was imprisoned again and sent to work in the West Indies.

In 1679, Archbishop James Sharp of St Andrews was brutally murdered. On 3 May 1679, while driving home in his coach with his daughter Isabella, he was attacked on Magus Muir by nine Covenanters led by John Balfour of Kinloch and hacked to death. Shortly after, on 1 June, government troops led by John Graham of Claverhouse, a relative of the great Montrose, were defeated at Drumclog, on the Borders of Ayrshire and Lanarkshire. But the Covenanters' victory was short-lived. At Bothwell Bridge in the same year, the King's illegitimate son, the Duke of Monmouth, mowed down the Covenanting army and took nearly twelve hundred prisoners who were marched to a camp set up near Greyfriars Kirk in Edinburgh. The wounded were lodged in George Heriot's Hospital and attended by the town's physicians. Within two weeks, all but 340 had signed a bond not to take up arms against the King. In November, 210 Covenanters who refused to sign were put on a ship bound for the plantations in the West Indies; but the vessel sank in a storm near the Orkneys and all were drowned.

The 1680s in Scotland became known as The Killing Time: the monarch was determined to have conformity. Scotland was to become part of England's Protestant empire, a concept that went back to the time of Elizabeth I. In their determination to stamp out extremist Covenanters, the government had billeted the 'Highland Host' in the south-west. As a contemporary writer noted, they were allowed to pillage at will:

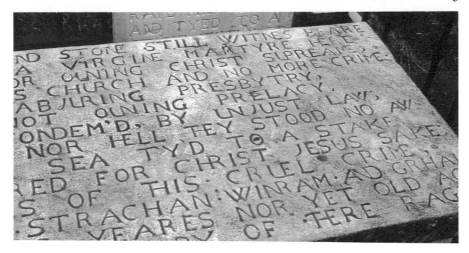

The grave of one of the Wigtown Martyrs, which names those who gave them up to the government authorities.   (*Author*)

> When the Highlanders went back, one would have thought they had been at the sacking of some besieged town, by their baggage and luggage. They were loaded with spoil. They carried away a great many horses, and no small quantity of goods out of merchants' shops.

The area abounds in memorials to those cruel years. In the old church at Loudoun, near Newmilns, is the grave of John Nisbet, tried first in Ayr and then in Edinburgh, who went to the scaffold rejoicing and praising the Lord. In the same churchyard lies John Law who helped eight Covenanter prisoners to escape only to die when dragoons attacked a Conventicle that was being held at Little Blackwood. In nearby Fenwick churchyard stands a memorial to James White who was shot dead on the spot when dragoons surprised an open-air service. The soldiers, it is said, cut off his head and played football with it.

In the churchyard at St Machatus in Wigtown in Kirkcudbrightshire are the graves of Margaret McLauchlin and Margaret Wilson, who, it is said, were tied to a stake and drowned by the rising tide for adhering to the Covenanting faith. At Dalgarnock, near Thornhill in Dumfriesshire, a cross commemorates the resting place of fifty-seven Covenanters from the surrounding countryside who died for their faith. They were martyrs in a Biblical sense. Feeling that at this time of great historic crisis civilization itself might be about to end, the Covenanters took intellectual refuge in the Second Coming – the concept that Christ would return to Earth and change everything, make it all perfect.

Hounded for their beliefs, the Covenanters took up arms to defend themselves. Richard Cameron, who was born in Falkland in Fife in 1648 had fought in Holland before he returned to Scotland. At Sanquhar on 22 June 1680 he openly declared war on King Charles.

> We for ourselves do by thir presents disown Charles Stewart, that has been reigning (or rather tyrannising as we may say) on the throne of Britain these years bygone, as having any right, title to, or interest in the said crown of Scotland for government as forfeited several years since by his perjury and breach of covenant both to God and his Kirk . . . As also, we being under the standard of our Lord Jesus Christ, Captain of salvation, do declare a war with such a tyrant and usurper and the men of his practices, as enemies to our Lord Jesus Christ, and his cause and covenants.

The government put a price of five thousand merks on Cameron's head and he was quickly trapped and killed by Royalist forces in a skirmish on Aird's Moss in Ayrshire. The war was carried on by his friend, Donald Cargill. When he, in turn, was caught and executed, the mantle fell upon James Renwick.

Renwick was nineteen when he witnessed Donald Cargill's execution in the Grassmarket in Edinburgh. So moved was he that he went to study theology at Gröningen, where he wrote:

> Courage for all that is come and gone. The loss of the men is not the loss of the cause. What is the matter though we all fall? The cause shall not fall.

He returned to Scotland in October 1683 and became the soul of the Cameronian movement. When he was finally captured, in January 1688, he had on him notes for a sermon on Psalm 46, Verse 10, 'Be still then, and know that I am God: I will be exalted among the heathen, and I will be exalted in the earth.' Charged with denying the authority of King James VII and II, James Renwick was the last Covenanter martyr.

The Covenanters declined in importance. An extreme manifesto, known as the Queensferry Paper, again committed Covenanters to the overthrow of the 'kingdom of darkness' in favour of the 'kingdom of Christ':

> We do declare that we shall set up over ourselves and over what God shall give us power of, government and governors, according to the word of God . . . That we shall no more commit the government of ourselves and the making of laws for us, to any one single person or lineal successor . . . this kind of government by a single person being most liable to inconveniences, and aptest to degenerate into tyranny as sad and long experience has taught us.

But few Scots really wished that the monarchy, however inept, would be abolished.

The end to the Killing Time came in an unexpected way. On 6 February 1685, Charles II had died and was succeeded by his brother, a Roman Catholic. James VII of Scotland and II of England conceded, by a Declaration of Indulgence in 1687, a general religious toleration throughout Great Britain. In Scotland, Catholics, like the Duke of Gordon who was made Governor of Edinburgh Castle, were given prominent posts. Holyrood Abbey was transformed into a Catholic Chapel and a school was set up in the Palace to train Catholic priests.

Scottish and English exiles in Holland plotted to depose James VII in favour of his nephew, the Protestant Duke of Monmouth. The attack was to be two-pronged. Monmouth was to land with his army in the west of England while Archibald Campbell, son of the famous Marquis of Argyll who had been executed for treason, was to raise a rebellion in the west of Scotland. At the beginning of May 1685, Argyll left Holland with three ships and 300 men. The army in Scotland was quickly called up and Covenanters thought likely to support Argyll were thrown into prison at Blackness and Dunnottar Castles. Argyll, however, failed to raise support and was captured at Inchinnan near Renfrew and executed.

So bitter were James VII's controversies with his English subjects that he was forced by April 1689 to throw in his hand and quit the country. The

English Parliament had asked his Protestant daughter Mary and her husband William of Orange to become joint rulers. In England, the revolution was almost bloodless and became known as Glorious. In Scotland, it proved a different story.

In 1689, a Convention of the Estates met to discuss whether James or William should be King. They took letters from both candidates. The one from James VII and II was so violent and stupid that it actually swayed the Estates in favour of William. William III of England and II of Scotland made Scotland Presbyterian once more. In 1690, the Westminster Confession, formulated in 1643, was once again adopted. The Confession, which was the result of an Assembly of English Presbyterians at which six Scots had been present as 'assistants', was the fulfilment of the Solemn League and Covenant. Four documents were involved. A Calvinist Confession of Faith, although rejected by the English Church, now became a cornerstone of the Scottish Kirk. So too did the Assembly's two Catechisms, the 'Larger' and the 'Shorter', designed to help ministers and elders instruct the young. Francis Rous, a Cornish MP and Provost of Eton College, had produced a Metrical Psalter, which, after revision, became an essential part of Scottish Presbyterian worship. The Convention of Estates did away with patronage; the government of the Kirk was restored. Over two-thirds of the existing ministry in Scotland were deprived of their parishes.

But the year before the Convention had witnessed the first example of the threat to stability that would now come from an exiled Stewart family. In 1689, John Graham of Claverhouse, now Viscount Dundee, raised the Standard of James VII in the Highlands and refused a summons to attend the Convention. Although a staunch Episcopalian, his antagonism to the Covenanters was far more political than religious. Like many of his contemporaries, Claverhouse considered the Covenanters a threat to order with the danger of civil war.

The Westminster Assembly sat for ten years. It was attended by over 120 divines who were paid four shillings a day expenses. Robert Baillie from Glasgow was one of the Scottish representatives who bewailed the 'longsomeness' of the proceedings. (*PW*)

Dundee rode north with fifty followers. While he set about raising his Highland army, Patrick Stewart, the steward of the Marquis of Atholl, who was in England, took over Blair Castle for the Jacobites, and the Duke of Gordon stubbornly continued to hold Edinburgh Castle for James VII.

General Mackay was ordered north with government troops to suppress the uprising. In March 1689, he set sail with 3000 foot soldiers while his cavalry travelled north by land. Blair Castle was strategically important and both Dundee and Mackay marched towards it. On the morning of 27 July, Dundee reached the Castle while Mackay was still making his way through the Pass of Killiecrankie. Dundee, with only 2500 men, placed his troops in the cliffs. An observer has left us an account of what happened:

> It was past seven o'clock, Dundee gave the word. The Highlanders dropped their plaids. It was long remembered in Lochaber that Lochiel took off what possibly was the only pair of shoes in his clan, and charged barefoot at the head of his men . . . In two minutes the battle was lost and won.

Mackay's troops were mostly new to battle and had been issued with a new weapon, bayonets, which were awkward to fit on their guns. He wrote of his troops:

> With the exception of Hasting's and Leven's regiments they behaved like the vilest cowards in nature.

Mackay lost 2000 men, killed or captured: the Highland army's losses were 900. But Dundee had been shot. In the past he had fought with William III and is even reported to have saved his life. Now the King was right when he remarked, on news of the Battle of Killiecrankie, 'Armies are needless. The war is over with Dundee's life.'

The Cameronians, who had formed a regiment on 14 May 1689, were sent to Dunkeld to halt the Highlanders' advance south. On 21 August 1689, 5000 Highlanders attacked the town and destroyed it. The Cameronian Commander, twenty-year-old William Cleland was killed but his troops drove the Highlanders out of the town. When their ammunition ran low the Cameronians made bullets from the lead on the roof of the Marquis of Atholl's house. In May 1690 the Jacobite army, the remnant of Dunkeld, finally broke up after being defeated at Cromdale on Speyside.

Scotland had torn itself apart for decades: the nation was exhausted and poverty-stricken. The British Civil War, often wrongly called English, ultimately discredited the Covenanters, and proved costly in both human lives and national wealth. It is estimated that 10,000 Scots, one per cent of the nation's population, were killed in one year alone. The thirty years that had followed Charles II's restoration had been years of misery, and the wounds inflicted by religious fanaticism, untreated, had become festering sores. Religious persecution brought about by the monarchy had made it impossible for Episcopalians and Presbyterians to trust one another, despite the fact that they had much in common when it came to practical worship.

With the accession of William and Mary, it was now the turn of trade, not religion, to become the preoccupation of people north and south of the border. The upper classes of Scotland, as their English counterparts, now looked for private financial gain, an ambition that fuelled the distrust and rivalry the two peoples already had for each other.

8

$\longleftrightarrow$

Disaster at Darien

SCOTLAND BY THE MIDDLE of the seventeenth century was an independent but poor country dominated by a land-owning aristocracy. A nation of a million people lived by the land and their wits. Four out of five Scots made their living from agriculture and fishing. The land, the main provider, gave niggardly returns. Only a quarter of the country was fit for any sort of cultivation at all. Mountains and peat-bogs made most of the Highlands and southern uplands of little use.

Scots still farmed as their medieval ancestors had done. Scottish land law moulded the very life of the nation, protecting the proprietor at the expense of the tenant. All land was held from feudal superiors and rights were scrupulously defined and precisely recorded. So the mass of farmers had little incentive to improve their land; if they dug ditches to drain the soil the landlord would either raise the rent or evict them.

Farming was backward in most of Scotland and rural poverty was widespread. Agriculture was at its most advanced in East Lothian. The infield, the best arable land, was manured regularly and kept constantly under cultivation. Often referred to as the 'croft', because it was continually cropped, the infield was usually divided into four to allow for a simple rotation of peas, wheat, barley and oats. Sometimes the arable land was divided into rigs – strips of land divided among the tenants. Sometimes, from four to sixteen tenants jointly worked the arable land in 'fermtouns'. The farmers paid their rent jointly and helped each other with the ploughing, although each tenant reaped his own harvest and kept what grain was left after the laird had been paid.

The laird often took more than his share. Some of his rent was paid in money, some in produce, and there was always a tribute to be paid by tenants in the form of livestock, or butter or cheese. In addition, tenants usually had to work for him for nothing, help transport his goods to market or cut his wood or peats. The laird frequently owned the local mill and forced his tenants to use it on penalty of a heavy fine if they chose to go elsewhere. From the middle of the seventeenth century, rack-renting was prevalent, and the old Scots saying 'Ane to saw, ane to gnaw and ane to pay the laird witha' summed up the gloomy picture.

Scottish towns were also troubled. The Royal Burghs, in particular, were in decline. Most like Culross in Fife were still small, and when an Act of

Prospectus Palatij & Oppidi CULROSSIÆ. *The Prospect of y⁰ House & Town of COLROSS.*

This Plate is Most Humbly Inscrib'd to the Hon.ble Colonel John Hope.

Culross in Fife as seen by the Dutchman, Captain John Slezer, a royal engineer in Scotland under Charles II. The burgh, founded by the Bruce family in the 1590s, prospered, mining coal, making salt and iron griddles which were exported. The pantiles used to roof the village were brought back from Holland as ballast. (*NLS*)

1672 deprived them of their trading privileges they never regained their old supremacy. The Scots still maintained a trading staple at Veere on the Dutch island of Walcheren; but when Rotterdam became the centre of trade with the Low Countries and the seaway into Veere silted up, the burghs of eastern Scotland suffered. The landed gentry were, however, slowly profiting from the country's limited economic development. If they found coal on their estates or had land on which cattle could be raised there was money to be made. England was a growing market for 'Scotch great coal', which was shipped regularly to London. England's capital was likewise the main market for Scotland's beef.

Edinburgh was Scotland's largest town, with a population of 40,000. Rich and poor lived cheek by jowl in the crowded dirty tenements and closes of the High Street. Even the residences of nobles and wealthy lawyers were cramped. Smallpox, tuberculosis and rheumatic fever were rife, and primitive, if heroic, surgery by the barbers of the town killed more than it cured. For the mass of the population, medical care was non-existent. Glasgow, with a population of twelve thousand, was a sober, hard-working burgh of trade and industry, with its own soap-works and sugar houses. The Scots, however, owned very few vessels themselves, relying on hired English ships to trade. In 1692, the nation's total tonnage was only ten thousand. Glasgow merchants owned fifteen ships, a tenth of Scotland's total.

Scotland's nobles had been tamed: disputes between them were more frequently settled in the courts of law rather than by force of arms. By the 1670s, the Faculty of Advocates had come together as a professional group and in 1681 Viscount Stair had published his *Institutions of the Law of Scotland* which, although a slim volume, was the first lucid exposition of Scottish law. The nobility looked to the law as a career for their sons. Land was the basis of Scots law and it was only natural that those who possessed land should manage the laws that governed it. Scotland's nobility, despite their limited means, were also outward-looking. The Grand Tour for the young Scottish laird was already commonplace and many of the nobility knew more about the Continent than about neighbouring England. Scots, eager to further their knowledge of law or medicine, went to Dutch universities, like Leiden. Scottish trading communities had been established in Poland, the Baltic and Muscovy.

The Kirk continued to discipline the nation. Calvinism meant there were two long sermons to sit through every Sunday, and the father of each Scottish household was responsible for leading his family in prayer and

James Dalrymple, 1st Viscount Stair (1619–95) served in the Covenanting army. He became an advocate in 1648 and was a Cromwellian commissioner for the administration of justice in Scotland; under William II he was Lord President.   (*FA*)

The Scots community at Veere in Holland had a Resident who regulated trade. These houses, now preserved as a museum, were homes of the Scottish merchants.   (*Author*)

keeping his children indoors on the Sabbath. Culturally, however, as a result of the Covenant, Scotland was a barren land. The 'profane arts', as the Covenanters called them, were suppressed and there was no permanent theatre and little painting done. Scots, as a literary tongue, was dying. To speak English was thought progressive. Although many Scots found written English difficult to master, and spoke it with trepidation, the tongue of the nation's neighbour was taking over.

Meanwhile London was prospering. The East India Company was bringing to England the riches of the Indian sub-continent and providing English manufacturers with a vast marketplace for their goods. To the west, the North American colonies were a rich source of raw materials and a ready market. England was making a vast variety of goods, like pots and pans, cheap earthenware, good quality linen, pins and needles, and glassware, which Scotland did not have the means to manufacture. The Scots imported these goods and paid for them with exports of fish, wool, cattle and coal.

Life in the Highlands was totally different from that of Lowland Scotland. The glens and straths housed a third of Scotland's population. Clan kinship, once strong in the Lowlands until the sixteenth century, was still the moving spirit. By the end of the seventeenth century, Lowland Scots, eager to improve their material well-being, were beginning to see war as an impediment to progress. The clans of the Western Highlands, on the other hand were, if anything, more warlike than before. Cattle raiding was still regarded as an honourable pursuit. Yet most of the Highland chiefs were well educated. Some spoke several foreign languages and had travelled extensively.

The chiefs and their people lived a pastoral life. The high rainfall of the Highlands and Western Islands produced lush pasture for raising cattle. In the summer months, in order to preserve the natural hay that grew in low-lying meadows, the cattle were taken to the hill pastures, the 'sheiling'. But the Highlander bred his cattle for quantity, not for their beef or milk quality. Far too many beasts were being raised and there was frequently no food for them during the winter.

If socially and economically, Highland and Lowland Scotland were developing in separate ways, politically there were also differences. Most Lowland Scots, except the most extreme Covenanters, had accepted William of Orange as their King. In 1691 Highland chiefs who had fought against William's accession were offered a pardon by the King. Under the impatient Lowland government of Lord Advocate Stair, son of the author of the *Institutions*, an order for the oath of allegiance to King William was made on 27 August 1691 and the clans of the north given until 1 January 1692 to swear it.

At Fort William in Inverness-shire, Colonel Hill, the Governor, had by way of firmness and conciliation managed to persuade most of the clan chiefs to take the oath. On 31 December Alasdair MacDonald of Glencoe presented himself at the garrison. The MacDonalds of Glencoe were Episcopalian and Royalist; the clan had fought at Killiecrankie and after the Revolution continued to support King James. Colonel Hill explained to MacDonald he could not administer the oath of allegiance and sent him to Inveraray with a letter to the Sheriff-Depute, Campbell of Ardkinglas,

William II (1650–1702) was the son of Mary, daughter of Charles I. He was married to Mary, daughter of James VII of Scotland.   (*SNPG*)

A view of London before the Fire of 1666.   (*NMM*)

hoping that the latter might be able to accept the submission of 'the great lost sheep, Glencoe'.

MacDonald reached Inveraray on 2 January, only to find that Campbell was absent until 5 January. After the old man pleaded, the Sheriff-Depute finally heard his submission on 6 January but warned MacDonald that his case would have to be referred to the Privy Council in Edinburgh. On 7 January the Master of Stair wrote from London to Sir Thomas Livingstone, the Commander-in-Chief in Scotland, that troops would shortly be ordered to ravage the lands of those chiefs who had refused to submit, and as joint Secretary of State, informed the King with some satisfaction that Mac-Donald had not subscribed to the oath by the appointed date:

> Glencoe hath not taken the oath at which I rejoice. It will be a proper vindication of the public justice to extirpate that sept of thieves . . . It were a great advantage to the nation that thieving tribes were rooted out and cut off. It must be quietly done, otherwise they will make shift for both men and their cattle . . . Let it be secret and sudden.

As an example Stair chose the MacDonalds of Glencoe, perhaps because it was the smallest and most unable part of the clan to defend itself, and because of its extremely isolated geographical situation. A total massacre of one particular branch of the MacDonalds would ensure that others would follow the wishes of the King.

Old enemies of the MacDonalds seized their chance. Persuaded principally by the Earl of Breadalbane, head of the cadet branch of the Campbell clan, William III of England and II of Scotland signed a document on

16 January ordering that the MacDonalds of Glencoe be annihilated. The officer to carry out the massacre was chosen with care: Robert Campbell of Glenlyon, a debauched spendthrift who had gambled away most of his estates. There was a long-running hatred between the clan Donald and the Campbells dating back to the MacDonalds' forfeiture of the Lordship of the Isles, from which the Campbells benefited, and exacerbated by the fact that the two clans fought on opposite sides during the Civil War. However, it was not the Campbell clan but one of the Argyll regiments that carried out the massacre, largely officered by Campbells and acting on direct orders from the King.

On 1 February 1692, Campbell quartered 120 men in Glencoe. As yet, he had no idea of the order that was to be given him and his protestation of friendship was genuine. For almost two weeks, the clansmen and the soldiers lived together, eating, drinking, gambling and playing shinty. The orders came on 12 February. Robert Duncanson, a Major in Argyll's Regiment, to Glenlyon:

> You are hereby ordered to fall upon the rebels, the MacDonalds of Glencoe, and put all to the sword under seventy. You are to have special care that the old fox and his sons do upon no account escape your hands. You are to secure all the avenues, that no man escape . . . This is by the King's special command, for the good and safety of the country, that these miscreants be cut off root and branch.

John Campbell, 1st Earl of Breadalbane (1635–1717) was one of Scottish history's most notorious double-dealers. Apart from the massacre of Glencoe, he was later imprisoned for dealing with the Jacobites and refused to vote for Union in 1706; yet he sat as a Scottish representative peer. Few knew which side he was on during the 1715 Jacobite Rebellion. (*SNPG*)

The massacre of Glencoe was a botched affair. Troops that were expected on the morning of 13 February to block both ends of the pass never arrived. Campbell of Glenlyon's soldiers hinted to the MacDonalds what their orders were. At five o'clock in the morning, however, the soldiers as ordered turned on their hosts.

Out of probably 150 MacDonalds, 38 were killed. The houses of others were burned and their cattle driven into the hills. Homeless, it is likely that at least as many MacDonalds died of exposure and starvation. Lieutenant Lindsay, one of Glenlyon's officers, was responsible for killing the old chief, who was shot in the back while he got out of bed. The troops stripped his wife and drew the rings off her fingers with their teeth.

The massacre caused a national outrage. Although in some ways it was no worse than earlier attempts to liquidate unruly clans, the abuse of MacDonald hospitality made Glencoe different. The Campbells were accused of 'Murder under trust'. In old Scots law, this meant an aggravated form of murder and so heinous a crime was it considered that it carried the same penalty as treason. An official inquiry was held at which Colonel Hill and three of his officers gave evidence. Ten MacDonalds related what had happened; but the tribunal never called any of Campbell's men to account for their actions. Few in Scotland doubted that William of Orange was behind the plan; but the official inquiry exonerated the King and placed most of the blame on the Master of Stair, who was forced to resign and given an Earldom in 1703.

Other events made King William's reputation even blacker. If agricultural output was stagnant in much of Scotland, the population was not. In the second half of the seventeenth century it steadily increased. Then came the 'Seven ill years of King William's reign'. Between 1695 and 1699 in a

Captain Robert Campbell of Glenlyon (1632–96). (*SNPG*)

The instructions of Major Robert Duncanson of the Argyll's Regiment, ordering the Massacre of Glencoe. Although only thirty-eight people were killed a nineteenth-century artist thought the massacre a worthy subject. (*NLS*) (*GAG, below*)

succession of bad harvests caused by wet summers and early frosts grain prices rose. Scots in their thousands died of hunger and typhus. People were found dead with grass in their mouths. One Scot in six was reduced to begging. At Dalkeith, the local Kirk Session ordered that a lime pit be dug for the bodies of vagrants from the Borders who had died while trying to get to Edinburgh. In the capital, a refugee camp was set up in Greyfriars kirkyard for the distribution of poor relief. The authorities of Stirling listed the town's poor by name so that they could be given help and the gates of the burgh were closed to all others. The matter was discussed in the Estates, and Andrew Fletcher of Saltoun summed up the nation's plight:

> There are at this day in Scotland two hundred thousand people begging from door to door. These are not only no way advantageous, but a very grievous burden to so poor a country . . . It were better for the nation they were sold to the galleys or West Indies, than that they should continue any longer to be a burden and curse upon us.

Patrick Walker, an itinerant peddler in the Highlands, wrote of the lean years:

> Meal became so scarce, that it was at two shillings a peck, and many could not get it. . . . I have seen, when meal was all sold in markets, women clapping their hands, and tearing the clothes off their heads, crying, 'How shall we go home and see our children die in hunger?' . . . Through the long continuance of these manifold judgements, deaths and burials were so many and common, that the living were wearied in the burying of the dead.

The Highlands suffered most. A Lowlander observed of a journey north:

> Some die by the wayside, some drop down in the streets, the poor sucking babs are starving for want of milk, which the empty breasts of their mothers cannot furnish them, everyone may see death in the face of the poor that abound everywhere.

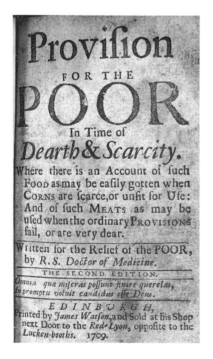

Sir Robert Sibbald (1641–1722) had studied medicine at Leiden and was Scotland's most famous botanist. (*RCP*) (*NLS, below*)

Sir Robert Sibbald, who was made Professor of Medicine at Edinburgh University in 1685, wrote a pamphlet proposing solutions to the problem of poverty. In his *Provision for the Poor in Time of Dearth and Scarcity*, he listed Scottish herbs and wild plants that were edible and even advocated the eating of cat flesh as a means of sustaining life. In many Scottish parishes the population fell by half. The Kirk attributed the famine years to the sins of the nation and ministers recommended fast days for the starving. The years of famine left those who lived off the land impoverished, landlords as well as tenants.

England's wars against continental Europe exacerbated Scotland's ills. The nation's trade suffered as a result of William of Orange's English wars. His campaign against the French was a war against Scotland's best overseas trading partner. Scottish exports of herring, salmon, coal and wool to France were disrupted and the import of wine, brandy and salt from the Continent could not get through the blockades. French privateers in an attempt to distract the English sailed into the Forth and Clyde. In 1692 Scottish Jacobites, with French support, captured the Bass Rock and made it a fortified base. They almost succeeded in cutting off the corn trade from the north-east of Scotland to Leith and Edinburgh. The Scots had no navy of their own, and the English fleet, otherwise preoccupied, did nothing.

William's three wars against the Dutch cut the Scots off from their other major trading partner. The merchants of the Low Countries were forced to look elsewhere for articles previously imported from Scotland.

In an attempt to alleviate the nation's economic difficulties the Bank of

Beggary was common in Scotland until well into the eighteenth century. David Allan (1744–96) drew this beggar with a donkey and children, asking a lady for alms outside one of Edinburgh's city gates.   (*NGS*)

Scotland was founded in 1695. An Englishman, John Holland, became its first Governor. The Bank made a quiet and unpretentious start. The staff was small and accommodation was rented in Mylne Square, off the High Street in Edinburgh. The Treasurer lived in the Bank House and was paid £100 a year. An additional allowance of £15 was made for the purchase of coal and candles to heat and light the office. George Watson, later to be the benefactor of a school, became the Bank of Scotland's first accountant. In 1696, the Bank moved to more suitable premises in Parliament Close then, after a fire, to Pearson's Close off the Lawnmarket, later renamed Old Bank Close. In the beginning the Bank acted as little more than a clearing house. No deposits were taken and cash credit was unknown. Paper notes, to replace Scotland's lack of uniform currency, were issued sparingly.

But the Bank of Scotland was unusual from the outset. It was forbidden to lend money to the state and, unlike the Bank of England, had no role as an agent of government. By its Royal Charter, the Bank had to depend wholly upon the opportunities afforded it by Scotland's agriculture, industry and commerce. The Bank of Scotland was the first joint-stock bank in Europe, formed by private individuals and solely dependent upon private capital with the express purpose of making a business out of banking. It was banking in its purest form, an innovation purely Scottish.

The act of the Scottish parliament that set up the Bank was but one of 145 acts passed in the year 1695, most of which were aimed at improving the nation's economy. Lack of enterprise and petty jealousy, however, constrained industrial and commercial development. The Estates gave help to the wrong industries. The Scottish woollen industry was given the unenviable task of trying to rival that of England. Parliament, by passing three Acts, tried to lend support to Nicholas Dupin, a Huguenot refugee, in his attempts to modernize the linen industry. But Dupin was unable to persuade the burghs to back his schemes and by the end of the century the linen business was in the doldrums. In an age of protectionism, Scotland found the economic world closing in.

England, out to guard her own trade, jealously excluded the Scots by Act of Parliament from trading directly with her North American colonies, although arrangements were made with the English proprietors to allow Scottish settlement. A small Scottish colony was founded in New Jersey, and in 1684 a group of Presbyterian Scots settled at Stuart's Town in South Carolina, where they were welcomed as a buttress against Spanish aspirations. Within a year, however, the little colony had been almost destroyed by Spanish raiders from Florida. What the Scots needed was a national plantation of their own, a trading colony.

The idea of a colony was first discussed by the Scottish Privy Council in 1681. Twelve years later, in 1693, the Estates passed an act to encourage foreign trade. London Scots, meanwhile, were giving thought to the possibility of forming a Scottish trading company similar to the English East India Company, a chance to make profit rather than an opportunity to help the old country. They knew, of course, that there would be much enthusiasm in Scotland for such a venture, and they hoped, with the backing of English merchants, to break the monopoly of the East India Company. In charge of the scheme was a Scot, William Paterson.

Born in 1658 in Tynwald, Dumfriesshire, Paterson had spent most of his early life in England. He had traded with the English West Indies and had helped found the Bank of England and become one of its directors. Paterson had organized North London's water supply and travelled extensively in the West Indies and the New England colonies of North America.

In June 1695 the Scottish Africa and India Company was founded. By an act of the Scottish parliament, the shareholders were to enjoy a monopoly of trade between Scotland, America, Africa and Asia and be exempt from customs and excise duties for twenty-one years. Public funds were to be available should economic disaster strike the Company. In an attempt to win the favour of Scots after the massacre of Glencoe, William of Orange gave the scheme lukewarm support and the company's books were opened in London in November 1695. To investors, the scheme was extremely attractive, and within two weeks, £300,000 had been raised. The directors had originally fixed the capital at £360,000 but the demand for shares was so great that they raised it to £600,000.

The East India Company took fright and lobbied English MPs to

George Watson (d. 1723) was a merchant in Edinburgh and the first accountant of the Bank of Scotland. William Paterson (*below*) (1658–1719) became one of the directors of the Bank of England in 1694; later he prepared a scheme for a Sinking Fund, consolidating what became Britain's National Debt. *(MCE)* *(BL, below)*

get the Scottish company proscribed. The English Parliament looked sympathetically upon the East India men's concern and threatened to impeach the Company of Scotland's English directors. The English investors withdrew. The Scots would have to look elsewhere for money, and to stop them raising it abroad, English consuls on the Continent were told to dissuade foreigners from investing. Sir Paul Rycaut, the English government's resident in Hamburg, informed the town's Senate that the King of England would view any support for the Scottish company as tantamount to a hostile act.

The Scottish directors, however, pressed on with the scheme and turned to the Scottish people. Popular subscription raised nearly £400,000, a sum that was almost equivalent to the entire value of Scottish coinage in circulation. The directors could now consider how they should go about founding a colony and organizing trade. They were persuaded to settle at Darien on the isthmus of Panama by Paterson, who claimed:

> The time and expense of navigation to China, Japan and the Spice Islands and the far greater part of the East Indies will be lessened by more than half, and the consumption of European commodities and manufactories will soon be more than doubled. Trade will increase trade, and money will beget money, and the trading world will need no more to want work for their hands, but will rather want hands for their work.

Sir Paul Rycaut, in April 1697, thwarted the attempt made by William Paterson to open the Subscription Book for the Scottish company in Hamburg. (*SNPG*)

Paterson's dream was that the Scots should penetrate the immense colonial empire of Spain. At Darien a great commercial emporium could be established, trading with the Pacific on one side and the Caribbean on the other. The Spanish claim to the area was tenuous. Indeed, the claim of Spain to the whole Caribbean was feeble: England had taken Jamaica without a fight and, like the Scots, had thoughts of planting a colony at Darien. It was not until 1776, in fact, when peace was made with the local Indians, that Spain could claim real control over this area of Central America.

Lionel Wafer, a surgeon on board a pirate ship, claimed to know Darien well and his glowing account helped persuade the directors of the Scottish company. The financial base of the Darien scheme was sound. The traffic of trade from east to west could be diverted from the long and dangerous passage round the Cape of Good Hope. In fact, centuries later, when the Panama Canal was being considered, serious thought was given to cutting the waterway across from the exact spot that the Scots were to settle. The Atlantic coast of Darien, however, has two seasons. From April to December, rainfall exceeds 200 inches, and during the dry season the prevailing wind blows on shore from the north-east, causing waves twenty feet high to crash against the granite shores. It is a land of hot humid jungle where malaria, yellow fever, tuberculosis and rabies are endemic. It was at Panama that Sir Francis Drake fell ill with fever before his death at Portobelo in 1596.

By 1698, four ships had been fitted out. The cargo contained the normal articles of trading, brandy, pitch, flour, biscuits, guns and ammunition; and also items uniquely Scottish, like bagpipes, blue bonnets, clay pipes and packages of leek and cabbage seed. Many of the supplies came from Europe. Ships were sent to Stockholm to buy salt, to La Rochelle in France to buy vinegar and wine, and to Amsterdam where supplies of raisins, spices and

A detail of the sailing orders to the intended colony of Caledonia. (*RBS*)

soap were purchased. Maps and charts for the voyage were bought from the most famous mapmaker in London. The first expedition, under the command of Captain Pennyquick, left Leith on 4 July 1698. Four ships, the *Unicorn*, *St Andrew*, *Caledonia* and *Endeavour*, contained 1500 men, women and children who were to settle the new colony. Only William Paterson, apart from the Captain of the little flotilla, knew of their destination. The Atlantic crossing was uneventful. Only seventy colonists died, which was considered par for the course. The Captain, on sighting the natural harbour of what is now called Puerto Escoces, noted in his journal:

> This harbour is capable of containing a thousand sail of the best ships in the world. And without great trouble, wharfs may be run out, to which ships of the greatest burden may lay their sides and unload.

To begin with, the Scottish settlers were delighted by their new home, which they thought an 'earthly paradise'. Their first task, however, was to decide where to build the settlement. The choice of site occasioned the first of many bitter arguments, as Paterson later wrote:

> The first place fallen upon was a place of landing but the sea counsellors were for a mere morass, neither fit to be fortified, nor indeed for men to lie upon. We were upon clearing and making huts upon this improper place near two months, in which time experience, the schoolmaster of fools, convinced our masters that the place now called Fort St Andrew was more proper for us.

Having wasted precious time, the settlers discovered in April 1699 that Darien was a hell hole. Torrential rains came, and with them malaria and yellow fever. By June, half the colonists were dead. The survivors sent a sloop to Hispaniola in the West Indies to gather fresh supplies. She returned with nothing, save news that King William had forbade any English ship or colony having anything to do with the Scottish settlement.

The Scots got news that the Spanish were mounting an attack on the colony and panic spread throughout the small unfinished town set within the Fort. The 700 remaining settlers fled for Jamaica. Only one ship, the *Caledonia*, out of the four returned to Scotland. The others were sold or lost at sea.

In Scotland meanwhile they knew nothing of the fate of the first settlers, and three more ships, full of supplies and a further 1302 colonists sailed for Darien. On arrival they discovered that there was nowhere to live and above all no protection from fever, as the Reverend Francis Borland wrote in his diary:

> We found nothing but a vast howling wilderness, the Colony deserted and gone, their huts all burnt, their fort most part ruined, the ground which they had cleared adjoining to the fort all overgrown with weeds; and we looked for peace but no good came, and for a time of health and comfort, but beheld trouble.

The new colonists set about rebuilding and reoccupying the settlement. Roger Oswald, who was to survive the expedition wrote:

> Every man . . . daily turned out to work by daylight, whether with the hatchet, wheelbarrow, pick-axe, shovel, fore-hammer, or any other instrument the case required, and so continued until twelve o'clock, and out at two again and stayed till night, sometimes working all day up to the

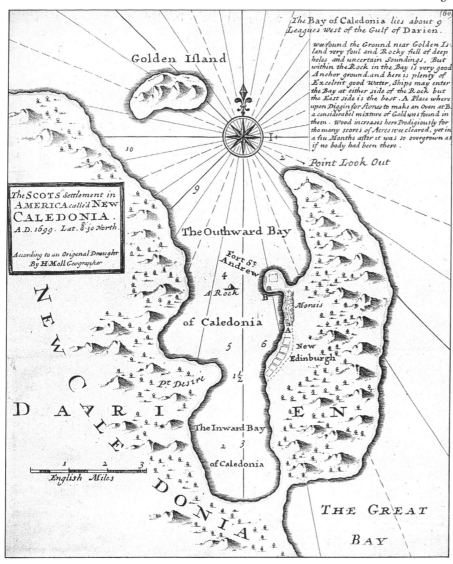

The Bay of Caledonia *lies about 9 Leagues west of the Gulf of* Darien.

wee found the Ground near Golden Island very foul and Rocky full of deep holes and uncertain Soundings. But within the Rock in the Bay is very good Anchor ground, and here is plenty of Excelent good Water, Ships may enter the Bay at either side of the Rock but the East side is the best. A Place where upon Diggin for Stones to make an Oven at B. a considerabel mixture of Gold was found in them. Wood increases here Prodigiously for tho many scores of Acres wee cleared, yet in a few Months after it was so overgrown as if no body had been there.

Herman Moll's map of New Caledonia, published in 1735, incorrectly placed New Edinburgh outside the Fort. *Above:* a view of the moat dug by the Scots settlers on the northern Bastion. (*NLS*) (*OD, above*)

headbands of the breeches in water at the trenches. My shoulders have been so wore with carrying burdens that the skin has come off them and grew full of boils. If a man were sick and so was obliged to stay within, no victuals for him that day. Our Councillors all the time lying at their ease, sometimes divided into factions and, being swayed by particular interest, ruined the public ... Though I preserved my life, yet I kept not my health. I was troubled with fever and ague that I raved almost every day and it rendered me so weak that my legs were not able to support me ... Our bodies pined away and grew so macerated with such allowance and hard work that we were like so many skeletons.

The Spanish did not allow the Scots to settle without a fight. On 13 February 1700, they attacked them at Toubaganti. Under the leadership of Captain Campbell a mixed force of Scots and local Indians beat the Spaniards off, but the colonists were too few in number to hold Darien for ever.

The new settlers rebuilt the huts and extended the fortifications, but the Spanish were bent on putting paid to Scottish aspirations once and for all.

A view of Panama in 1702. The new city, built after Henry Morgan had sacked and burned the town in 1671, was the home of the Spanish Provincial Governor.   (*NMM*)

Under the command of the Governor, General Pimiento, a large fleet sailed from Cartagena and an army marched from Panama. In March 1700 Fort St Andrew capitulated. Reverend Francis Borland described the short siege:

> It was a great loss to us that since the Spaniards had got so near our Fort they debarred us from our watering-place, which was about half a mile distant from our settlement . . . And as for other liquors at this time to give to the sick and dying, we had little or none, or any other substance that was suitable or comfortable, and moreover, our surgeon's drugs were now almost all exhausted, and our Fort indeed like a hospital of sick and dying men.

The settlers withdrew. As Borland noted, they were crowded together in the boat:

> . . . like so many hogs in a sty or sheep in a fold, so that their breath and noisome smell infected and poisoned one another . . . Malignant fevers and fluxes were the most common diseases, which swept away great numbers from among us. From aboard one ship, the *Rising Sun*, they would sometimes bury in the sea eight in one morning.

It had been in an attempt to prevent Spain from allying herself with France that William of Orange forbade England's colonists in America and the West Indies from giving the Scots any help. But his actions were seen as hostile by the Scots and gave credence to claims that the English were responsible for the disaster at Darien. News of the first expedition did not reach Scotland until October 1699, when the Scots asked William to allow three English frigates in harbour at Burntisland in Fife to be put at the disposal of the Company. King William curtly refused and the Scottish parliament was furious. On 27 May 1700, the Estates declared that the settlement of New Caledonia was legal and that they should lend the Company support. The mood became bitter: Anglophobia set in. There were riots against the King in Edinburgh and a Convention of the Estates was called for, to defy his government.

When the handful of settlers who had managed to escape from Darien finally returned to Scotland the true tragedy of the adventure became known. Two thousand young Scots had died in the attempt to found the colony. On hearing that the colony had been totally abandoned, William of Orange felt able to act. He asked Spain to release Scots captured during the first expedition and held under sentence of death. But he had little real interest in his northern kingdom. As he wrote to his Dutch court:

> I am sorry to be obliged to tell you that affairs go on very badly in the Scotch parliament ... What vexes me in particular is that this affair retards my departure for Holland, for which I long more than ever.

The Scots refused to allow William to forget. A furious assembly of the Estates threatened to deny him his taxes, but James Ogilvie, Earl of Seafield, with the help of the Earl of Argyll, managed to dampen the anger. Ambitious nobles were bought off and the matter of Darien was dropped.

The Scottish company survived the disaster at Darien. Trade continued, on a limited scale, with Africa and the Far East. But the company's deficit was £232,884 by 1706 and its shareholders scattered throughout the length and breadth of Scotland had nothing to show for their investment. The disaster fed national disillusionment. The seeds of Jacobitism were sown. Many now saw the restoration of the Stewarts as the only way to right the wrongs of William of Orange's reign. The English court, fearful of the Scots desire for independence, realised the northern kingdom would have to be brought firmly and for ever under control, and William himself expressed the opinion that a Union of Parliaments would be for the best. A union of the two nations, which the parliaments of neither side wanted, was seen as the only solution.

A selection of some of the artifacts from the Scottish colony which Operation Drake discovered in 1979, including a cannon ball, musket shot, knife blades and decorated pottery. (*OD*)

9

Act of Union

THE QUESTION OF a more complete union between the Scots and the English was raised not by the people but by the monarchy. Historically, it was not the first time. James VI of Scotland and I of England had told the English Parliament in 1603:

> I am the husband and all the whole Isle is my lawful wife. I hope therefore no man will be so unreasonable as to think that I, that am a Christian king under the Gospel, should be a polygamist and husband to two wives.

The old Royal Coat of Arms of Scotland before James VI became King of England, to be found at Whithorn in Kirkcudbrightshire. (*Author*)

His concept of unity was simple – there should be one religion in Scotland and England, the two kingdoms should be uniformly governed and should share the same laws. He appointed commissioners to recommend how his kingdoms should be merged and had even drawn up a 'British' flag.

The Scots, curiously, had not been against James's aspirations; in 1607, the Estates had passed an act approving Union. But the English were deeply suspicious. England was seen as a rich pasture threatened by a herd of famished cattle. When Union came to be debated in the English Parliament, one member remarked that the Scots were peddlers and not merchants. Another, dipping into the history of Scotland to prove English superiority, remarked in a gross misrepresentation of Scots history, 'They have not suffered above two kings to die in their beds these two hundred years.' James had been forced to shelve his grand design.

James's second son, Charles, was virtually an Englishman. Although born in Dunfermline, he had spent all his life from the age of three in England and when he became King the personal link with the Scottish people that had helped his father rule Scotland was gone. When Charles I attempted to impose his brand of religion upon the Scots, they rebelled and established Presbyterianism.

Under Oliver Cromwell, Scotland had been annexed to England by military force. The union had been short-lived and bitterly resented, and when Charles II was restored to the British throne, the two parliaments gladly went their separate ways. From 1660, however, the Scots had again been ruled by an absentee king who by necessity had to tailor his policies, both foreign and domestic, to English needs. England, after all, provided

Charles II with £1,500,000 in taxes, whereas he could raise little more than £60,000 in Scotland. The Estates, under Charles II, rarely met and the nation was managed by an administration appointed from London, men often Scots but puppets of the English Court.

During the reign of William of Orange the Estates were given the chance to assert themselves. The King needed money to finance his costly European wars, and the Scots blackmailed him by threatening to withhold taxes unless he agreed to legislation passed by the Scottish parliament. When peace came, of course, William was able, like monarchs before him, to ignore the Scots' parliament and have his Dutch favourite, the Earl of Portland, manage Scottish affairs. The exertion of authority by the Estates, however, though brief, proved important.

Prince Charles, presenting the King and Queen of Bohemia to his father James I, sitting in the English Parliament.   (*BM*)

The only known illustration of the Estates, the Scots parliament, first published in Nicolas de Guedeville's *Atlas Historique* in 1721. The Riding of Parliament, namely the procession from Holyrood to Parliament House, and the scene within the House itself, are shown. (*STV*)

William and his Stewart wife, Mary, had no children. In 1689 the English Parliament, anxious about the succession, decided with the Declaration of Right that Mary's sister, Anne, should become Queen when they died. The Scottish Estates agreed, passing the Claim of Right on 11 April 1689. Mary died in 1694. Anne, the heir apparent, married Prince George of Denmark. She was eighteen times pregnant and five children were born, but only one, the Duke of Gloucester, survived infancy. In 1700, the young Duke died, and the following year the English Parliament passed an Act of Settlement which gave the Crown of England, on Queen Anne's death, to the Electress Sophia and the German House of Hanover. In 1702 William died. Anne became Queen and, as the Scots had refused to follow the example of England's Parliament and name her successor, Anne reassembled the Estates. Because the Scottish parliament comprised the same members as had passed the Claim of Right, she hoped that the question of her heir could be resolved by the Scots' agreeing to some form of political union.

But when parliament met in Edinburgh in June 1702 the forty-four-year-old 4th Duke of Hamilton refused to recognize the assembled Estates. 'By the fundamental laws and constitutions of this kingdom,' he declared, 'all parliaments do dissolve by the death of the King or Queen.' He was right. William had died on 7 March and fresh elections should have taken place in Scotland because the Estates had not been called by the new Queen within twenty-one days of his death. On 9 June, Hamilton walked out of the assembly together with seventy-three members.

In their absence, the 2nd Duke of Queensberry persuaded the remaining 120 Scottish parliamentarians to pass an act that enabled Queen Anne to appoint delegates to treat for Union. The two sets of Commissioners – Scottish and English – first met in the Cockpit at Westminster on 10 November 1702. Arguments about trade dominated the proceedings. Sir Edward Seymour summed up the English attitude:

> What a bother is here about a Union with Scotland, of which all the advantage we shall have will be what a man gets by marrying a beggar; a louse for her portion?

Since the English rarely turned up in sufficient numbers the Commission was postponed eight times, and on 3 February 1703, Queen Anne adjourned proceedings and called for fresh elections in Scotland. The new parliament, which met in May 1703, was hardly what the Queen had hoped for. The members expressed anger at the existing constitution and many felt they were free to break the Union of Crowns and choose a different monarch to succeed Anne in Scotland.

Among the dissidents was Andrew Fletcher of Saltoun. Born in 1653, he had first been elected to the Estates at the age of twenty-five. Fletcher had been exiled in 1681, and had fought with William of Orange against the Turks in Spain. In 1689, when the Scottish Convention declared that James VII had forfeited the Crown of Scotland and offered it to William and Mary, he returned to Saltoun Hall, near Pencaitland. With a keen interest in commerce and agriculture, he was elected to Queen Anne's new Scottish parliament at the age of fifty-five. Now he told the new Estates that Scotland had suffered since the Union of Crowns in 1603:

> When our kings succeeded to the crown of England, the ministers of that nation took a short way to ruin us, by concurring with their inclinations to extend the prerogative in Scotland . . . All of our affairs, since the union of crowns, have been managed by the advice of English ministers, and the principal offices of the kingdom filled with such men, as the court of England knew would be subservient to their designs: by which means they have had so visible an influence upon our whole administration, that we have, from that time, appeared to the rest of the world more like a conquered province, than a free independent people.

Fletcher knew well that until 1603, the Estates had had some say in the ruling of the nation. Now the Scots, he rightly claimed, had lost control over their own foreign policy and the disposal of revenue raised in Scotland. The dual monarchy had failed. No king of both countries could give justice to Scotland. England, being the larger and more powerful, got the lion's share.

Since the Union of the Crowns England's wars had harmed Scotland's traditional trade links, as Fletcher pointed out:

> Our trade was formerly in so flourishing a condition that the shire of Fife alone had as many ships as now belong to the whole kingdom; that ten or twelve towns, which lie on the south coast of that province had at that time, a very considerable trade, and in our days are little better than so many heaps of ruins; that our trade with France was very advantageous, by reason of the great privileges we enjoyed in that kingdom; that our commerce with Spain had been considerable and began during the wars

Andrew Fletcher of Saltoun (1653–1716) was the leading anti-Unionist but unfortunately for the cause he was not a very good speaker in the Estates. (*SNPG*)

> between England and that nation; and that we drove a great trade in the Baltic with our fish, before the Dutch had wholly possessed themselves of that advantageous traffic. Upon the Union of the crowns not only all this went to decay, but our money was spent in England, and not among ourselves; the furniture of our houses, and the best of our clothes and equipage, was bought at London; and though particular persons of the Scots nation had many great and profitable places at court, to the high displeasure of the English, yet that was no advantage to our country, which was totally neglected, like a farm managed by servants, and not under the eye of the master.

Certainly Scotland's economic state prior to the Union was deplorable by any standards, and it was generally considered to be either the poorest country in Europe or the second poorest – next only to Galicia in Poland. Scottish cargoes were being arrested on the high seas and it was clear that some kind of commercial agreement between Scotland and England had to be worked out.

Fletcher saw two possible solutions to the dilemma. Scotland could either choose a different successor to follow Queen Anne or, like the English, choose the House of Hanover but demand that effective power in Scotland be transferred to the Scottish parliament, which would meet annually and appoint Scotland's administrators. His ideas, in essence, were embodied in the Act of Security which was passed on 13 August 1703 by a majority of fifty-nine. The Act contained a vital clause which prevented the successor to the Crown of England from becoming the Scottish monarch unless Scotland's conditions were met.

Lord Godolphin, in charge of Scottish affairs, viewed the Act of Security as tantamount to revolt. The self-interested English court could not accept that the Scottish parliament was independent and feared a revival of the Auld Alliance with the French, with whom the English were at war. Jonathan Swift pointed out:

> It was thought highly dangerous to leave that part of the island inhabited by a poor, fierce northern people, at liberty to put themselves under a different king . . . And so the Union became necessary, not for any actual good it could possibly do us, but to avoid a probable evil.

James Douglas, 2nd Duke of Queensberry (1662–1711). (*SNPG*)

The Duke of Queensberry, Queen Anne's Commissioner to the Estates, was told to withhold the Royal Assent from the Security Act.

The English war with France, that had begun in 1701, dragged on for twelve years and proved a major factor in determining attitudes towards Union in both England and Scotland. The War of the Spanish Succession, as it was called, the first trade war of the eighteenth century, was a struggle between England and France for commercial supremacy. The war was disruptive to Franco-Scottish trade, and there was genuine resentment in Scotland that the struggle was involving Scottish troops. The Cameronians suffered heavy losses at the Battle of Blenheim. At Steenkirk, the Scots Greys won great distinction. The war affected many Scots homes; one Ayrshire family, for example, lost four out of five sons.

The Estates passed an Act Anent Peace and War which gave the Scots parliament, in future, a say in whether the British Crown declared war or made peace. In an attempt to placate the Scots Anne gave Royal Assent to the Wine Act, allowing the Scots to renew their old duty-free trade with France.

But the concession made no difference to a Scottish parliament that was proving intractable.

James VII and II followed the proceedings with interest. At St Germain-en-Laye outside Paris, the exiled Stewart court wrongly assessed the situation. Some of James's advisers saw Scottish nationalist feeling as pro-Jacobite sentiment, and when the French government showed some interest in a plan to invade Scotland the Earl of Perth advised the Old Pretender to exploit the situation. Simon Fraser was chosen to act for the Pretender in Scotland but he betrayed the Jacobite plan to the Duke of Queensberry, who used the information to try and discredit other nobles. He told the Queen that the Dukes Hamilton and Atholl and the Earls of Seafield and of Cromartie were leaders of what came to be known as 'the Scots Plot'. Anne refused to believe Queensberry and instead dismissed him as her Commissioner.

James VII (1633–1701) had gone into exile after a Scottish Convention declared he had forfeited the throne on 4 April 1689.   (*NTS*)

The Scots Plot, however, worried the English Parliament. In 1704, the Lords, after an investigation, claimed that there had been a genuine conspiracy to raise a rebellion with French military help. Scotland was referred to by Bishop Burnet as England's 'back door'; the only way to secure England's northern frontier was to make the Scots accept the English Act of Succession. Accordingly the Queen instructed the 1st Earl of Seafield, Lord Chancellor of Scotland, to put pressure on those in the Estates who objected to the Hanoverian Succession. She concluded:

> As to such of them as you cannot prevail with to concur you are to endeavour at least to soften them in their opposition or to get them to be absent.

Anne's hope of a treaty to determine the relationship between Scotland and England posed a problem of interpretation. In the early eighteenth century, the word 'Union' did not have the specific political meaning that it now has. 'Union' then meant the opposite of conflict. Andrew Fletcher spoke of 'Union' with England in order to do away with 'bloody and destructive wars'. 'Union', to the Scots, meant co-operation, a chance to encourage industry and trade between the two countries, as Fletcher pointed out.

> This is the only just and rational kind of Union. All other coalitions are but the unjust subjection of one people to another.

Fletcher wanted the two independent countries to share the same monarch, co-operate over defence and foreign policy and have a trading relationship based upon a legal treaty. Neither party, however, should be allowed to interfere with the internal affairs of the other. The concept was novel, but ahead of its time.

The relations between the two countries were soured by an incident that had more to do with trade than politics. In August 1704, an English ship, the *Worcester*, entered the Firth of Forth for repairs. The Scots believed – wrongly – that the ship belonged to the English East India Company. In retaliation for the English having seized a Company of Scotland ship, the *Anandale*, on the grounds that it was infringing English colonial trading privileges, the Secretary of the Scottish company asked that the *Worcester* and her crew be arrested. When the Estates refused his request, Roderick Mackenzie, the company Secretary, boarded the *Worcester* and had the ship's Captain and some members of her crew put in prison.

James Douglas, 4th Duke of Hamilton (1659–1712) spent much of his youth abroad. He had supported the Jacobite cause when William II came to the throne and defended the interests of the Company of Scotland. He was killed in a duel.   *(SNPG)*

James Ogilvy, 1st Earl of Seafield (1664–1730) acted as Chancellor from 1702 to 1704 and from 1705 to 1708; he was also a Commissioner for Union. *(SNPG)*

Captain Green and fourteen of his crew were tried on 14 March 1705 by the Scottish Court of Admiralty. Charged, on a rumour that they had destroyed a Company of Scotland ship, the *Speedy Return*, they were found guilty. When the mob of Edinburgh got wind that the captain and his crew might be reprieved, they attacked the Earl of Seafield's carriage and threatened to break into the Tolbooth prison and execute the Englishmen themselves. On 11 April 1705, Captain Green, his mate and gunner were executed on the sands of Leith. They died protesting their innocence, and innocent they were. The English House of Commons took revenge.

In March 1705, an act was passed sanctioning the Scots. Estates owned by Scotsmen in England were to be confiscated and exports of linen, cattle and coal to England were to be forbidden. After Christmas Day 1705, according to the act, all Scots who were not resident in England, Ireland and the English colonies, or serving in Queen Anne's army and navy, were to be declared aliens. Daniel Defoe was shocked by the severity of what came to be known as the 'Alien Act'. 'It was the most impolitic, I had almost said, unjust,' he wrote, 'that ever passed that great assembly.' Uncompromising in its terms, the act was little more than an attempt to call the bluff of the Scots to get them to accept the Hanoverian succession.

In January 1705, the English House of Lords had attempted to exert military blackmail by informing the Queen:

> It is highly requisite for the safety of this kingdom that speedy and effectual orders be given to putting of Newcastle into a condition of defence, for securing the port of Tynemouth, and for repairing Carlisle and Hull.

The Lords suggested that the militia of the four northern English counties should be trained and armed and regular troops sent north to augment them. War, the Lords insinuated, between Scotland and England was imminent.

The question of again appointing Commissioners to discuss union was brought before the Scots parliament on 1 September 1705. The Earl of Seafield hoped that the Scots Commissioners would be appointed by the Queen, and an amazing *volte-face* on the part of the Duke of Hamilton resolved the issue. On 1 September 1705 Hamilton, leader of the opposition to union, demanded a vote. His resolution astounded the Estates, and over a dozen of his anti-union colleagues left the assembly in disgust, enabling the motion to be carried by eight votes. The Duke's action is seen by some as one of the most unscrupulous acts of political treachery in Scottish history for it ensured that the Queen would choose both sets of Commissioners. The Treaty would not now be the subject of negotiation but rather the meeting of two sets of Crown appointees discussing details.

The Duke of Hamilton switched sides for money. He was heavily in debt and the promise of honours was irresistible. After the Act of Union was finally passed in 1707, he was made an English Duke, given the Order of both the Thistle and the Garter and subsequently appointed British Ambassador to Paris. He had secretly made a deal with Robert Harley and Godolphin of the English court to sabotage the anti-Union lobby, which he had done with considerable skill. Hamilton could with justification write on 11 September 1705, 'Our Parliament is now drawing to a close. I have done her Majesty signal service in it.' Even so it was to take eighteen months to get

The town of Hamilton from John Slezer's *Theatrum Scotiae* (*NLS*)

union accepted by the Scots. To get it through the Estates the English court used bribery, a common method of winning the political day in the eighteenth century. Government jobs down to quite junior levels, 'places', as they were called, were promised to the Scots, together with 'pensions', awards of money for services to the Crown. The Earl of Mar, Anne's Scottish Secretary of State, kept London informed of the names of those who opposed union and could be won over. Some of the Scottish nobility openly bartered their support. The 2nd Duke of Argyll, who had succeeded to the title in 1703, was serving with the Duke of Marlborough in the War of the Spanish Succession. He demanded from the field of battle that he be made a major-general before agreeing to return to Scotland to support union. Apart from military promotion, the young Duke of Argyll was subsequently given an English peerage for himself and a Scottish one for his brother.

The 2nd Duke of Queensberry, in 1706, again found himself in favour with the court, after being disgraced by the Scots Plot. Acting as the Lord High Commissioner to the Estates, he was to be chiefly responsible for finally getting Union through the Scottish parliament. The 'Union Duke', as James Douglas was nicknamed, won an English Dukedom for his services and an annual pension of £3000 for life. The facts concerning bribery came to light in 1711, when the British Parliament enquired into what had happened to £20,000 that had been secretly advanced by Queen Anne to the Earl of Glasgow on 12 August 1706. The parliamentary Commission discovered that the Scottish Lords had demanded that the court pay off arrears in salaries before they would agree to support Union with England; and it was claimed that of the £20,000, over £12,000 had been handed over in cash to the Duke of Queensberry alone.

The court also used propaganda. In February 1704, Daniel Defoe had started the most important of his periodicals, *A review of the State of the*

John Erskine, 11th Earl of Mar (1675–1732) with his son; he was called 'Bobbing John' because he changed sides so many times. (*SNPG*)

Daniel Defoe (1660–1731), a supporter of the Protestant religion and the accession of William II. His most famous work, *Robinson Crusoe*, was published in 1719.   (*NPG*)

English Nation. Union with Scotland was not popular among many classes of Englishmen and the *Review* was an attempt to persuade them of its advantages. Then in October 1706 Defoe was sent to Scotland by Lord Godolphin to act as an English spy. He was given instructions by Robert Harley, Speaker of the English House of Commons:

> You are to use utmost caution that it may not be supposed you are employed by any person in England; but that you came there upon your own business, and out of love to the Country.

Defoe was told to send reports at least once a week addressed to a Mrs Collins, who lived at the Posthouse, Middle Temple Gate in London. The reports were to be sent anonymously, for Harley's attention. Defoe's task was to make clear to the Scots the necessity of union, as Harley pointed out:

> You must shew them, this is such an opportunity that being once lost or neglected is not again to be recovered. England was never before in so good a disposition to make such large Concessions, or so heartily to unite with Scotland.

Defoe infiltrated Edinburgh society with great success. He was accepted by a Committee of the Scottish parliament as an expert in trade and taxation and taken into their confidence. His main task was to persuade the Scots that union would not be prejudicial to the Kirk. Defoe, brought up a Presbyterian, was trusted, as he informed Harley:

> They take me for a friend. I am in the Morning at the Committee, in the Afternoon in the assembly. I am privy to all their folly, I wish I could not call it Knavery, and am Entirely Confided in.

Defoe produced numerous pamphlets urging the Scots into union. As a political propagandist, he proved a genius. There were others in the English court's pay. William Seton of Pitmedden, a member of the Scottish parliament, was rewarded for writing pro-Union pamphlets, as was William Paterson, the architect of the Company of Scotland and the Darien adventure.

If bribery and propaganda should fail, the English court made clear to the Scots that they were preparing for a military conquest. English troops were moved north, and the Earl of Mar was told:

> The troops on the Borders are three regiments of foot, and in the North of Ireland, three of horse, one of foot, and one of dragoons, and they have the necessary orders . . . There is eight hundred horse marched from this to the Borders by advice of the Duke of Marlborough, for he thinks they will be more useful than twice their number of foot.

A book, written by the anti-Union Scot James Hodges, entitled *War Betwixt the Two British Kingdoms Consider'd*, admitted that the Scots would not be able to resist an English attack although the English would find it difficult to maintain a permanent presence in a hostile Scotland. By December 1706, a strong English force was ready to move if Queensberry felt it necessary. Against this background of espionage, bribery and military pressure, the so-called discussions between Scottish and English Commissioners took place.

Thirty-one representatives from each country were to talk terms. Only one Scot, George Lockhart of Carnwath, a Jacobite who at first refused to serve as a Commissioner, was not a court appointee. Negotiations began in the Cockpit of the Palace of Westminster on 16 April 1706, where the two sets of Commissioners met separately in different apartments. Only once, when the time came to discuss the number of Scots who would sit in the new parliament, did both groups confer.

The Scots made a hollow show. A token stand was made for federal union; but when the English objected the idea was never raised again. The Earl of Stair wisely suggested that the Commissioners should consider achieving union in stages, so that it might be more popularly accepted on both sides of the border. Godolphin, the English Lord Treasurer, objected and the Scots were told to busy themselves with details, not principles. But the union might have been more fair if the Scots concept of federalism had not been so readily dismissed.

The first four Articles of the agreed Treaty laid down the essence of the Union. Two kingdoms, Scotland and England were to become one, called Great Britain. Scottish subjects were to have the same rights in England as Englishmen, and were to be able to trade freely with their southern partner and her rich colonies. The Protestant Succession, as defined by the Act the English Parliament, was to apply to Scotland as well. One new Parliament, called the Parliament of Great Britain, was to replace the two.

The question of Scottish representation in the new parliament was complex. Representation in the early eighteenth century was to do with wealth, not population. England was probably over thirty times richer than Scotland, although her population was only five times as great. The English had proposed that the Scots should have 38 seats in the new House of Commons. The Scots objected and it was finally agreed that the Scottish nation should be represented by 45 MPs – one more than the English county of Cornwall. The representation was grossly unfair: 513 English MPs and 45 Scots, a ratio of 11 to 1. In the Lords, England was to have 196 seats to Scotland's 16. Scottish Lords lost their automatic right to sit in parliament; the 16 would be elected from 154. Although in theory the treaty created a new parliament, in reality the English Parliament carried on unchanged.

The English made some concessions. The Scottish legal system was to remain; but could at some future date be amended by the Parliament of Great Britain. Laws concerning the public were to be made the same throughout Britain; but Scottish civil law was to continue unaltered. The ancient Royal Burghs of Scotland were guaranteed their rights and privileges but would be able to trade freely with England and her overseas colonies. They would have to adopt English weights and measures and English coinage and English duties and customs and excise would now be applicable throughout Scotland. The Kirk, and the Scottish education system nurtured by it, were guaranteed. The union, therefore, was to be less incorporating than the English would have wished. Scotland's separate identity, it seemed, was not to be destroyed, only impaired.

The union of Scotland and England is unique, the only instance in history of two sovereign nations coming together to form one by treaty. But it was a patrician bargain, a deal done by two ruling classes; and the terms agreed were themselves a bribe to the Scottish nobility. Their special legal rights and privileges were to remain intact; and the nobility stood to gain most from the Equivalent, the sum of money England agreed to pay Scotland for accepting a share of the English National Debt.

By 1697, the English National Debt was nearly £14,500,000. It represented loans and investments that had been made by privileged organizations, like the East India Company and the newly formed Bank of England. The loans were regarded by both parties as permanent, but the government paid annual dividends from taxation to those who had underwritten its debts. Scotland's National Debt, on the other hand, was small, less than £200,000. The Scots, after all, had not been involved in costly European wars, and had not shared the English obsession with territorial conquest. As a result of the bargain, Scottish taxes would rise after the union to help pay the dividend. The Equivalent amounted to £398,085 10s 0d, and the English Commissioners agreed that a further cash payment would be made after seven years to balance the increased revenue that would come to the new British government from increases in Scottish customs and excise. By 1714, however, the British National Debt had exceeded £36,000,000.

More than half the Equivalent money, which would be recouped by taxation, was used to make good the losses suffered by the stockholders of the Company of Scotland, plus an additional five per cent. It was a generous offer, which must have influenced many members of the Scottish Estates – an overt and effective bribe. Greed gave credence to the English claim that, by paying the Equivalent, they had bought the right to tax the Scots, in perpetuity, as they saw fit.

All twenty-five Articles of Union had been agreed by most of the Commissioners. Only two, the Archbishop of York and the Jacobite Lockhart, refused to sign them on 22 July 1706. When the terms became known in Scotland there was uproar. The mobs of Edinburgh and Glasgow took to the street with the cry, 'No Union, No Union!'. In Dumfries, the terms were publicly burned.

The Estates met to discuss the deal on 3 October 1706. The session was to last over three and a half months and the members were to talk long into the night. The debate was tense and the terms agreed in London were strongly contested. Although few records exist the speech made by Lord Belhaven has survived:

> I think I see a free and independent kingdom delivering up that which all the world hath been fighting for, since the days of Nimrod, to wit, a power to manage their own affairs by themselves without the assistance and counsel of any other.

Having pointed the accusing finger at Scotland's nobility, Belhaven went on to list the consequences of union with England. Scotsmen, he claimed, would be used to win and maintain England's colonies, while Scottish merchants would be impoverished by new taxes.

> But above all, I see our ancient mother Caledonia, like Caesar sitting in the midst of our Senate, ruefully looking about her, covering herself with her royal garment, attending the fatal blow, and breathing out her last with a *Et tu quoque mi fili*.

The pro-union case was put by William Seton of Pitmedden, who attacked the idea of federation as impracticable and unworkable. He asked the anti-union opposition in the Estates:

Sir John Clerk of Penicuik (1676–1755) was a Commissioner for Union and is said to have been responsible for working out the Equivalent. He later was a Scottish MP at Westminster.   (*SNPG*)

Whether there can be any sure guaranty projected for the observance of
the articles of a federal compact, stipulated betwixt two nations, whereof
the one is much superior to the other in riches, numbers of people, and
an extended commerce?

But Lord Belhaven spoke for the Scottish people, who were overwhelmingly
against the Articles of Union:

> When I consider this treaty as it hath been explained and spoke to before
> us these three weeks past, I see the English Constitution remaining firm,
> the same two Houses of Parliament, the same taxes, the same customs,
> the same excises, the same trade in companies, the same municipal laws
> and Court of Judicature, and all ours either subject to regulations or
> annihilations; only we have the honour to pay their old debts, and to have
> some few persons present for witnesses to the validity of the deed, when
> they are pleased to contract more. Good God! What, is this an entire
> surrender?

John Hamilton, 2nd Lord Belhaven
(1656–1708) opposed the accession of
James VII and was put in prison. He
had subscribed £1000 to the Company
of Scotland and had dealings with the
Jacobites.   (*SNPG*)

On 8 and 9 November 1706, the mob of Glasgow rioted and a national revolt
seemed possible. The Estates forbade Scotsmen to carry arms, but this only
provoked further violence. The Glasgow mob broke into the Tolbooth and
ransacked homes in search of weapons. It was not until a detachment of
dragoons succeeded in arresting the leaders that peace came to the town.
Daniel Defoe thought the matter of union with England had nothing to do
with the mob:

> As to all the rest of the People of Scotland who have no right to elect
> representatives, I affirm, and think the nature of the thing demonstrate
> it, they can have no right to direct those who they have no part in
> constituting . . . They are meddling with what they have no right to be
> meddling with, nor in any way concerned in.

Petitions, however, had poured into the Scottish parliament urging the
Estates to vote against the terms, from a third of the Scottish shires, a quarter
of the Royal Burghs and from Presbyteries – ninety petitions in all. Not one
shire or burgh sent an address in support. The Estates refused to consider
them. Despite the fact that the majority were an honest reflection of the
feelings of many Scots of all classes, the young Argyll suggested they should
be used to make paper kites. On 7 January, the Duke of Atholl, declaring,
'There is not one Address from any part of this Kingdom in favour of this
Union', demanded an election so as to have a parliament that reflected the
mood of the country. His motion was defeated. Instead, the Estates issued
a Proclamation forbidding people to come to Edinburgh in support of their
petitions.

John Murray, Marquis of Atholl
(1659–1724) was Secretary of State
between 1696 and 1698. He was
created Duke of Atholl in 1703 but
opposed the Union.   (*A*)

   When it became clear that patronage and bribery were working, the
anti-union lobby made three desperate attempts to stop the terms being
steam-rollered through the Scots parliament. First an armed rising was
planned, involving Presbyterians from the south-west and Jacobites from the
north. It was proposed that the two armed groups, estimated at some 7000
men, should meet in the town of Hamilton and then march on Edinburgh,
where they would 'raise the parliament'. The Duke of Hamilton was to lead
them. He postponed the rendezvous at the last moment.

   It was then proposed that those entitled to vote should come to Edinburgh and approve an address asking Queen Anne to call a new parliament
and allow the General Assembly of the Church of Scotland to meet and

Sir James Steuart of Goodtrees (1635–1713).   (*SNPG*)

Queen Anne (1665–1714). A detail of the statue, outside St Paul's Cathedral, London, to the last Stewart sovereign. (*Author*)

discuss the terms more fully. Again Hamilton frustrated the scheme, and proposed instead that those parliamentarians against the terms of the treaty should send a Protestation, a plea, to London. He also insisted on a clause supporting the Hanoverian Succession.

The Protestation was drafted by the Lord Advocate of Scotland, Sir James Steuart. Its signatories declared:

> I do for myself, and in the name of all those who shall adhere to this my Protestation, protest against this union in the terms of these articles now before this House, as manifestly tending to subvert that original, fundamental and indissolvable Constitution, by which the people of this ancient kingdom are joined together in a society amongst themselves.

When the day came to present the Protestation, the Duke of Hamilton was conveniently at home with toothache; but may well have heard from James VII and II, who hoped to exploit political unrest, that he should not oppose the union.

On 16 January 1707 the act agreeing to the Articles of Union was passed by the Estates. The vote was 110 in favour, 69 against. Forty-two peers voted in favour and 19 against. The vote of members for the Scottish shires was 38 to 30 and that representing the burghs 30 to 20. The document had been accepted by a majority in each Estate. It was not, strictly speaking, a treaty unless regarded as a treaty made by Anne, Queen of Scotland with herself as Queen of England. It was an agreement between two entirely independent sovereign states creating a new single sovereign state.

Bitterly, Lockhart of Carnwath remarked that 'the Union was crammed down Scotland's throat'. 'The Articles were confirmed in the parliament of Scotland contrary to the inclinations of at least three-fourths of the kingdom,' remarked Sir John Clerk of Penicuik, who had been responsible for working out the Equivalent. Andrew Fletcher decided to quit Scotland, remarking that in his opinion the country in future would be 'only fit for the slaves who sold it'. The last sitting of the Scottish Estates was adjourned on 19 March and nine days later they were formally dissolved.

The 2nd Duke of Queensberry packed his bags. When he reached Barnet, outside London, Queen Anne's ministers were there with forty-six coaches and hundreds of horsemen to lead him in triumph into Great Britain's new capital, where he presented the Scottish part of the treaty to the Queen. The English Parliament, without much ado, voted in favour on 6 March 1707, and in St Paul's Cathedral in London, on 1 May 1707 – the first official day of union – Anne gave thanks for what she regarded as the greatest political achievement of her reign.

In Edinburgh, church bells also rang out; they played a different tune, 'How Can I be Sad Upon My Wedding Day?' As the bells of St Giles tolled a lament for independence lost the Earl of Seafield made his famous poignant remark, 'There's ane end of ane auld sang.' The present-day frustration of the Scottish people, with its origins in the Union of the Crowns of 1603, is equally rooted in 1707.

10

An Imperfect Match

IT WAS TO ST GERMAIN-EN-LAYE, overlooking Paris, that the Stewart King, James VII of Scotland and II of England went with his exiled court in 1688. There the deposed King lived a life of religious gloom, beating himself in penance and praying half the day. Ungracious and bigoted, the Catholic monarch was despised by most who had dealings with him. He insulted loyal Protestants who had chosen to follow him into exile and constantly rejected their advice. James VII regarded his own daughter, Mary, who had married the Protestant William of Orange, as a traitor, and when she died of smallpox in 1694 refused to allow mourning at his French court. When Anne, his other daughter, became Queen, she too was banished from her father's mind.

James VII and II, before his exile, had helped found the British Navy, whose fleets ironically, thwarted his attempts to regain the throne. (*SNPG*)

James Drummond, 4th Earl of Perth, was among the Scottish nobles who followed him into exile. James's court was a small community, and very poor, dependent on the French King for charity, and there was constant intrigue. But hope at St Germain-en-Laye burned eternal. Jacobites in England as well as Scotland believed it was just a matter of time before James VII and II would regain his thrones.

In 1696 William of Orange had offered to recognize James's son as his heir in exchange for an end to Jacobite plotting. James bluntly refused, afraid his son would be brain-washed into becoming a Protestant; he also declined the invitation to have the boy elected King of Poland.

The Treaty of Ryswick in 1697 put an end to Stewart political ambitions. The peace settlement, signed by France, England, the Netherlands, Spain and the Holy Roman Empire ended the war of the Grand Alliance that had dragged on nine long years. Under the terms, Louis XIV recognized William as King of England and Anne as his successor. Four years later James VII and II died. His one lasting achievement as Duke of York, had been the creation of the British Navy, an accomplishment which subsequently again and again stopped the Stewarts from regaining the throne.

James VII's claim passed to his thirteen-year-old son and he was recognized by Louis XIV as King James VIII of Scotland and III of England. On 19 July 1696, James VII had made the Earl of Perth Governor of his young heir, drawing up twenty-five paragraphs instructing the Earl how the boy was to be brought up. He was to keep his Catholic religion and treat people with tolerance and generosity. Of Scotland, James VII had advised:

Mary of Modena (1658–1718), Queen Consort and second wife of James VII, whom she married in 1673. James Francis Edward was her only surviving child. (*BQ*)

Take all care to let no alterations be made in the government of that kingdom. They [the nobles] will stand by the crown and the crown must stand by them [adding] . . . except the Campbells . . . The true interest of the Crown is to keep that kingdom separate from England and to be governed by their own laws and constitutions.

The Kings of France and Spain acknowledged James Francis Stewart as the King *de jure*. His mother, Mary of Modena, ruled the Jacobite faction as Regent. In 1701, however, the Act of Settlement made the Electress Sophia, granddaughter of James VI of Scotland, and her children, heirs to the English throne on Queen Anne's death, although few relished the thought of the crown passing to the House of Hanover.

William III of England, II of Scotland died in 1702. He broke his collar bone when his horse tripped on a mole-hill and unseated the King, who died of pneumonia a few days later. Jacobites everywhere toasted the mole, who was referred to as 'the little gentleman in black velvet'. The time looked ripe for the teenage James VIII of Scotland and III of England to return. In England there was a run on the Bank of England and Parliament saw fit to suspend *Habeas Corpus*. Those suspected of Jacobite sympathies were arrested. Had the Pretender seized the opportunity and returned to Scotland, he might well have become King, but James did nothing and the chance of success without an armed rebellion was lost.

In 1707, Scotland became North Britain. Almost immediately the new British Parliament at Westminster breached the terms of the Treaty of Union. The Equivalent, the money paid to the Scots in return for their subsidizing England's National Debt, was three months late. As the carts, ostensibly laden with money, passed through Northumberland, the crowd jeered, angry that the Scots were being given good English gold. When the detachment guarding the bullion reached Edinburgh, the mob also jeered: rumour had spread that the chests contained rocks and that the Scots had been duped. When the chests were opened, three-quarters of the Equivalent was in suspect English Exchequer Bills, and only a quarter in coin as had been agreed.

In May 1708, contrary to the spirit of the Treaty, the Scottish Privy Council was abolished. In the same year, the Scottish Court of Exchequer was completely reconstituted and English forms and procedure introduced. Judges were appointed, under the titles they bore in England, including a Chief Baron of Exchequer. Despite opposition the system remained in Scotland for nearly 150 years. The English Treason Act that dated from 1350s was applied to Scotland from 1709, an Act that was barbarous compared with the old Scottish act it replaced. It was provided specifically under the terms of union that the Court of Admiralty in Scotland was to continue, but its jurisdiction was gradually undermined and it was finally abolished in 1830.

The breaches of the terms of union sprang from ignorance and arrogance. The new parliament of Great Britain was 400 miles away. Communication between London and Scotland was tortuous and the government was without the plethora of information modern British administrators have at hand. A predominantly English House of Commons, moreover, thought in terms of their own country. Ignorant of the law of Scotland they regarded their own system as superior.

Louis XIV (1638–1715) exploited the Stewart monarch's exile, but his death on 1 September 1715 put paid to French support for the Rising.   (*BQ*)

Queen Anne's Union of the parliaments proved unpopular. She is seen here receiving the Scottish 'Treaty' from the Duke of Queensberry.   (*PW*)

The English paid little attention to the Scottish MPs in their midst. Often they claimed they could hardly understand what they were saying, let alone care. The Scots allowed themselves to be manipulated, became tools of the two English political parties, the Whigs and the Tories. Scots peers and MPs were wooed with favours to keep them amenable. But many were quickly disillusioned.

On 14 June 1708, the Earl of Mar, who had been enthusiastic about the union and instrumental in bringing it about, informed Queen Anne:

> I think myself obliged in duty to let your Majesty know that so far as I understand the inclinations and temper of the generality of this country is still as dissatisfied with the Union as ever, and seem mightily soured.

By then, James VII had been dead seven years and Scots had begun to forget his shortcomings. The exiled Stewart court began to plot. Colonel Nathaniel Hooke, a French agent, visited Scotland. He returned to report to Louis XIV that Jacobite sympathy could be put to political use. The Pope promised money if the King of France sent troops to Scotland and Louis decided on a Scottish diversion to embarrass and, he hoped, unseat the British monarch. But the planned invasion went awry. James contracted measles, and the French fleet, carrying some 5000 troops was delayed and failed to rendezvous with the Scottish Jacobite forces in the Firth of Forth. A superior British squadron, led by Admiral Byng, forced the French to flee.

The root of Scottish discontent was that the country did not immediately enjoy the economic benefits union had promised. When a Bill was brought before Westminster aimed at stimulating the Scottish linen industry the Irish lobby, afraid of competition, quashed it. Robert Harley, now the Earl of Oxford, attempted to improve the administration of Scotland by setting up a Commission of Chamberlaincy and Trade to replace the defunct Scottish Privy Council. Set up in 1711 to distribute part of the Equivalent money and encourage trade and manufacture, the Commission failed to make any real impact. The English Board of Trade objected to its existence on the grounds that it infringed its authority.

The case of the Reverend James Greenshields brought Scotland into open revolt. An Episcopalian minister, he was imprisoned in 1710 by the magistrates of Edinburgh because he had used the English Liturgy and was flouting the authority of his local Presbytery. The decision of the lower court was upheld by the Scottish Court of Session and Greenshields decided to appeal to the British House of Lords, although the terms of union gave him no right to do so.

The Patronage Act of 1712 which angered Scots Presbyterians. (*NLS*)

With no Scottish lawyers in their ranks and unaware of the legal implications, the English Lords reversed the Court of Session's decision and found in favour of Greenshields. Then two Acts were passed by Westminster in 1712. The Toleration Act allowed the Scots' Episcopalian clergy to use 'the liturgy of England', and the Patronage Act restored to Scottish landowners their right to choose and appoint parish ministers. Contrary to the terms of union, this legislation enraged the Scottish Presbyterians.

Angry Scots peers hinted to Queen Anne that the union was in danger. By the end of 1711, the Earl of Mar had written to his brother:

> The English as most of the Scots are, seem to be weary of the Union . . .
> If we saw a possibility of getting free of the Union without a civil war, we
> would have some comfort, but that I'm afraid is impossible.

The Scots boycotted Parliament when English MPs, in 1713, decided to apply the English tax on malt to Scotland. This tax was also against the terms of union, and Scots openly demanded that both countries again go their separate ways. On 2 June 1713, Viscount Seafield, who had worked hard to bring about the union, moved in the House of Lords to have the union dissolved. The motion was defeated by 71 votes to 67; a majority of 4. Only 16 Scottish peers sat in the House at that time. Had the motion been put before the House of Commons, the union might well have been dissolved. The court in London, determined that the union should hold, placated the more vociferous Scots.

Jacobitism, support for the exiled Pretender, was to be more than a Scottish phenomenon. When Queen Anne died in 1714, there were disturbances all over England. In Oxford, a Hanoverian undergraduate shot a Jacobite student. In Manchester, Jacobite sympathizers pulled down a Presbyterian meeting-house. In Somerset, in protest to the House of Hanover, they rang church bells and toasted the health of James III of England. In Bath, Lord Lansdowne collected cannon and firearms and planned for him to land near Plymouth. The rebellion in the west country was only stifled when its leaders, including six MPs, were arrested.

Scotland's fortifications were in a chronic state of disrepair; the British government had neglected the country's defences. In December 1714, however, a Commission of Police was set up to keep a strict watch on suspect Papists, and many Scots, particularly Highlanders, felt bridled. Unwittingly, the government helped bring about the Earl of Mar's rebellion. So too did an act 'for Encouraging Loyalty', passed by Westminster on 30 August 1715, which required a long list of suspects to present themselves in Edinburgh to take an oath of allegiance to the House of Hanover. Many, fearing they were marked men, openly looked to the Earl of Mar.

On 27 August 1715 at his castle at Braemar in Aberdeenshire Mar organized a deer hunt at which plans for an armed rebellion were drawn up. At this meeting news came of the death of Louis XIV, which doomed the Rising before it began; but the rebels felt that they were already too far committed to draw back.

With the support of the Earl of Huntly and George Keith, the Earl Marischal, the call went out for recruits. Mar's own tenants were unwilling to turn out for the cause and he had to force them by threatening to burn their homes. On 6 September 1715, the Standard of King James VIII was raised at Braemar Castle. With a small army, drawn mainly from the Episcopalian north-east, the Earl of Mar marched south. En route, Highlanders from the west joined him: Cameron of Lochiel and his men because they were Episcopalian, the clans of the Western Isles because – as much as anything – the Campbells were on the other side.

The town of Perth fell on 14 September, and two weeks later Mar made the town his headquarters. But time was wasted while he waited for support to arrive and the element of surprise was lost. In Northumberland, on 6 October, Thomas Forster, an English MP, raised a force in support of the Jacobite cause. In southern Scotland, Viscount Kenmure raised a few

George Keith, 10th Earl Marischal of Scotland (1694–1778) and his younger brother, Field-Marshal James Keith, were both involved in the Jacobite Rebellions of 1715 and 1719. (*SNPG*)

Thomas Forster, MP and English Jacobite. (*SNPG*)

hundred troops. Mar, unaware of either of these risings, yet in command of an army of well over 10,000 men at Perth, was paralysed by chronic indecision and failed to take the advice of professional soldiers on his side.

The Duke of Argyll, Commander-in-Chief of the government forces in Scotland, had only 4000 troops at hand. Most were ill-trained Lowland militia wary of fighting Highlanders. An experienced soldier, Argyll knew, like many before him, that Stirling Castle would be the key to the campaign, and Mar played into his hands. On 12 October 1715, Brigadier William Mackintosh of Borlum was ordered to join up with the southern Jacobites and prepare to attack Argyll's army from the south.

John Campbell, 2nd Duke of Argyll (1678–1743), had been made Earl and later Duke of Greenwich for his support of the Union. Before 1715 he had served under Marlborough in the war of the Spanish Succession.   (*BQ*)

Borlum, however, wasted time trying to take Edinburgh, which stubbornly resisted, and it was not until 20 October that he finally met up with the Jacobite forces of Northumberland and Dumfriesshire. Thomas Forster insisted on striking south into England, convinced he could raise, 'loyal Lancashire'. At first it seemed the right action. As he passed through Cumberland, his troops put the local militia to flight, but success was short-lived and Forster was forced to surrender to government troops at the English town of Preston on 14 November 1715.

In Scotland Inveraray Castle, Argyll's stronghold, had been attacked by Jacobites in October in the hope that the government's Commander-in-Chief would be distracted but the strategy had failed. Mar had to make a move if all was not to be lost, and at Sheriffmuir on 13 November 1715, the Jacobite army faced the British. Mar's forces outnumbered those of Argyll by four to one; but the battle was a comedy of errors. There was ill-feeling between the Jacobite leaders and once again Mar refused to take good professional advice. As he dithered John Gordon of Glenbuchat, recalling Claverhouse, cried out in exasperation, 'Oh for an hour of Dundee!'

At Sheriffmuir, each army routed the other. The right flank of Mar's army got the better of the left flank of Argyll's, while the latter's right pushed back the left flank of Mar's force. The result was indecisive; Rob Roy and the MacGregors, watching from a hill, realized this and failed to intervene. Sheriffmuir was a psychological victory for Argyll: Mar's Highlanders, in retreat, drifted back to the glens.

James VIII, the Old Pretender (1688–1766), landing at Peterhead; from a contemporary Dutch print. (*SNPG*)

On 22 December, the Old Pretender James VIII landed at Peterhead. He was too late. Had he seen fit to arrive and take command of his forces earlier he might have won the day, but he was hampered by bad communications. As it was his troops were demoralized by news that the Duke of Argyll's army had been reinforced with 6000 seasoned Dutch troops. On 4 February 1716, James VIII headed back to France followed by the leaders of his army. Many, like the King himself, would never see Scotland again. During his exile the Earl of Mar was sometime chief minister at the Jacobite court but later he became disillusioned and took no further part in politics. He died in 1732, at Aix la Chapelle.

The rebellion that might have succeeded failed. The time had been right; but the leaders were not. If Mar had been anything like competent, Scotland would have been the Pretender's for the asking. So too, perhaps, might England, where many saw the ruling Whigs as villains. A distrusted minority before the Hanoverian Succession, the Whigs had scrambled to power in a sort of bloodless *coup d'état*. In office, they preyed upon the fears of Jacobitism, which became equated with Toryism. Many reacted in horror to

George I (1660–1727), the first Hanoverian to rule, did not endear himself to the British people. He never learnt to speak English and was out of Britain much of the time, leaving the Whigs to run the country. (*NPG*)

their excesses, and there was a genuine dislike of the Hanoverian regime with the non-English speaking King George at its head. The disillusionment of many in Britain was never fully exploited.

Those leaders of the rebellion who did not flee the country were taken to London and imprisoned. Some, like Brigadier Mackintosh of Borlum and the Earl of Nithsdale under sentence of death, managed to escape. From the Queen's House in the Tower, Nithsdale was daringly rescued by his wife and fled to France; in the end only two rebel lords paid the ultimate penalty. The Earl of Derwentwater, who with Thomas Forster had raised the rebellion in the north of England, went to the scaffold, along with the 6th Viscount Kenmure, who had raised the Borderers. He never expected to be beheaded, believing an accommodation would be reached, so he was executed wearing a brown suit because, expecting to be released, he had not ordered himself any black clothes.

Other Scots Jacobites were taken to Carlisle for trial. The government feared they would never be found guilty by a Scottish court but the Scots were rightly angered by a decision that was felt to be in breach of the Union. Sir James Dalrymple, the Lord Advocate of Scotland who was strongly anti-Jacobite refused to prosecute at the trials, as did his Deputy, Duncan Forbes of Culloden. Money was raised by public subscription to help pay for their defence. Tried by an English court, many were sentenced to death; but few suffered the axe and in 1717 an Act of Grace and Pardon was passed under which Jacobites still in prison were allowed their freedom.

The British government wreaked economic vengeance on those families who had taken part in the 1715 Rebellion. The estates of the Earl of Mar, the Earl Marischal of Scotland, MacDonald of Sleat and MacKenzie of Applecross were confiscated by the government and sold. Some, like the MacLeans, were punished by their Scottish enemies. The MacLeans had fought at Killiecrankie and later at Sheriffmuir. Now the Campbells landed soldiers on Mull and took Duart Castle, the MacLean stronghold.

Many of the forfeited estates went to the York Buildings Company, speculative London investors who hoped to establish industries in the Highlands. In 1728, the company took the lease on the Abernethy pine forest, believing that the 60,000 trees there could be used as masts for the Royal Navy. When they proved too small the trees were used for charcoal and a small ironworks was built. The London-based company also built a sawmill at Abernethy and, at Strontian in Argyll, they mined for lead; but their investment was to prove unwise and the company went into liquidation.

Jacobite leaders, exiled in Europe, continued to plot and scheme. In 1719, they attempted another rebellion, with the help of Catholic Spain. Two fleets sailed for Scotland. The larger, under the 2nd Duke of Ormonde, carried 3000 troops. The smaller, with only 300 men aboard, was led by George Keith, the Earl Marischal of Scotland. Ormonde was driven back to Spain by severe storms; but Keith reached the Western Isles. On landing, he learnt that James VIII, tactless as ever, had appointed Lord Tullibardine, the Duke of Atholl's second son, as commander, a man for whom the Earl Marischal had no respect.

On 25 April 1719, the small force gathered on the shores of Loch Alsh and made Eilean Donan Castle their base. Over a thousand Highlanders

James Butler, 2nd Duke of Ormonde (1665–1745), supported William of Orange in 1688 and served under him. A firm Tory, he opposed George I and in 1714 was attainted. He participated in the Rebellion of 1715 and spent the rest of his life in exile. (*NPG*)

rallied to their call; but there was little discipline. Keith and Tullibardine hated each other so much that they set up separate camps three miles apart. At Glenshiel on 10 June, their forces were scattered by the artillery of the government forces led by General Wightman. Jacobite aspirations were again shattered. Yet the seed-bed of the movement remained. Many, in Lowland as well as Highland Scotland, were still disillusioned.

The problem facing the British government after the Rising of 1715 and the abortive attempt of 1719 was to make sure that rebellion could never happen again. In 1725, Westminster passed a second Disarming Act, which forbade Highlanders to carry arms and ordered that they hand in those they already possessed. In practice, the Act achieved nothing. In 1726, however, the government made an appointment that had more far-reaching consequences. General George Wade, an Irishman, became Commander-in-Chief in Scotland with a brief to pacify the Highlands. Having carried out the first thorough survey ever made of the area, Wade built a line of forts across northern Scotland and a series of smaller barracks, like that at Ruthven, were constructed to keep the peace. Many were 'toy' forts with a superficial warlike appearance that could never have resisted any serious artillery attack. The hope, bearing the cost to the British taxpayer in mind, was to frighten Highlanders into submission, to impress natives thought to be ignorant.

The Old Pretender had been aboard a French ship which failed to rendezvous with the Jacobites in 1708. After his brief visit to Scotland in 1715 he spent most of his remaining life in Rome. (*SNPG*)

Like the Romans before him, Wade saw his forts as part of a chain, linked by military roads and bridges. In 1733, he completed the construction of Garva Bridge, which spanned the River Spey and carried the road that linked Fort Augustus at the southern end of Loch Ness with the barracks at Ruthven near Kingussie. It took three summers of hard labour to build a road to link Perth with Inverness and its construction employed nearly 600 men, divided into two groups. One party worked south from Inverness, the other north from Dunkeld. Given the weather conditions, the men worked on the roads and forts from April until October and then went home for the winter.

The labourers were men of the Black Watch. Wade revived the idea of using Highlanders with proven loyalty to the Crown. He raised them in 1725 at Aberfeldy when six companies of some 500 men were drawn from the clans Campbell, Grant, Fraser and Munro. The Black Watch also policed the Highlands. They were authorized to disarm clansmen, prevent cattle stealing and act as guides for Hanoverian redcoats and dragoons. Believing it to be in the government's interest that the men of the Watch be kept happy in their remote camps, Wade established breweries for his men. In 1739, a year after the major road-building programme was finished, the six companies were increased to ten and the Black Watch Regiment was formally constituted. Wade went south to assume another post in 1734. He had supervised the construction of some 235 miles of road and 28 bridges in just 6 years. The first steps had been taken towards taming the Highlands, where, before Wade, travel had been on foot or horseback over grass or gravel tracks. To communicate in safety people or goods had gone by sea.

George Wade (1673–1748) became Commander-in-Chief in Scotland in 1724, and a Field-Marshal in 1743. (*SNPG*)

Wade's successor, General William Caulfield, carried on the road-building programme; but the Highlanders were difficult to subdue. Cattle thieving in remote glens was a worthwhile occupation. Upwards of 150,000 beasts were driven south to the market held three times a year at Falkirk and they were easy prey.

Chief among the cattle rustlers were the MacGregors. Although the clan

Ruthven Barracks near Kingussie, Inverness-shire, built by the government in 1718. *(STB)*

Rob Roy MacGregor (1671–1734). Arrested more than once, his escapes became legendary. *(MS)*

had been outlawed and condemned to death in 1590 for persistently breaking the law, they had survived. When they emerged to show their loyalty to James VII, they had been again proscribed in 1695. Rob Roy MacGregor was born at Glengyle at the head of Loch Katrine in 1671. He took his mother's name of Campbell and farmed at Balquhidder, operating also as a cattle dealer. Rob Roy became an outlaw as a result of an unwise financial speculation, in which he lost not only his own savings but also money entrusted to him by the Duke of Montrose. He was declared bankrupt and a warrant was taken out for his arrest.

From the braes of Balquhidder, Rob Roy and a band of about twenty took revenge. He became Scotland's Robin Hood, raiding Montrose's cattle and lands whenever possible. He also ran a protection racket. For a time, Rob Roy was one of the Highland Constables, a body organized to try to prevent Highlanders from stealing from Lowland farmers. Their wages were paid by the Lowland farmers on the basis of the number of cattle and sheep that each farmer owned. When they were not losing cattle some of them stopped paying. Rob Roy pointed out that the reason they were not losing anything was because of his operations and if they did not pay him his due, usually in black meal, they might live to regret it, and this, in all likelihood, is the origin of the term blackmail.

Stealing cattle and raiding the rich farmland south of the Highland Line were the mainstays of the old Highland economy. (*CAC*)

Rob Roy, arrested more than once, always managed to escape. In 1726, while in Newgate Prison in London he was saved from transportation by a pardon and retired to Scotland to spend the remaining eight years of his life. By the time he died at the age of sixty-three the Highlands had roads and, with improved communications, law and order. He had lived during the last period in Highland history when behaviour such as his was possible.

At Westminster, the Scottish nobility who accepted the Hanoverian monarchy proved they were more interested in themselves than in the lot of the Scottish people. Daniel Defoe noted their behaviour after the Union:

> The great men are posting to London for places and Honours, every man full of his own merit and afraid of everything near him: I never saw so much trick, sham, pride, jealousy and cutting of friends' throats as there is among the noblemen.

In 1713, the British Parliament had pushed the Malt Tax through; but Scottish opposition had been effective enough to ensure that the tax, although passed, was not levied. By 1724, English Tory squires in the House of Commons, disgruntled by the heavy land taxes they were having to pay, decided to increase the tax on Scottish ale by sixpence a barrel. Robert Walpole, the Prime Minister, realized that such a demand was swingeing and would cause trouble. He reduced the tax to threepence a barrel on every bushel of malt, but the concession made little difference to Scottish anger.

In June 1725, Scots in Glasgow rioted. Daniel Campbell, the local MP, was the main target of the mob, as he was said to have voted in favour of the tax. His house, Shawfield, was looted and razed to the ground. Duncan Forbes, the Lord Advocate of Scotland asked the army, under the command of General Wade, to restore order and the captain of the troops ordered his men to fire on the mob. He was later tried and found guilty and condemned to death. Only the granting of a royal pardon saved him from execution. The legality of Forbes's action was questionable; but the city was brought under control. The townsfolk were fined to compensate Campbell and several of the rioters were sentenced to transportation.

When the tax on malt was imposed, the Scots turned to smuggling. 'Free Traders', as euphemistically the smugglers were called, operated out of fishing towns like Eyemouth and had the sympathy of the public. Tax in Scotland fell into drastic arrears. In 1715, nearly £18,000 was collected in Scottish customs. By 1745, the revenue had fallen to a third of that sum. The Scots were not a taxable people.

In Pittenweem, in Fife, James Stark, the local exciseman, was robbed in 1736 and the people of Edinburgh took to the streets in support of two smugglers who had been arrested. One managed to escape; but the other, Andrew Wilson, was executed. The mob threatened 'Black Jock' Porteous, a professional soldier employed in 1715 to train the City Guard, who had seen to the execution of Wilson. Captain Porteous ordered his men to fire on the crowd and some were killed, others wounded. He was tried and condemned for his actions. When the mob heard he was to be reprieved, they forced open the doors of the Tolbooth prison in Edinburgh and hanged him. The British government believed the rumour that Porteous had been murdered with the connivance of Edinburgh's civil authorities, and the House of Lords demanded that the city be punished. The Provost of Edinburgh was sacked and disqualified from holding public office for life. The city was heavily fined and the Nether Bow Port demolished so that it would be easier in future for government troops to enter the town to quell rebellion.

Despite occasional riots, the economic benefits of Union with England slowly came. Trade and manufacturing industries began to prosper in Scotland. The Jacobite ranks seemed to thin and by 1739 it was found necessary to form a Jacobite Association to keep interest from flagging. In France, the exiled Stewart court was to become the victim of wishful thinking, and once again the Pretender was to mistake anti-Hanoverian and anti-Whig feeling for Jacobite zeal.

The Porteous Riot.   (*CAC*)

11

The '45 and the Aftermath

JAMES FRANCIS STEWART, the Pretender, was twenty-seven when he failed to regain his throne in 1715. He had married the seventeen-year-old Princess Clementina Sobieski, first by proxy and then, in 1719, in person and, forced to leave France, had set up his exiled court in Rome. There on 31 December 1720, was born Charles Edward Louis Philip Casimir Stewart – the Young Pretender.

The prince was never academically outstanding but he grew up to be a good shot, a master of the crossbow and an accomplished golfer. At the age of twenty-two Charles, who had been brought up with an almost Messianic sense of mission, resolved to win back by force the throne of Britain for his father. Events in Europe made such a scheme far from harebrain. In March 1744 Britain and France were at war over the question of the Austrian Succession; the French were eager to help the Stewart cause.

The plan was to invade England as well as Scotland. Three thousand troops were to be landed in the Highlands, where, it was assumed, there would be an uprising of Jacobite clans in support of the exiled Stewart King; at the same time the Young Pretender, Prince Charles, was to be put ashore near London with an army of at least 12,000. The invasion was no fantasy. On the scale envisaged the French plan would certainly have precipitated a financial crisis in London which would have restored France's position in Europe. Even before the rising of 1745 there was savage and hysterical anti-Jacobite and anti-Scottish propaganda in England, which only went to encourage these aspirations.

But the French invasion of 1744 floundered. Much of the fleet at Dunkirk, made ready by Marshal Maurice de Saxe to land troops in the Thames, was destroyed in a storm, and the French abandoned their plan. The British Navy had been alerted by spies including, perhaps, the Earl Marischal of Scotland, and the Scottish supporters urged Prince Charles to abandon the rising. With typical Stewart disregard for good advice, he set about organizing an invasion on his own.

He pawned the Sobieski rubies, his mother's dowry, for £4000 and bought 1800 broadswords, 1500 muskets, 20 small pieces of artillery and ammunition. Two Jacobite shipowners supplied him with transport: Antoine Walsh lent a frigate, *du Teillay*, and Walter Routeledge his ship *L'Elisabeth*. Seven were to accompany him on his voyage to Scotland, among them Sir

The marriage of Prince James Francis Edward Stewart, the Old Pretender, and Princess Clementina Sobieska, the sixteen-year-old daughter of King John of Poland, which took place, to the anger of King George of England, in September 1719. (*SNPG*)

Thomas Sheridan, his former tutor, Aeneas MacDonald, a Scots-born Paris banker, and John William O'Sullivan, an Irishman of dubious military ability. On 5 July, dressed as a divinity student, Charles boarded *du Teillay* at Minden at the mouth of the Loire, but after five days at sea *L'Elisabeth* was attacked by the British man-o'-war *Lion* and, badly damaged, had to return to France with all the arms and ammunition.

After landing on the island of Eriskay off South Uist in the Western Isles, the Prince eventually made contact with the local chief, MacDonald of Boisdale, who told him to go home. The Prince is said to have replied, 'I am come home, sir,' although he had never set foot in Scotland before in his life.

On 25 July, Charles sailed for the Scottish mainland and established a base at Borrodale near Arisaig. There he met with Donald Cameron of Lochiel, who was critical of the scheme and also suggested the Prince return to France. The Prince persuaded him by casting doubt on his courage and loyalty. 'Lochiel,' he said, 'may stay at home and learn from the newspapers the fate of his Prince.'

The fifty-year-old Cameron of Lochiel, whose father had been attainted after the 1715 rising, had devoted his life to improving his estate and before meeting the Prince had been planting a beech avenue. When he heard the Prince had landed he put the young trees into a trench very close together meaning to place them properly later. But Lochiel never did come back, and the trees grew up close together in the trench where he put them. They are there to this day.

Others refused to support the Prince. The then Mackintosh of Mackintosh, for example, was a captain in the Black Watch in command of a company, and when Bonnie Prince Charlie made his appearance he simply remained with his regiment and true to his oath of allegiance.

The MacDonalds had raised more than any other clan to fight for the Old Pretender in 1715, but in 1745 they too were hesitant. Sir Alexander MacDonald had had his lands restored at great personal cost in the late 1720s, and although he inwardly supported the Jacobites he outwardly appeared to support the government and gave his word that he would not put

Prince Charles Edward Stewart (1720–88), *de jure* Charles III, otherwise styled the Young Pretender. (*SNPG*)

men in the field. MacDonald managed to give the Prince considerable moral and financial support without actually sending men to fight.

The Forty-Five Rising split families. Lord Boyd, the son of Lord Kilmarnock, fought on the Hanoverian side, while his father stood loyally behind the Prince. The chief of clan Chisholm had sons fighting on both sides in order to ensure that the family would not suffer as they had done after the Fifteen; no matter the outcome, someone would be on the winning side and forfeiture would be averted.

A contemporary account estimates that 20,650 clansmen were on hand at the time of the rebellion of 1745. Of this number 4800 fought on the Hanoverian side and 3400 chose to take no part in the campaign. The Prince, therefore, rallied little over half of the fighting strength of the Highlands to his cause. Most of those gave their support for feudal reasons; others, Episcopalian and Roman Catholic, for religious reasons. Few took up arms because they believed in the rebellion politically. The Young Pretender's appeal to the clans also had an economic base. Many Highlanders saw the forthcoming campaign as a chance to revive, on a grand scale, the traditional rape of the Lowlands.

On 19 August 1745, Charles waited at Glenfinnan for the clans to arrive. After three hours only 150 men from clan Ranald had joined him. Then Lochiel appeared with six to seven hundred Camerons at his back, and after them 300 MacDonalds from Keppoch arrived and a few MacLeods. Eventually some twelve hundred had assembled at Glenfinnan to hear the Old Pretender declared King for the second time.

Using the Highland road system the British government had built, the Prince made a brisk beginning. In the first few months of the campaign he scarcely made a wrong move; while Sir John Cope, the commander-in-chief of the British government forces in Scotland made a feeble showing. Ignorant of the Young Pretender's arrival until 8 August, Cope was able to raise only around 1400 raw recruits. Belatedly, he set off from Stirling Castle to face Prince Charles, who by 27 August was encamped at Garva Bridge in Inverness-shire. Cope had to decide whether to challenge the Prince at the Bridge or not. When told by his scouts that Charles's army was twice the strength it really was, he decided it would be safer to halt his footsore and weary redcoats at Ruthven Barracks and then march north to Inverness to get supplies of food and ammunition. The way south was thus left open to Prince Charles, and on 4 September, he took Perth, where many rallied to his side.

Some, like the twenty-four-year-old David Wemyss, Lord Elcho, felt the chance had come to correct the grievances that many Scots felt, despite the Union with England which in 1707 his father had ardently supported. At school at Winchester, Lord Elcho had been slighted because of his Scots ancestry and accent, and he had not found London life easy, whereas in France Scots aristocrats like him were accepted as equals by the French. Even so, he did not join Prince Charles on rash impulse. He sent a message to Perth asking how many troops were there in the army. Murray of Broughton, who was secretary to Bonnie Prince Charlie, replied saying that there were 6000 currently with the Jacobite army and 6000 were expected with a French general in command. On the basis of this information Elcho met the Prince in Edinburgh about a week later. In fact there were only 2000 Highlanders at that stage and no French at all. Elcho joined under false

Donald Cameron of Lochiel (c 1695–1748), the 'Gentle Lochiel'. He had regained the estate his father John had lost after the 1715 Rebellion, and was devoting his efforts to agricultural improvement, when 'Bonnie Prince Charlie' landed.   (CL)

The Banner which Lochiel and clan Cameron took into battle at Culloden. Lochiel himself was badly wounded but escaped to France, where he died. (CL)

pretences and this made him very bitter in later years, as did the fact that his loan of 1500 guineas, made when the Prince had only £50 in his treasury, was never paid back.

James Drummond, 3rd Duke of Perth, and Lord George Murray, the younger brother of the Duke of Atholl, were made joint commanders in the Prince's army. But since the Duke of Perth was in no way an ambitious man, they made an arrangement by which he and George Murray were each to command a day in turn. It was a fine recipe for confusion, although luckily the Duke of Perth was content to leave Murray in total charge of the military operations.

In his late forties and a veteran of the Fifteen and the abortive attempt made in 1719, Murray proved a commander of ability. He had been pardoned in 1726 and returned to Scotland from France, but unfortunately he was regarded with suspicion by those followers of the Prince who had travelled with him, especially John William O'Sullivan, Charles's Quarter-master-General. If Murray was the Young Pretender's efficient commander, O'Sullivan was the Prince's fool. He had been a captain in the French army and was supposed to know about staff work, but throughout the rebellion he was to advise the Prince wrongly and fail to supply his army adequately. In the first few months of the rebellion, however, O'Sullivan's shortcomings were not perceived.

Lowland Scotland was in panic. On 17 September, the town of Edinburgh, but not the castle, fell without resistance and government officials quit the town for the safety of Berwick. Cope, meanwhile, having scoured the north-east in search of the rebel army, shipped his troops from Dundee to Dunbar and met the Prince at Prestonpans, otherwise called Gladsmuir. The battle took place on 21 September 1745. Both armies were of roughly equal size, 2300 men. Cope had rightly chosen the open ground just outside the village of Preston and beneath the village of Tranent for the fight; but his dragoons were in a bad state. Their commander, Colonel Gardiner, was sick, and the horses were in a poor condition after their sea voyage.

Fortune favoured the Prince. The evening before the battle, as the two armies faced each other across an almost impassable morass, a local man agreed to guide some of Charles's men along a safe route that would take them within half a mile of Cope's east flank. The Highlanders advanced under cover of the morning mist and it was not until six-thirty in the morning that they were challenged by a patrol of dragoons. Cope barely had time to order his forces to wheel into position before the surprise attack was launched. His dragoons panicked and, in a battle that lasted only ten minutes, the government forces were routed. The Prince, after the battle wrote to his father:

> I cannot let slip this occasion of giving a short account of the battle of Gladsmuir fought on the 21 September which was one of the most surprising actions that ever was; we gained a complete victory over General Cope who commanded three thousand foot and two regiments of the best dragoons in the island, he being advantageously posted, with also batteries of cannon and mortars, we having neither horse or artillery with us and being to attack them in their post and obliged to pass before their noses in defile and bog. Only our first line had occasion to engage, for actually in five minutes the field was cleared of the enemy. On our side we only lost a hundred men between killed and wounded.

Lord George Murray (c 1700–60), son of the 1st Duke of Atholl. He took part in the 1715 and 1719 Rebellions before joining Prince Charles Edward Stewart.   (*A*)

Colonel James Gardiner (1688–1745), born in West Lothian, had fought at the Battle of Blenheim in 1704. He was killed in the Battle of Prestonpans. (*SP*)

The frontispiece of *The Several Journals of the Court of Directors of the Company of Scotland*. Although normally associated with the disastrous attempt to found a colony at Darien on the isthmus of Panama, the Scottish Company also traded with Asia and Africa until it was liquidated by Article Fifteen of the Treaty of Union of 1707. (*RBS*)

The

Several Journals

of the
Court of Directors of the
COMPANY of SCOTLAND

Trading to

Africa and the Indies;

Together with that of the Nominees in the Act of Parliament for establishing the said Company commencing the 14.th day of February, 1696. and ending the 15.th day of July 1698.

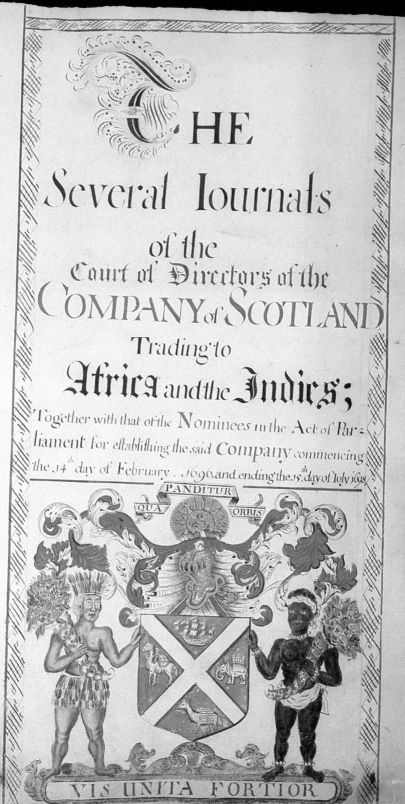

PANDITUR

QUA   ORBIS

VIS UNITA FORTIOR

After the disgrace of Prestonpans, Cope was court-martialled, General Wade, now a Field-Marshal, presiding. Cope was acquitted though it was the view of many in England that he could have extinguished the Jacobite rebellion at the start. As it was, the Prince now had complete control of Scotland and recruits poured into his army from the north. Within six weeks of his crushing victory, the Young Pretender commanded an army of over 5000 men and 500 cavalry. The British government was in a state of confusion and despair, and at Drury Lane Theatre in London the audience sang a new verse of the National Anthem, calling upon Field-Marshal Wade to put an end to the upstart Stewart's ambitions – curiously to a tune that is probably Jacobite in origin:

Sir John Cope (*d.* 1760), fleeing to Berwick after his army had been routed at Prestonpans.   (*SNPG*)

> God grant that Marshal Wade,
> May by thy mighty aid Victory bring,
> May he sedition hush,
> And like a torrent rush,
> Rebellious Scots to crush,
> God save the King.

After Cope's defeat at Prestonpans, the British government took swift action, as Tobias Smollet, a London Scot, recalled:

> Immediately after the defeat of Cope, six thousand Dutch troops arrived in England, and three battalions of guards, with seven regiments of infantry, were recalled from Flanders for the defence of the kingdom. They forthwith began their march to the North, under the command of General Wade, who received orders to assemble an army. The Duke of Cumberland arrived from the Netherlands, and was followed by another detachment of dragoons and infantry. The train bands of London were reviewed by his Majesty: the county regiments were completed: the volunteers in different parts of the kingdom employed themselves industriously in the exercise of arms: and the whole English nation seemed to rise up as one man against this formidable invader.

Despite success, all was not well in the rebel camp. Charles wrote petulantly to his father:

> I, with my own money, hired a small vessel, ill-provided with money, arms or friends; I arrived in Scotland, attended by seven persons, I publish the King, my father's declarations, and proclaim his title, with pardon in one hand and in the other liberty of conscience; and the most solemn promises to grant whatever a free parliament shall propose for the happiness of the people ... Why then, is so much pains taken to spirit up the minds of the people against this my undertaking? ... The reason is obvious; it is, lest the real sense of the nation's present sufferings should blot out the remembrance of past misfortunes, and of the outcries formerly raised against the royal family. Whatever miscarriages might have given occasion to them, they have been more than atoned for since.

Against the advice of Lord George Murray and others, Charles decided to invade England. The march began on 3 November, his troops taking two routes south to confuse the Hanoverian army, led by Field-Marshal Wade, which had just reached Newcastle. The Prince's forces reunited at the Border.

On 15 November 1745, amid heavy snow, Carlisle surrendered without

A view of Edinburgh from Calton Hill, showing the neo-classical memorial to the philosopher Dugald Stewart designed by William Playfair in 1822. Born in London, Playfair (1789–1857) contributed greatly to the architecture of the New Town; he also designed the National Monument on Calton Hill, Donaldson's Hospital and Surgeons' Hall, and was responsible between 1823 and 1836 for the design of the Royal Institution for the Encouragement of Fine Art (*below*), now the Royal Scottish Academy.   (*SG*)

a shot being fired. The Prince dismissed Murray but the Highland chiefs refused to serve under any other leader and the Prince was forced to reinstate Lord George. By 25 November the Jacobites had taken Penrith and Lancaster. On 26 November Preston fell, followed by Manchester three days later. By 4 December the Prince was at Derby. But the Prince's speedy campaign south was not matched by support for his cause. One of the Jacobite officers noted:

> The road betwixt Preston and Wigan was crowded with people standing at their doors to see the army go by, and they generally professed to wish the Prince's army success; but if arms was offered to them and they were desired to go along with the army they all declined, and said they did not understand fighting.

By the time the Prince reached Derby he had been joined by only 200 Englishmen, mostly from Manchester. London, however, was in a state of panic. As the novelist Henry Fielding noted:

> When the Highlanders by a most incredible march got between the army of the Duke of Cumberland and the metropolis, they struck a terror into it scarce to be credited.

The shops of London closed, and the Bank of England, fearing a run on money, paid out in sixpences. The rumour that George II had made contingency plans to return to Hanover was Jacobite fantasy, but there is perhaps truth in the belief that the Duke of Newcastle, his Prime Minister, contemplated a quick conversion to the Jacobite cause.

Charles and his Irish favourites demanded an advance on London. Given the consternation there it is not impossible that London might have fallen. Lord George, however, was against the scheme. With Cumberland at Lichfield, Wade at Wetherby, and a large militia at Finchley in North London, Murray argued that the Prince was surrounded by upwards of 30,000 men. The Highland chiefs agreed and urged a sullen Charles to retreat back to Scotland. As Lord Elcho noted:

> The Prince heard all arguments with the greatest impatience, fell into a passion and gave most of the Gentlemen that had spoke very abusive language, and said that they had a mind to betray him. He continued all that day positive he would march to London, but at night the Prince sent for them and told them he consented to go to Scotland. And at the same time he told them that for the future he would have no more Councils, for he would neither ask nor take their advice, and he was as good as his word.

On 6 December, 'Black Friday', the Jacobite retreat began. When the army reached Carlisle, Charles insisted that 400 men remain to garrison the castle although he was advised not to leave them to face the Duke of Cumberland, who later bombarded the castle with heavy cannon for two days. The Jacobites were forced to surrender; the officers were hanged and the men transported to the West Indies. But a victorious, not beaten, army had skilfully withdrawn, and on Christmas Day, entered Glasgow.

The city was strongly Hanoverian. When, previously, the Prince had demanded of it £15,000 the burgesses had refused. Nor were there volunteers to be raised; Glasgow produced 500 men to fight for the government. Provost Andrew Cochrane recorded that the Young Pretender . . .

George II (1683–1760) was a keen soldier and the last British monarch to take part in battle, acquitting himself bravely at Dettingen in 1743. *(NPG)*

... appeared four times publicly on our streets, without acclamation or one huzza; no ringing of bells, or smallest respect or acknowledgment paid him by the meanest inhabitant. Our very ladies had not the curiosity to go near him, and declined going to a ball held by his chiefs.

The Prince stayed at the newly rebuilt Shawfield House, where he met and fell in love with Clementina Walkinshaw, who later in exile became his mistress. Charles demanded clothes for his troops; the burghers of Glasgow said no. The hawks in his army wanted to sack the city, but Lochiel persuaded Prince Charles it would be a mistake. The councillors of Glasgow were so grateful that they promised to ring the bells of the Tolbooth whenever Lochiel's descendants visited the city.

While Charles and his army were in England General Henry Hawley had retaken Edinburgh. As the Prince attempted to prise supplies out of Glasgow, Hawley erected gibbets anticipating an early victory.

Charles stayed in Glasgow for ten days while he waited for the town to refit his army. Reluctantly, the citizens provided twelve thousand shirts and six thousand waistcoats, coats, bonnets, shoes and stockings.

On 3 January 1746 the Jacobites left the town. The Prince remarked that nowhere in the world had he found so few friends as in Glasgow. Within a fortnight, he had linked up with a further 4000 Jacobites who had rallied at Perth and prepared to meet the government army, led by General Henry Hawley and marshalled at Falkirk.

Hawley was a brutal, blustering and incompetent Englishman. He took no notice of the first warning of Jacobite approach. When they attacked on 17 January 1746, the Hanoverian regiments broke, and only the rearguard held while Hawley's troops beat a disorderly retreat to Linlithgow. He lost 400 to Jacobite losses of 40 and blamed his men. Over 30 of his own dragoons and an equal number of infantrymen were shot or hanged on charges of cowardice.

William Blakeney, who defended Stirling Castle after Prince Charles's victory at Falkirk. (*SNPG*)

The Jacobite victory was helped by welcome supplies of stores and ammunition sent from France, and by the addition of new troops raised in Scotland, some by families who were fighting on the government side. Lady Anne Mackintosh, a very spirited young lady aged twenty-two, raised about 300 men and sent them to the south of Scotland, where they joined up with the Prince's army just before the battle of Falkirk.

Flushed by victory at Falkirk, Prince Charles wasted time trying to capture Stirling Castle, but failed and retreated north. On 18 February the Jacobites entered Inverness and two days later the town's castle surrendered. On 3 March they laid siege to Fort Augustus, which succumbed two days later. But from 7 March to 4 April, nearly a month was spent laying siege to Fort William which refused to surrender.

The government, shocked by the news of Falkirk, sent William Augustus, the Duke of Cumberland, north with reinforcements. The third son of George II, Cumberland was twenty-five years old and had made a name for himself in the War of the Austrian Succession which Britain had been fighting for two years.

Meanwhile the sloop *Hazard* had run ashore near Tongue in Sutherland after being pursued north by British vessels. The ship was captured by Lord Reay's Mackays, who commandeered the supplies and £12,000 in gold from France intended for the needy Prince. Charles sent the Earl of Cromartie

William Augustus, Duke of
Cumberland (1721–65), third
son of George II.　(*SNPG*)

A contemporary drawing of Prince
Charles in campaign dress at
Inverness.　(*SNPG*)

with 1500 men to recover the treasure, but the Jacobites were attacked by the loyal Earl of Sutherland and Lord Reay and taken prisoner.

By 14 April, the young energetic Duke of Cumberland had made his way up the east coast and was camped with his army at Nairn on the Moray Firth. O'Sullivan had chosen Drummossie, a totally indefensible moor, as the Jacobite base despite the fact that Murray's suggestion of Dalcross Castle provided a better defensive position. Unable to listen to the right man at the right moment, Charles agreed with O'Sullivan, against Murray's better judgement, that a surprise attack be made on Cumberland and the Jacobite army was forced into a badly-organized, ill-guided, night march towards the Hanoverian camp. It was not until after eight o'clock at night that the hungry force began the ten-mile march to Nairn. Then, two miles short of the English camp, a drumbeat was heard: the English were awake. Wearily, the Jacobites retraced their steps and were back in camp by about six o'clock in the morning, exhausted and dispirited. Many deserted the ranks on the march back to hunt out food. After the abortive night raid, as Lord Elcho noted:

> The men were prodigiously tired with hunger and fatigue, and vast numbers of them went into Inverness, and the villages about, both to sleep and to pick up what little nourishment they could get. The principal officers went all to the house of Culloden and were so much tired that they never thought of calling a Council what was to be done; but every one laid himself down where he could.

It is clear from Lord Elcho's memoirs that the Stewart Pretender was quite unable to place trust in those who might have helped him win the day and he had an almost paranoid suspicion of Lord George Murray. For instance, on the march from Culloden when the Highland army tried to get behind Cumberland, two men were detailed to accompany Murray and to shoot him if he attempted to betray the Jacobite cause.

Cumberland, aware of the night's march, wasted no time. In the knowledge that the Jacobite troops were tired and hungry he set off with his army at five o'clock in the morning and sighted the Jacobites six hours later. By one o'clock in the afternoon of Wednesday, 16 April 1746, the two armies had taken up their positions, separated by some four to six hundred yards. The half-starved Jacobites waited in a freezing cold gale, with rain and sleet blowing in their faces on the desolate moor. Out of a possible seven to eight thousand men, the Prince could muster only 5000, an army that ranged in age from fourteen to fifty. Many were not professional soldiers. His first line of battle consisted mainly of Highland units. The second line, drawn up seventy yards behind, was a third of the strength, composed mostly of the Lowland regiments and Scottish and Irish units from the French army. Behind was what remained of the Jacobite cavalry, under the command of Lord Balmerino and Lord Elcho. At Culloden, the young Prince assumed personal command for the first time.

A quarter of a mile away were Cumberland's 9000 well-provisioned and well-equipped men. His superior forces comprised 15 regular British battalions. He also had the Argyll Militia and a company of Loudoun's regiment, an additional 600. Cumberland, moreover, could call upon 800 mounted dragoons and his superior artillery. The Prince could only call upon 13 assorted guns, of varying calibres, which made the supply of ammunition difficult.

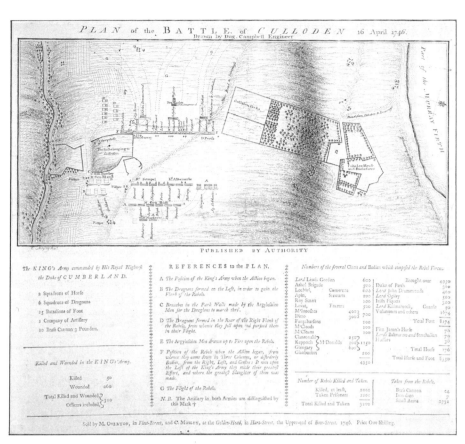

PLAN of the BATTLE of CULLODEN 16 April 1746.
Drawn by Dug. Campbell Engineer

PUBLISHED BY AUTHORITY

The KING's Army commanded by His Royal Highness the Duke of CUMBERLAND.

2 Squadrons of Horse
6 Squadrons of Dragoons
15 Battalions of Foot
1 Company of Artillery
10 Brass Cannon 3 Pounders.

Killed and Wounded in the KING's Army.

Killed   50
Wounded   260
Total Killed and Wounded,
Officers included,   310

REFERENCES to the PLAN.

A The Position of the King's Army when the Action began.

B The Dragoons formed on the Left, in order to gain the Flank of the Rebels.

C Breaches in the Park Walls made by the Argyleshire Men for the Dragoons to march thro'.

D The Dragoons formed in the Rear of the Right Flank of the Rebels, from whence they fell upon and pursued them in their Flight.

E The Argyleshire Men drawn up to Fire upon the Rebels.

F Position of the Rebels when the Action began, from whence they came down in Three Columns, or disorderly Bodies, from the Right, Left, and Centre: It was upon the Left of the King's Army they made their greatest Effort, and where the greatest Slaughter of them was made.

G The Flight of the Rebels.

N.B. The Artillery in both Armies are distinguished by this Mark †

Numbers of the several Clans and Bodies which composed the Rebel Forces.

Lord Lewis Gordon		600	Brought over	4950
Athol Brigade		500	Duke of Perth	300
Lochiel,	Camerons	600	Lord John Drummond	400
Apin,	Stewarts	200	Lord Ogilvy	500
Roy Stuart		100	Irish Piquets	300
Lovat,	Frasers	500	Lord Kilmarnock, Guards	50
M'Intoshes	400	700	Volunteers and others	1074
Ditto	300		Total Foot	8174
Farquharsons		200		
M'Goods		100		
M'Cleans		100		
Clanronalds	250		Fitz James's Horse	70
Keppoch } M'Donalds	300 }	1150	Lords Balmerino and Strathallan	70
Glengary	600		Hussars	36
Glenbucket		200		
			Total Horse	176
		4950	Total Horse and Foot	8350

Number of Rebels Killed and Taken.   Taken from the Rebels.

Killed, at least,	2000	Brass Cannon	22
Taken Prisoners	3200	Iron ditto	7
Total Killed and Taken	5200	Small Arms	2732

Sold by M. Overton, in Fleet-Street, and C. Mosley, at the Golden-Head, in Hart-Street, the Upper-end of Bow-Street. 1746. Price One Shilling.

A plan of the Battle of Culloden, drawn in 1746 by D. Campbell, an engineer. Drummossie Moor (*below*), on 16 April 1746 (A) (*WHM, below*)

The Hanoverian leader had made a careful study of the Highland way of fighting. He drew up his men in two lines, expecting the Jacobites to break through the first; they would then encounter the second, where his troops were ranged three deep, a rank kneeling, a second leaning forward and the third standing. Their combined fire power would thus be heavy and almost continuous.

The Battle of Culloden was a slaughter. From one o'clock in the afternoon, the Jacobites were subjected to a sustained attack by Cumberland's artillery. Accounts vary as to the length of the Hanoverian bombardment – from nine to twenty minutes – and the Jacobites could do little in reply. The wind that day was so strong that the clansmen were blinded by their own gunsmoke, and when they finally charged, they did so in ragged fashion. As the Highlanders approached, the Hanoverian artillery commander Colonel Belford changed from round shot to grape with devastating results. The Jacobites succeeded in piercing the Hanoverian left wing but by two o'clock in the afternoon it was all over. Cannon and sheer weight of numbers had won the day. Twelve hundred Highlanders were killed while only 364 government troops lost their lives. Although Lord George Murray had his horse shot from under him, he fought on and was one of the last to leave the field. Before the battle was over, however, the Young Pretender had fled. Yet many, like Lord Elcho, felt that the day was not altogether lost, for the Scots who had come out had risked everything and so had nothing to lose by a last ditch stand. Indeed Elcho is said to have met Bonnie Prince Charlie flying from Culloden and to have urged him to make one last effort, believing they could yet win the day. Bonnie Prince Charlie is said to have replied that he intended to save his own life and that he recommended Lord Elcho to do the same. To which, the story goes, Elcho replied: 'There ye go for a damned cowardly Italian!' They never saw each other again.

At Culloden the fighting strength of the Jacobite army was by no means destroyed. The Prince still had an army of over 4000. In addition, there were those stragglers from the night attack who had missed the battle, and Lord Cromartie, the MacKinnons and other clansmen who had been carrying the war into Caithness and Sutherland and were still fit for the fight. In case of defeat no rendezvous had been arranged for the Jacobite forces. The Prince is said to have suggested Fort Augustus, but most believed they were to remuster at Ruthven Barracks. Some 1000 to 1500 men, the remnants of the battered Jacobite army, met at Ruthven on 17 April to await fresh orders. But Prince Charles did not arrive, and Murray, angered by the needless defeat on Drummossie Moor, wrote to his commander:

> It was highly wrong to have set up the royal standard without having positive assurance from his most Christian majesty [the King of France] that he would assist you with all his force, and as your royal family lost the crown of these realms upon the account of France, the world did and had reason to expect that France would seize the first favourable opportunity to restore your august family.

He went on to blame the slaughter on O'Sullivan's failure to provide adequate provisions so that a third of the army was scattered while those that remained were 'really faint for want'.

Charles sent an arrogant farewell to the Highlanders who had fought for his cause:

Lord Elcho probably met up with Prince Charles as he crossed the River Nairn. *(WHM)*

I see with grief I can at present do little for you on this side of the water, whereas, by my going into France instantly, however dangerous it may be I will certainly engage the French court either to assist us effectually and powerfully, or at least to procure you such terms as you would not obtain otherwise.

The slaughter at Culloden had been bloody and ruthless. The Hanoverian troops regarded the Highlanders as savages, though, in truth, their conduct throughout the campaign was more civilized than that of their professional enemies. Most of those who served with the British army were drawn from the dregs of society and after the battle reprisals made little distinction between innocent and guilty. The young Hanoverian Duke of Cumberland refused to quarter the prisoners and the wounded and encouraged senseless cruelty. Ghastly atrocities earned him the nickname, 'Butcher'.

One of Cumberland's surgeons counted 750 dead on the field, but perhaps at least the same number again were killed in pursuit. Those found in hiding were brought back to the Moor and shot. Seventy deserters who had gone over to the Prince were captured. Twenty-nine of them, mostly Scots, were swiftly hanged at Inverness.

Twelve wounded Jacobites were removed from a cottage on the grounds they were to be attended by a surgeon, and then shot. Thirty more men were found in a barn near the Moor. They were locked in and the barn burnt to the ground. Cumberland's troops slaughtered innocent bystanders, men, women and children. A man with his nine-year-old son, found ploughing a nearby field, were among their victims.

The day after the battle, Cumberland's men buried their own dead and continued to search for fugitives. The Duke had told his men a lie. He claimed that Lord George Murray had ordered his troops to spare 'no quarter'. A copy of Lord George's order had indeed been captured, but the phrase about sparing no quarter had been clumsily forged at the end of it.

On the afternoon of the battle, some 300 were thrown into the Inverness Town Jail. As more prisoners were indiscriminately taken, the town's churches, cellars and ships lying in the harbour were commandeered as make-shift prisons. They were given no food or water for the first two days. Stripped of their clothing many died of the cold as well as untended wounds. The dead were tossed in unmarked trenches.

The rebel leaders were made to suffer. On 18 August 1746, Lord Kilmarnock and Lord Balmerino were publicly beheaded. Lord Cromartie, also sentenced to death, was spared the axe and imprisoned for life. Charles, Earl of Derwentwater, like his brother after the 1715 rising, was tried and executed. Lord Lovat, captured after Culloden by a Lowlander, John Fergussone, was sent to London for trial, although he had taken no active part in the battle. Despite the fact he conducted an able defence, Lovat was the last peer condemned and executed in Britain, in 1747.

Simon Fraser, 11th Lord Lovat (c 1667–1747), had this portrait painted by William Hogarth shortly before his execution.   (NPG)

By May 1746, there were twenty regular battalions and three full regiments of dragoons in Scotland. Military occupation of the Highlands was to last nearly a hundred years. Cumberland became dictator of Scotland, bent on the extermination of the Highland Scot. He wrote to the Prime Minister:

Jacobite rebellious spirit is so rooted in the nation's mind that this generation must be pretty well wore out before this country will be quiet.

Dr Archibald Cameron (1707–53), the younger brother of Donald Cameron of Lochiel, was executed for his part in the Jacobite Plot.   (*SNPG*)

Duncan Forbes (1685–1747), although he rendered valuable service to the British government at the time of the Forty-Five, always tried to maintain Scottish interests.   (*SNPG*)

The commemoration medal struck in honour of the Duke of Cumberland's victory at Culloden.   (*WHM*)

The glens were to be ravaged. Men were shot or hanged, women were raped, homes were burnt, everything of value stolen. Highland chiefs like MacLeod of MacLeod of Skye helped with the work. Cumberland's men systematically 'harried the glens' – Glenmoriston, Strathglass, Lochaber, Keppoch, Glen Nevis, Appin and west to Moidart. In gratitude, a grateful British government increased the Duke's Civil List allowance from £15,000 to £40,000.

The castles of those who had aided the Prince were burned. Lochiel's house at Achnacarry was destroyed as were the homes of Glengarry, Lord Lovat, Macpherson and Chisholm. Forty Jacobite chiefs lost their lands. The forfeited estates were administered by the Barons of the Exchequer; but so impoverished were many of them that the British government was forced to sell them to pay off their bad debts. Thousands of head of cattle were driven south. By the end of July 1746, over 8000 cattle had been driven into Fort Augustus, together with flocks of goats and sheep. Traders came from Yorkshire to buy the plundered beasts from the Hanoverian troops. The Highlander was to be robbed of any wealth, whether he had supported the Prince or not, and left in the hope that, homeless and without any means of support, he would die.

In London, Parliament discussed what should be done. Some members suggested that all Jacobite women be sterilized. Others advocated destroying all seed-corn north of the Highland Line 'so as to extirpate the inhabitants of the cursed country'. Others suggested clearing the Highlands totally and re-colonizing them with 'decent God-fearing people from the South'. Lord Chesterfield, famous for his letters to his son, was Lord Lieutenant of Ireland during the rebellion. He blockaded the Highlands during and after the Prince's abortive campaign in an attempt to starve the Jacobites to death.

Lord President Forbes protested at parliament's new Disarming Act of 1746. As supreme Law Lord in Scotland he was never consulted about the new legislation nor about the contents of the Act for the Abolition of Heritable Jurisdictions, applied to all clan chiefs whether they had been Jacobite or not. In contravention of the Treaty of Union 160 Scottish courts of Heritable Jurisdiction were abolished. Only the small baron courts were allowed to continue to try minor civil cases and help keep the peace in country villages.

When Cumberland returned to London he was given a hero's welcome. A service of thanksgiving was held at St Paul's; Handel composed 'See the Conquering Hero Comes' and special Culloden commemoration medals were struck. The King bestowed the title Baron Culloden on his son.

For five months, the Young Pretender hid in the Highlands and islands of Scotland before leaving for France, with a price of £30,000 on his head. His wanderings gave rise to legend and romance. In hiding, Charles received a letter from his father which had been written before Culloden, with advice too late to heed:

> If you really cannot maintain yourself in Scotland do not for God's sake drive things too far; but think of your own safety on which so much depends . . . so that you should really have no temptation to pursue rash or desperate measures at this time . . . In fine, my dear child, never separate prudence and courage.

Flora MacDonald, born in 1722 was the most famous of many Highlanders to risk their lives to protect the Prince. Prince Charles first met her on 20 June 1746 at Ormaclete on the isle of South Uist. For eleven days she shielded the Prince. Dressed as Flora's serving maid, 'Betty Burke', the Prince sailed from Benbecula to Skye, from where, on 1 July 1746, he returned to the mainland of Scotland, promising to reward Flora for her help.

Flora was then arrested and taken to London. There, she was treated royally and even the King's son Frederick, Prince of Wales, is said to have visited her. In July, as a result of a general amnesty, she was released and within three years was again living in Skye.

'Betty Burke'.   (*SNPG*)

Charles had a genuinely hazardous time. He slept rough in the heather and in bothies, learnt to smoke and took to drink. Finally, on 20 September 1746, he took leave of Scotland and boarded the French ship *L'Heureux* at Arisaig on Loch Nan Uamh. His attempts to gain further support in Europe were in vain. In 1748, by the Treaty of Aix la Chapelle, Charles was banished from France. In 1750, he visited London incognito and may have been received into the Anglican faith in an attempt to court support for his lost cause.

His father, the Old Pretender, died in 1766 and Charles took the title King Charles III of Great Britain and Ireland. In 1772, realizing that he needed an heir, he married Louisa, Princess of Stolberg. They had no children. Wrecked by drink and debauchery, the once-dashing Prince died aged sixty-seven on the last day of January 1788.

His younger brother, Henry, Cardinal Duke of York, gave Charles a royal funeral, buried him at Frascati, near Rome. He assumed the title Henry IX and amassed a large fortune, but was financially ruined during Napoleon's occupation of Italy in 1799. George III took pity on him and awarded him a pension of £4000 a year. When Henry died in 1807, the male line of the House of Stewart became extinct. In 1819, Pope Pius VII commissioned a monument to the exiled House of Stewart, and the Prince Regent, later King George IV, donated £50 to its cost.

Prince Charles Edward Stewart in old age.   (*SNPG*)

In his will, Prince Charles left nothing to his loyal Scots. Flora received not a penny. Charles's daughter, Charlotte, Duchess of Albany, born to him and Clementina Walkinshaw in 1753, was the main benefactor. His brother, Henry, was left a piece of silver valued at 1000 Roman crowns. John Stewart, the Master of his Household, was amply rewarded with a pension, as were dozens of Italian servants.

After Culloden, Lord George Murray quit Scotland and went to Rome in 1747. Charles refused to see him and asked his father to place Murray under house arrest. Later, when Lord George tried to see the Prince in Paris, he was physically threatened by the Young Pretender and told to leave. He died in exile in Holland in 1760.

Some of the rebels, like Lady Anne Mackintosh, found themselves pardoned more easily. Two years after Culloden she attended a ball given by the Duke of Cumberland, and he asked her to dance. She then said, 'Well I've danced to your tune. Will you dance to mine?' She then asked for the 'Old Stewarts Back Again' and they solemnly danced to that.

To the English, then and now, the rebellion of 1745 was thought of as a 'Scotch rebellion', although it would be more correct to call it a Scottish civil

Henry Benedict, Cardinal Duke of York (1725–1807), second son of James Francis Edward Stewart; he made no attempt to assert his royal claims after his brother's death.   (*BCA*)

war. Three Scottish regiments, the Royal Scots, the Royal Scots Fusiliers and the King's Own Scottish Borderers, fought on Cumberland's side. Many Highland clans remained aloof or fought against the Young Pretender: the Mackays, the Munros, the Macphersons, the Grants, the MacLeods, the MacNeills, the MacDonalds of the Isles, and of course the Campbells. More Scots took up arms against the Prince than supported his cause.

It is wrong too to see the Forty-Five rebellion as the death blow of Gaelic civilization. Even by 1715, a number of clan chiefs were already cosmopolitan in outlook, personally absorbed into the wider world of Britain and the world. Most of the Scottish Jacobite leaders were cultured men. Nor was the rebellion of 1745 a romantic mad fling for the throne. Before Culloden the Jacobites defeated superior government forces in battle. At the time, as the vast quantities of propaganda produced by the Whigs proves, the threat was real enough. The Old Pretender might well, in fact, have made a good constitutional monarch. His reputation and importance, however, have been clouded by the brave antics of his self-centred, stubborn son. Mementoes of his brief campaign are found in a dozen museums or more throughout Scotland. Locks of hair, writing desks, letters, miniature portraits, combine with local legend to promote the lost cause.

Two acts passed by the British government allowed the Highlands to be terrorized for nearly a decade, and were not repealed for nearly forty years. The more cruel of the two was the act which banned the wearing of Highland dress and which was proclaimed in every village and glen; 'No man or boy within that part of Great Britain called Scotland . . . whatsoever, wear or put on the clothes commonly called Highland clothes (that is to say) the Plaid, Philabeg, or little kilt, Trews, Shoulder belts, or any part whatsoever of what peculiarly belongs to the Highland Garb.'

Troops were ordered to kill anyone, save loyal Highlanders, seen wearing Highland dress. By the Disarming Acts of 1716 and 1725 Highlanders had already been forbidden to bear arms, even the dirk, which was used primarily for eating. After Culloden, they were forced to take an oath:

> I swear as I shall answer to God at the great day of judgment, I have not and shall not have in my possession any gun, sword, or arms whatsoever, and never use tartan, plaid or any part of the Highland garb, and if I do so I may be accursed in my undertakings, family and property, may I never see my wife, nor children, nor father, mother or relations, may I be killed in battle as a fugitive coward, and lie without Christian burial in a foreign land far from the graves of my forefathers and kindred; may all this come upon me if I break this oath.

James Moray of Abercairney (1739–68). This portrait was painted while the wearing of tartan was prohibited. (A)

Fort George, near Inverness, is evidence of the paranoia that gripped the British government after the Forty-Five. Designed to hold two infantry battalions – 1600 men – and an artillery unit, the fort took twenty-four years to complete. It was estimated that the cost of building would be £92,673 19s 1½d. When finished in 1769, it had cost almost double. Practically all the building materials, together with labour to build the fort, were brought up by sea from the loyal Lowlands. It was the largest construction ever undertaken in the Highlands and when completed its guns were kept at constant readiness for an attack that never came.

As well as repairing and garrisoning Field-Marshal Wade's old forts, the

British government extended the road system. By 1767, there were over 700 miles of roads in the Highlands and towerhouses like Corgarff and Braemar were converted into army barracks to guard the military highways. Highlanders were thought alien and every method was used to come to terms with the people. In 1747, the Commander of Fort Augustus advised his subordinate officers:

> The commanding officer at each station is to endeavour to ingratiate himself in the favour of some person in his neighbourhood by giving him a reward, or filling him drunk with whisky as often as he may judge proper, which I'm confident is the only way to penetrate the secrets of these people.

Landlords replaced chiefs as the lands of those who had fought with the Young Pretender were confiscated and government Commissioners appointed to administer many of them. The British government delivered a psychological blow as Dr Johnson noted when he made his famous Tour with Boswell in 1773:

> Their pride has been crushed by the heavy hand of a vindictive conqueror, whose severities have been followed by laws, which, though they cannot be called cruel, have produced much discontent, because they operate on the surface of life, and make every eye bear witness to subjection. To be compelled to a new dress has always been found painful. Their chiefs being now deprived of their jurisdiction, have already lost much of their influence and as they gradually deteriorate from patriarchal rulers to rapacious landlords, they will divest themselves of the little that remains.

For years after Culloden, Highlanders were rounded up by government troops. (*NGS*)

Many came to see emigration as an alternative to living in a Britain hostile to Highland ways. The changes in ownership of land made for excessive rents and evictions. The anti-Jacobite legislation removed by law the ties and restraints – social and military – that had previously held their society together. The old system of tacksmen, whereby the chief granted leases or tacks to close relatives in return for rents and military service was broken, and when the tacksmen found they could no longer raise their own rewards as their tenants became poorer it was they who organized the first great wave of Scottish emigration, between 1749 and 1775. Between 1763 and 1773 20,000 Highlanders emigrated. Pamphlets distributed in the Highlands, listing the advantages and attractions of the New World, together with letters from those already established in the American colonies, encouraged many to quit Scotland. On one ship, *Bachelor of Leith*, which sailed from Caithness in 1774, over half of those on board were emigrating as a direct result of countrymen and relatives who had gone before them.

By 1732, just seventeen years after the first major rebellion, three Highlanders had taken out grants of land near Cape Fear in North Carolina. They found the land easy to work and fertile, and seven years later 350 from Argyll settled in the area, encouraged by a Lowland Scot, Gabriel Johnston, the Governor of the colony. In 1740, he agreed to a Bill that gave newcomers ten years' grace on their taxes.

Governor Johnston knew many of the Scottish chiefs who had fought with the Prince personally and had gone to school with some. It was said that after the Forty-Five, he turned poor Germans off their land in Carolina to make way for immigrants from the Scottish Highlands. In 1768, he per-

Flora MacDonald (1722–90). She was imprisoned in London after Culloden; on her release married Allan MacDonald of Kingsburgh, in 1750.   (*SNPG*)

suaded the Colonial Assembly of North Carolina to establish a trading town on the upper Cape Fear River, called Campbelltown, now Fayetteville; and by the outbreak of the American Revolution in 1776, it is possible that as many as 12,000 Highlanders had settled in North Carolina alone. Most who came from Scotland were Presbyterians, some of them recent converts from the Catholicism or Episcopalianism of their Jacobite grandfathers. Because of their Gaelic language, they stuck together in the New World. Ironically, in North Carolina they settled in a county called Cumberland.

Among those who decided to emigrate in 1774 were Flora MacDonald, with her husband Allan, and two of their sons. When in March 1775 there was colonial unrest, leading Highlanders, among them Flora's husband Allan, raised a force to fight for the Hanoverian King George III. On 10 February 1776, 1500 Highlanders were at Cross Creek. Meanwhile the American revolutionaries had organized a force of Minute Men who set up earthworks and two cannon at the bridge over the Creek to stop the Scots.

At one o'clock in the morning of 28 February, the Highlanders charged with the cry, 'King George and broadswords'. The Americans opened fire. About fifty Highlanders were shot or drowned and the remainder took flight. The battle, the first in the American Revolution, lasted three minutes. Allan MacDonald and his son, Alexander, were taken prisoner and the following year Flora MacDonald was deprived of the family's plantation because she refused to take an American Oath of Allegiance ordered by the rebellious North Carolina Congress. The MacDonalds went to Nova Scotia and then Flora and Allan returned to Skye, where she died on 4 March 1790. Her funeral was unique to the island. Thousands paid homage in a procession that was over a mile long. She and her family remain the most famous examples of a phenomenon – Scots once loyal to the Stewart monarchy who after the failure of the Forty-Five rebellion transferred an equally strong British monarchy they had once contrived to overthrow.

After Culloden, Highland loyalty was brutally disillusioned. The Stewart Royal House not only expected loyalty, but had demanded it; their arrogance forced Highlanders to seek refuge in the New World. Unwittingly in defeat they helped bring about an Empire.

Moore's Creek, North Carolina, now maintained as an American National Park.   (*Author*)

12

Athens of the North

AFTER THE UNION OF 1707, Edinburgh ceased to be a national capital. Men at far-off Westminster now made the political decisions; but Scotsmen resolved that Edinburgh would not become a provincial backwater. By the late eighteenth century, Scottish lawyers, writers, philosophers, doctors and painters had made the town the intellectual hub of Europe.

The reasons for the phenomenon were complex. This flowering of Scottish indigenous talent had little to do with the nation's being linked politically to a neighbour the Scots had struggled against for nearly a thousand years, although peace with England put an end to the historical drain on the nation's money and men. But the economic benefits of Union were slow in coming; indeed the Jacobite movement had exploited with skill a nation's disappointment.

First and foremost, the Scottish Enlightenment was the culmination of a national system of education that had its roots in the far-off days of the Reformation. By the middle of the eighteenth century the desire of the Calvinists like Knox to have a school in every parish had become a reality, certainly in Lowland Scotland, and the fruits of a nation's near-obsession with education showed themselves in the late eighteenth century and well into the nineteenth. The second factor was the aftermath of the Jacobite rebellions. After the Forty-Five, all that was Scottish was distinctly under threat. The English, assuming *all* Scots were Jacobites, were determined to rid Britain of Scotland's individualism, and one aspect of the Scottish Enlightenment was a calculated, determined effort to rescue for posterity the culture of what had once been an independent nation. In consequence an attempt was also made to assess the nature of human society and plan for a future that a loss of nationhood and the old ways had put into question.

After union, with no parliament of their own, the influence of the nobility in Scotland declined rapidly, and in increasing numbers they drifted south in search of power. A new class, distinctly secular in outlook, emerged to fill the social and political vacuum. These 'literati' were men of learning and letters determined to show the world that, if their country was now but a component part of Great Britain, they as men of intellect could outstrip the English by creating works of international importance. This national determination to leave a mark produced a galaxy of historians, philosophers, novelists, literary critics, scientists and scholars.

Allan Ramsay (1686–1758), bookseller and publisher. (*SNPG*)

James Thomson (1700–48), poet. (*SNPG*)

The Treaty of Union provoked a strong sense of outrage. The nation, after all, had petitioned against incorporation with England, and many felt their pride deeply wounded. So the Enlightenment was in large part a period of patriotic nostalgia. Many became obsessed with collecting, editing and imitating old Scottish poetry. Some saw it their duty to get the poetry of old on paper before it was lost for ever.

Between 1706 and 1711, James Watson, a native of Aberdeen, published three large volumes entitled *A Choice Collection of Comic and Serious Scots Poems, both Ancient and Modern* in an attempt to reinstate the independent Scottish poetic tradition which had been in decline since the loss of court patronage after the Union of Crowns in 1603. This printed collection, culled from private manuscripts and old printed broadsides, stimulated a revived interest in vernacular poetry.

Allan Ramsay, born at Leadhills in Dumfriesshire in 1686, was initially apprenticed to an Edinburgh wigmaker. In 1719, fascinated by the works of early Scottish poets, he set up as a bookseller. The bards of old, he believed, were the true interpreters of Scottish culture, now under threat:

> When these good old bards wrote, we had not made use of imported trimmings upon our clothes, nor of foreign embroidery in our writings. Their poetry is the product of their own country, not pilfered and spoiled in the transportation from abroad: their images are native, and their landscapes domestic; copied from those fields and meadows we every day behold.

In 1728, in an attempt to make native literature available in Edinburgh, Ramsay opened the first circulating library in Scotland. His *Tea Table Miscellany*, published in four volumes between 1724 and 1732, was an anthology of old and new Scots songs. His popularity was assured by *The Gentle Shepherd*, published in 1725. A pastoral drama set to music, the work

'An oyster cellar in Leith', painted by John Burnet (1784–1868). (*NGS*)

established the ballad-opera tradition in Scotland three years before Gay's *The Beggars' Opera*. Allan Ramsay paved the way for Scotland's more well-known poets, Robert Fergusson and Robert Burns.

Fergusson, one of the most gifted poets of his day, was born in Cap and Feather Close in Edinburgh in 1750. The son of an Aberdeenshire clerk, Robert was intended to read Divinity at St Andrews University. When his father died, however, he abandoned his studies and walked to Edinburgh to search for a job. At eighteen he became the family breadwinner working as a copyist in the office of the clerk of the Commissary Court. He penned his first poem at the age of twenty-two. Called 'The Daft Days', it was about the life and squalor of his native city. Fergusson's masterpiece, however, was 'Auld Reekie', a racy survey of eighteenth-century Edinburgh. Describing a typical day, Fergusson includes portraits of local characters, including the ladies of the night:

> Near some lamp-post, wi' dowy face,
> We' heavy een, and sour grimace,
> Stands she that beauty lang had kend
> Whoredom her trade, and vice her end.

Fergusson, like many of the 'literati' was a member of one of Edinburgh's numerous clubs. In 1772, he was elected to the Cape Club, whose members included the artist Alexander Runciman and the landscape painter Alexander Nasmyth. Over suppers of oysters and gin, ale and dried salt haddock, the Cape Club met regularly in James Mann's Tavern in Craig Close off Edinburgh's High Street.

In his tragically short life, Fergusson reawakened the tradition of Scottish poetry. But sadly he became a religious maniac, and after a fall that damaged mind and body, died in a madhouse on 17 October 1774 at the age of twenty-four.

After the Union the Edinburgh City Council agreed that if their city, no longer a political capital, was to prosper as a British city, it must grow. In 1759, the Nor Loch was drained and a bridge was built to link the Old Town on Castle Hill with the rich plains to the north. A New Town was to be built, an ideal city, laid out rationally, symmetrically and with elegance. James Craig, a little known architect, aged twenty-seven, submitted the winning plan. His uncle was James Thomson, the poet who wrote the words of 'Rule Britannia'.

Craig conceived the New Town on a grand scale. His was to be a town to equal London in elegance and stature. The street names, George Street, Frederick Street, Princes Street, Charlotte Square, purposely reflected the happy harmony that, thanks to the Hanoverian monarchy, existed in Britain. The design was classical: Edinburgh was to be the Athens of the North. Pastiches of ancient Greece were to grace Calton Hill. Edinburgh's Acropolis was later to have its Parthenon in the shape of a National Monument. Designed by William Playfair, the Monument was begun in 1824 to commemorate the Napoleonic Wars but was never completed. The New Observatory, also designed by Playfair, was Edinburgh's Temple of the Winds; Thomas Hamilton's design for a new Royal High School, the Temple of Theseus. The philosophy of the Enlightenment was in no way revolutionary. The golden means of classical architecture reflected an age

A detail from 'The Clubbists', a drawing by Sir David Wilkie (1785–1841).   (*NGS*)

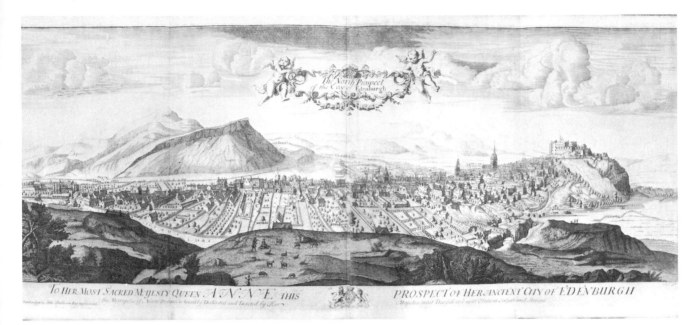

A prospect of Edinburgh from the 1797 edition of Slezer's *Theatrum Scotiae*. (*NLS*)

James Craig (*c* 1740–95), architect in 1767 of the winning plan for the New Town of Edinburgh. (*CAC*)

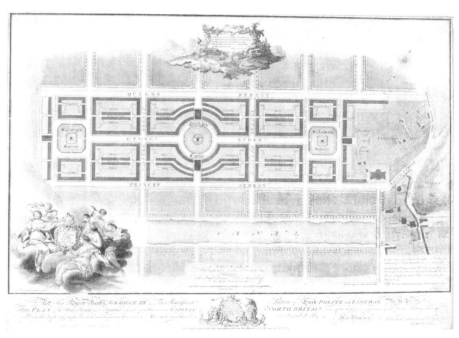

that sought social and intellectual balance. A monument to the belief in reason, progress and gentility, Scotland's capital city still reflects the inheritance of the Enlightenment, a city that praises education and propriety, repudiates the vernacular, yet asserts a Scottishness.

With the building of the New Town, Edinburgh's social classes divided for the first time. Lawyers and judges, made important and wealthy by the Treaty of Union, deserted the Old Town for the New.

David Hume was born in Edinburgh on 26 April 1711. Like many of the Enlightenment, his education was somewhat haphazard for he decided from

The New Town was spacious and elegant. 'A Dining Room Scene', by the Edinburgh-born Alexander Carse, shows a typical interior. (*SG*) (*BQ, below*)

an early age that all knowledge was derived from experience and refused to train formally for any profession. He was the first man in Britain to make a living as a man of letters.

In 1734, aged twenty-three, Hume took himself off to France. For the next three years, he worked on his *Treatise on Human Nature* expounding his theory of knowledge, but the book received scant attention. By 1749, he was in London, having spent a further year on the Continent, and two years later he published *The Enquiry Concerning the Principles of Morals*, quickly followed by his *Political Discourses*. Although orthodox thinkers did not take kindly to him, Hume appealed to the general public and he returned to the town of his birth a prosperous and contented man:

> I have fifty pounds a year, a hundred pounds worth of books, a great store of linens and fine clothes, and near a hundred pounds in my pocket, along with order, frugality, a strong spirit of independency, good health, a contented humour, and an unabating love of study. In these circumstances, I must esteem myself one of the happy and fortunate, and so far from being willing to draw my ticket over again in the lottery of life, there are very few prizes with which I would make an exchange.

David Hume (1711–76), philosopher and historian.   (*SNPG*)

Hume became Keeper of the Advocates Library in Edinburgh. It contained over 30,000 books, among them a copy of every volume published since 1710. With this wonderful source material to hand Hume turned to history, which he believed was in essence the outward manifestation of the progress of the mind. History was, in his own words, 'Philosophy teaching examples'. The first volume of his *History* was published in 1754. The book was an instant success and established Hume's reputation once and for all. But restless, and disillusioned with Edinburgh, Hume tried twice more to live in London. On each occasion he became bored by the company of 'the barbarians who inhabit the banks of the Thames'. By 1769 he was back in Edinburgh for good. But his health was declining and in 1776, at the age of sixty-five, David Hume died.

Hume had been proud to be Scottish. Throughout his life he spoke a Scots more broad than Robert Burns. He once remarked to a friend:

> Is it not strange that at a time when we have lost our princes, our parliaments, our independent government, even the presence of our chief nobility, are unhappy in our accent and pronunciation, speak a very corrupt dialect of tongue, which we make use of; is it not strange, I say, that in these circumstances, we should really be the people most distinguished for literature in Europe?

Allan Ramsay (1713–84), painter. (*SNPG*)

The written English of the 'literati' was precise and formal. Hume, like many of his contemporaries, even sent his manuscripts to English friends to ensure that his Scotticisms were removed. The problem of correct pronunciation and vocabulary became an obsession. For Lowland Scotland after the Union still spoke Braid Scots. A vigorous, expressive language, akin to Old English and given its greatest expression by Robert Burns, Braid Scots had its own vocabulary, idiom and pronunciation. Indeed during the first sessions of the new British Parliament the English members found their Scottish colleagues unintelligible.

In 1754 the Select Society of Edinburgh founded by Allan Ramsay, the son of the poet, decided to help Scots improve their mode of speech. Thomas Sheridan, father of the noted dramatist, was invited from London to give elocution lessons. He constructed a course that covered all aspects of speech – articulation, pronunciation, emphasis, pauses and stops, as he called them, pitch and management of voice. In 1787, Professor James Beattie of Aberdeen University published *Scotticisms, arranged in Alphabetical Order, designed to correct Improprieties of Speech and Writing*, for the benefit of those wishing to purge themselves of the language of their forefathers.

Thomas Sheridan, father of Richard Sheridan, who wrote *The School for Scandal*.   (*BM*)

During the Enlightenment, Scotland produced some of the finest writers of English poetry and the English novel. James Thomson, the son of the local parish minister, was born in Ednam in 1700. He rejected his planned future in the Kirk and at the age of twenty-five took himself off to London. His poem 'Winter' was published in 1726, the first poem in English to take nature as its theme. 'Winter' was followed up by poems on the other three seasons. Thomson later wrote 'The Masque of Alfred', which included 'Rule Britannia'.

Tobias Smollett was born in Dunbartonshire in 1721. He turned his back on a promising career in medicine and went to London at the age of eighteen. In 1748, his first successful novel, *Roderick Random*, was published and he went on to pen *Peregrine Pickle* and *Humphrey Clinker* as well as a *History of England*.

The most famous of these Augustans, primarily because of his association with Dr Samuel Johnson, was James Boswell. Typical of many Scots of his day, Boswell was reared in one culture and spent his entire life trying hard to assimilate another. Many of the vices he exhibited throughout his life – his snobbery, his boasts, his touchiness – were a result of never quite fitting in to the society of England of which he so craved to be part.

Thomas Carlyle, born in Ecclefechan in Dumfriesshire in 1795, continued the literary drift south. He lived over half his life in London where he was fêted for his histories.

For those who chose to remain in Scotland life during the Enlightenment was sophisticated and convivial. Most of the 'literati' belonged to one or more of the many literary and social clubs. The soirée was another social device that kept men of differing intellectual disciplines in touch with one another. Over many glasses of claret, ideas were exchanged, knowledge broadened. Drink was a vital ingredient in eighteenth-century Edinburgh. Most respectable people started the day with a 'morning glass' of ale, followed by claret served with breakfast. By about eleven-thirty, it was time to visit Edinburgh's taverns. The closes, or alleyways, that ran off the High Street were full of hostelries. In polite circles, dinner was served in the early afternoon. Claret, champagne, brandy and whisky were liberally on hand during the meal and drinking would continue apace for the rest of the day.

Lord Kames, one of the Lords of Session, was a typical Man of Reason. Schooled in the law, versed in letters, he was also an historian and agriculturalist. Like most of the Lords of Session, Kames stubbornly continued to speak the Scots tongue and was a hard drinker. Even while trying cases, bottles of strong port were set down beside the bench with glasses, carafes of water and biscuits. In his less demanding moments Kames also dabbled in the new almost exclusively Scottish sciences of sociology and economics – political economy as it was then termed.

On 9 March 1776, two volumes, of over 500 pages each, were published in London. The cost of the two books was £1 16s and there was no great rush to buy them. The work, *An Inquiry into the Nature and Causes of the Wealth of Nations* was written by a fifty-three-year-old Scot, Adam Smith. Since publication, more than 200 years ago, Smith's *Wealth of Nations* has never been out of print. Adam Smith was born on 5 June 1723 in Kirkcaldy in Fife. His father was a Writer to the Signet, a Scottish solicitor. At the age of fourteen he went to Glasgow University, where he was greatly influenced by Francis Hutcheson, the Professor of Moral Philosophy, who impressed

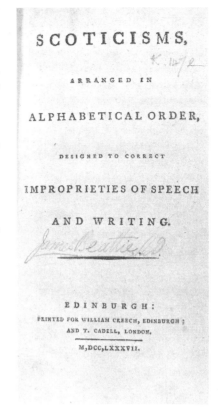

SCOTICISMS,

ARRANGED IN

ALPHABETICAL ORDER,

DESIGNED TO CORRECT

IMPROPRIETIES OF SPEECH

AND WRITING.

EDINBURGH:

PRINTED FOR WILLIAM CREECH, EDINBURGH;
AND T. CADELL, LONDON.

M,DCC,LXXXVII.

Such was the obsession of James Beattie, author of *Scoticisms*, that he refused to allow his son to be educated in Scotland, determined he would grow up a Briton. (*NLS*)

James Boswell (1740–95) entered London society in 1760. He met Samuel Johnson in 1763 and brought him to Scotland ten years later. (*SNPG*)

'Dowie's Tavern' by George
Cattermole. (*CAC*)

the young man with his common sense and optimistic view of human nature.

Adam Smith managed to win a small Exhibition to Balliol College, Oxford, a college much favoured by Scots, in part because it had been founded by John Balliol, father of the hapless Scottish King. There Smith made excellent use of the college's fine library. In 1751, the University of Glasgow elected Smith Professor of Logic. Four years later he became Professor of Moral Philosophy and remained in the post for the next nine years. He published his first major work, *Theory of Moral Sentiments*, in 1759. It won him a European reputation overnight and resulted in his being made a doctor of law. When, however, Charles Townshend, the English politician suggested that Smith accompany him on a Grand Tour of Europe, Smith could not resist the generous terms offered, and he abandoned the academic life. In France, he met the Physiocrats, or Economistes, as they were often called, who believed in setting up an economic system that would operate through its own intrinsic harmonies and balances. Smith was much impressed by their 'laissez-faire, let alone', philosophy and in the spring of 1767 returned to his native Kirkcaldy to work on his own ideas of political economy. Every morning, he dictated to a secretary, and after five years the manuscript of *The Wealth of Nations* was complete, although Smith spent a further three years revising the work before agreeing to its publication. He became a Commissioner of Customs and moved to Edinburgh, where he lived a happy and successful life, and in 1787 was elected Lord Rector of Glasgow University. A few days before his death on 17 July 1790, he ordered that all his unfinished manuscripts be destroyed, regretting that he had done so little with his life. He was buried in the graveyard of the Canongate Church in Edinburgh. He left behind a book that, apart from the Bible and *Das Kapital*, perhaps did more than any other to change the Western world.

Adam Smith (1723–90), philosopher and economist.   (*SNPG*)

The Wealth of Nations is not a book about Smith's native Scotland. It concerns Britain, with London as its capital. Nor is it simply a textbook in economics; but a history of the age in which Smith lived. He saw Britain as a country poised to experience revolutions, in agriculture and industry; but of limited trade, for he questioned the morality of merchants and feared Britain would become, as he termed it, 'a nation of shopkeepers'. To him the source of all wealth was labour, and society was held together by the division of that labour. People, Smith argued, bargained to help each other. Individuals made up society; but unconsciously they worked for the common good. The new industrialized world would be one of materialism for the masses. Enlightened self-interest would be its mainspring, but regulated by what Smith called the 'Invisible Hand', namely God; and God had in mind for human society the wealth and welfare of everyone. In Smith's scheme of things, happiness was what political economy was all about.

Adam Smith's work is still one of the most important books ever written. In Victorian times, it was revered in Britain, and it was only when political power became more centralized and began to unite government with big business that the great age of Adam Smith's concept of society came to an end. In recent times, it has become the Bible of post-war industrialized Japan.

William Robertson (1721–93), the historian who, like so many 'literati', was a son of the manse.   (*SNPG*)

Throughout the period of the Scottish Enlightenment, Scotsmen proved themselves to be methodical and practical thinkers. William Robertson, often called the Father of the Enlightenment because he placed so many students on the road to greatness, was one of the finest historians of the age. In 1762, he became Principal of Edinburgh University and as such not only taught but furthered plans for new accommodation and helped to create Edinburgh University's Old College. William Robertson was one of the first historians to work from original source material. In 1759, he published a *History of Scotland During the Reigns of Mary and James VI* which set new standards of scholarship and in its day was the best history in existence of any nation. Ten years later he wrote an equally celebrated *History of Charles V*, which was followed in 1791 by a *History of America*. His concepts of education and scholarship became the basis of education in the United States.

Scholarship during the Enlightenment was not the prerogative of the Lowland Scot. Sociology as a science was the invention of a Highlander,

Adam Fergusson. Realizing that the Highlander's way of life was earmarked for extinction, Fergusson sought to praise this ancient Celtic society. He was born in Logierait near Pitlochry in 1723, and served as a chaplain in a Black Watch regiment between 1745 and 1757, witnessing at first hand the government-inspired destruction of the Highlands. David Hume, a Lowlander, condemned the clan system; Fergusson was better able to see its merits. Appointed Professor of Natural Philosophy and later of Moral Philosophy at Edinburgh, he made a careful examination of Highland society, then published three books to set out his theories: *Essay on Civil Society* in 1766, *Institutes of Moral Philosophy* in 1772 and finally *Principles of Political Science.*

Fergusson claimed that in the clan system there was no social gulf between the chief and his clan. In smaller societies, however primitive, a

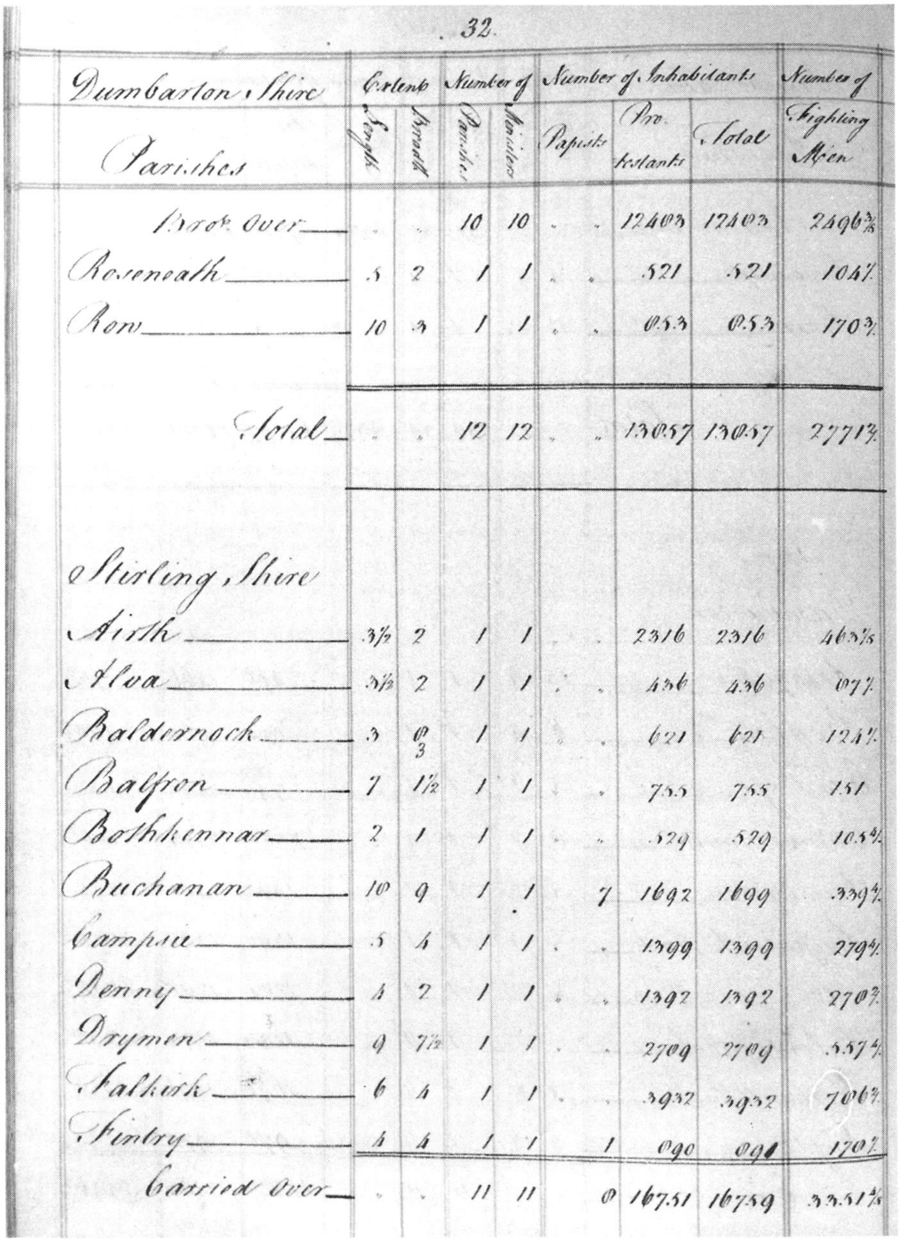

32.

Dumbarton Shire	Extent		Number of		Number of Inhabitants			Number of
Parishes	Length	Breadth	Parishes	Ministers	Papists	Protestants	Total	Fighting Men
Brot. Over	.	.	10	10	.	. 12403	12403	2496 3/5
Roseneath	5	2	1	1	.	. 521	521	104 1/5
Row	10	3	1	1	.	. 853	853	170 3/5
Total	.	.	12	12	.	. 13057	13057	2771 2/5
Stirling Shire								
Airth	3½	2	1	1	.	2316	2316	463 1/5
Alva	3½	2	1	1	.	436	436	87 1/5
Baldernock	3	2/3	1	1	.	621	621	124 1/5
Balfron	7	1½	1	1	.	755	755	151
Bothkennar	2	1	1	1	.	529	529	105 4/5
Buchanan	10	9	1	1	7	1692	1699	339 4/5
Campsie	5	4	1	1	.	1399	1399	279 4/5
Denny	4	2	1	1	.	1392	1392	278 2/5
Drymen	9	7½	1	1	.	2709	2709	541 4/5
Falkirk	6	4	1	1	.	3932	3932	786 2/5
Fintry	4	4	1	1	1	890	891	178 1/5
Carried Over	.	.	11	11	8	16751	16759	3351 4/5

Alexander Webster (1707–84) produced his Census with the help of Robert Wallace (1697–1771), a minister also concerned with the social problems relating to population. (*NLS*)

more perfect relationship between the individual and society was to be found while a tradition of fighting made for better social cohesion. His claim that all was not wrong with Scotland's Celtic traditions made little impact in Britain but Fergusson was highly respected in the new United States of America and his works were also, during his lifetime, translated into French, German and even Russian.

During the Enlightenment the Scots invented statistics, and the Reverend Alexander Webster produced the world's first census. The son of the minister of Edinburgh's Tolbooth Kirk, Webster excelled in mathematics. He succeeded his father and in 1753 was Moderator of the General Assembly. Then, with another minister, Robert Wallace, Webster tried to ascertain what nobody up to that time knew – the exact population of Scotland. The census, relying on local ministers to do the count, as well as collecting data from the missionary charity schools set up by the Society for Promoting Christian Knowledge, was completed in 1755. Scotland's population amounted to 1,265,380. One half lived north of the River Tay, and nearly a third of the country spoke only Gaelic.

Sir John Sinclair of Ulbster in Caithness resolved to make a thorough survey of every parish. A circular containing 160 questions concerning history, geography, as well as the number of livestock, dovecots, and mineral springs to be found, was sent to every minister. The object was to find out what the people of Scotland had, with a view to creating in future their wealth, health and happiness. The first volume of his *Statistical Account* was published in 1791. Seven years later the final volume appeared, concluding the findings of two hundred thousand letters of inquiry.

Edinburgh became one of Britain's great publishing cities. By 1790, the

Sir John Sinclair of Ulbster (1754–1835) succeeded to extensive estates in 1770. An MP for thirty-one years, he was President of the Board of Agriculture for eight years, as well as instrumental in preparing the first *Statistical Account of Scotland*. (NGS)

Encyclopaedia Britannica was not published until 1781, with Andrew Bell (1726–1809), as co-proprietor. (NLS)

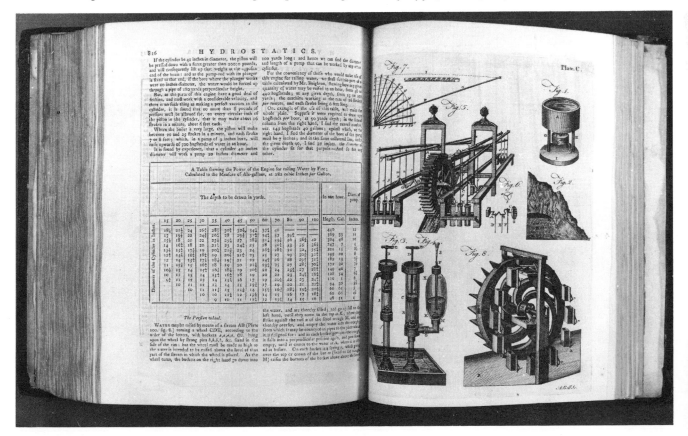

William Creech (1745–1815), another son of the manse, published the works of Adam Smith as well as Robert Burns. He was Lord Provost of Edinburgh from 1811 to 1813. (*SNPG*)

Robert Burns (1759–96), as painted by Alexander Nasmyth (1758–1840), a pupil of Allan Ramsay. (*SNPG*)

Sir David Wilkie, a minister's son from Fife who became one of London's most famous painters. (*NGS*)

town could boast sixteen printers, among them William Smellie, who was also the editor and chief contributor to the *Encyclopaedia Britannica*, founded in 1768 and yet another example of the desire of the age to put down in factual, logical form what man knew. A less philanthropic publisher was William Creech who, by buying copyrights for a pittance, made himself a fortune; one of his most successful clients was Robert Burns.

Robert Burns arrived in Edinburgh in 1786 to arrange for the publication of his poetry, which had proved hugely successful when published in Kilmarnock. The son of a tenant farmer, Burns was born in Alloway in Ayrshire on 25 January 1759. The boy's education had been sound. Robert's father and a few neighbours had hired the services of John Murdoch to teach their children, and under Murdoch Burns was steeped in the poetry of Thomas Gray and Shakespeare and learnt a little French.

By 1784, Robert Burns had become the tenant of Mossgiel Farm near Mauchline; but his real love was poetry, and the Edinburgh 'literati' quickly took to this sparkling conversationalist, full of wit and learning. The Earl of Glencairn became Burns's patron and arranged for the gentlemen of the Caledonian Hunt to pay for the printing of his second collection of poems. The publication of *The Edinburgh Edition* by William Creech proved Burns to be one of the outstanding British poets of his day.

Burns was a writer of genius, Scotland's greatest poet. His satire is earthy and biting, and his narrative poems, like 'Tam o'Shanter', racy and brilliantly descriptive. As a song writer, Burns ranks among the greatest the British Isles has produced. In both poetry and song he captured for posterity a rural Scotland that was quickly to vanish and his love of rural life proved universal. Apart from William Shakespeare, no other British poet has been translated into so many languages.

In 1788, Burns took land at Ellisland, near Dumfries. The skills of the farmer, however, eluded him and within three years he became an exciseman in Dumfries, where he lived until his death in 1796 at the tragically young age of thirty-seven. Robert Burns died of rheumatic fever, contracted after falling asleep by the roadside on his way home from a heavy drinking session. He was buried with full military honours – as befit a member of a volunteer regiment, raised to protect Britain from the disease of the French Revolution. In July 1801, five years after his death, the first Burns Club was formed at Greenock. Burns quickly became a legend, and in the years since his death both the man and his poetry have become scapegoats for a nation's nagging sense of inferiority. The schizophrenia of identity that bedevils many a Scot finds expression in the 'here's-tae-us, wha's-like-us' celebration.

Others during the Enlightenment recorded the passing of rural Scotland not in poetry but in painting. David Wilkie, son of David Wilkie, minister of Cults, concentrated on homely themes in his native Fife and is remembered for his first important work, 'Pitlessie Fair'. Henry Raeburn, born in Stockbridge in Edinburgh in 1756, became one of the Enlightenment's greatest portrait painters. In his studio, in York Place in Edinburgh, open between the hours of nine to five precisely, he produced some of Britain's greatest portraiture. He also designed one of Edinburgh's finest residential streets, which he named after his wife, Ann, and presented her with the plans as a birthday present.

Even more successful, however, was Allan Ramsay, the son of the poet.

Having studied painting in Edinburgh, London and Italy, he worked in Edinburgh for eighteen years. In 1756, he became the Royal portrait painter. Ramsay was so much in demand that he delegated a deal of his commissions to lesser artists. Nevertheless he was the first major portrait painter Britain, let alone Scotland, had produced.

Yet the greatest Scotsman of the age was Sir Walter Scott. The inventor of the historical novel, Scott more than any other individual brought together Scotland's past and welded it into the coherent entity to which the nation still clings and which many outside Scotland believe to be reality. He was born in 1771 in a house at the top of College Wynd in Edinburgh. His father was a well-to-do lawyer and because the young Walter contracted polio amid the relative squalor of the Old Town, his parents moved to the New Town elegance of George Square. He left the old Edinburgh High School with, as he said . . .

Sir Henry Raeburn (1756–1823), like Wilkie, became a famous painter, producing some 600 portraits including all the notables of his day.   (NGS)

> . . . a great quantity of general information, ill-arranged indeed, and collected without system, yet deeply impressed upon my mind; readily assorted by my power of connexion and memory, and gilded, if I may be permitted to say so, by a vivid and active imagination.

His imagination had been stirred by his childhood sojourns at his grand-father's farm at Sandyknowe in the Borders, but his studies, both at the High School and at Edinburgh University, were interrupted by recurring child-hood illness, and in 1786, aged fifteen, he was apprenticed to his father's law firm. It was then, at the house of Professor Adam Fergusson, that Scott met Robert Burns.

He began to visit the Borders in search of antiquities and local ballads, providing material for *Minstrelsy of the Scottish Border* which he published in 1802. In 1799 he became Sheriff of Selkirk. The duties were light, affording time for writing, and before the age of forty Walter Scott had penned all his greatest poems – 'The Lay of the Last Minstrel', 'Marmion', and 'The Lady of the Lake'. Outraged by the Anglomania of the age, he deliberately stuck to the Scottish tongue, encouraged in this by the Irish writer Maria Edgeworth. After all, as Scott himself wrote:

Walter Scott (1771–1832), as a young man.   (FA)

> Every Scottishman has a pedigree. It is a national prerogative as unalienable as his pride and poverty.

Already a poet of distinction, Scott turned to novel writing, preserving in his first and best the memory of a Scotland that had passed.

In 1811, Scott bought a small and unattractive farmhouse near Melrose for £4000. He was to transform the estate, at a cost of over £25,000, into Abbotsford. It took fourteen years to complete the building and landscaping. Inside Scott crammed Abbotsford with antiquarian memorabilia, Flora MacDonald's pocket book, a quaich (cup) that had once been owned by the Young Pretender, Rob Roy's sporran, a tumbler Robert Burns had used, a crucifix once owned by Mary Queen of Scots, even a fragment of oatmeal, uneaten by a starving Highlander who had fought at Culloden.

Walter Scott had required large advances from his publishers Archibald Constable to pay for Abbotsford. When Constable crashed Walter Scott fell with him. He had lived on credit and was unaware of his debts, which amounted to £116,838 11s 3d. Ruin stared him in the face; but Scott was determined to weather the storm:

Adam Fergusson (1723–1816), sociologist.   (SNPG)

Archibald Constable (1774–1827), the publisher whose bankruptcy in 1826 forced Walter Scott (*below*), created a baronet six years earlier, virtually to write himself to death. (*SNPG*) (*CAC, below*)

> I have lost a large fortune, but I have ample competence remaining behind, and so I am just like an oak that loses its leaves and keeps its branches . . . Others will regret my losses more than I do.

Offers of financial help poured in but Scott was adamant. He wrote book after book to pay off his debts himself.

In a serious attempt to preserve the past Walter Scott started the Blair-Adam Club. Each year from 1816 until 1830, he and his friends spent a weekend in June in Kinross in Fife. From Friday until Tuesday morning, the group sought out Scotland's history; Loch Leven Castle, that had once been Mary Queen of Scots' prison, Castle Campbell, Dunfermline's great Abbey associated with Malcolm III and his Queen, Margaret, and St Andrews Cathedral and Castle were all visited, examined and discussed. The Reverend John Thompson, a member of the Club, painted the places visited, creating in oil the romantic image of Scott's historical novels.

In 1823 Scott also helped found the Bannatyne Club to republish some of Scotland's older literary and historical works. The thirty-one members were responsible for the printing, and therefore salvaging, of the few historical sources of a nation's past. In the nine years during which Scott was President of the Club, forty-three volumes of historical and literary texts were produced. The old Scottish institution of the Club was adopted in the service of a new almost scientific concept of the nature and use of historical evidence. The desire to preserve the nation's past became a national movement. In Glasgow, the Maitland Club was founded in 1828, with an original membership of fifty. Like the Bannatyne, the Maitland Club was fired by a sense of purpose – to make available to present and future generations the source material of Scotland's history.

This phenomenon of antiquarian clubs was unique and explained in part by the political and social position in which Scots found themselves. In 1780 the 11th Earl of Buchan founded the Society of Antiquaries of Scotland and carried out restoration work at Dryburgh and Inchcolm Abbeys. In his own words, he claimed:

> Such has been the accumulation of disgrace and discomfiture that has fallen on us as a people since the last wretched twenty-four years of the British annals, that I turn with aversion from the filthy picture that is before my eyes and look back for consolation to the times which are past.

Dozens of local antiquarian societies followed.

For over a century after union with England, nobody had seen the Honours of Scotland, the crown, sword and sceptre of kingship. On 4 February 1817, Scott and his colleagues forced open two sealed doors in Edinburgh Castle and discovered a large oak chest in which were found Scotland's ancient Honours that no British monarch since Charles II had bothered to claim. Their discovery, with the visit of George IV three years later, crowned a golden age.

Sir Walter Scott stage-managed the Royal Visit which, he believed, should be 'the codification of Scottishness'. He wrote a pamphlet, *Hints, Addressed to the Inhabitants of Edinburgh and Others* to advise Scots:

> Let our king see us as nature and education have made us – an orderly people whose feelings, however warm, are rarely suffered to outspring the restraint of judgment – whose blessings have always been (like their

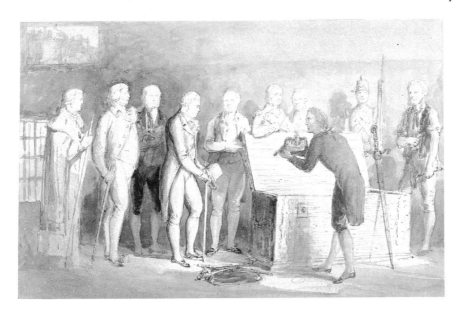

Walter Scott and his colleagues discovering the 'Honours of Scotland', the Crown, Sceptre and Sword of State, which are now on view in Edinburgh Castle.   (*NGS*)

curses) 'not loud, but deep' . . . We are The Clan, and our king is The Chief.

Scott was a leading light of the European Romantic movement that sprung from the new liberal and secular view of man. The Royal Visit would be a Celtic pageant, a celebration of the culture of Gaelic Scotland that had brought fame to the Scottish nation through the literary works of James Macpherson. The alleged translations of the poems of Ossian by Macpherson created a literary stir at home and abroad and inspired Goethe and Italian poets. Macpherson's *Fragments of Ancient Poetry*, published in 1760, gave a massive impetus to the growing interest in Britain in the Scottish Highlands, and Sir Walter Scott regarded George IV's visit as the royal seal of approval to the romantic Celtic revival.

Over 300,000 Scots, a seventh of the country's entire population, converged on Edinburgh for the Royal Visit in August 1822. The sixty-year-old monarch stayed with the Duke of Buccleuch at Dalkeith, as Holyrood was thought too uncomfortable and depressing. The Duke was only sixteen years old so the King thoughtfully brought his own cooks and servants with him.

On the first night there were firework displays, and the nobility of Scotland, anxious that the best of impressions be made, were glad to note that the ordinary folk of Edinburgh did not disgrace themselves. The daughter of Grant of Rothiemurchus noted, 'with their clean best clothes, the common people seem to have put on their politest manners'.

On 17 August, the King held court at Holyrood, and wore a kilt. Although proud of his legs he was advised out of decorum to wear flesh-coloured tights. Sir William Curtis, the Lord Mayor of London, who hailed from Wapping, was similarly attired for the state occasion.

Five days later there was a grand procession from Holyrood to Edinburgh Castle, with the newly-found Honours of Scotland given pride of place. George IV braved the rain to wave to the city's populace from the Castle's battlements and remarked as he surveyed the New Town:

> Good God what a fine sight, I had no conception that there was such a scene in the world, and to find it in my own dominions.

On 23 August, there was a military review on Portobello Sands and on the same evening a ball in the city's Assembly Rooms. It was marred, however, by a Highland guest accidentally dropping his pistol on a royal foot. The injured monarch stayed only an hour and a half before a painful toe sent him hobbling back to Dalkeith.

Few in Scotland, given the political feelings of the day, viewed George IV's two week visit as anything but an exercise in public relations, as Lord Cockburn remarked:

> In giving the people a spectacle at which they gazed exactly as they would have done at a Chinese Emperor with his gongs, elephants and mandarins, his visit accomplished all that could be reasonably anticipated.

The Scotsman noted in its editorial:

> None can deny that His Majesty's visit was an act of gracious kindness and condescension on his part; but we are not of the number of those who expect that it will be productive of any considerable or solid advantage.

Those critical of the Royal Visit had cause for concern. The flowering of intellectual talent in Scotland had been brought about in large part by a crisis of identity. The great literature and art of the Enlightenment was produced against a curious background of conflict, confidence and doubt: a situation not unlike the 'stasis' that had produced a golden age in ancient Greece and more recently the Renaissance in the Italian city states. Scotland had been torn apart during the Covenanting period and by the eighteenth century the theology of Calvinism was in question. The Kirk that had done so much to educate the mind of the nation was divided. Economically, Scotland had suffered William's Seven Lean Years and the disastrous attempt to found a colony at Darien had wounded, though not killed, pride and confidence. The Union with England had been the culmination of a century of strife and hardship. The beginnings of the revolutions in agriculture and industry prompted doubt and fear for the future. The obliteration of the past by an overpowering English culture made a nation feel uncertain. Jacobites took to arms to express their fears; some took to the more peaceful pen and brush, and by so doing benefited mankind as well as Scotland. Others, impressed by the revolutions in France and America, came into conflict with a British political system that refused to reform itself.

13

Of Government and Men

IN 1707, THE SCOTS had agreed to their system of government being dismantled, but the Treaty of Union made no provision for an adequate replacement. Instead of the 159 who had been elected to the Estates, 45 Scottish MPs now served at Westminster. As in England, those with the vote in Scotland were the freeholders; but an act of the old Scottish parliament made for widespread electoral corruption in Scotland's counties. In 1681, the Estates had granted the right to vote in Scotland to those with property valued at £400 Scots. By an ingenious device invented by lawyers, people of property could easily multiply their votes, by surrendering the land charter to the crown and then appoint a number of friends to whom the crown then parcelled out lots. At the end of the eighteenth century, the total number of real voters in the counties of Scotland was only 1390, with an estimated additional 1201 fictitious voters.

The burghs of Scotland were unfairly represented. Glasgow, with a population of over 77,000, was, for parliamentary election purposes joined with the towns of Renfrew, Rutherglen and Dumbarton to elect a single MP. He, in turn, was chosen by 32 members of the Town Councils, who in fact elected themselves. Edinburgh, Scotland's largest city, was represented by 1 MP, chosen by just 33 people. The other 14 members that represented Scotland's burghs were chosen by a grand total of 65 delegates, all of whom were self-elected Town Councillors. By the end of the century, when there were 2,000,000 people living in Scotland, the nation's 45 Westminster MPs were chosen by only 3844 Scots.

The election of Scotland's representatives to the House of Lords was a hollow formality. The English ministry of the day sent up a list of the sixteen Scottish peers they wanted and the Secret Service fund was used to buy support from Scottish nobles. Under British Prime Ministers like Sir Robert Walpole the affairs of Scotland were managed. Money and position were used to keep the Scots subservient and willing. The English-dominated government of Britain did not need to send Englishmen north to Scotland to have done what they wished; there were Scotsmen enough eager to place their country under England's political thumb.

Archibald Campbell, younger brother of the 2nd Duke of Argyll, who as part of the family bribe to support Union had been made the Earl of Islay in 1706 and later, in 1743, succeeded his brother as 3rd Duke, together with

David Stuart Erskine, 11th Earl of Buchan (1742–1829), founded the Society of Antiquaries in Scotland in 1780 and helped to free the election of Scottish peers from government interference. (*SNPG*)

John Campbell, 2nd Duke of Argyll (1678–1743). (*SNPG*)

Archibald Campbell, Earl of Islay (1682–1761), succeeded his brother as 3rd Duke of Argyll. (*SNPG*)

Henry Dundas, 1st Viscount Melville (1742–1811). (*SP*)

Duncan Forbes, Lord Advocate from 1725, dispensed patronage and blatantly rigged elections.

Under the Union, the representation of Scotland and England had been based on the comparative wealth of the two countries, and with one twelfth of the MPs allocated to England, Scotland in terms of population was grossly under-represented. Forty-five Scots could achieve little of benefit to their country, faced with a solid English opposition of 513 members. When Scottish opposition did show itself, however, it often materially altered the face of British politics. Scottish votes were vital to the survival of any ministry in the eighteenth century, and the 'Scotch interest', as it was called could make or break governments. In the General Election of 1741 the 2nd Duke of Argyll openly opposed Walpole's war against Spain that had begun in 1739, and with his allies captured nearly half of Scotland's forty-five seats. By so doing, Argyll paved the way for Walpole's resignation in the following year. The 3rd Duke of Argyll succeeded at the age of sixty-one and, for nearly twenty years, kept the Scottish electorate an exclusive upper-class preserve.

After the Union, Scotland was ruled by lawyers. They were the agents that administered the policies of the British government. Scotland was politically unique, a country with an independent judiciary but no means of making her own laws: an executive without a legislature.

The Kirk was the other remaining bastion of Scottish nationhood. However, the Patronage Act of 1712 had restored to the nobility the right to choose ministers, a choice that in practice became political. By the 1760s, most ministers favoured lay patronage, since they themselves held office from a local lay patron, while a few belonged to the landed families and naturally supported the existing order. The Kirk thus became part of the tightly woven web of political power.

The greatest problem facing the Westminster parliament after the Union was how to raise revenue in Scotland. The Court of Exchequer, remodelled on English lines, was an attempt to ensure that rents due to the King and government taxes were paid. Commissioners of Supply, who had existed since 1667, were given new powers. They not only levied, 'Cess', the King's taxes, but looked after schools and maintained jails. In effect they were embryo county councils and continued to function until those bodies were officially set up in 1889.

When the 3rd Duke of Argyll died in 1761, Lord North and his ministry looked to Henry Dundas to act as a political manager. Dundas came from one of the smaller landed families, whose legal background had made them important. Sir James Dundas, who died in 1679, begat a legal dynasty. Four generations of sons that bore the Christian name Robert had held the top legal posts in Scotland, including Solicitor General, Lord Advocate and Lord President. Henry Dundas went to Edinburgh University and trained as an advocate. His father had died when he was twelve, and his mother, Ann Gordon, was the great influence on his life. In 1766, at the age of twenty-four, he became Solicitor General and began to wield undisputed power. Affable and pragmatic, he was the epitome of the eighteenth-century politician. By 1780, he personally controlled 12 out of the 45 Scottish seats and could ensure that, apart from 4 MPs, all the Scots supported Lord North's ministry.

World events, however, conspired to challenge his cosy political system. The American War of Independence brought about the final downfall of Lord North's administration in March 1782 and Dundas used his Westminster group to support North's successors in return for personal rewards. Dundas was made Treasurer of the British Navy, a Privy Councillor and granted the Keepership of the Scottish signet for life. By 1783, he had committed himself to William Pitt the Younger. In the General Election of 1784, Dundas delivered him 22 of the 45 Scottish seats.

Dundas was a genuinely popular despot, for he used his positions to reward those who did as he asked. When he became President of the Board of Control for India he awarded posts to Scots in the East India Company and secured pensions for relatives and friends. In 1792, Dundas used the Pension List of Scotland to give 175 pensions at a cost of £24,842. Most were granted to the wives of those in his political pocket. In 1802, he was made Viscount Melville and two years later became First Lord of the Admiralty. Within a year, however, Dundas was found out.

The British Admiralty was notoriously corrupt, and an inquiry in 1805 revealed that a Scot, Alexander Trotter, had used public funds to speculate on his own behalf. Dundas, aware of Trotter's indiscretion, was impeached. Although the monies had all been returned to the public purse, the scandal was enough to force Melville to resign in April 1805. The Scots could scarcely believe his fall. For all his faults, Viscount Melville had firmly established the Scots in British government, and the very fact that he became so powerful stopped much of the derision current in England about the Scots. With Henry Dundas to bargain with, nobody dared joke about Scotland any more!

The Dundas family continued to dominate Scottish politics. Robert, Melville's son, became political manager of Scotland, and the Viscount himself continued to have influence in his native land until he died in 1811.

Many Scots grew angry at the cynical management of their country. In 1768, the 11th Earl of Buchan openly condemned the way in which Scotland's sixteen representative peers were elected, and his protest encouraged others to take a hard look at a political system that was continuing to deny a say to increasingly important elements of society.

Because Scotland's traditional ruling class, the aristocracy now exercised minimal power, merchants, lawyers, academics and doctors increased in wealth and importance more rapidly than in England. But this rising class was still excluded even from burgh government. Edinburgh's burgh Council was the most important and typical. Lord Cockburn described how it operated:

> The council met in a low blackguard-looking room, very dark, and very dirty, with some dens off it for clerks. Within this pandemonium sat the town council, omnipotent, corrupt, impenetrable. Nothing was beyond its grasp, no variety of opinion disturbed its unanimity.

When any public work was to be undertaken in the city, a preference was given to councillors as a matter of course, and the council controlled the town's land and other sources of income.

The French Revolution was the catalyst that showed up latent antagonism. In the beginning the events in France were welcomed by all classes. To the labouring poor, in particular, many of whom had been ousted from the

John Wilson (1785–1854), 'Christopher North'. (*HA*)

Henry Thomas, Lord Cockburn (1779–1854), a critic of the wide powers of the Lord Advocate. (*FA*)

Robert Dundas, 2nd Viscount Melville (1771–1851). (*SNPG*)

John Kay (1742–1826), an Edinburgh barber turned caricaturist, produced some 900 drawings. Here he depicts two Edinburgh town councillors supervising the levelling of the High Street. (*SNPG*)

Ann Gordon, Henry Dundas's mother; she toured Edinburgh's bookshops in search of seditious literature, like Paine's *The Rights of Man*. (*SP*)

The grave of Neil Campbell from the island of Lewis in the Old Kildonan churchyard in what is now Winnipeg in Canada.

A monument at Pictou, Nova Scotia, commemorates the Scots from the *Hector* who settled in 1773, when thirty-three families and twenty-five single men arrived from Ullapool on Loch Broom.

At the Highland Village museum at Iona in Nova Scotia, Scots Canadians enact a 'milling-frolic', and sing the old songs as they shrink the tweed, as their Highland forefathers did. (*Author*)

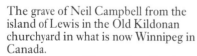

land by agricultural improvement, or, like the weavers, had witnessed wages drop with the onset of machines, the events in France were a revelation. When Thomas Paine published the first part of his book *The Rights of Man* in 1791, he became a hero. Over a million copies were sold and it was even translated into Gaelic.

In 1792, the London Corresponding Society was founded by an émigré Scottish shoemaker, Thomas Hardy. Later that year, Societies of Friends of the People sprung up throughout Scotland and attracted professional men as well as artisans. The leading light of the Glasgow association was Thomas Muir.

1792 proved to be a year of economic hardship in Scotland. A bad harvest sent the price of bread soaring and radicals of all classes were restless. In May, as a result of the second part of *The Rights of Man* being published, the government issued a Proclamation banning seditious meetings and publications, including Paine's much sought after treatise. On 4 June, the King's birthday, hungry crowds in Edinburgh burnt Henry Dundas in effigy, and Sheriff Pringle sent in the troops. The government's high-handedness was heavily censored by men like Colonel Norman MacLeod of MacLeod, the MP for Inverness, who wrote:

> The present ministry is extemely odious from three causes: the Proclamation; the resistance to the Borough reform; and the firing on the mob on the King's Birthday here for burning Dundas in effigy. The pension of £100 a year given immediately to Pringle the Sheriff who ordered the troops to fire and creating the Provost a Baronet, have greatly aggravated the insult. The conduct of Government seems a mixture of timidity and cunning; afraid of insurrections, they court and provoke them.

Few reformers, however, wanted revolution, as Colonel MacLeod noted:

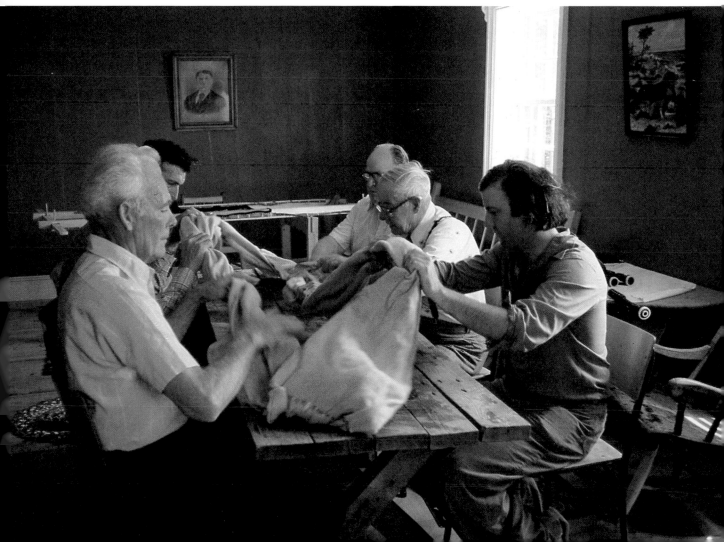

TO THE MEMORY OF
ANGUS MAC DONALD
HUGH MAC DONALD
JOHN MAC PHERSON
SOLDIERS OF PRINCE CHARLIE.
THEY FOUGHT FOR SCOTLAND IN THE
CLANRANALD REGIMENT AT THE
BATTLE OF CULLODEN IN 1746.
BORN IN MOIDART SCOTLAND 1712-16
CAME TO MOIDART NOVA SCOTIA 1790-91

I have attended two of their meeting, one in Glasgow and one here (Edinburgh); both composed of delegates from various associations. I found much order, much coolness and great desire for Reform in general. The people were neither very rich nor very poor; certainly not in the least like a rabble.

The first Convention of the Scottish Friends of the People opened in Edinburgh on 11 December 1792. Over 150 delegates representing 80 societies from 35 towns and villages attended. Their aim was to draw up a petition to send to the British Parliament in support of electoral reform.

Thomas Muir, a Glasgow barrister with a reputation as a man of principle, had helped organize many of the societies. He had also, before the Convention, been in contact with the United Irishmen movement, a group of professional men in Dublin also bent on political reform. Against the advice of his colleagues, Muir read an address the United Irishmen had sent which urged the Edinburgh Convention to 'openly, actively and urgently' will Parliamentary reform.

On the last day of the Convention, a Petition to parliament was read and approved; but it was suggested that the Convention arm itself so as to be able to help magistrats put down riots that might occur in support of reform. An emotional evening session ended with delegates swearing the French oath, 'To live free or die'.

The government at Westminster misread the situation. The Home Office files bulged with reports from spies. As informers were paid piece-rate many had put down gossip as fact, and rumour spread that the delegates were preparing themselves for insurrection. The government panicked and on 2 January 1793 arrested Muir.

His trial opened in Edinburgh on 30 August 1793. He was accused of making seditious speeches, of circulating Paine's *Rights of Man* and of defending as well as reading the Address from the United Irishmen. Muir turned down an offer made by Henry Erskine, the Dean of the Faculty of Advocates, to defend him and conducted his own defence:

> I am accused of sedition and yet can prove by thousands of witnesses that I warned the people of that crime, exhorted them to adopt none but measures which were constitutional, and entreated them to connect liberty with knowledge and both with morality.

The trial lasted sixteen hours, the evidence heard by five judges and a jury. But the proceedings were dominated by Lord Braxfield, of whom Lord Cockburn wrote:

> Strong built and dark, with rough eyebrows, powerful eyes, threatening lips, and a low growling voice, he was like a formidable blacksmith. His accent and his dialect were exaggerated Scotch; his language, like his thoughts, short, strong, and conclusive. He was the Jeffreys of Scotland. 'Let them bring me prisoners, and I'll find them law', used to be openly stated as his suggestion, when an intended political prosecution was marred by anticipated difficulties.

Muir's flowery address to the jury lasted three hours but fell upon deaf ears.

> I have devoted myself to the cause of the people. It is a good cause, it shall ultimately prevail, it shall ultimately triumph.

Braxfield, who had arrogantly dismissed the evidence of Muir's twenty-one witnesses, summed up:

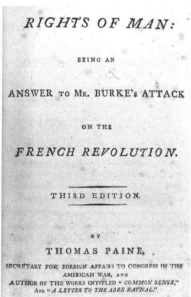

Thomas Paine (1737–1809). His *The Rights of Man*, published in two parts (1790–2), greatly influenced Scottish as well as English radicals.   (*SNPG*) (*NLS, below*)

A cairn near Arisaig in Nova Scotia poignantly recalls how the outlawing of clan society after the Battle of Culloden in 1746 made many Scots take boat for Canada. (*Author*)   The Scottish military tradition also helped win and settle Britain's Empire. Highlanders fought in the American Revolution and at Waterloo in 1815 (*right*). (*SG*)
During the Indian Mutiny (*below*), Scottish military commanders and soldiers helped restore British authority. The 93rd Highlanders are shown storming the Shah Najaf in 1857. (*NTS*)

Robert MacQueen, Lord Braxfield (1722–99) was born in Lanarkshire. An expert on land law, he was employed by the Crown in connection with the forfeited estates after Culloden. After Thomas Muir's trial he gained a reputation as a 'hanging judge'.   (FA)

Government in this country is made up of the landed interest, which alone has a right to be represented; as for the rabble, who have nothing but personal property, what hold has the nation of them? What security for the payment of their taxes? They may pack up all their property on their backs, and leave the country in the twinkling of an eye.

The jury found Muir guilty, and Braxfield sentenced him to fourteen years' transportation to Botany Bay, a novel sentence then tantamount to the death penalty.

After 1783 Britain had looked to Australia as a substitute for the American colonies to take the overflow from Britain's prisons. The first fleet of eleven vessels had carried nearly 800 convicts, and had arrived at Sydney Cove on 26 January 1788. Many subsequent ships sank before reaching Australia; many convicts died of dysentery or typhoid en route, and by the time of Muir's sentence horror stories about Britain's embryo prison colony abounded. Scots were shocked by the sentence. Robert Burns was moved to write, 'Scots Wha Hae' in protest, a song which was immediately banned as seditious. The newspapers gave Muir's trial enormous coverage and three editions of the court's proceedings were published, two of them in America. After sentence, Muir was taken to the Tolbooth and on 14 November put on board the *Royal George* bound for London. His mother and father presented him with a pocket Bible with the inscription, 'To Thomas Muir from his Afflicted Parents'.

A view near Woolwich in Kent, showing the employment of the convicts from the Hulks.   (NMM)

The state trial of Thomas Muir did not deter the parliamentary reformers. On 19 November 1793 English delegates joined Scots at an all-British Convention in Edinburgh. The government authorities arrested the Convention's leaders, Skirving, Margarot and Gerrald, who like Muir, were sentenced to fourteen years' transportation. The trio quickly became known as the Edinburgh Martyrs; in its over-reaction to middle-class radicalism, the government had stirred up a hornets' nest.

The British newspapers gave detailed coverage of Muir's imprisonment in the convict hulks at Woolwich, outside London, and fearful that he might die on them, the authorities were forced to move him to Newgate Prison.

'Transported for sedition, being portraits of the Scottish Martyrs and a view of Botany Bay'. A contemporary woodcut on linen in the State Library of New South Wales, Australia. (*NSWL*)

Thomas Muir (1765–1798), born in Glasgow, became an advocate at the age of twenty-two.   (*FA*)

The question of his sentence was raised five times in Parliament; but on 13 February, Muir, together with Skirving, Gerrald and Margarot, set sail for Botany Bay. The filthy, stinking, mutinous voyage took nearly six months. Because they were political prisoners Muir and the Edinburgh Martyrs were not obliged to work like the other convicts. Thomas purchased a small farm near Sydney Cove and called it Huntershill, after his father's Scottish home.

On 24 January 1796, the *Otter*, an American ship from Boston, visited the colony and the night before she set sail Thomas Muir managed to board her. His escape, after just sixteen months in the colony, proved a timely one. Within a month of Muir's bid for freedom, Gerrald died at the age of thirty-six and Skirving succumbed to dysentery.

After many adventures Muir eventually reached France, where he was given a hero's welcome at Bordeaux, and thence conveyed to Paris where the Revolutionary government held a banquet in his honour. But his last years were marked by sad decline, both physical and intellectual. Although he had not seen Britain's shores for four years, he set himself up as an expert on his country's affairs. Talleyrand, the French Foreign Secretary, allowed him a small pension; but once the French had exhausted Muir's propaganda value he became an irrelevance. He died at Chantilly outside Paris in 1798, more extreme in his views and more full of his own importance than ever.

The British government, meanwhile, had become obsessed with the need to stamp out the reform movement. In England, the Act of *Habeas*

Henry Erskine (1746–1817), son of the 10th Earl of Buchan. He was the Dean of the Faculty of Advocates for eleven years but lost his job in 1796 because of his Whig principles. (*SNPG*)

Corpus, and in Scotland the 1701 Act against wrongful imprisonment were suspended. In 1794, the authorities discovered a cache of pikeheads in Edinburgh and were sure that a revolutionary coup was planned. The government played the Pike Plot, as it was known, for all it was worth. Two of its alleged leaders, Robert Watt and David Downie, were tried for High Treason; the former was hanged, the latter transported.

But Britain's declaration of war on France in 1793 did more than state trials to turn public opinion against parliamentary reform. In April 1794, Sir Walter Scott took part in a pitched battle in an Edinburgh theatre when a group of Irish medical students booed the British National Anthem. He subsequently joined the Edinburgh Light Horse, one of dozens of volunteer companies raised in Scotland to protect the realm from French invasion. Radicalism was smothered: Scots suspected of liberal tendencies ostracized. Henry Erskine, who had offered to defend Muir, was relieved of his job as Dean of the Faculty of Advocates. John Millar, Muir's old teacher, a supporter of American Independence and a firm advocate for reform, quit Scotland for America with his family because no one would give him a job. In July 1799, the British government outlawed all radical societies. There was not, as Samuel Taylor Coleridge wrote . . .

> . . . a city, no, not a town, in which a man suspected of holding democratic principles could move abroad without receiving some unpleasant proof of the hatred in which his supposed opinions were held by the great majority of the people.

Tradesmen, suspected of democratic sympathies, were denied bank credit. In protest, they later banded together in 1810 to found the Commercial Bank of Scotland. Only the printing presses carried on the battle for parliamentary reform.

In 1782, only eight newspapers were published in Scotland: within eight years, there were twenty-seven, many radical in outlook. The *Dundee Advertiser* made its first appearance in 1801, followed five years later by the *Aberdeen Chronicle*. The greatest Scottish Whig paper, *The Scotsman* with Charles MacLaren as its first editor appeared in 1817. The most influential organ of reform, however, was to be a magazine, the *Edinburgh Review*. After the Peace of Amiens, when Britain was again at peace with France, young Scottish Whigs felt safe to voice their opinions without being thought subversives. The first edition of 750 copies quickly sold out when it appeared in 1802. Edited by Francis Jeffrey and published by Archibald Constable, the *Review* became one of the nineteenth century's great moulders of Whig opinion, not only in Scotland but in Britain as a whole. By 1807, the journal had a circulation of 7000; within a decade 14,000 copies were being sold.

Alexander Maconochie (1777–1861), an MP and Lord of Session. He was dismissed from office and created Lord Meadowbank in 1819 as a result of the farcical state trials of weavers. (*SNPG*)

Made anxious by the success of the *Review*, Scottish Tories produced a rival magazine. In 1817, William Blackwood started *Blackwood's Edinburgh Magazine*, which began to make its mark when John Wilson, 'Christopher North', became editor and published a political satire in the form of an Old Testament story called the *Chaldee Manuscript*.

If peace after war with France again breathed life into political debate, it near mortally wounded the Scots economy. As in England the textile industry in Scotland had over-extended itself to meet the needs of war, and the first decades of the nineteenth century proved hard for the Scottish labouring classes. Trade fluctuated violently, prices soared, and wages fell.

By 1816, as the depression deepened, handloom weavers, in particular, suffered. In just eight years, their average wages fell by nearly half.

In Glasgow, they turned for help to Alexander Richmond, once a weaver himself. Under an Act of 1661, Richmond asked the town's magistrates to arbitrate on a fair wage, which they duly did. The employers refused to accept the magistrates' ruling and appealed to the Court of Session. When the Court upheld the award, the employers refused to implement it and the weavers of Glasgow and the surrounding district went on strike.

Thinking the Phoenix of popular radicalism was again to rise, the British government coerced the strikers and arrested their leaders. The weavers were tried in March 1813, found guilty, and sentenced to eighteen months. Cynically, the government repealed the 1661 Act and looked to other means of ensuring that radicalism was quashed.

Kirkman Finlay, the son of the founder of James Finlay and Company, owned cotton mills and had considerable trade with Europe, India and America. Like many industrialists, Finlay had suffered badly as a result of the post-war recession; but as MP for the Glasgow burghs, he lived in mortal fear that the radical troubles of Europe would engulf Britain. From 1816, he set up an intricate intelligence system that infiltrated the ranks of the Scottish radical weavers, and then informed the British Home Secretary of his findings. By degrees Finlay managed to inveigle Alexander Richmond to work for him. Richmond, once the weavers' hero, was paid money for the information passed on, and eventually he could afford to give up his own business altogether to become a full-time government agent. In January 1817, he persuaded two weavers, Stewart Buchan and Andrew McKinley to take an oath based on the one formally used by the United Irishmen. When he passed the wording on to Kirkman Finlay and the Lord Advocate, Alexander Maconochie, they promptly arranged for the arrest of some twenty radical leaders. But the state trials of 1817, the first for sedition in fifteen years, proved a political disaster. Only two radicals were sentenced, Alexander McLaren, a weaver, and Thomas Baird, a grocer. Then one of the main prosecution witnesses, a weaver, John Campbell, astonished the court when he admitted that the Lord Advocate's Deputy, Henry Home Drummond, had attempted to bribe him into giving evidence against his friend Andrew McKinley. The prosecution case collapsed and all other radicals awaiting trial had to be released.

In 1819 at St Peter's Fields in Manchester an incident made the British government panic once again. On 16 August a peaceful crowd listening to a radical speaker were charged by the local yeomanry. Several in the audience were trampled and sabred to death in what came to be known as the Peterloo Massacre. Lord Liverpool, the Prime Minister, fearing revolution was nigh, passed six repressive parliamentary acts. In Scotland news of Peterloo led to riots in Paisley, more arrests and more trials of radical supporters. Samuel Hunter, the editor of the *Glasgow Herald* asked for permission to raise a Glasgow Yeomanry regiment to defend the town and over a thousand were recruited to his Glasgow Sharpshooters. Both sides, it seemed, were preparing for a showdown. On 9 November 1819, Lord Advocate Hope wrote to Lord Melville:

> All disguise is now thrown off – even the flimsy pretence of Radical Reform is laid aside – a complete revolution and plunder is avowed their object.

Kirkman Finlay (1773–1842), a Glasgow cotton manufacturer and MP for the Glasgow burghs. (*SNPG*)

'Andrew McKinley on trial' by John Kay (1742–1826). (*SNPG*)

Massacre at St Peter's or "BRITONS STRIKE HOME"!!!

The 'Peterloo' Massacre, 16 August 1819. *(BM)*

John Hope, Lord Justice-Clerk (1794–1858). *(SNPG)*

1820 was the year of the so-called Scottish Insurrection. The events, which were to culminate in the execution of three weavers for high treason, were, however, in large part the expression of the resentment many in Scotland felt for having fought for Britain against Napoleon only to return home and find themselves treated as seditious rabble and industrial scrap.

Attempts had been made by the authorities, after the Napoleonic War, to relieve the hardship caused by unemployment. The Town Council of Glasgow, for instance, employed 324 workless to restyle Glasgow Green. Relief centres were also opened up in the town; but charity did little to ameliorate what was seen as the root of the problem. If the disaffected, as the government called them, were to continue to be intransigent, there was but one solution, namely to create a head-on collision that would put the radical movement in its place.

In 1820, government spies once again were ordered to infiltrate the radical ranks. They encouraged the radicals to form a Committee of Organization for Forming a Provisional Government, and on 1 April placards appeared on the streets of Glasgow, calling for an immediate national strike and a rising on 5 April:

> To show the world that we are not that lawless, sanguinary rabble which our oppressors would persuade the higher circles we are but a brave and generous people determined to be free.

The Proclamation, making reference, as it did, to the Magna Carta and the English Bill of Rights, was probably written by a government spy.

Throughout Scotland some 60,000 stopped work on 1 April. Yet unknown to the rank and file of the radical movement, twenty-eight members of the so-called provisional government were in Glasgow jail and had been since 21 March when they had been quietly arrested. On April Fool's Day 1820, the streets of Glasgow were lined with troops. The government had called out the Rifle Brigade and the 83rd Regiment of Foot, together with the 7th and 10th Hussars, under the command of Sir Richard Hussey Vivian, the government's leading expert in cavalry tactics and expressly sent north by the Duke of York in case of disturbances. Samuel Hunter's Glasgow Sharpshooters were also on hand, under his personal command. There was a brief encounter in the evening when three hundred radicals skirmished with a party of cavalry, but no one came to harm that day.

Baron Richard Hussey Vivian (1775–1842). (*NPG*)

At Fir Park, now Glasgow's Necropolis, seventy radicals had been directed by government agents to go to Falkirk, where English sympathizers, it was said, would join up with them and help take the Carron Iron Works. When the small band got there, they found nobody and half of them dispersed. Thirty radicals were resting at Bonnymuir, near Castlecary, when a troop of the 7th Hussars advanced towards them. Andrew Hardie, one of the radicals, recalled the scene:

> Some of our men were wounded in a most shocking manner, and it is truly unbecoming the character of a soldier to wound, or try and kill any man whom he has it in his power to take prisoner, and when we had no arms to make any defence.

Forty-seven radicals were ultimately rounded up and taken to the military prison at Stirling Castle. Twenty-four were tried and sentenced to death. One of the three hanged was a sixty-year-old weaver, James Wilson.

A special English Court of Oyer and Terminer, a royal commission court with power to hear and determine criminal causes, was set up in Glasgow. Wilson made an impassioned speech to the court:

> You may condemn me to immolation on the scaffold, but you cannot degrade me. If I have appeared as a pioneer in the van of freedom's battles – if I have attempted to free my country from political degradation – my conscience tells me that I have only done my duty. Your brief authority will soon cease, but the vindictive proceedings this day shall be recorded in history.

Sentence was passed by Lord President Hope. Wilson was to be drawn on a hurdle to the place of execution, hanged, then his head severed from his body and his corpse quartered. Twenty thousand people witnessed James Wilson's execution on Glasgow Green. His remains were spared quartering and were ultimately allowed to rest in Strathaven, the village of his birth, where in his younger days, it is said, he had invented the purl stitch.

Two other radicals, John Baird a thirty-two-year-old weaver from Condorrat, and Andrew Hardie, a weaver from Glasgow aged twenty-eight were executed in Stirling, watched by a crowd of 2000. The night before Hardie wrote to his girlfriend:

> I shall die firm to the cause in which I embarked, and although we were outwitted and betrayed, yet I protest, as a dying man, it was done with good intention on my part . . . No person could have induced me to take up arms to rob or plunder; no, my dear Margaret, I took them for the

The account of the expenses incurred executing Andrew Hardie and John Baird at Stirling on 8 September 1820, a bill which the authorities took their time in settling. *(SPL)*

Abstract of Account of Expenses relative to Execution of ~~Baird~~ and ~~~~ Hardie & John Baird at Stirling 8th Sept. 1820. for High Treason.

		£		
To Amount of Mr Littlejohns Account		10	4	11
" Mr Cockraiths Do		3	10	10
Do Peter McGibbons		2	17	7
Mr Traquairs Filling up Scaffold		6	13	6
2 Town Officers &c		8		
1 Mr Duncan McLaren			13	6
4 Executioner		40		
3 James McPherson		4	2	9
5 Alex Calder		14	10	2
~~Mr Traquair ~~~~~~				
6 Thomas Thenie		3	3	
7 James McNab Grave Digger			4	
Mr Adam Steel		15		

restoration of those rights for which our forefathers bled, and which we have allowed shamefully to be wrested from us . . .

The authorities had trouble in finding someone who would chop off the heads of the two radicals at Stirling. Nine days before the execution two town clerks were sent to 'engage an executioner'. One went to Glasgow, where he witnessed James Wilson's execution and noticed he was first hanged by an executioner and then had his head severed by another masked man 'in a long robe'. Glasgow's hangman demanded ten guineas per victim and, grudgingly, the Stirling Town Clerk agreed to pay it. The decapitator was found in Edinburgh. He demanded twenty guineas per victim for what was regarded as a more dangerous job as the crowd would almost certainly react to his gory task.

The sentences of nineteen other radicals captured after Bonnymuir were commuted to transportation to New South Wales, seven for life and twelve for fourteen years. Peter Mackenzie, a Glasgow journalist, campaigned to have them pardoned. He published a small book entitled, *The Spy System, including the exploits of Mr Alex. Richmond, the notorious Government Spy of Sidmouth and Castlereagh, in the years 1819–1820*. Richmond took a libel action against the publication but in court the defence tore his arguments to pieces and the judge ruled that the plaintiff was non-suited. In July 1835, King William IV of England, III of Scotland was persuaded to pardon those transported.

Meanwhile most of the nineteen radicals transported had made good. Thomas McCulloch and his second wife from Glasgow, Sarah, ran the Sydney Arms, a public house which made enough money for him and his sons to purchase land in the town and in the country areas of New South Wales. On one such property, Buckinbah, purchased by his son Thomas, McCullochs still live to this day. Thomas's son, Andrew Hardie, so-named because he was born on the day of the Stirling executions, became an attorney in the New South Wales Supreme Court. In turn his son, Andrew Hardie Junior became a solicitor, and was a member of the Legislative Assembly of New

South Wales. Other McCullochs became medical men. Dr Stanhope Hastings McCulloch, grandson of the radical, became an authority on obstetrics and practised in Sydney for over fifty years. The family has made good the remark the radical Thomas made in a letter he wrote to his wife Sarah in 1821 to encourage her to join him:

> If you will only come out, a steady man and woman can do well, as they are very rare articles to be found here.

Scotland's loss became Australia's gain.

An inquiry, meanwhile, into Scottish local government had proved that corruption had been responsible for bankrupting Edinburgh, Aberdeen, Dundee and Dunfermline. In 1823, Lord Archibald Hamilton drew the attention of parliament to the defects of county representation:

> I have the right to vote in five counties in Scotland in not one of which do I possess an acre of land; and I have no doubt that if I took the trouble, I might have a vote for every county in that kingdom.

His motion, calling for parliamentary reform, was defeated by only thirty-five votes. Reform there would have to be, sooner or later.

In 1832 two Reform Bills were passed by the Westminster Parliament, one for England, the other for Scotland. The number of county constituencies in Scotland was to remain at thirty, but some counties were fused into a single entity, like Ross and Cromarty. The number of burgh constituencies was raised from fifteen to twenty-three. Edinburgh was given a second Member of Parliament and Glasgow received two of her own. The Reform Act of 1832 increased the number of voters in Scotland from 4500 to 65,000. But the act did not sweep away abuse. The practice of fictitious votes continued; legislation just made them cheaper. Estate tenants, now enfranchised, were to feel honour bound to follow the political leanings of their landlords without the benefit of financial and legal trickery.

In the same year as the great Reform Act of 1832, Sir Walter Scott died peacefully in his sleep at Abbotsford. A nation mourned his passing, and a public subscription was got up to raise a memorial to the man who had done so much to promote Scotland. On 15 August 1840, a public holiday was declared so that people could witness the laying of the foundation stone of the Scott Monument in Edinburgh. In all, the people of Scotland contributed £15,650 to honour their greatest writer. Most of the leading sculptors of the day helped the architect, George Kemp, adorn the monument. The masons who crafted the statue were so enthusiastic that at one stage they offered to work for a fortnight without pay so that minor alterations could be made. The monument, the largest ever erected to a writer in Britain before Scott or since, was finally finished on 17 August 1846.

Two years before, other Scots had helped raise a more modest obelisk, to Thomas Muir and the Edinburgh Martyrs, who, with the passing of the Reform Act, were now thought respectable. Possibly better than any other Scot, Muir had voiced Scottish radicalism. Sir Walter Scott had celebrated its rural, conservative past, but his Scotland was not of the real world now. Scotland was fast becoming an urban nation. A revolution in agriculture was helping drive Lowlanders into Scotland's growing industrial towns or abroad.

The drawing made by the architect, George Meikle Kemp (1790–1844), of the Scott Monument, Edinburgh. (*CAC*)

14

The Improvers

THE ENLIGHTENMENT of the eighteenth century was to have far-reaching consequences in Scotland. The 'literati' of Edinburgh were not content just to talk about the nature of human society over glasses of claret. If happiness was what life was about, then changes would have to be made. Agriculture, Scotland's major employer, had in the past provided niggardly returns. Despite hard work, those who worked the land had frequently been brought to starvation by bad or non-existent harvests.

Long before Scotland's 'enlightened' agricultural improvers got to work, steady if limited advances had been made. The process of bringing more land into use had been ceaseless since the Middle Ages. As peat bogs were cut for fuel, more ground had been made available for pastoral or arable farming. Scotland's forests had been cut down over the centuries for ships and housing and again farmers had striven to put the land left to good use.

Before the Union of 1707 agricultural innovation was already popular. Many Scots, who had served or studied in Europe brought back new ideas. In 1697, James Donaldson, who had served abroad in the army, wrote *Husbandry Anatomized*, and both Andrew Fletcher of Saltoun and the 2nd Lord Belhaven, who had together vigorously opposed Union, were keen agricultural reformers. Belhaven was the first in Scotland to examine the ideal layout of farm buildings. In *Country-Man's Rudiments* he proposed they should be built around a square with a central midden, and his plan was adopted throughout much of the Lowlands. The use of lime also became popular and by the middle of the eighteenth century enclosure to form individual and separate farms, with fields bounded by stone dykes, was common. Many lairds, like the Jacobite Mackintosh of Borlum and the 6th Earl of Haddington, stimulated advance by improving their own estates.

The catalysts of the agricultural revolution were war and England's growing industrialization. Between 1702 and 1815, the British crown was almost constantly preparing for war or fighting. In 1702, the War of the Spanish Succession broke out and Britain's army and navy had to be supplied for eleven long years. In 1740 came the War of the Austrian Succession and another eight years of fighting. In 1756, the Seven Years War determined whether France or Britain would be imperial masters of the Western world. Between 1775 and 1783, Britain struggled with her American colonies. Ten years later, in 1793, Britain declared war on the

Thomas Hamilton, 6th Earl of Haddington (1680–1735), a supporter of the Union and a keen agricultural Improver. (*SNPG*)

Revolutionary France and with the exception of a year's peace, the fight lasted twenty-three years.

The effects on Scotland of Britain's imperial wars were considerable. Long wars put demands on Scotland's farmers; there were troops and factory workers to feed and clothe. The century of battle also socially altered the face of Scotland. Between 1740 and 1815, no fewer than eighty-six Highland regiments were formed and an almost equally large number of regular and volunteer troops were raised in Lowland Scotland and elsewhere. Many went to war never to return.

Soon after the union of 1707 the first improvements in Scottish agriculture were aimed at satisfying England's need of Scots cattle. Indeed, those who prospered by raising livestock had been among those most fervent for the union, and the owners of estates in the south-west of Scotland made fortunes sending cattle south to feed England's growing towns. Cattle-raising in the Highlands also prospered. By the 1770s, over 1500 cattle were being exported from the island of Islay alone and Scotland as a whole was annually sending south over 100,000 head. In the century after union, cattle prices rose fourfold.

John McNeill of Colonsay and Oronsay (1767–1846) was one of the first to bring improved agriculture to Scotland's islands. (*SNPG*)

Enclosure first took place in the south-west counties of Dumfries and Galloway. Unlike their counterparts in England, Scottish landowners did not need special acts passed by the British Parliament to reorganize their estates. Legislation passed by the old Scottish parliament in 1695 made blocking out of farms into larger units possible. Also, unlike England, there were few significant revolts against enclosure, although in 1724, the annual horse fair at Keltonhill in Dumfriesshire was the scene of angry protests by tenants who had been evicted to make way for larger farms. The Levellers, as they were called, pulled down the newly built dykes. In Kirkcudbright, also in the south-west, dispossessed tenants banded together and published a manifesto condemning the local lairds. The government sent troops and some of the Levellers were transported to North America. Similar outbreaks of violence took place in Wigtownshire.

The agricultural revolution in Scotland did not, to begin with, make for fewer people working the land. Lairds improving their estates needed labour to build dykes, manure the fields and plant trees, and it was only much later in the century, when many improving lairds went bankrupt because they had over-invested, that farm labourers in large numbers began to drift abroad and to Scotland's towns.

George Dempster (1732–1818), MP for Forfar and for the Fife boroughs from 1762 to 1790. (*SNPG*)

For most tenant farmers the way they worked the land changed slowly. George Dempster, a Scottish MP between 1762 and 1790 and a keen agrarian improver noted:

> The farmers having no leases, or short ones, were extremely poor. They were also bound to grind their corn at the mill of the barony (this obligation was known as thirlage) and to employ the proprietor's blacksmith. They paid double price for their work at the mill and the blacksmith's shop and were besides saucily and ill served. The proprietor received a rent on this account from the miller and the blacksmith.

The isle of Arran, off the Clyde coast, was typical of the state of much of Scotland's agriculture. By the middle of the eighteenth century, the people of Arran lived round the coast and in the glens convenient to the open fields. They lived in clachans, compact clusters of Black Houses and outbuildings.

Walter Geikie (1795–1837) was a deaf and dumb Edinburgh artist noted for his sketches of his native city and of rural life. (*CAC*)

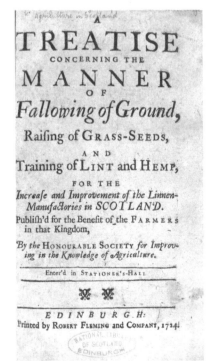

The title page of a publication of The Society of Improvers in the Knowledge of Agriculture. (*NLS*)

The arable land closest to the clachan was the infield, cultivated year after year. Cattle, together with horses and butter, were the island's main exports. Land was allocated and shared by a system called run-rig, strips, or rigs of constant width but varying length. These were shared out according to a family's function, ability and needs and also determined each family's rent. The clachan worked as a community, the land being allotted by the 'man of the clachan', usually the tacksman or middle man responsible for collecting and delivering up to the laird each year's rent. It was subsistence farming. The clachan grew peas, beans and oats and latterly potatoes when they came into fashion and they salted sheep, goats and fish. Beef beasts were too valuable for their own use and were sold at Greenock. In the autumn they sold some butter and fishing nets made out of home grown flax. The land was used in rotation; cultivated one year, next left fallow, then for grazing. These run-rigs were not all grouped together. In order to keep the rotation of land, all the crops would be in one area, all the grazing in another and all the fallow in a third. This was time-consuming to work, and it also meant that if one man didn't look after his land properly, the next year, when another family had it, the poor husbandry would affect their crop. It was not altogether a satisfactory system. Famine was just round the corner a lot of the time.

In the eighteenth century land was thought to be a secure and profitable investment and estates in Lowland Scotland were eagerly sought after. Profits from Scotland's increasing trade after the Union and salaries from public office were poured into land and agricultural improvement. The merchants of Glasgow, growing fat on the new post-Union trade with America, saw land as a sensible investment. By the last quarter of the eighteenth century 103 Glasgow traders were owners of 145 estates. Besides, land was seen as the source of political power.

Meanwhile, in this Age of Reason, philanthropy and profit motive went hand in hand. Throughout Scotland clubs and societies were formed to promote new ways and agricultural shows and competitions became com-

mon. Lawyers, like Lord Kames, were in the forefront of agricultural innovation. So too were Scottish MPs like Sir John Cockburn of Ormiston. As
one of the Lords of the Admiralty Cockburn had a substantial income and,
based in London, improved his estate by means of correspondence with his
gardener Bell. Between 1727 and 1741 he sent instructions about all aspects
of agriculture, animal husbandry and forestry by packet boat between
London and Leith. He took a dim view of Scottish agriculture:

> It is commonly our Scots way to do little business but squeeze up high
> prices, whereas it would much more real advantage to enlarge the
> business, have the profit, though small upon it, yet many smalls to make
> a great.

It was the job of the farmer, he argued, to meet the growing needs of towns
like Edinburgh and provide a more varied diet:

> All the people in Scotland are not so void of taste or their other senses as
> you incline to think them. It is the not being able to get good things which
> makes people not have them and if they whose business should lead
> them to furnish good things were at more pains in supplying with good at
> all seasons and to introduce them to some customers it would soon take.
> I remember since little garden stuff was to be got to buy at Edinburgh a
> gardener said, 'Why shall we raise them, nobody will buy them'. The
> moment they were to be had everybody bought.

Sir John Cockburn of Ormiston
(1679–1758) sat in the British
Parliament until 1741. (*SNPG*)

Cockburn built a new village at Ormiston, and his tenants were given long
leases of thirty-eight years or more to encourage them to improve the land,
for he realized that his best interest was served by having a prosperous and
contented tenantry.

Yet by the time Sir John retired in 1741, he was nearing bankruptcy.
Expenditure in improving his estate was not matched by profit and he was
£10,000 in debt. In 1747, he was forced to sell his estate to the Earl of
Hopetoun. After nearly 400 years the Cockburn family quit Ormiston. But
John Cockburn's far-seeing policy earned him the nickname 'the father of
Scottish agriculture'; by planting trees, his great passion, and enclosing his
fields with hedges, he had shown the way. He had also founded the Ormiston
Society, which met in the village inn to discuss farming topics. Ormiston
Hall, however, which he began in 1745, was the *folie de grandeur* that forced
him to sell up.

William Cullen (1710–90). (*SNPG*)

Science was brought to bear on Scottish agriculture. James Hutton, born
in Edinburgh, turned from the study of medicine to chemistry. He produced
sal ammoniac from soot, and having studied agriculture in England, bought a
small estate in Berwickshire. Hutton's *Theory of the Earth* which he wrote in
1785, is regarded as 'the foundation of modern geology', and his estate at
Bunkle with its advanced methods of husbandry helped make Berwickshire
one of the leading agricultural districts of Scotland by the end of the
eighteenth century. William Cullen, born in Hamilton, became Professor of
Chemistry at Edinburgh University in 1756 and turned his mind to solving
the problems that beset the farmers of Scotland's poorer soil. William Dick
studied animal genetics and went on to found the Edinburgh Veterinary
College in 1823, and by the beginning of the nineteenth century, Edinburgh
University had acknowledged the scientific approach to farming by appointing a Professor of Agriculture.

William Dick (1793–1866). (*SNPG*)

From the 1760s farming became mechanized. James Small, a Berwickshire ploughwright, invented the swing plough which could be drawn by two horses instead of the ten often required for the old Scotch plough that it replaced. In 1828 Patrick Bell from Auchterhouse in Angus produced the world's first reaping-machine which revolutionized harvesting. At Prestonkirk Graveyard in East Lothian are buried three Scotsmen involved in the agricultural revolution. Andrew Meikle, born in 1719, was the son of the inventor of 'fanners' used to winnow grain and became a mill-wright at Houston, near Dunbar. In 1768 he patented his machine for dressing grain and then turned his hand to threshing machines which he began producing in 1789. John Sherriff was a pioneer in the discovery of new strains of wheat and oats and John Brown became the editor of the first farming journal published in Scotland. In 1723, the Honourable Society of Improvers in the Knowledge of Agriculture was founded, and in 1784, the Highland and Agricultural Society first met in Edinburgh and it was to have a huge and permanent influence on Scottish farming. In 1822, the Society held its first show.

As the range of vegetables and flowers grown in Scotland increased, horticulture took hold. From the middle of the eighteenth century the Scots were to become world-famous as gardeners. The vegetable that revolutionized Scottish agriculture was, as in Ireland and much of Europe, the potato. Easy to grow and relatively cheap, it enabled more valuable crops of grain to be sent to market for profit. Yet it began life as an expensive luxury. Grown purely as a garden plant, the tubers, if eaten at all, were reserved as a

'Boiling Potatoes', a study by Walter Geikie. (*NGS*)

delicacy for the laird. In 1739, Robert Graham of Kilsyth planted half an acre of potatoes on his estate; but Lowlanders were slow to accept the crop as food. To begin with farmers used the potato to help clear the ground for other crops.

The benefits of better farming were shared by most classes. The real wage of the agricultural labourer rose and Scotland's people were, by and large, better fed and healthier than they had ever been. As a result of improvement, the rent of farm land rose. In 1793, it was estimated that the total annual rent of Scotland's farms stood at £1,500,000. Within two decades it had risen to six million.

Meanwhile the nation's towns were growing and young countryfolk were attracted to quit the land for manufacturing industry and the promise of steady wages. Highlanders had begun migrating south to Glasgow and Edinburgh well before the Jacobite rebellions of 1715 and 1745. After Culloden, young Highlanders flocked south in their thousands. By the end of the eighteenth century, a census in Glasgow established that there were 20,000 Gaelic-speaking Highlanders there. The Highland community of Glasgow had its own Presbyterian church which helped migrants by making very substantial loans to enable people to set up their own business.

But voluntary migration to Scotland's growing towns was not in itself enough to make many estates viable. In 1766 the 7th Duke of Hamilton was a minor, and the trustees of his estates, influenced by the work of the improvers, asked agriculturalists John Burrel and Boyd Anderson to try and make the Duke's island estate of Arran more profitable. Burrel's remit was the enclosure of land and also to report on what possible development there could be in Arran. He did a survey and started a slate quarry. He also began salt pans and searched for coal. Burrel suggested that the Duke should open lime quarries and the tenants should be allowed to take the lime at their own expense to improve the soil.

In 1773, Arran had 99 farms, supporting 1110 families. Under Burrel, the Duke's tacksmen were abolished and tenant farmers were made responsible directly for the rents and the management of their land. Run-rig made way for larger farms. Henceforth the land was only to be leased to men who themselves could stock, work and improve it. In the new leases, Burrel laid down that crop rotation was to be introduced and that all arable land was to be regularly manured. Tenant's rights to common pasture were withdrawn and pasture was divided out as part of the new enlarged farms. Under Burrel's plan, Arran was to support only 250 families and had the ambitious scheme gone through, over 750 families would have been denied land. But two developments, the consequence of Britain's long wars against the French, forced Burrel to revise his plan.

'Coastal fishermen' by Geikie.   (*CAC*)

After 1787, a bounty was given to inshore fishermen, which made the industry profitable; and the kelp industry of Arran also helped absorb those that enclosure of land was making homeless. Imported alkalis, required in the manufacture of soap and glass, were made expensive by the war and the making of alkali by burning kelp, seaweed, flourished throughout much of the Highlands and islands.

When peace came in 1815, the Duke of Hamilton, like many Scottish landlords, looked to sheep as a way of making his island estate profitable. His new factor, a minister named Headrick, brought sheep from the Border to Arran. He felt that the north end of the island should be given over to the beasts because, apart from a strip of about a hundred yards near the sea, there was little to cultivate there. The people in the towns required more and more wool and meat, and blackface Cheviot sheep were better producers of both than the little brown animals that Arran had before.

The Duke arranged for subjects made landless by sheep farming to emigrate and paid half the fare of their passage to Canada. The first eighty-six emigrants left Lamlash for Quebec in April 1829. The following month, another thirty boarded ship. Some of the Arran islanders went to Chaleur Bay, whilst others were settled in Megantic County, which was then still virgin forest. The islanders wrote home and encouraged others to join them. By 1843, 222 from Arran had made new homes in Megantic County alone.

Other Scots migrated to North America as a direct result of Britain's wars. Before the Union of the Crowns in 1603, Scottish soldiers had joined battle abroad for the monarchs of Europe. They fought alongside Joan of Arc and had later lent their services to the kings of Sweden, Bohemia and Denmark as well as France. In 1422, a troop of Gendarmes Ecossais formed part of the French royal forces. Twenty-three years later when the Maison du Roi was founded Scots continued to act as the French King's close bodyguard. The Gendarmes and the Gardes Ecossais had fought against the Duke of Marlborough and, of course, fellow Scots.

The Swedes and the Dutch had also raised Scottish regiments. Gustavus Adolphus of Sweden, like the French King, had a Scottish bodyguard. Scots had also fought in the Wars of Dutch Independence. In 1572, companies were raised in Scotland for service in the Netherlands and saw almost continuous action for twenty years. During the War of the Austrian Succession Scots fought in French, Dutch as well as British uniforms. Daniel Defoe remarked in 1707 that the Scots were the best soldiers in Europe and should be in British service, 'instead of cutting each other's throats in the service of foreign princes'. During the eighteenth century, the arrival in France of exiled Jacobites enabled six regiments of Infantry of the Line to be recruited. The Royal Ecossais, raised in 1744, fought at Fontenoy in 1745 and a year later were part of the French contingent at Culloden where they opposed the British Royal Scots.

After the union of 1707, Britain needed troops to win and hold her growing colonial empire. Between 1739 and 1800 no fewer than twenty-four regiments were raised in the northern areas of Scotland. Most were employed to fight the particular war at hand – first the Seven Years War and subsequently the War of American Independence – and were then usually disbanded. An example of the contribution made by Scots during this period is the Isle of Skye. Between 1775 and 1815, it is estimated that the island produced more than 20 generals, 600 officers and 10,000 soldiers to fight in the British army. During the Napoleonic Wars the Highland and Lowland regiments were augmented by units raised for home defence. Forty Fencible regiments were raised in Scotland; between 1794 and 1815 some 50,000 men served in the part-time Militia Volunteers or Local Militia. Not all Scots fought on land. By 1809, it was estimated that more than 5000 Shetlanders and Orcadians were serving in the Royal Navy.

In 1797, when the war with France was going badly, the government

Highland troops at the Battle of Vimiera during Britain's long wars against France. (*SG*)

passed a Militia Act to supplement Britain's regular army. Six thousand Scots were to be compulsorily enlisted, chosen by ballot from parish registers. But the Militia Act was resented as a class measure. Those of the upper classes who were not enrolled as volunteers could hire substitutes to take their place. When the act became operative in August 1797, teachers in Scotland, often in charge of parish registers, were terrorized and their ballot lists burned. The coalminers of Tranent refused to be called up and the government was forced to send in troops to quash the revolt. Eleven people were killed, including a thirteen-year-old boy. When the battle was over, nobody was brought to task and the government refused to compensate Tranent for the pillage and robbery that had taken place. Two years later there were similar riots in Bathgate against the act.

The Highlanders had already shown their dislike for fighting in wars they thought were of more concern to the English than the Scots. In May 1740, 1000 men of the Black Watch, formed after the rising of 1715 to police the Highlands, were called to muster near Aberfeldy on the pretext that King George II wished to inspect them in London. Although the men had been promised they would never be asked to leave Scotland, the government had secretly decided to send them to Flanders. When the Black Watch reached London, they were reviewed by General Wade and about a hundred met on Finchley Common on 17 May 1743 and decided to make for home. The deserters were captured at Oundle in Northamptonshire seventy miles from London and imprisoned in the Tower. They were persuaded to plead guilty; but the government showed no mercy. Corporal Samuel MacPherson and Corporal Malcolm MacPherson from Badenoch were shot, along with Private Farquhar Shaw of Rothiemurchus. The other deserters were drafted into regiments serving overseas in Gibraltar, Minorca, Georgia and the Leeward Islands. Few saw Scotland again. Of the Black Watch mutineers sent into exile, nine were Camerons and four Stewarts. Perhaps it was no accident that the chiefs of the MacPhersons and the Stewarts of Appin, together with Cameron of Lochie were to answer Prince Charles Edward's call to rebellion in 1745.

Between 1743 and 1804, no fewer than sixteen Scottish regiments resorted to mutiny because they felt that the Hanoverian government had cheated them. Scots regarded soldiering as an honourable profession and

SAM.ᴸ MᶜPHERSON   MALCOLM MᶜPHERSON   FARQUAR SHAW

Corporal Samuel MacPherson, Corporal Malcolm MacPherson and Private Farquhar Shaw of the Black Watch, shot for desertion in 1743. (*CAC*)

A view of the Highland deserters at the Tower of London, 31 May 1743. (*CAC*)

historically had never been docile cannon fodder. Clan chiefs had had to justify the cause for which they wished their followers to fight. But, in fact, it was the Lowland Royal Scots who were responsible for the first Mutiny Act, passed in 1689. They had been given a foreign Colonel, Friedric Hermann Schomberg, and refused to obey orders until the King allowed a Scot of their choice to command the first battalion.

The British government paid its soldiers as little as it dared and even in peacetime pay was seldom issued regularly. By 1795, each soldier received tenpence a day, of which sixpence was regarded as pay and the remainder was for board and keep. The food provided was sparse. Daily rations, as late as the Peninsular War (1808–1813), were often no more than a biscuit. When regiments were sent abroad, shipwreck and disease decimated the troops before they ever got near the fight. In 1805, half a Cameronian regiment, bound for Germany, drowned.

After Culloden, little was done to improve life in the Highlands as the traveller, John Knox, wrote:

> No villages, magazines or harbours were formed, or manufactures introduced, by which the people might be usefully employed; nor hath the smallest ray of hope been held out, whereby they might expect to see better days. On the contrary it seems to be a political maxim with many persons, that the Highlands of Scotland are to be considered merely as a nursery for soldiers and seamen; that the inhabitants, formed admirably by nature for the fatigues of the campaign and the ocean, are to be employed in these capacities alone; and that, to facilitate the business of recruiting, it is necessary to keep them low.

Fraser's Highlanders, the 78th Regiment, was raised in 1757 by Simon Fraser. They were first of all posted to Ireland and then went on to British North America, where they took part in the attack on the French at Quebec led by General James Wolfe, who had fought for the Hanoverians at Culloden. In 1758 they scaled the Heights of Abraham at night to win Canada. The Regiment was disbanded in 1783 and the men were offered land in Canada by the British government instead of the passage home. Many Scots who settled in Quebec in time became entirely French in their outlook, and there are still something like 100,000 Frasers in Canada as a whole.

Many Highlanders, however, returned home to Scotland after fighting was over. Findlay Mackenzie fought at Louisburg in 1758 and, once disbanded, returned to his native island of Barra. He and a fellow soldier, Donald McNeill sailed home via Cape Breton in Nova Scotia and so impressed the people of Barra with tales of Canada that in 1802 nearly 300 left the island to settle in Nova Scotia. To islanders, Canada's virgin forests were a new experience, as one of Findlay's descendants, Archibald Macken-zie, makes clear:

> Some of them never saw a tree; most of them never had an axe. What a challenge it was to go into the forest but my God they were strong, hardy men. In a few years they cleared enough land that would grow potatoes. As soon as they cut down the trees they planted potatoes between the stumps. And of course they wrestled with the stumps until they could pull them out of the ground.

Cape Breton, Nova Scotia. (*Author*)

Pictou, Nova Scotia (*above*).
A reconstruction (*below*) of the log
church the Scots built at Loch
Broom.   (*Author*)

In 1773, one hundred and eighty-nine Scots arrived in Nova Scotia aboard
the *Hector*. The ship had sailed from Greenock, via Ullapool in Loch Broom,
where the captain had taken aboard thirty-three families and twenty-five
unmarried men. All but one of the Highland passengers were Presbyterians
forced by famine the previous Spring and high rents to quit Scotland. All,
given the promise of free passage, a free farm and a year's supplies, had
volunteered to settle in Canada. The *Hector* dropped anchor at Pictou on the
west coast of Nova Scotia on 15 September 1773. Wherever they went they
named their settlements after home – Gairloch, Glengarry, Lorne and
Arisaig. Their descendants became bankers, businessmen and politicians
like Ulysses Simpson Grant, eighteenth President of the United States, who
claimed descent from a *Hector* immigrant.

To the early Pictou settlers religion was important. In 1786, the Reverend James Drummond MacGregor arrived there from Scotland and with
the help of his congregation built a log church on the banks of Loch Broom,
Nova Scotia. From 1791, Catholic Highlanders began to arrive and, like the
Presbyterian Scots, clung to their faith.

Others from Scotland settled western Canada long before 1800, as
employees of the Hudson's Bay Company. Founded in 1670 by Charles II,
the company had been granted the vast hinterland of western and northern
Canada. When the British military conquest of the country was complete,
trade speedily followed the flag. The traders of the company moved west and
set up their forts and trading posts. Many of those employed by the Hudson's
Bay Company came from the Orkney islands. William Sinclair, a graduate of

Edinburgh University was attracted into the company's employ in 1792. He was twenty-six years old and was immediately sent out to establish a trading post.

William Sinclair married Nahovway, the daughter of a local Indian chief. As the company relied on the Indians to trap the precious furs of the beaver and the bear, his choice of wife had its advantages. From 1792 until the present day, at least one member of every generation of the Sinclair family has been an employee of the Hudson's Bay Company.

By 1800, the company was recruiting three-quarters of its workforce in Orkney. John and James Inkster were encouraged to settle in Canada by their uncle John, who had emigrated from Orkney in the 1790s and was farming near what is now Winnipeg in Manitoba. Nephew John turned part of his first house into a trading post and married Mary, the daughter of William Sinclair and Nahovway. The couple raised nine children and John built a mansion for his family, the only two-storey house in the district.

Throughout the eighteenth century ministers of the Kirk and Catholic priests encouraged emigration, as did the old clan tacksmen, who after Culloden lost their privileged status and sought wealth and prestige in the New World. With the connivance of unscrupulous ship's captains and government agents eager to populate Canada emigration from the north was established long before the ideas and economic philosophies of the Lowland improvers could be applied beyond the Highland line.

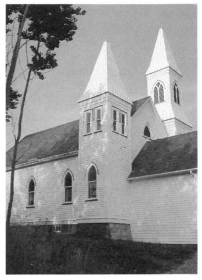

The Presbyterian church founded by Scots settlers at Whycocomagh in Inverness County, Cape Breton. The Post Office at nearby Iona (*left*), proof that Gaelic is recognized in Nova Scotia as the third language.   (*Author*)

15

The Clearances

ON THE NORTH BANK of Loch Naver in Sutherland the ruins of the townships of Grummore and Grumbeg are preserved as Ancient Monuments. The clearing of the people who once lived there was witnessed in 1819 by a local stonemason, Donald MacLeod, who wrote about the event twenty years later in *Gloomy Memories*:

> This calamity came on the people quite unexpectedly. Strong parties, for each district, furnished with faggots and other combustibles, rushed on the dwellings of this devoted people, and immediately commenced setting fire to them, proceeding in their work with the greatest rapidity till about three hundred houses were in flames! The consternation and confusion were extreme; little or no time was given for the removal of persons or property – the people striving to remove the sick and the helpless before the fire should reach them – next, struggling to save the most valuable of their effects. The cries of the women and children – the roaring of the affrighted cattle hunted at the same time by the yelling dogs of the shepherds amid the smoke and fire – altogether presented a scene that completely baffles description: it required to be seen to be believed.

The evicted were tenants of the Countess of Sutherland and her English husband, the Marquis of Stafford, later Duke of Sutherland, who by the early nineteenth century were the richest noble family in Britain. Their actions, or rather those done in their name, have never been forgotten; the word 'Clearance' still conjures up emotions of bitterness and anger. The Reverend Donald Sage, the missionary at Achness, witnessed the Clearances at Grummore and noted the event in his *Memorabilia Domestica*:

> At an early hour on a Tuesday, Mr Sellar, escorted by a large body of constables, sheriff-officers and others commenced work at Grummore, the first inhabited township to the west. They gave the inmates an hour to pack up and carry off their furniture and then set the cottages on fire. To this plan they ruthlessly adhered. The roofs and rafters were lighted up into one red blaze.

The events in Sutherland at the beginning of the nineteenth century were real enough. Thousands of tenants who felt the land they worked was their ancestral home were forced to leave, their houses and crops burnt so that nothing remained to encourage them to return. But the stories have been

George Granville Leveson-Gower, 1st Duke of Sutherland (1758–1833), diplomat and magnate. (*NPG*)

coloured by the recollections of Donald MacLeod who, himself evicted, emigrated to Canada and was to conduct a war against the Sutherland family for forty years, and by the poets and writers who, at the time and since, have clouded economic reality with Scottish sentimentality.

After Culloden in 1746, the estates of those who had fought with Prince Charles Edward Stewart were confiscated. Commissioners were appointed to manage them and the new ideas of farming so fashionable in Lowland Scotland were slowly brought to bear on the more pastoral Highlands. As in the Lowlands, many tenants were granted long leases on condition that they enclosed land and worked larger farms. Agricultural innovation, certainly in north-east Scotland, was not new. Lairds like the Earls of Huntly had for centuries tried to keep abreast of new ideas. At the time of James VI, when the Gordon family were in political eclipse, the Earl had built bridges and planted trees on his Aberdeenshire estates, and before the eighteenth century, lairds like the Gordons prepared to take personal responsibility for their estates were able to make them economically viable. The major obstacle, certainly in north-east Scotland, was distance from a marketplace rather than the poor state of their lands.

Alexander Gordon, 4th Duke of Gordon (1743–1827), Keeper of the Great Seal of Scotland and agricultural Improver. (*NTS*)

Long before Culloden, the social structure of the Highlands had shown its inadequacies. The people of the glens for the most part had scraped little more than a subsistence living, and famine had never been far away. Even by the beginning of the eighteenth century the old economy of the Highlands was already not viable. Of old, chiefs granted large parts of their estates by lease, or 'tack', to men of substance, often kinsmen. The leaseholder, or 'tacksman' as he was called, then let out smaller holdings to the rank and file of the clan. As the middle man, the tacksman lived on the surplus by which the rents he received exceeded the tack he paid to his chief. The object of the system had been to maintain the maximum number of tenants on the clan territory, and had evolved when the clan's existence depended upon its ability to defend itself from raiding neighbours. After Culloden, legislation outlawed military tenure, and the advent of the potato and improved medical knowledge reduced mortality. By 1800 the population of the Scottish Highlands was well over a quarter of a million. Encouraged by tacksmen, who no longer received good rents, emigration became the escape from poverty.

James Boswell, who persuaded Samuel Johnson to visit Scotland with him, wrote in 1773:

> We performed a dance which I suppose the emigration from Skye has occasioned. They call it 'America'. The dance seems intended to show how emigration catches, till a whole neighbourhood is set afloat. Mrs M'Kinnon told me that last year when a ship sailed from Portree for America, the people on shore were almost distracted when they saw their relations go off; they lay down on the ground, tumbled and tore the grass with their teeth. This year there was not a tear shed. The people on shore seemed to think that they would soon follow. This indifference is a mortal sign for the country.

After the American War of Independence emigration began again. The harvests of 1782 and 1783 were bad and rents could not be paid. Now it was not only a story of well-to-do, but hard-pressed tacksmen taking their tenants with them. The destitute were leaving a land that could no longer maintain them. Between 1800 and 1803, twenty-three ships – all but one from an island or Highland port – took nearly 5,400 to the New World. But many landowners, with estates by the sea, like the 5th Duke of Argyll, were opposed to emigration. Indeed in 1803 the Duke helped to instigate the Passenger Vessels Act, aimed at obstructing this drain of labour from their lands.

Chiefs became caught up in the new Lowland concept of commercial landlordism. Most of the Highland nobility were educated men, who shared the more polite culture of Lowland Scotland, and many began to better their estates on the Lowland model. Although Argyll managed them from London through regional chamberlains or baillies, he was a conscientious, well-meaning landlord. In three years, between 1779 and 1782, the population of the Argyll estates rose by a fifth and the Duke attempted to stimulate industry and fishing to provide a living for some of his people. Kelp manufacture, the burning of seaweed to produce alkali, boomed during the long wars with France and gave tenants work. In the 1760s, kelp prices were about £2 a ton. Within thirty years, the price per ton had risen

The Georgian village of Inveraray and the Duke of Argyll's castle. (*STB*)

to £10, and by the early 1800s the landlords of the Hebrides alone made profits of £70,000 on an annual export of fifteen to twenty thousand tons of kelp. But when peace came in 1815 the kelp industry waned and only a high import tax on foreign alkali made from barilla kept the Scottish industry alive until 1823. At Inveraray in 1743, the Duke of Argyll began to build a new Georgian village. Inveraray, the Duke hoped, would become a base for herring fishing in Loch Fyne; but the cost of building the town was immense, and he like many other lairds relied overmuch on the boom in kelp prices to finance its construction.

The 3rd Earl of Breadalbane, head of the cadet branch of the Campbells, was determined not to be outdone by the Duke of Argyll, the senior Campbell chief. In 1760 he too began constructing a model village, at Kenmore at the gates of his castle by Loch Tay. With the help of £1000 from the Commissioners of Forfeited Estates he built a new bridge over the Tay in 1774. Between 1750 and 1790, dozens of new villages were constructed. Sir Ludovic Grant planned Grantown-on-Spey as an industrial village. He hoped to make the new Georgian town a centre for the manufacture of

John Campbell, 3rd Earl of Breadalbane (1696–1782). (*SNPG*)

woollen and linen goods and the timber trade. Farther north the Gordon family followed suit. The 4th Duke built Fochabers at the end of the eighteenth century. The elegant town was planned by John Baxter, mason to William Adam, when the building of an extension to Gordon Castle meant the destruction of the old village.

New towns became an obsession. New Deer was the largest of four villages founded by James Ferguson of Pitfour. Born in 1734, Ferguson went on to drive turnpike roads throughout much of Buchan and planted miles of hawthorn hedges. On his own estate he constructed a forty-five-acre lake and adorned it, in the true spirit of the Enlightenment, with a miniature copy of the Temple of Theseus in Athens. His other creations were Longside, Mintlaw and Fetterangus, which he began to build as his first new village in 1772.

The British Fisheries Society was founded in London in 1786, with the 5th Duke of Argyll as governor, in an attempt to halt Highland emigration. The Society established fishing stations at Lochbay in north-west Skye, Ullapool, and Tobermoray. The most successful was set up in 1786 at Pulteneytown near Wick. By 1806 it was clear, however, that the Society had failed to stem depopulation, despite employing Thomas Telford, perhaps the greatest planner Britain has produced.

North of Inverness lay some of the most infertile land in Europe. Sir John Sinclair of Ulbster, laird of thousands of acres in Caithness, had travelled extensively abroad and returned to his estate bent on making life more happy and prosperous not only for himself but for his tenants. The difficulties were immense:

> They who live in a part of the island that has already made progress [he wrote] cannot form an idea of the obstinacies which must be sur-mounted when towns and villages must be erected and centres of communication and business; when roads and harbours must be made for the sake of domestic and foreign intercourse, when manufactures or fisheries must be established to provide employment for surplus popula-tion which an improved system of agriculture and the enlargement of farms necessarily occasion.

Under Sinclair, Scrabster was developed as an anchorage, as was the new town of Thurso. New industries were to be stimulated, mining, brewing, tanning, bleach and lint mills. Sinclair believed that his northern home should be as good a place in which to live as any. But the economic reality that faced him, and has subsequently faced individuals and governments bent on improving and developing the Highlands of Scotland, was the distance from the marketplace. Thurso was nearly 300 miles from Scotland's growing towns.

Sinclair waxed large about the virtues of the sheep:

> The Highlands of Scotland may sell at present, perhaps from two hundred thousand to three hundred thousand pounds' worth of lean cattle per annum. The same ground will produce twice as much mutton and there is wool in the bargain. If covered with the coarse woollen breed of sheep the wool might be worth about three hundred thousand pounds, whereas the same ground under the Cheviot, or true Mountain breed, will produce at least nine hundred thousand pounds of fine wool.

From the 1770s, the demand for wool had increased, its price doubling in a decade. Yet Sir John saw sheep as but a component of the economy, and he did not advocate turning northern estates exclusively over to sheep-runs.

> Nothing could be more detrimental than the mode now used of converting cattle into sheep farms in the Highlands. The first thing which is done is to drive away all the present inhabitants. The next is to introduce a shepherd and a few dogs and then to cover the mountains with flocks of wild, coarse-wooled and savage animals which seldom see their shepherd. The true plan of rendering the Highlands valuable would be to follow a different system. As many as possible of the present inhabitants ought to be retained. They ought to be gradually brought to exchange their cattle for a sufficient flock of valuable sheep. A flock of three hundred sheep might be maintained on the generality of Highland farms as they are at present.

But like many Improvers Sinclair ran into debt. Although he gave up being an MP and took a job in the Excise, the £2000 a year salary was not enough to finance his ambitious schemes. Digging ditches, building dykes and reclaiming land meant a vast investment on which there was no immediate return.

Admiral Sir John Lockhart-Ross of Balnagown is credited with having been the first landlord to rear sheep north of Inverness. When Sir John, a Lowlander, retired from the Navy, he decided to devote his life to improving his estate in Easter Ross. Black-faced sheep were imported and Lowland shepherds enticed north to take charge of them. The black-faced Linton was popular, with its characteristic coarse wool; and the Cheviot proved surprisingly hardy when it was imported from the south. Turnips helped to provide winter fodder, and huge areas of land were turned over to sheep-runs. Plots that had supported eight or nine families were patrolled only by a solitary Lowland shepherd and his dog.

Only once, in 1792, did the Highlanders attempt to halt the invasion of sheep. Starting from near Lairg, some 400 men from Ross marched south, forcing shepherds and their flocks before them. By the time they reached Alness, they had rounded up some 6000 beasts. On hearing that the military were to be brought out against them they disbanded. Five men, allegedly the ringleaders, were tried and sentenced to transportation.

In 1784 Donald Cameron of Lochiel bought back his lands from the Board of Trustees for Annexed Estates for £3433 9s 1d. He was fifteen years old and his factors in Lochaber brought in flocks of sheep to replace some of the Cameron clan, who had voluntarily raised money to support their chief and his family in French exile. Some were moved to more fertile ground at Corpach and a few tacksmen became sheep farmers in their own right, but most quit the land of their ancestors for Canada. Lochiel's income increased, as rents doubled, trebled and quadrupled; but when he died in 1832 he left a massive debt of £33,000. Although his successor, unlike many clan chiefs, was not forced to sell up entirely, gone from his land were the sons of those who had followed Gentle Lochiel into battle at Culloden.

Robert Southey felt that the forfeited estates would have been managed better if they had remained in the hands of the Crown, or sold to new owners. In his *Journal of a Tour in Scotland*, he remarked:

> A few of the Highland lairds are desirous of improving their own estates by bettering the conditions of their tenants. But the greater number are fools at heart: their object is to increase their revenue and they care not by what means this is accomplished.

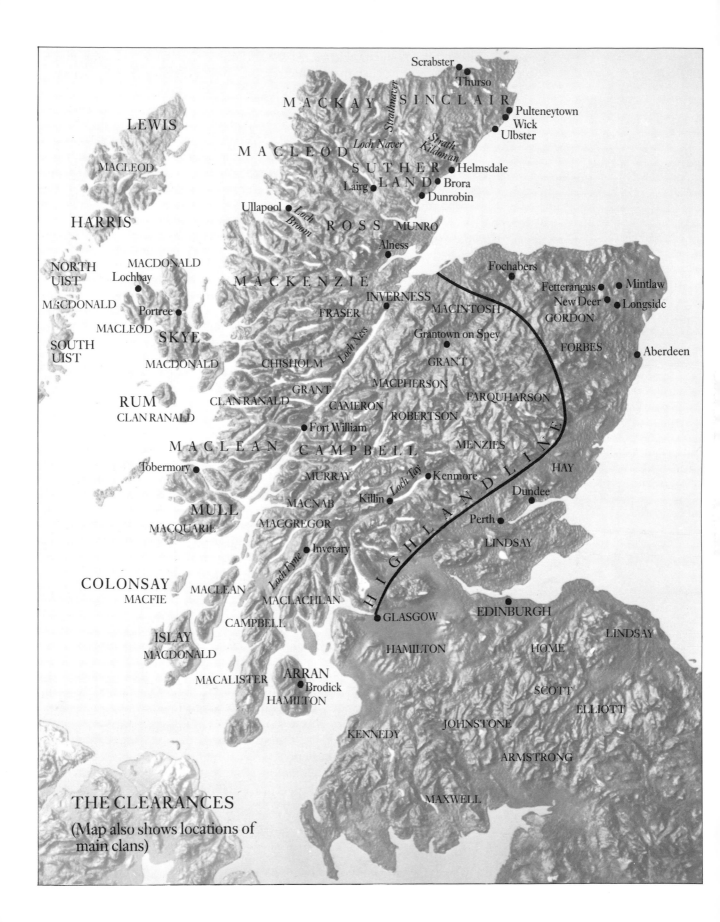

Scrabster
Thurso
Pulteneytown
Wick
Ulbster

MACKAY SINCLAIR

MACLEOD

Strathnaver

Loch Naver *Strath Kildonan*

SUTHER LAND

Helmsdale
Brora
Dunrobin

Lairg

Ullapool *Loch Broom*

ROSS MUNRO

Alness

Fochabers

Fetterangus Mintlaw
New Deer Longside

LEWIS

MACLEOD

HARRIS

MACKENZIE

INVERNESS

MACINTOSH

GORDON

FORBES

Aberdeen

NORTH UIST

MACDONALD

Lochbay

MACDONALD

Portree

MACLEOD

SKYE

MACDONALD

FRASER

Loch Ness

Grantown on Spey

GRANT

SOUTH UIST

CHISHOLM

GRANT

MACPHERSON

FARQUHARSON

CLAN RANALD

CAMERON

ROBERTSON

RUM

CLAN RANALD

Fort William

MENZIES

HAY

MACLEAN

CAMPBELL

Tobermory

MURRAY

Loch Tay Kenmore

Dundee

Killin

Perth

MULL

MACNAB

MACGREGOR

LINDSAY

MACQUARIE

Inverary

COLONSAY

MACFIE

MACLEAN

Loch Fyne

MACLACHLAN

CAMPBELL

GLASGOW

EDINBURGH

LINDSAY

ISLAY

MACDONALD

HAMILTON

HOME

MACALISTER

ARRAN
Brodick

SCOTT

ELLIOTT

HAMILTON

JOHNSTONE

KENNEDY

ARMSTRONG

MAXWELL

HIGHLAND LINE

THE CLEARANCES

(Map also shows locations of
main clans)

Francis Macnab of Macnab
(1734–1816) strikingly painted in
Highland dress by Raeburn.
(*Dewar's*)

Archibald Macnab of Macnab
(*c* 1781–1860), the colonizer of
Upper Canada.   (*SNPG*)

Yet still the population grew. At the middle of the eighteenth century, the population of Lochaber was about 3000. Within thirty years it had risen to about 4500. Even in 1810, despite massive migration, nearly 6000 still lived in the area.

Clan Macnab traditionally occupied the lands round Killin in Perthshire. Francis Macnab, the 16th chief, led a life of extravagance and in 1816 his nephew Archibald not only inherited the estate but his uncle's vast debts. With the help of his cousin, Buchanan of Lennie, Archibald quietly quit Scotland for Canada to escape his debtors. He managed to get a grant of 81,000 acres on the Ottawa River and persuaded some of his people to join him. The first of his Perthshire tenants, after a succession of poor harvests, joined him in 1825. He ruled his Canadian estate like a despot, and those who had followed him ultimately petitioned the British government in 1839:

> For the last fifteen years we have been persecuted, harassed with lawsuits, threatened with deprivation of our lands and subjected to threats by the Macnab. The said chief has impoverished many families and completely ruined others. Your petitioners have hitherto resisted, and will continue to resist, any attempt to impose the feudal system of the Dark Ages on them or their descendants.

An inquiry stripped Macnab of his power over the community and he retired to Orkney in 1848, claiming that he had been 'betrayed by his own serfs'. As a result of Macnab of Macnab's attempts to solve his own financial crisis Macnabs are found all over the world, not only in Canada and the United States but also in Australia, New Zealand, France and Argentina. Of the name Macnab, only the present clan chief and his family live in Killin.

Between 1800 and 1806, nearly 20,000 were evicted from the Highlands and islands of Scotland. Few communities were not affected but by far the most famous Clearances took place on the lands of the Countess of Sutherland, who inherited her estate at the age of one. Both her parents, William, 18th Earl of Sutherland and his wife, were never strong and their first born Catherine died at the age of two. When William went to Bath to take the waters he fell ill with fever and died shortly after. His wife Mary followed him to the grave three weeks later and they were buried in the same grave in Holyrood Abbey.

Before his death, the 18th Earl of Sutherland had appointed trustees to administer the estate for his orphaned daughter. In 1771, after a legal battle that went to the House of Lords, Elizabeth was granted the succession, which Sir Robert Gordon of Gordonstoun and George Sutherland of Forth contested. As a child the young Countess of Sutherland was brought up by her maternal grandmother in Edinburgh, where she witnessed men raised on her estate on parade before being sent to fight in the American War of Independence. She also spent time in London before visiting Dunrobin, ancestral home of the Sutherlands, for the first time aged seventeen. Three years later her engagement book notes, 'September 4, 1785, was married to Lord T'. Lord Trenton was the son of Lord Gower and later 2nd Marquis of Stafford. The couple went to Paris, where Elizabeth's husband was British Ambassador. The young Countess managed to get herself imprisoned for helping Marie Antoinette; and before returning to Britain bought furniture for Dunrobin Castle.

When he married the Countess of Sutherland, Stafford may have thought he had married a kingdom. But his wife's estate was almost a million acres of barren infertile land. In his *Tour of Scotland* Thomas Pennant described the people of Sutherland as they were in 1772:

> Almost torpid with idleness and most wretched; their hovels most miserable, made of poles wattled and covered with thin sods. There is not corn raised sufficient to supply half the wants of the inhabitants. Numbers of the miserables of this country were now migrating: they wandered in a state of desperation; too poor to pay, they madly sell themselves for their passage, preferring a temporary bondage in a strange land to starving for life in their native soil.

Forty years before the notorious Clearances the people were leaving this 'rural slum'.

Unable to speak Gaelic, the Countess and her husband had to rely on factors. At first they tried to alleviate hardship by the traditional importation of meal and grain when harvests were bad. Then, in 1803, Lord Stafford inherited a vast landed and industrial empire in the English Potteries and also came into an enormous cash fortune. His uncle, the Duke of Bridge-

'Last of the Clan' by Thomas Faed (1826–1900), a romantic view of Highland emigration.   (*GAG*)

water, left his nephew a life interest in the income from the canal that bore his name. The Marquis decided to rehabilitate his wife's estate, bring about in effect a massive re-development of the region. In concept, his plan differed little from those of other lairds like Sir John Sinclair. Those parts of the estate inland that could not provide much of a living were to be given over to sheep, and those who lived there would be moved to the coast. New townships with stone-built houses were planned and new industries like fish-curing would give the tenants employment. At Brora the people were to work in the new brewery, saltworks, brickworks, and the coal mine dating from 1529, the oldest in Scotland, was to be enlarged. Helmsdale, at the foot of Strath Kildonan, was to be a new harbour and village. In 1814 a Morayshire firm was asked to build a curing shed at Helmsdale at a cost of £1200. Other Lowland firms were paid to start up other industries and within five years the Marquis had invested £14,000 in creating this modern fishing port alone. Roads and bridges were built, together with coaching inns to help open up the vast hinterland of Sutherland to incomers and trade.

Colin Mackenzie, a lawyer acting as factor, did most of the early resettlement of the people, many of whom made the move successfully. Few, however, wanted to go to sea. William Young, a corn-chandler from Morayshire, continued the work. An ardent Improver, Young, as Commissioner and later Chief Factor, reset the farms of Sutherland where the land made them a profitable venture and was responsible for the early evictions in the west. In 1816, James Loch, an Edinburgh lawyer, took over management and improvement of the Sutherland estates. Loch was friendly with Edinburgh's leading Whigs, including Lord Cockburn, and like many was a devotee of Adam Smith's view of political economy. In 1798, the Reverend Thomas Malthus published his *Essay on the Principle of Population as it Affects the Future Improvements of Society*, which argued that the increase in population could not be matched by a similar increase in production. Since population was limited only by natural disasters such as famine, a growing population could only get poorer. Loch became an ardent Malthusian, and although he – like many Lowland Improvers – profited from his work in the Highlands, in many respects he viewed the Highlands of Scotland just as seriously as contemporary concerned minds consider the Third World. His view of the Countess of Sutherland's tenants, although it now seems to smack of Lowland bigotry, was probably not far from the truth:

> The men being impatient of regular and constant work, all the heavy labour was abandoned to the women, who were employed, occasionally, even in dragging the harrow to cover the seed. To build their hut, or get in their peats for fuel, the men were ever ready to assist; but most of the time, when not in pursuit of game, or illegal distillation, was spent in indolence and sloth.

Stubborn tenants were removed by force. As a result of what happened at Strathnavar in June 1814 Patrick Sellar was charged with the murder of an old woman who had died five days after being badly burned. 'Damn her, the old witch,' he is reported to have said; 'she has lived too long; let her burn.' The trial was held at Inverness, and the jury, made up of local landowners, found Sellar Not Guilty. Robert McKidd, the Sheriff-Substitute, who had courageously brought the charge, lost his job. Patrick Sellar became tenant of the sheep-run that replaced the people of Strathnavar and he was allowed by James Loch to continue with his work.

In 1811, the factors of the Sutherland estate told the Board of Agriculture:

> The number of Cheviots are now about 15,000. More ground will be laid off for the same mode of husbandry, without decreasing the population. Situations in various ways will be fixed on for the people. Fishing stations, in which mechanics will be settled; inland villages, with carding machines; moors and detached spots calculated for the purpose will be found, but the people must work. The industrious will be encouraged and protected, but the slothful must remove or starve, as man was not born to be idle, but to gain his bread by the sweat of his brow.

The Duke of Sutherland's revenue from the Bridgewater Canal, however, was finite, as the present Countess of Sutherland explains:

> The Duke was a fairly elderly man and only had a life interest in this income. He and the Countess wanted to do all their building quickly and the factors they employed were in a great hurry. I think Loch thought afterwards that he'd done the thing too fast and perhaps left too much to other people. The ideas were good and perhaps there should have been a pilot scheme to show people how good life could be on the coast. I think they didn't realize how much Highlanders cling together and what a strong clan feeling there was.

By 1811 some 15,000 tenants on the Sutherland estate had been moved to make way for sheep; but despite the social hardship caused, the Duke's scheme seemed to make economic sense. So important had the wool trade become that mill-owners from Halifax, Wakefield and Huddersfield came north to Inverness to purchase upwards of 15,000 stones of fleece a year, much of it from Sutherland. But the hundreds of thousands of pounds spent on improving met with failure. The Duke's fishing fleet failed to rival the fishermen of the north-east and fish prices, like those of wool after the Napoleonic War, slumped. For over twenty years the Duke and his wife received not a penny profit from their investment. They had succeeded only in inflicting lasting misery on the Countess's tenants.

In an attempt to rectify the worst abuses caused by haphazard emigration at the hands of the unscrupulous, as well as provide a select labour force for his own plans in North America, Thomas Douglas, the 5th Earl of Selkirk, organized planned emigration to the New World. In 1803, at the age of thirty-two, Selkirk personally led eight hundred emigrants chosen from Skye, Ross, Inverness and Argyll to Prince Edward Island, where they founded a Scottish colony. Two years later he settled Baldoon, now called Wallaceburg. In 1811, he sponsored his most famous venture, the settlement by Scots of the Red River in what became Manitoba. The government refused to support his scheme to colonize the great north-west unknown of Canada, so Selkirk turned to the Hudson's Bay Company, whose Royal Charter gave them control of western Canada. Having bought an interest in the Company, he obtained a grant of 116,000 square miles of territory called Assiniboia, it is said for ten shillings. Although the land was cheap Selkirk under the terms of the grant had to bear the entire cost of transporting the emigrants and was also made solely responsible for negotiating with the local Indians and for building the new settlement.

The statue of Thomas Douglas, 5th Earl of Selkirk (1771–1820), outside Manitoba State House. (*Author*)

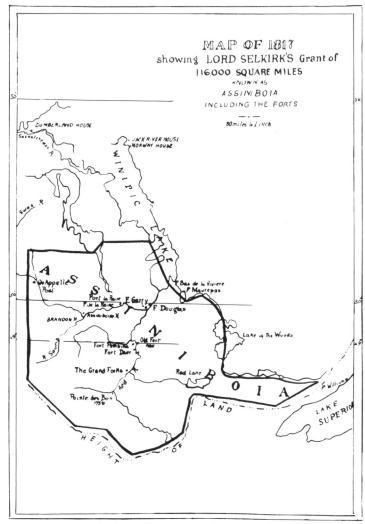

Map illustrating Prof Bryce's Paper on the Five Forks of Winnipeg
Proceedings of The Royal Society of Canada 1885 Vol III Sec II Pole 3.

A contemporary sketch of the 5th Earl of Selkirk's grant from the Hudson's Bay Company. (*HBC*)

Main Street, Winnipeg, the town that grew out of Selkirk's Red River Settlement. (*PAC*)

A Hudson's Bay trading store in the 1840s. (*HBC*)

From the outset, Selkirk's scheme was bitterly opposed by the rival North-West Company, who saw his scheme as a threat to their profitable fur trade. No sooner had the Earl enlisted colonists in Sutherland than the North-West Company's agents set about dissuading the emigrants with tales of hardship and hostile Indians.

The crofters who joined Selkirk's parties were not destitute. They were required to pay ten pounds per head for transportation and the promise of a year's supply of provisions. Each would be granted 100 acres of land, at a cost of five shillings an acre. The Red River scheme was a business venture, not a charitable exercise.

Captain Miles Macdonell, born in Scotland, became the first Governor of Assiniboia. With his father, he had fought for Britain in the American War of Independence. He and his men of the advance party left Stromness on 24 July 1811. The following spring the party made their way south by boat and foot from York Factory on Hudson's Bay, a journey of over 700 miles, and reached the site of the settlement just six weeks before the arrival of the first emigrants, who left Stromness on 24 June 1812. All were immediately put to work building Fort Douglas for protection, and the land on the west side of Red River was divided out. Each plot was two miles long and between five and ten chains wide. Although inconvenient for farming, it was Selkirk's view that such a division would enable the settlers to live close together as they had done in the Highlands, both for security and for companionship. The Earl also set aside land for churches and schools, and planned roads and bridges. More emigrants came out and twice the North-West Company attacked with the help of half-caste Indians. After the Battle of Seven Oaks on 19 June 1816 Fort Douglas was taken and the settlers told to quit.

In 1817, Lord Selkirk visited his settlers who had returned to Red River and promised them a Gaelic-speaking Presbyterian church. He asked that the parish be named Kildonan, after the one in Sutherland from which so many had come. But the long legal battles with the North-West Company over ownership and settlement of the area broke his health and Selkirk returned to Europe a sick man. He died in Pau in southern France in April 1820. Ironically a few months after his death the two giant fur companies united under the name of the Hudson's Bay Company. Sir Walter Scott, who knew Selkirk well, provided a fitting epitaph:

> I never knew a man in my life with a more generous and disinterested disposition or one whose talents and perseverance were fitted to bring great and national schemes to a successful conclusion.

It was not until 1851 that the community at Red River was to receive its first minister, the Reverend John Black from Scotland, who set about building the first Presbyterian church in the west of Canada. In the graveyard of his church at Old Kildonan are the remains of the early pioneers, the Bannermans, Sutherlands, Rosses and Hendersons.

Unlike many of his contemporaries, Lord Selkirk saw that emigration from Scotland and the development of Australia, New Zealand, Canada and elsewhere was of far-reaching significance. In Canada, if there had not been

Old Kildonan Church. In the graveyard are the remains of the Presbyterian Scots who helped open up and settle Western Canada. (*Author*)

The Reverend John and Mrs Black.
(*MA*)

a British settlement on the Red River, it is likely that the Americans would have gone straight up to Hudson's Bay, and Canada as it is today would have been impossible. Selkirk's dream came true. His pioneer settlement on the edge of the prairie prospered and became Winnipeg.

But in Scotland the 5th Earl of Selkirk's enlightened attitude scarcely scratched the surface. The depopulation of Scotland's Highlands and islands continued throughout the nineteenth century and well into the twentieth. Then came the charges, particularly after the Second World War, that the Clearances of the eighteenth century alone had started the exodus, made life for those who were left behind impossible.

Historical evidence is to the contrary. Mass migration from the Highlands had begun long before sheep were introduced by improving landlords, and the deterioration of Highland life had its roots in Scotland's past, when the Stewart Kings wanted the power of Highland Scotland broken. The monarchy, quite rightly, had wished to tame the warlike way of life of Highland Scotland; clan society was only viable through battle and theft, usually at the expense of Lowland Scotland. Left to itself, the Highlands could not have existed in perpetuity on the fringe of a different, wealthier civilization. The Stewarts were the first in a long line of Scots who tried to change life in Highland Scotland, but they had no idea what to put in its place. They were not, however, like the agricultural Improvers of the eighteenth century, bent on destroying the Gaelic way of life; but rather on attempting to improve it, to bring the Highlands within Scotland as a whole. For poets, novelists and journalists, the Clearances remain a source of inspiration, and the human tragedy still moves Scots at home and abroad; but few of those who blame the Highland-improving lairds can give alternative solutions to the problem with any economic reality. The soil of Scotland's most beautiful landscape could not provide a living for the mass of folk who wished to live in the glens.

The attention given to the events in Sutherland has distorted reality. The Countess's estate was untypical. Both she and her husband almost certainly felt that what they were doing was in the interest of their tenants in the long run. True they wished to make their vast estate profitable; but few could have expected them to keep their people on the land by charity indefinitely. Some form of reduction in the Highland population had to take place, or the people might have suffered a worse fate.

Sheep from Lowland Scotland were but one solution in a long list of attempts to make Scotland's more remote areas economically viable. Kelp manufacture, fishing, iron smelting and other industries were tried in the eighteenth and nineteenth centuries to bring work. In more recent times, large companies as well as governments with great resources to call upon have also tried and often failed.

In the eighteenth century, the Highlands and islands of Scotland ceased to be an economy of kind and slowly became one of cash. To the young educated Highlander Scotland's growing towns, especially Glasgow, were magnets. Few rural communities did not have some relative or friend established in the town. The faith of Calvin, moreover, made people wish to better themselves and encouraged migration. Britain's imperial wars also added to the disintegrating process, leaving the glens to the very young, the old and the widowed, weakening the communities of the north.

The Highland Clearances, however sad and traumatic, cannot be seen in isolation. Scotland by the late eighteenth century was a fast changing society, grappling with the problems of industrialization and growing population caused by improved agriculture and medical knowledge. It was a restless, changing age, and as in all such periods of history sections of society, often inadvertently, get hurt.

16

Made in Scotland

AT THE TIME OF THE UNION with England Glasgow was one of the most beautiful cities in Britain. The River Clyde was but a placid stream, fifteen inches deep at low tide, and the burgh took pride in the riverside meadow where the broom grew so charmingly they called it the Broomielaw and used it to graze their cattle. Less than 13,000 'tame and sober' people inhabited the town that had grown up round the great medieval Cathedral of St Mungo.

Within a hundred years Glasgow and the county of Lanarkshire of which she was part was to spawn the Scottish working class. By 1804, Glasgow's population had risen to over 70,000. Her growth was founded upon a new trade – the import and re-export of tobacco from the American colonies. Britain demanded that all goods from her colonies pass through British ports, and the Scots were quick to take advantage of a trade which for centuries England had jealously guarded as her own. Glasgow was several hundred miles closer to America than any English port, and the chronic state of war that existed between Britain and much of Europe during the eighteenth century meant that the Scottish burgh was safer than Bristol. The Tobacco Exchange was at 33 Virginia Court, where a little window that can be seen to this day is said to have been the auctioneer's box. By the 1720s, Glasgow was importing over half of all the American tobacco brought into Britain.

In return the American colonists needed manufactured goods like linen, paper and wrought-iron. In the beginning, Glasgow had few exports of her own, as Alexander Carlyle pointed out in 1743 in his autobiography:

> There were not manufactures sufficient, either there or at Paisley, to supply an outward-bound cargo for Virginia. Manufactures were in their infancy. About this time the inkle manufactory was first begun and was shown to strangers as a great curiosity.

The making of inkle, cloth tape, was a huge success and is remembered to this day by Americans who refer to modern adhesive transparent tape as Scotch Tape.

The tobacco community was so close that, even by the 1770s, only thirty-seven companies, involving fewer than eighty merchants, monopolized Glasgow's trade. A tightly-knit group, the Tobacco Lords, as they came to be known, were often linked by blood and marriage.

John Glassford, 'Tobacco Lord', and family. (*PP*)

George III (1738–1820), grandson of George II. His mentor was the Scotsman John Stuart, 3rd Earl of Bute, whom George described as his 'dearest friend'. (*NPG*)

John Glassford was typical of those who made fortunes. He owned twenty-five ships and his business was worth over £500,000 a year. Glassford was also a partner in the Glasgow Tanwork Company, one of the largest leather workers in Europe, and a partner in two of Glasgow's banks. He had large interests in the Cudbear Dyeworks and the printfield at Pollockshaws. Besides all this he had made three successful marriages and owned a large estate at Douglaston and a town house, Shawfield, which on his death was sold for £9850.

William Cunninghame became one of the richest Tobacco Lords. Realizing in advance that the American Revolution might cut off supplies, Cunninghame shrewdly bought up all the tobacco he could lay his hands on and then warehoused it until the price rose from the pre-war level of sixpence a pound to three shillings and sixpence.

During the war, the tobacco trade virtually collapsed. In 1777 less than half a million pounds found their way up the Clyde instead of the normal forty-six million, and by 1783 Britain had not only lost her colonies but also her monopoly on American tobacco. Heavy losses were taken by those Glasgow merchants who owned plantations; but most had developed other trade, particularly with the West Indies. The loss of the American colonies contributed to the forming of a Chamber of Commerce in Glasgow; founded by Provost Patrick Colquhoun, it was the first in Britain. King George III granted the Chamber a Royal Charter in March 1783. By the turn of the century, Scottish merchants also had interests in Asia, South America and Australasia. They had shown that the Scots, although officially banned from trading with England's rich colonial empire before the union, had nevertheless developed business acumen in their long mercantile links with Europe. From an early date, Scotland was drawn into the world economy, and trade became more diverse as a result of improvements in domestic industries.

In 1707 Scotland's linen industry was primitive. Those who worked up the cloth were cottagers and farmers first, spinners and weavers second. Home was their factory to which an agent brought flax returned to him as finished cloth. Spinners owned their own wheels and weavers their looms. When merchants moved into the industry, they cut out the middlemen by originating manufacture themselves. In 1746, the British Linen Company was formed to provide the capital required to import flax; when it was renamed the British Linen Bank, given the fact that the industry was nationwide, the bank pioneered the establishment of branches.

Patrick Colquhoun, Lord Provost of Glasgow, who at the age of thirty-eight helped organize the town's Chamber of Commerce. (*GCC*)

Spinning was mostly done in the north-eastern counties, and other areas specialized in weaving particular types of cloth. Perth was famous for linen sheetings, shawl-cloths, calicoes and muslins. In Fife, they made coarser linens and canvas sails for the British Navy. The weavers of Dunfermline made their name producing fine table linen, and from 1725, Glasgow had a prosperous industry in fine lawns and damasks. In 1727, a Board of Trustees for Manufactures was set up by the British government to help stimulate Scotland's linen and fishing industries. The money came from the promised part of the Equivalent not paid in cash but owed the Scots under the Treaty of Union. Weavers and flax-dressers from the Low Countries were brought over to instruct the Scots in new technology, and thread-twisting machines and presses for folding finished cloth were also imported. Scots were encouraged to adopt new methods such as the use of chloride of lime in bleaching, and throughout the eighteenth century the production of linen in Scotland increased. By 1778 there were over 4000 handlooms at work in and around Glasgow alone. Dundee could boast nearly 2000 weavers, Paisley over 1300; by 1760 ten million yards of cloth were produced each year.

The Bounty Act of 1742 gave financial incentives to exporters and Glasgow in particular thrived on a growing trade in linen with America. The linen industry, however, suffered booms and slumps. When the American colonists became independent, they turned away from buying British goods if they could, and flax prices had begun to rise steadily from the middle of the eighteenth century. Linen became costly and cotton was looked to as a substitute.

Introduced from the Caribbean to the American mainland, cotton quickly became cheaper than flax as a raw material. Eli Whitney's invention of the cotton gin, which enabled fibre to be separated easily from seed, kept prices low. At Penicuik, outside Edinburgh, the first water-wheel powered cotton mill in Scotland was established in 1778. At Rothesay, on Bute, a second mill was opened in the same year, using cargoes of raw cotton from the West Indies landed at Glasgow.

The British Linen Bank, Ingram Street, Glasgow, which united with the Bank of Scotland in 1969.   (*M*)

In Britain the inventions that revolutionized the cotton industry such as the flying shuttle and spinning jenny were English and ensured that Lancashire would lead the world in the industrial production of cotton. In Scotland, to begin with, cotton was woven on old-style linen frames and weavers became the aristocrats of industry able to command high wages. Their superiority was, however, short-lived. In 1807, at Catrine in Ayrshire, the first power-loom in Scotland was installed; the age of the machine and the industrialized worker had arrived. The town was founded by Sir Claude Alexander of Ballochmyle in 1787 who, with the help of David Dale of Glasgow, set up a cotton mill. Where once had stood a tiny hamlet a town of over 1300 millworkers grew.

At Stanley in Perthshire, the Duke of Atholl and Sir George Dempster, the MP, built a cotton mill in the late 1780s with the help of the English inventor, Richard Arkwright. Their plan included the construction of a new village to house the workers at a cost of £2000. By 1795, the Stanley mill was employing 350, of whom 300 were women or children under the age of sixteen.

The parish of Neilston near Glasgow also became a mill town. In his report for the *Original Statistical Account*, the minister noted:

David Dale (1739–1806) acquired his first cotton mill at Rothesay in 1778. (*PP*)

> The rapid increase of manufactures is neither friendly to the health nor morals of the people. In cotton mills a multitude of children spend a considerable part of their life there and are often exposed not to the best example. It is to be feared that a total ignorance of Christianity may become prevalent. The children in these works, confined as it were to the very point of a spindle, must of course have narrow and contracted minds. While the work is going on, the finer parts of the cotton, flying off by friction, fill the atmosphere in which they breathe with unwholesome particles, and it is probably from this cause that their appearance is so pale and sickly.

Old handloom workers fought a losing battle against industrialization. In 1814, the weekly wage of Scottish weavers was £1 1s 6d. By 1830, many were fortunate to earn six shillings a week. By the 1830s more than 85,000 were employed in weaving in Scotland, most in cotton factories. By the 1880s, there were over 100,000, the vast majority women.

Only in Paisley did the craft of the weaver live on. Shawls, copies of those that had been brought back in the 1770s by soldiers serving in Kashmir in India, were produced in Norwich in England as well as Paisley. The intricate design meant that in the beginning they could not be worked on power looms. When Napoleon stopped the importation of silk thread into Britain by the Berlin Decree, many weavers, like William Coats of Paisley, began to produce cotton sewing thread. Coats flourished and became one of the few Scottish companies big enough to dominate British and world markets. Even as early as 1840, they were exporting three-quarters of their production to the United States. When the Americans put on tariff barriers Coats responded by building their own cotton mill at Rhode Island in 1870.

Paisley in the 1820s.   (*M*)

The fate of the handloom weaver, William Carnegie of Dunfermline, was typical. When factories forced him out of business, he saw no alternative but to take his family to the New World, including his son, Andrew. Others, more privileged, found fortune by moving with the times, like David Dale who had once been a weaver in Paisley. He was born in 1739 in Stewarton and, realizing the days of the handloom were numbered, became a cloth dealer. In 1778 he had acquired his first cotton mill at Rothesay and by the end of the century was employing large numbers of factory weavers. In 1795 he started the New Lanark Mills, which within ten years was employing 1334 workers. A typical capitalist manufacturer, Dale realized that to make profit he had to make his cotton as cheap and preferably cheaper than the fabric produced in Lancashire. Scottish workers could be paid less and the abundance of local water power made mechanization easy. Even as early as the eighteenth century, industrial advance in Scotland, given the greater distance from the marketplace, was only possible if it could be competitive.

Mill workers in Scotland were housed in meanly designed tenements and women and children formed a large proportion of the ill-paid workforce. Most came from the countryside or from the poorhouse. At New Lanark, all the occupants of one of Dale's tenements were paupers from Edinburgh and Glasgow. Children were especially favoured because, apart from being cheap, they were able to crawl under the machines and sweep away fluff during spinning. Most owners believed that only children employed before the age of twelve could be trained to become good workers, and at New Lanark hundreds of orphans were brought in to work eleven-and-a-half hours a day. Housed in a special building, they slept three to a bed and were obliged to attend the factory school for two hours each day after work. Their diet consisted of oatmeal and milk twice a day with for their main meal barley soup, bread, potatoes, meat or herrings and cheese. At New Lanark, given the background of most children, they were treated well. David Dale, a godly man, made benevolent use of child labour.

David Dale's New Lanark.   (*SG*)

The recruitment and training of labour were problems hard to solve. The discipline of factory life was difficult for rural folk, who found long and regular hours at the machines for a meagre weekly wage difficult to bear. The turnover of labour in the mills was staggering. At Newton Stewart in 1800 fewer than half the workers stayed the full twelve months.

Cotton mills ceased to rely on rivers for power when in 1765 James Watt patented his famous condenser and the steam age began; but in Scotland the introduction of steam was slow because of the abundance of running water.

By 1787 there were nineteen cotton mills in Scotland. In less than half a century there were nearly two hundred, half of them in or around Glasgow. By the middle of the nineteenth century 400,000 Scots were employed by the industry, three-quarters of them in the county of Lanark. Most specialized in fancy cloth, leaving Lancashire to supply common cottons, and most Scottish companies were small. But other industries were competing with cotton for industrial capital. Scotland was richer underground than above.

At Leadhills and Wanlockhead, lead as well as gold and silver had been mined for centuries. The highest villages in Scotland, they were nicknamed 'God's Treasure Chest'. The lot of lead miners was hard. They received no day-to-day wages but entered into a bargain whereby they were paid after they had driven deep into the hills and brought out the metal. If men were killed their wives, according to contract, had to complete their husband's unfinished work before payment was made. Although from 1738 Leadhills had a lending library, fewer than one in ten Scottish miners were literate.

Coal was Scotland's greater mineral, required to power steam engines and bring heat to the houses of Britain's industrial workers. By the end of the eighteenth century many Scots lairds were leasing mineral rights on their extensive lands. Each year the Duke of Hamilton drew more than £100,000 in royalties, £10 for every miner employed in the pits under his estates. Underground workers were paid fourpence a ton for the coal they dug out with their bare hands. The man under whose land they laboured received one shilling and fourpence.

Coal miners were serfs, bought and sold with the mine. Even as adults it was impossible for them to obtain their freedom and they were advertised for sale regularly in Edinburgh newspapers.

Coal mining was a family affair. While children worked fourteen hours a day in darkness up to their waists in water, their mothers acted as hauliers, dragging coal trucks on all fours up from the steep seams to the surface. By custom mining areas were outside the mainstream of Scottish life, and the squalid homes of colliers were proof of the country's lack of concern. Special galleries, with their own outside staircase like the one still found at Newton Parish Kirk, were built to keep miners and their families apart from the rest of the congregation on Sundays. Hugh Miller, the Scottish geologist, visited a typical mining village near Edinburgh:

Hugh Miller (1802–56), self-taught geologist who, unable to reconcile his religious views with science, took his own life. (*HA*)

> It was a wretched assemblage of dingy, low-roofed, tile-covered hovels, each of which perfectly resembled all the others, and was inhabited by a rude and ignorant race of men, that still bore about them the soil and stain of recent slavery. All the older men of that village, though situated little more than four miles from Edinburgh, had been born slaves.
>
> The collier women of this village – poor over-toiled creatures, who carried up all the coal from underground on their backs, by a long turnpike stair inserted in one of the shafts – continued to bear more of the marks of serfdom still about them than even the men . . . It has been estimated that one of their ordinary day's work was equal to the carrying of a hundred-weight from the level of the sea to the top of Ben Lomond. I have seen these collier women crying like children, when toiling under their load along the upper rounds of the wooden stair that traversed the shaft; and then returning, scarce a minute after, with the empty creel, singing with glee.

By the end of the eighteenth century, various Acts of Parliament had given miners their freedom; but the legislation was brought about by economic rather than human concern and women, together with children, continued to work long shifts. Wives, God willing, worked on until they were fifty. To earn eightpence a day, they hauled thirty-six hundredweight to the surface. In 1842, Margaret Drysdale, aged fifteen and a coal putter, told a government inquiry:

> I don't like the work, but mother is dead and father brought me down; I had no choice. I have harness on like the horse and pull carts. Large carts hold seven and a half hundredweight.

After the union, Scotland's iron industry was centred in the north-west. English ironmasters had come north to set up furnaces to smelt ore shipped up to Scotland from the south. At Bonawe, east of Oban, an iron smelting furnace was established in 1753, the high cost of transporting English ore from Furness more than offset by the ready supply of cheap charcoal. The company, Richard Ford of Lancashire, continued to work at Bonawe until 1873 and represented the only real success in attempting to industrialize the north-west Highlands.

Fifty years after Abraham Darby had pioneered a new method of smelting iron ore with coke, the Carron iron works were founded near Falkirk. Again the money and expertise were English. Only one of the founding partners was a Scot, William Cadell, a merchant from Cockenzie in the Firth of Forth. The prime mover in the scheme was John Roebuck. Carron began operations in 1760 and quickly gained a reputation for grates, stoves, iron pipes and nails. In 1776, the iron works was responsible for a new light gun called the Carronade which found fame far and wide and was used, it is said, by both sides at the Battle of Waterloo. By 1800 Carron had become the largest munitions works in Europe.

But because of the cost of transporting ore from the south, the Scottish iron industry expanded slowly. In 1786 the Clyde Iron Works was set up at Tollcross near Glasgow to manufacture bar iron and other companies were founded in Ayrshire and Lanarkshire. By 1796, there were sixteen iron works in Scotland. Then a discovery was made in the Monkland area of Scotland's central belt that brought about rapid development. In the early 1800s, David Mushet, the manager of the Calder iron works, discovered a rich vein of ironstone known as 'Mushet's Blackband'. Found in vast quantity, blackband ironstone was in fact coal that contained anything up to thirty-five per cent raw iron. Scotland's fledgling iron industry no longer had to rely upon the importation of raw material and new methods of working the metal were swiftly introduced.

In James Neilson, Scotland produced her first major iron-age inventor. Born in Shettleston in 1792, Neilson worked first as an engine-wright at Irvine and became the foreman of the Glasgow Gas Works in 1817. In 1828 he introduced the hot blast method of smelting iron which required a quarter of the coal previously needed. With Neilson's hot blast system, the Coatbridge area became one of the centres of iron smelting. The village of Airdrie became a burgh and the population increased almost three times. Labourers from Ireland and skilled workers from Staffordshire in England swelled the population. In 1755, the population of the parish of Old Monkland was

An engineer in the railway works at Cowlairs, Glasgow, c. 1890, by which time Scotland's iron and steel industries were foremost in the world. (*PP*)

1183. By 1861, 29,543 people lived in the town. By 1847 Scotland was responsible for a quarter of Britain's total output of iron.

The output of coal also rapidly increased. By the middle of the nineteenth century, Scottish mines produced eight million tons of coal a year and within fifty years were to produce four times as much. Most of Scotland's coal, and iron, was exported; home demand was as yet slight.

Baird's of Gartsherrie was the largest Scottish iron company to emerge in the second half of the nineteenth century. By 1870 they employed over nine thousand and were responsible for the production of a quarter of Scotland's iron at their twenty-six Ayrshire and sixteen Lanarkshire furnaces.

Scotland's industrial revolution created a huge demand for labour. Peasants from Ireland and the Highlands were drawn to the towns where they had to learn new skills. They worked with dangerous equipment in an age when no legislation protected them and the social cost of industrial expansion was great. Overcrowding and poor health were the lot of most and industrial paternalism was the keynote of the age. Iron workers were forced to live in tied houses and had to use company shops. Factory workers lived in tall steep tenements without plumbing and water.

As the wealth of Scotland became increasingly centred on the Lowlands, so were the country's people. By 1840, a third of Scotland's manufacturing labourers lived in one county, Lanark. In 1740, Glasgow had just over 17,000 inhabitants. In less than fifty years the population had grown to 66,000. By 1831, there were over 200,000; thirty years later nearly 400,000 were crammed into the city.

Whole families were employed in factories, and when gas lighting was introduced in the early part of the nineteenth century, workers were able to put in longer hours. The abuse of children was the greatest evil of the age. By 1830, children of six or seven were put to work in cotton mills for less than two shillings a week. In Dundee, children got up at four o'clock in the morning in order to walk to the factory and be at the machines by five to five. They were expected to work all day until half past seven at night. Often they had to be beaten with straps to keep them at their machines. One Dundee mill owner employed Edinburgh orphans whom he housed in a building locked and barred at night to stop them running away.

Women were expected to work thirteen to fourteen hours a day; but seventeen-hour days were not unknown. For this they were paid wages of four to eight shillings a week. Their health probably suffered more than that of their husbands. Pregnant women stayed by their machines until the last possible moment and went back to work as soon as their babies were born. Chronic pelvic disorders among women workers were common. In 1861 a quarter of the children born to women cotton workers died before they were a year old. Mothers whose babies survived had no alternative but to leave them at home.

Industrial workers survived on a diet of porridge and potatoes and, badly fed, succumbed to disease. Rickets was endemic and tuberculosis rampant among cotton spinners and miners. Smallpox was hideously nicknamed 'the poor man's friend'. Epidemics of the disease, it was argued, at least relieved the hardship caused by too many children. Smallpox became the scourge of Scotland. By the middle of the nineteenth century it was estimated that one

Blackfriars Wynd, Edinburgh, 1868.   (*CAC*)

death in ten in Edinburgh and one in six in Kilmarnock was caused by the disease. After smallpox was slowly brought under control by immunization, cholera came from the Far East. In fifty years, from 1831, Glasgow suffered four major cholera epidemics. In Britain as a whole in the second half of the century, people could expect to live on average forty-six years. In Glasgow, average life-expectancy was thirty.

In 1840 it was claimed that in terms of housing and health Glasgow was the worst city in Europe. Edinburgh, Scotland's capital, was only a marginally better place to live. Scottish doctors did their best and many were convinced that poor housing and malnutrition were wreaking havoc with the nation's health. But the Scottish middle-class turned a blind eye and businessmen did nothing for fear of losing profits.

Industrial workers took to the bottle. Happiness, however fleeting, came in a glass. A Glasgow minister wrote in the 1793 *Statistical Account*:

> There is now a great deal more industry on six days of the week, and a great deal more dissipation and licentiousness on the seventh. Great crimes were formerly very uncommon; but now robberies, housebreakings, swindling, pickpockets, pilferers, and consequently executions, are becoming more common. These delinquents, as well as common prostitutes, are often little advanced above childhood; and yet a healthy child of 7 to 8 years, or at most 10 years of age, can now earn a very decent subsistence from some of the numerous manufactories established among us.

Argyll Street, Glasgow, in the eighteenth century.   (*PP*)

The High Street, Glasgow in the middle of the nineteenth century, with its lodging houses sandwiched between off-licences and the offices of the Glasgow Abstainers. A photograph by Thomas Annan (1830–87), one of the city's pioneers of photography.   (*M*)

By 1832 there was a dealer in spirits in Glasgow to every fourteen families. Nine years later it was estimated that the Scots were drinking twenty-three pints of spirits annually while their English industrial counterparts drank four.

A few industrialists attempted to rectify the social abuse they had helped to create. Robert Owen was one. Born in Wales in 1771, Owen was a mill-owner in Manchester before becoming the son-in-law of David Dale. In 1800, Robert became the manager of New Lanark and began to run the mills in a revolutionary way. Regarded as the founder of the co-operative movement, Owen encouraged his workers to form friendly societies and use the subscriptions to help sick and injured members. He opened a company store where his workers could buy basic goods more cheaply. The town was kept clean and refuse collection was organized on a regular basis. In the mills, the working day was reduced to ten and a half hours and Owen refused to employ children until they were ten years old. Until that age, they went to Owen's Institution and learnt history, geography and botany as well as reading, writing and arithmetic. On 1 January 1816, Robert Owen addressed the inhabitants of New Lanark regarding his Institution for the Formation of Character:

> The Institution has been devised, to afford the means of receiving your children at an early age, as soon almost as they can walk. By this means, many of you, mothers of families, will be enabled to earn a better maintenance or support for your children; you will have less care and anxiety about them; while the children will be prevented from acquiring bad habits, and gradually prepared to learn the best.

In 1819, Owen had helped secure the passage of the Factory Act which banned children under nine working in cotton mills and limited the working day of those aged between nine and sixteen to no more than twelve hours. Yet Robert Southey remarked in his *Journal of a Tour in Scotland*:

Robert Owen (1771–1858), born in Montgomeryshire. Son-in-law of David Dale, he became manager of New Lanark in 1800. (*SNPG*)

> Owen in reality deceives himself. He is part-owner and sole Director of a large establishment, differing more in accidents than in essence from a plantation: the persons under him happen to be white, and are at liberty by law to quit his service, but while they remain in it they are as much under his absolute management as so many negro slaves ... Owen keeps out of sight from others, and perhaps from himself that his system, instead of aiming at perfect freedom, can only be kept in play by absolute power.
> Yet I admire the man, and like him too.

Owen's workers were sceptical. Because of his age limit on the employment of children, family income was reduced and his compulsory dancing classes were bitterly resented. He was disliked by other mill-owners, and in 1828 he went to America and established a colony in New Harmony in Indiana.

Samuel Smiles was another enlightened spirit of the industrial age. Born in Haddington in 1812, he studied to become a doctor but was better known as a writer. Smiles believed that the humblest worker could better himself by hard work and in 1859 published his most famous book, *Self Help*. He toured the country lecturing and told the working men of Leeds:

Samuel Smiles (1812–1904). (*SNPG*)

> The education of the working classes is to be regarded, in its highest aspect, not as a means of raising up a few clever and talented men into a higher rank of life, but of elevating and improving the whole class – of raising the entire condition of the working man. The grand object aimed at should be to make the great mass of the people virtuous, intelligent, well-informed, and well-conducted; and to open up them new sources of pleasure and happiness. Knowledge is of itself one of the highest enjoyments ...
> We believe in a 'good time coming' for working men and women – when an atmosphere of intelligence shall pervade them, when they will prove themselves as enlightened, polite, and independent as the other classes in society.

William Quarrier, born in 1829, began work at the age of seven in a pin factory. By the age of twenty he was in business for himself and resolved to help Glasgow's destitute children. In 1871 he founded his famous homes at the Bridge of Weir where children of the tenements were given proper food, fresh air and education. He was also responsible for opening the first tuberculosis sanitorium in Scotland.

In Scotland poor relief was mean. Only the destitute qualified and those out of work because of slumps or illness received nothing. Relief was in the hands of the Kirk but most Kirk Sessions did little more than help the poor with their rent and the provision of food was left to private charity. Whereas in England Poor Relief could mean anything up to seven shillings and sixpence a week, in Scotland grants rarely exceeded one shilling and sixpence. Calvinists found it hard to square the ethic of hard work with unemployment and frequently Kirk leaders saw moral reasons as the cause of poverty rather than the single-minded demands of a capitalist industrial economy.

Drink was the demon, and Glasgow, with its large immigrant Irish

William Quarrier (1829–1903), his wife and a view of the homes he opened at Bridge of Weir in 1876. (Q)

population, was a rich ground for salvation. Temperance societies were established and by the 1840s at least 30,000 Irishmen in the city belonged to societies organized by their Catholic priests. Then as hundreds of thousands of immigrants crossed the Irish Sea in search of work, rivalry for jobs in Glasgow came to be expressed in terms of religious differences. The Irish were often willing to accept wages below those demanded by Scots workers and there is some truth in the Protestant claim that the Catholic Irish helped keep the standard of living lower than Scots workers would have tolerated. The Irish and their priests were blamed for the town's poverty, crime and drunkenness.

Scotland's major problem was housing. In 1838 in Edinburgh a tene-

The joiners' workshop. The children of Scotland's industrial slums were taught a trade by Quarrier, and (*below*) received health care denied them in the city.   (*Q*)

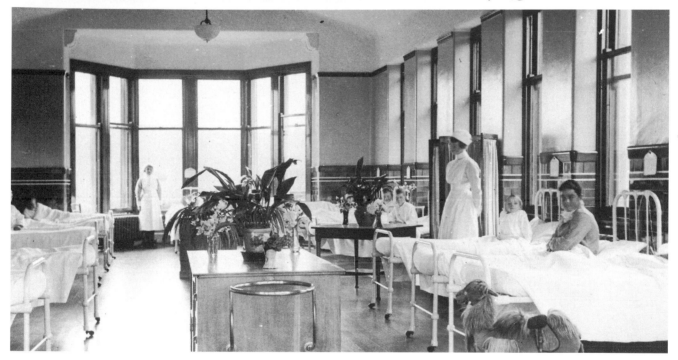

ment of fifty-nine rooms was home to nearly 250 people who had no water supply of any kind. When the census was taken in 1841, it showed that more than a third of Scotland's families – a million people – lived in one-room homes. Eight thousand had rooms with no windows. The situation deteriorated. By 1870, over forty per cent of Paisley's population lived in single rooms, in Dundee thirty-seven per cent, in Aberdeen thirty-five per cent and in Edinburgh and Glasgow thirty-four. Public opinion tolerated the scandal. People used to rural hovels, it was thought, should require no more than a 'single-end'. The 'one apartment houses', as newspapers liked to call them, were in truth no more than rural hovels stacked one upon another. City dosshouses, in which many unmarried labourers lived, were urban bothies.

Scotland's towns were killing more people than natural population increase could match. Only the continual influx of Highlanders and Irishmen kept cities growing.

The tenement was a Scottish phenomenon. As land in the growing cities was at a premium housing went upwards. At first middle-class merchants had lived in the tenements and it was only when they became more wealthy that they began to purchase land outside the town to build more spacious homes; in Glasgow the names of the new streets – Virginia Street, Jamaica Street – indicated the source of their wealth. As they moved out factory workers crowded into their old homes, which were divided and subdivided by greedy landlords. New cheaply built tenements were often thrown up where there had once been a back garden. Called the back lands, they were entered by narrow closes. In the 1840s, one writer described the housing available in Glasgow to the majority of incoming Highlanders:

Children of the Calton district of Glasgow, c. 1890.   (PP)

> We entered a dirty, low passage like a house door, which led through the first house to a court immediately behind, which court, apart from a narrow path around it, was occupied entirely by a dunghill of the most disgusting kind. There were no privies or drains there, and the dung-heaps received all filth which the swarm of wretched inhabitants could give. Inside the houses we saw half-dressed wretches crowding together to be warm, and in one bed, although in the middle of the day, several women were imprisoned under a blanket, because as many others who had on their backs all the articles of dress that belonged to the party, were then out of doors.

In 1866, the City Improvement Trust was set up to help alleviate Glasgow's problems of overcrowding and ill-health. The Trust built common lodging houses, where for threepence a night a man could get a bed in a large dormitory divided into cubicles by wooden partitions. Glasgow's houses were 'ticketed'. All homes of three rooms or less were carefully measured and the number of occupants allowed to live in them laid down by law. A metal plate or 'ticket' stating the number was nailed firmly to the door. By the 1880s, there were nearly 25,000 ticketed houses in Glasgow, over half of them 'single-ends'. Sanitary inspectors made visits without warning in the middle of the night to ensure the regulations were kept. Often they discovered people in every corner of the house, in cupboards, under beds or attempting to avoid detection by climbing on to the roof. People in fact often slept in tiers: some on the mattress, others among the bedclothes on top.

Ticketed house tokens.   (PP)

Those able to afford two-roomed apartments frequently restricted life to one. They ate and slept in the kitchen and reserved the front room for special occasions such as weddings and funerals. In the kitchen was usually a bed recess and landlords always tried to supply metal beds. Wooden ones rarely lasted long: they were chopped up by tenants and used as firewood. Under the main bed was usually a mattress for the children, pulled out at night and called the 'hurley bed'.

From 1855, an ambitious and far-sighted scheme brought fresh water to Glasgow. A submerged aquaduct, thirty-four miles long, brought the water of Loch Katrine in Perthshire to Glasgow. Curious arrangements brought sinks to the tenements. Usually they were installed on an outside stair with a timber canopy over them for shelter. These became known in Glasgow as 'jaw-boxes' because housewives gossiped there while at the sink.

A photograph of the Close at 118 High Street, Glasgow, taken by Thomas Annan. (*M*)

As the old burgh of Glasgow could no longer contain the town's vast population, Glasgow spread, absorbing what had once been picturesque villages. On the south bank of the Clyde, Govan had enjoyed a long history of its own; but after 1864 large tenement blocks replaced the rural village. Govan and Clydebank became working-class suburbs at a time when Glasgow was fast gaining a world reputation for building ships.

At the end of the Napoleonic Wars, shipbuilding in Scotland was a fairly insignificant industry. Small yards, mostly on the east coast and employing between twenty and thirty men, made small trading and fishing vessels. Aberdeen and Leith had dominated the industry, together with the lower Clyde towns of Greenock and Port Glasgow.

In 1802, William Symington and Patrick Millar launched the *Charlotte Dundas* on the Forth and Clyde canal. Symington was born in Leadhills in 1763 and had studied for the ministry before becoming a civil engineer. He invented a method of applying steam power to a road vehicle by chains and ratchets before turning his mind, under the patronage of the Duke of Bridgewater, to perfecting a steamboat. Patrick Millar, a director of the Bank of Scotland and a shareholder in the Carron company, was also experimenting with a system of propelling ships by paddle wheels with his children's tutor, James Taylor. After some twenty years of work, the three men finally launched the boat that brought about a revolution in shipping. In 1812, steamships were given a further boost by Henry Bell. In January, Bell's tiny *Comet* was launched on the Clyde, the first commercial steamship in Europe to sail in open water. The pride of Helensburgh, the *Comet*, plied for years between Glasgow and Greenock.

By 1832, 95 steamships had been built in Scotland, 72 of which were

Henry Bell (1767–1830). (*SNPG*)

William Hall's shipyard, Aberdeen, 1862.   (*NMM*)

The SS *Aquitania* launched in 1914 at John Brown's yard, Clydebank. (*NMM*)

constructed on the Clyde. Of the number, 40 had been sold abroad. *Sirius*, the first transatlantic steamship, was built in 1838 at Leith, with engines made in Glasgow. Steam and steel vessels, pioneered by Dennys of Dumbarton in the 1880s, were powerful rivals to sailing clippers like the *Cutty Sark*.

Glasgow became world-famous for her marine engineers. In 1853 Charles Randolph and John Elder introduced the marine compound expansion engine that cut the amount of fuel needed by over a third. Nine years later James Howden perfected the cylindrical tank, the famous 'Scotch Boiler'. Glasgow shipbuilding companies attracted orders from the Cunard Shipping Line, founded in 1839 by George Burns and Robert Napier. George and his brother James had helped pioneer steam navigation from Glasgow. Robert Napier from Dumbarton built his first steam marine engine in 1823 and his cousin had established steam travel between Greenock and Belfast. The Scots formed the shipping company in conjunction with Samuel Cunard from Halifax, Nova Scotia, and the first four vessels for the new line were all built on the Clyde. Companies like John Brown and Stephens of Linthouse, moved to the Clyde and made the area world famous for warships and merchant and passenger vessels.

Shipbuilding and marine engineering were Scotland's particular contribution to the industrial revolution, but for the shipyard workers life was hard. Children acted as riveter's boys, working on high precarious wooden scaffolds, tossing white hot rivets to the man who hammered them into place. Because of the noise, children frequently split their ear drums and became permanently deaf. When there were orders, there was work. In more lean years the social problems of drink and malnutrition again showed themselves.

Management, in an attempt to hold on to their best labour, brought demarcation into the yards. Boilermakers, shipwrights and carpenters were encouraged to stay in one yard rather than another on the guarantee that their particular craft would be protected, sowing seeds of trouble to come. Meanwhile, with shipbuilding, Scotland's three prime industries – engineering, iron and steel, and coal – flourished. Labour was relatively cheap, versatile and highly skilled; a sophisticated Scottish banking system provided credit. There were decades of profit. The sheer hard work of the masses made Glasgow Britain's most gracious Victorian city and in terms of industry and wealth the town became Scotland's first. Glasgow's entrepreneurs died as rich as any in Britain.

Elsewhere Scotsmen found other ways of making money. In West Lothian James Young discovered torbanite, a shale-like coal that when gently heated gave up crude oil. In 1851, having patented his process, Young set up the first commercial oil works in the world at Bathgate in West Lothian: Young's Paraffin Light and Mineral Oil Company Limited. When the supply of torbanite at Bathgate ran out, Young built the Addiewell Works, near West Calder. Reputed to be the largest oil works in the world, Addiewell produced naptha, wax and lubricating oils as well as paraffin. When the patent for Young's process expired in 1864, Scotland's shale oil business boomed. Some 120 companies were begun, and by the beginning of the twentieth century the six largest were producing some six million tonnes of oil and gave work to thousands.

Beardmore's Engineering Works, *c.* 1900.   (*PP*)

Thomas Pennant noted in 1776 in his *Tour of Scotland* how Dundee's industry had grown:

> The manufacture of Dundee are linen, especially of Osnaburghs, sail-cloth, cordage, threads, thread-stockings, buckrams (a new work in Scotland), tanned leather and shoes for the London market; hats, which has set aside their importation from England for the supply of these parts; and lastly, a sugar house, erected about seven years ago, which does considerable business.

By the middle of the nineteenth century, Dundee had become 'Juteopolis', the leading jute manufacturing town in Britain. Jute was brought up the Tay

A typical Dundee weaving shed, *c.* 1800.   (*SP*)

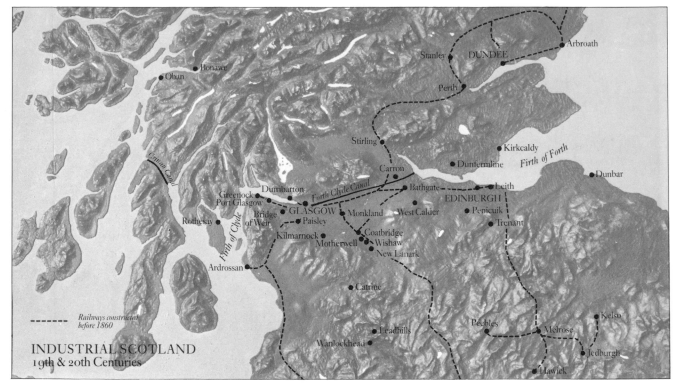

INDUSTRIAL SCOTLAND
19th & 20th Centuries

Railways constructed
before 1860

from Calcutta, Bombay and Karachi to be worked up. Half the town's population was employed making sacks and backings for carpets and linoleum. Kirkcaldy in nearby Fife became the centre of the linoleum industry.

The Borders and their traditional woollen industries also flourished. Local sheep and fleeces imported from Australia provided the raw material, the Rivers Tweed and Gala the water power. In Hawick, the woollen industry was started by a local magistrate, John Hardie, who brought the first four knitting frames in Scotland to the town. By 1816, there were over 500 frames turning out more than 320,000 pairs of socks a year. In its heyday, the woollen industry of Hawick had over 1200 frames at work and in the Crimean War began to make sweaters when Lord Cardigan asked for a garment that his men could wear under their uniforms to protect them from the cold. But when the war was over there was unemployment in the town: redundant knitters were given what was called 'tramping money', twelve shillings to go to Nottingham or Leicester to find work. The weaving of tweed was not begun until after 1818. The cloth originally was called 'tweel' but a London clerk misspelled it and the name stuck.

By the second half of the nineteenth century Scotland was beginning to attract foreign investment. At Ardeer in Ayrshire the Swede, Alfred Nobel, set up the British Dynamite Factory in 1871 which grew into a major chemical works. American capital was behind the North British Rubber Company which built a factory at Fountainbridge in Edinburgh in 1856. The previous year Robert Thomson had invented and patented the principle of the air cushioned wheel. Born in Stonehaven, he was a merchant in Charleston, South Carolina before returning to his native land to take up engineering. A man of remarkable talent he also invented the fountain pen

The PS *Mercury* going 'doon the Watter'. From the late nineteenth century, Glasgow's workers sailed down the Clyde to the coast resorts of Largs and Saltcoats. (*PP*)

and machinery for sugar making, and was one of the first to use electric charges to fire explosives during demolition work.

The American Singer Company came to Clydebank in 1884. Isaac Singer, a German-American, decided to build a factory in Scotland, perhaps influenced by his Scottish Vice-President, George McKenzie. The Scottish connection began at Love Loan off John Street in Glasgow. Production moved to Bridgeton in 1869, where 600 sewing machines a week were produced. Then Singer decided to construct at Kilbowie the largest factory in Europe. Building began in 1882 and, when finished two years later,

Children on the beach at Saltcoats, *c.* 1890s.   (*PP*)

The Broomielaw Bridge, Glasgow, *c.* 1880s. A photograph by George Washington Wilson.   (*AU*)

occupied forty-six acres. By the end of the century Singer had a workforce of 5000.

If the world began to invest in Scotland, Scots were investing in the world. Before the First World War, Scottish capital investment in North America was well over £200,000,000, and almost as much had been invested in Asia and Australasia.

Robert Fleming, frequently called the father of the investment trust movement, was born the son of a farmer near Dundee. He began his working life as a secretary in Baxters' jute mills in Dundee and in 1870 was asked to visit the United States and report on investment possibilities. As a result the First Scottish American Investment Trust was born, allowing investors' money to be put into various ventures spreading the risk. The Scottish investment trust movement financed the Atcheson, Topeka and Santa Fe Railroad, the Denver and Rio Grande Railroad and even the railways of Cuba.

The Scots also invested in American cattle and land. The largest ranch of all, the Matador Land and Cattle Company which ultimately spanned much of Texas, Montana, Dakota and north into Canada, was based on a ranch founded by an American of Scottish descent, Harry Campbell. It reached its zenith in the years from 1884, branding from 18,000 to 25,000 calves a year. But Harry Campbell soon fell out with the Scottish directors over what they regarded as his expensive purchase of new land and Scotsmen were put directly in charge. William Somerville was sent over to act as manager and he in turn was succeeded by a magisterial Scot, Murdo Mackenzie. Under Mackenzie's rule, the Matador cowboys claimed, you could not buy a length of rope without Dundee knowing about it. The ranch remained in Scottish hands until it was sold in 1951.

While Scotland, within a century, became a leading industrial nation there had been other developments of far-reaching consequence. The problem of communication that had plagued the nation's progress since the beginning of time had been gradually solved by a group of brilliant Scottish engineers. Other Scots had turned their attention to the health of the nation and become world famous.

Murdo Mackenzie, the Scots-born manager of the Matador Land and Cattle Company.   (*ITC*)

Matador Ranch hands, 1883.   (*ITC*)

17

Communication and Disruption

JOHN KNOX AND THE PROTESTANT REFORMERS had laid great stress on the need to educate the laity. Their Calvinist ideal, however, of a school in every parish was a slow reality. It was eighty years after the Reformation of 1560 before the children of the parish of Cardross in Dumbartonshire were given a disused Catholic chapel at Kilmahew by the local laird to use as a schoolroom. Every pupil at Cardross school paid six shillings and eightpence Scots a quarter if they came from the parish. They were also expected to provide the teacher with a gift at Christmas. Pupils from outside the parish paid double. Poor children were paid for by the local Kirk Session. Until 1843, Cardross had no other school but by the late nineteenth century two children of the parish were taking an honours degree in mathematics at Cambridge University.

Walter Geikie's drawing 'A Grandchild Reading'. (*NGS*)

In 1696, the Scottish parliament passed an Act for Settling Schools, to reinforce the wish that every parish should have a school, its schoolmaster paid for by the local landowners and supervised by the Kirk. Although schoolhouses were often no more than rude hovels and teachers' pay low, there were soon a substantial number of effective schools. In 1711, the Society for Propagating Christian Knowledge, founded to promote education north of the Highland Line, opened its first school in remote St Kilda, and within four years had established twenty-four more in the Highlands and islands. By 1738 the education offered was widened to include instruction in practical subjects and the Society went on to fund and administer 134 schools.

As Scots began to make their mark in medicine, engineering and the arts, the myth was born of the 'lad o' pairts' – the able boy from humble background who, by dint of hard work and ability, worked his way through the parish school and went to university. From the outset, Scottish education was meritocratic, and the Reformers would not have wished it otherwise. Even by the seventeenth century a large number of able Scots children were realizing that educational attainment and the acquisition of formal qualifications were the means to escape from poverty.

Scotland's universities were unique. The students at Edinburgh, Glasgow, Aberdeen and St Andrews were for the most part drawn directly from parish and burgh schools. Unlike England's two universities of Oxford and Cambridge, those in Scotland were open to all ranks of society. The poor

Highland student, armed with a sack of oatmeal and a barrel of salted herring to keep him during the university terms, was indeed a reality, although perhaps not as numerous as some Scots would imply. In 1690, the Scottish parliament set up a Commission to examine the four universities. Intellectually stagnant, medieval in outlook, all were hampered by a lack of funds. Apart from Andrew Melville's reforms at Glasgow, little happened until William Carstares became Principal of Edinburgh University in 1703. The son of a Presbyterian minister, Carstares had spent much of his life exiled in Holland until William of Orange succeeded to the throne. In 1708, Carstares abolished the system of teaching by Regent, whereby one teacher taught a class of students all the subjects throughout the three years of their course, and reorganized Edinburgh on the lines of the Dutch universities, with individual professors responsible for teaching their own specialized subjects. By the end of the eighteenth century this fundamental reform had been accepted by all four Scottish universities, although until 1727 all teaching was still in Latin.

The great names of the Scottish Enlightenment had by and large come from the upper classes and the towns, or the manse; by the 1860s, however, a third of all Scotland's university students were drawn from remote parish schools like Cardross. The sons of small farmers, masons, weavers, bootmakers, shepherds and common labourers were given the chance to further their education. In no other country in the world in the early nineteenth century did such people dream of going to university and education became a Scottish obsession: knowledge was the way to escape from poverty, from the narrow hard life of the glen or the urban slum.

At school as well as university the son of the laird sat with the son of the ploughman. By 1864, one out of every 205 Scots went to secondary school. In Prussia the ratio was one in 249; in France, one in 570; and in England, one in every 1300. Merchants and artisans made Edinburgh famous for her schools. George Heriot, who had amassed a fortune as James VI's jeweller, bequeathed his fortune to found George Heriot's Hospital. Part of his bequest later helped found the Watt Institute and School of Arts in 1852. Its first report declared:

> The great object of this institution is to supply at such an expense as a working tradesman can afford, instruction in the various branches of science which are of practical application to mechanics in their several trades . . . for the purpose of giving you real and substantial instruction, not to amuse a vacant hour and excite your wonder by exhibiting some curious and showy experiments . . .

When the Institute became Heriot Watt College it went on to expand into many branches of engineering and science.

In 1681 the Merchant Company of Edinburgh was incorporated. Within twenty years the town's businessmen had founded the Merchant Maidens Hospital for orphaned girls. With a donation from Mary Erskine, the widow of James Hair, an Edinburgh druggist, the Mary Erskine School was founded to educate the daughters of Edinburgh burgesses. George Watson, James Gillespie, Daniel Stewart and other Edinburgh worthies founded further excellent schools. Other Scottish burghs could also boast good education. In Glasgow George and Thomas Hutcheson had left money in the seventeenth century to found a school for poor boys. In Aberdeen,

George Heriot (1563–1624), known as Jinglin' Geordie, was goldsmith to James VI and a money-lender. (*CAC*)

Heriot's fortune built a 'Hospital' in Edinburgh, which later became a school. (*NGS*)

Robert Gordon, a merchant who had made his fortune trading with the Baltic, set up a hospital for the education of boys. But Scotland's institutions of learning were never to be as wealthy as those of England. The revenues of Eton and Winchester alone outstripped those of Scotland's four universities together.

The classics were the chief subjects taught in the burgh schools; but by the eighteenth century other subjects were thought necessary. In 1760 the people of Perth petitioned the Town Council, arguing that

> ... things begin to be valued according to their use, and men of the greatest abilities have employed their skill in making the sciences contribute not only to the improvement of the physician, lawyer and divine, but to the improvement of the merchant, mechanic, and farmer in their respective arts.

Archibald Pitcairne (1652–1713) qualified in medicine and became a Professor at Leyden. (*RCP*)

Perth Academy was founded in the same year. The pupils would be taught Natural Science, Mathematics, Navigation and Astronomy as well as English. Edinburgh Academy was later built by private subscription. The academy was a peculiarly Scots invention. Perth was probably the first of a long list founded to teach subjects not included in the classical curriculum of grammar schools.

The products of Scotland's schools and universities had by tradition looked for jobs in the ministry of the Reformed Kirk. The Kirk not only gave Scotland an education system but also, as Knox would have wished, reaped the fruit. The secular nature of the Scottish Enlightenment, however, made other disciplines fashionable. By the end of the eighteenth century Edinburgh in particular was offering students the most advanced medical training to be found in Britain.

Edinburgh's Medical School had been established in the days of Charles II. Archibald Pitcairne, born in Dalkeith in 1652, had been its inspiration. A man of wit, a playwright, a poet and a hearty drinker, Pitcairn studied theology and philosophy at Edinburgh University before going to Paris where he became interested in medicine and, having taken a medical degree at the University of Rheims, became a professor at Leyden University in Holland in 1692. He returned to Scotland to become a professor at Edinburgh's Royal College of Physicians and to give birth to the scientific approach in Scotland. Only facts should be considered; in future doctors should be taught sensibly and systematically.

John Monro (*d.* 1737). A portrait by William Aikman (1682–1731). (*RCS*)

At the same time, Robert Sibbald from Fife was busy establishing a Physics Garden near Holyrood Palace. Like Pitcairne, Sibbald had studied at Leyden where Clusius had shown the way with his famous *Hortus Botanicus* in which herbs and plants of medical virtue were grown. Sibbald's garden was begun in 1667 and under him botany became a university subject. Sibbald had helped found the College of Physicians in 1681 and four years later became Professor of Medicine.

John Monro also trained in Leyden and became a doctor. His son, Alexander, became Professor of Anatomy at Edinburgh in 1719, at the age of twenty-two, and held the chair for fifty years. His *Anatomy of Human Bones and Nerves*, published in 1726, was a standard textbook for over a century. Within six years of Alexander Monro's appointment, Edinburgh could boast professors of botany, chemistry, midwifery and the theory and practice of medicine. In 1726, Alexander together with the Lord Provost of Edinburgh

William Hare probably died a pauper in London in 1860. (*CAC*)

William Burke (1792–1829). (*CAC*)

Robert Knox (1791–1862). (*CAC*)

launched an appeal to raise funds to build a hospital where patients could be studied and treated. A further call on private funds paid for a new building to accommodate 228 more patients in 1741. The new infirmary was staffed by professors and members of both Royal Colleges, Physicians and Surgeons. The rivalry helped to stimulate the study of medicine, and from 1746, professors were giving their students practical teaching in the wards of the Royal Infirmary. Monro was an inspired lecturer and attracted students from far and wide. So great was the pressure on his time that he called upon his son, Alexander Monro Secundus, to be joint professor with him from 1754. He succeeded to his father's professorship in 1769 and held the chair until he too retired in 1808. Like his father he contributed greatly to medical knowledge, and his published works, *Treatise on the Lymphatics*, *The Structure and Functions of the Nervous System* and *The Brain, the Eye and the Ear* became standard textbooks. Secundus was in turn joined by his son, Alexander Tertius in 1798, and he became Professor of Anatomy in 1808. When Tertius, much criticized for using his grandfather's lecture notes, retired in 1846, the Monro family had dominated the study of anatomy for over 120 years. The Edinburgh Medical School had several family dynasties. The Gregory family produced sixteen professors in five generations.

But for the anatomists, the problem was finding enough dead bodies for dissection. Hanged criminals were the only source and, given the expansion of the School, supply could not meet demand. Body snatching was the solution. Robbers euphemistically called 'Resurrectionists' desecrated graveyards and relatives of the dead were forced to take precautions to protect the interred. Guards were employed to watch graves, railings were thrown up round tombs and bodies were buried in sealed iron coffins called 'mortsafes'. Demand for corpses was so great that murders took place.

On 29 November 1827, an old man called Donald died in Tanner's Close, West Port, owing £4 rent to his landlord William Hare. To recover the debt Hare decided to sell his corpse to the Medical School and, with the help of another of his lodgers, William Burke, took the cadaver to Dr Robert Knox, keeper of the Anatomy Museum in Edinburgh, who paid the pair £7 10s.

Burke and Hare realized that profit could be made. In the boarding house another lodger was in bed with fever and Burke and Hare smothered him. Knox paid £10 for this superior specimen. Fourteen more people were murdered before the body of Margaret Docherty, Burke and Hare's last victim, was recognized by one of the school's students who had seen her alive and well a few days before.

At the trial in November 1828, Hare turned King's Evidence and was released. William Burke, aged thirty-seven, was hanged. Their exploits quickly became part of Edinburgh's folklore and children sang:

> Up the close and doun the stair
> But and ben wi' Burke and Hare,
> Burke's the butcher, Hare's the thief,
> Knox the boy that buys the beef.

Hare may have died a pauper in London. Knox was exonerated by Burke in his confession and by a committee of inquiry but he failed to become a professor in Scotland and left for London where he became a pathologist at the Brompton Cancer Hospital. The scandal, in fact, caused a public outcry which did not subside until the passage of the Anatomy Act in 1832, which made it possible for schools of anatomy to obtain bodies from hospitals and other institutions where people died without friends or relatives.

For Edinburgh's medical students life was hard. Some came to the city very poor, unable to afford candles to study by. Many came from England and America, like Benjamin Rush of New Jersey. Some took a few classes, others took the full three-year course that could result in the prized Doctor of Medicine degree. The final examination was searching. Students were examined orally by two professors as well as having to show how they would treat two specimen medical cases. In addition, a thesis in Latin had to be submitted.

Not all Scotland's doctors confined their activity to Edinburgh. The Hunter brothers were among the greatest natural geniuses the country ever produced and were responsible for taking the knowledge of Edinburgh's Medical School to London. Born on a Lanarkshire farm, John Hunter was poorly educated but, as he wrote in later life, had an inquisitive mind:

Alexander Monro (1697–1767), 'Primus'. (*RCS*)

> When I was a boy I wanted to know all about the clouds and grasses, and why the leaves changed colour in the autumn; I watched the ants, bees, birds, tadpoles and caddis worms: I pestered people with questions about what nobody knew or cared anything about.

John's brother, William, had abandoned his divinity studies for medicine and became a surgeon at St George's Hospital in London where he made obstetrics an acceptable branch of medicine. He became physician to Queen Charlotte, wife of George III, and attended at the birth of the Younger Pitt. He became President of the English Royal College of Physicians in 1781 and built up a vast collection of art and artefacts later acquired by Glasgow University. William Hunter made his fortune suddenly. In 1759 his account at Drummond's Bank was £2000. Three years later he had £28,000 to his credit. John joined William in London in 1748. Trained by his brother, he served as a military surgeon before he enjoyed an illustrious reputation in London's hospitals.

Alexander Monro (1733–1817), 'Secundus'. (*RCS*)

Practical Scots brought about a revolution in surgery. James Syme, the son of a prosperous Edinburgh lawyer, was Professor of Clinical Surgery at Edinburgh for thirty-six years and constantly experimented with new techniques. In 1828 he carried out one of his most famous operations when he removed a fifteen-inch tumour from the mouth of Robert Renman. Others had refused to operate on the growth, but in twenty-four minutes, with Renman strapped in a chair, Syme cut the tumour out and his patient went on to live a completely normal life. But without anaesthetics surgery was a grim business; everything depended upon the speed of the surgeon's hands. Robert Liston, a minister's son from West Lothian, like Syme, developed great skill. As a surgeon at the Royal Infirmary, Liston could amputate a leg in less than a minute and remove gallstones in less than two. In 1834, he became Professor of Clinical Surgery in London and twelve years later was the first in Britain to use ether as an anaesthetic. His experiments attracted the attention of James Young Simpson.

Simpson was born in Bathgate in West Lothian in 1811. His father was a baker with a family of eight children to feed. But with the help of older

Alexander Monro (1773–1859), 'Tertius'. (*RCS*)

Sir James Young Simpson
(1811–70). (*RCP*)

John Loudon MacAdam
(1756–1836). (*NPG*)

working brothers James's parents found the money to send him to Edinburgh where he proved to be one of the Medical School's most able students. At the age of twenty-eight, he was appointed Professor of Midwifery and was the first to use ether to help ease childbirth. In 1847, Simpson began experimenting with other gases and discovered chloroform.

Meanwhile other Scots had turned to Scotland's oldest problem – communication. The nature of the land had for ever hindered economic and social progress. General Wade's road system constructed after the Jacobite Rebellion of 1715 was of little use in the development of trade and industry. By the middle of the eighteenth century, it still took a month for mail to get from Edinburgh to London and even a parcel or letter to Selkirk, thirty-eight miles away from Scotland's capital, could take a fortnight. The sea was still the only adequate method of transport. Towards the end of the century, however, efforts to improve the roads in Lowland Scotland were being made, but the expense was crippling. Where tracks existed, travellers went on foot or horseback. North of the Highland Line coaches were a useless luxury and it was not until 1749 that there was a regular coaching service between Edinburgh and Glasgow. It took upwards of twelve hours to make the forty-six-mile journey.

Yet Scotland became famous for her coachbuilders. In 1738, John Home set up business in Edinburgh. He assigned different craftsmen different jobs and his mass-produced coaches were sold all over Europe. In time, Edinburgh became the hub of coaching services in Scotland, with services that linked Aberdeen, Stirling and Dumfries with Carlisle and London, and by the end of the eighteenth century there were regular coaching services out of Glasgow as well.

But coach and cart wheels needed a decent dry surface to run on. John Loudon MacAdam became interested in road building while serving with a Volunteer Regiment in the Napoleonic Wars. In 1816, at the age of sixty, he became a professional road engineer as Surveyor General of the Bristol Turnpike Trust. His method of road construction, based on a layer of small stones laid on a drained surface which pressure bonded together, was widely adopted. When MacAdam roads finally came to Lowland Scotland they enabled great strides to be made in agriculture. The farm cart became common: manure could be easily transported to fields, as could produce for the market.

The problem of transport in the Highlands was not solved until the nineteenth century. In 1803, the British government appointed a Commission for Highland Roads and Bridges led by Thomas Telford. The son of a Dumfriesshire shepherd, Telford had no formal education save a grounding in reading, writing and arithmetic. At the age of fourteen he was apprenticed to a stonemason and in 1779 took his trade to Edinburgh. Three years later he went to London where he worked on the building of Somerset House and studied civil engineering. Eventually he became an engineer of brilliance who understood the social significance of his work, anticipating John Maynard Keynes by over a century in his emphasis on the benefits of public works.

Although railways were introduced into England from 1786, Scotland had to wait another forty years before the first line was constructed. Meanwhile, the Scots put faith in canals. The Forth-Clyde Canal, linked to

Monkland, proved the most important, enabling iron ore from Lanarkshire to be moved east and west. In 1790, the first ship passed from Leith to Greenock in the west. By the middle of the century the canal complex of central Scotland was transporting over three million tons of goods a year and thousands of passengers on ships like the steam-packet *Victoria*.

Thomas Telford was fascinated by canals. Before he built his famous Caledonian Canal that linked Inverness to Corpach near Fort William, such was the long and hazardous sea voyage round Scotland's north coast that a ship leaving Newcastle for India could reach Bombay before another, departing from Newcastle the same day, berthed at Liverpool on the west coast. Telford began the Caledonian Canal in 1803. It took nearly twenty years to complete at a cost of a million pounds with a complex system of locks along the sixty-mile-long waterway, thirty-seven of which made use of the Lochs Ness, Oich and Lochy. It was not until 1842, after another twenty years of modification and reconstruction, that the canal proved reasonably satisfactory for shipping. But in the end Telford's Caledonian Canal was one of his failures; less than three per cent of Scottish shipping bothered to use his waterway.

Thomas Telford (1757–1834). (*GAG*)

Telford's major Scottish contribution proved to be his roads and bridges. By 1820 he had supervised the construction of 875 miles in Scotland alone and earned himself the nickname – 'The Colossus of Roads'. He saw his task as helping to unite Britain: Scotland had to be made more accessible and therefore more attractive to industrialists. Like many a Scottish engineer, he was hard to please. He referred to his work-force as 'slaves' and drew detailed plans to show exactly what he wanted. His great love was bridges. He built a thousand in Britain alone. At Dunkeld, he bridged the River Tay and in Edinburgh he built the Dean Bridge which shortened by many miles the journey from the town to the Queen's Ferry across the Forth.

The Industrial Revolution in Scotland was brought about as much by English money as by Scottish minds, and Scotland's inventors, like her doctors and engineers, were not parochial. They put ambition first and exploited fully what England had to offer. The benefits of their inventions, therefore, frequently came to the English long before they reached the Scots.

John Rennie (1761–1821).   (*SNPG*)

John Rennie was a contemporary of Telford. Born at Phantassie House in East Linton in 1761, he was educated at the local Prestonkirk school. His father died when John was five, leaving his mother to bring up nine children. The eldest son, George, took over the family farm and became one of Scotland's leading agricultural Improvers. At the age of six, John began making models, and the local mill-wright, Andrew Meikle, lent him tools. At Dunbar High School he was such a distinguished pupil that they offered him a post as schoolmaster; but he quickly became bored with teaching and returned to Phantassie where by day he worked at Houston Mill and by night studied mathematics and mechanics. When he was nineteen John won his first contract to design the building and machinery for a new mill at Invergowrie near Dundee. He was also called in to renovate Aitchison's Mill at Bonnington in Edinburgh and the success of these two ventures established him as a mill-wright. Rennie earned enough money to go to Edinburgh University, where he studied Natural Philosophy and French and

James Watt (1736–1819).   *(PP)*

German so that he could read foreign engineering textbooks. During the long summer vacations he worked on more mill contracts to earn money to keep him at university.

In 1784, Rennie set off with a letter of introduction to James Watt, then working in Birmingham. Watt was impressed by the twenty-two-year-old and asked him to design new machinery for the Albion Mills near Blackfriars in London. They took four years to build and established Rennie as a mechanical engineer. By the time he was thirty, John Rennie was Britain's leading consultant engineer. Like Telford, he found the challenge of England irresistible. He built Waterloo and Southwark Bridges to span the River Thames and was commissioned to construct the Rochdale Canal and drain the Fen country. He constructed the new London Docks of the East India Company and improved naval dockyards at Chatham and Portsmouth. In Scotland Rennie began to build one of his finest bridges at Kelso in 1800. The bridge took three years to construct and was the model for Waterloo Bridge in London, built in 1811. Rennie also spanned the River Esk at Musselburgh with Britain's first level bridge.

Rennie worked himself to death. By the time he was sixty he was worn out. When he died in 1821 a grateful Britain laid him to rest in St Paul's Cathedral in London. In Scotland, it was not until 1936 that a sundial and a bronze plaque were erected in his memory near his birthplace, Phantassie House, at a cost of £180. It was not the first, nor the last time, that the worth of a Scotsman with a world-wide reputation was ignored by his native land.

New roads, bridges and methods of travel, highlighted the problems of a postal system. Peter Williamson, born in Hinley in Aberdeenshire in 1730, led an adventurous life. As a boy he had been kidnapped and transported to America. On his return to Scotland he became an Edinburgh bookseller and in 1786 set up a penny-post in Edinburgh. His mail service between Edinburgh and London reduced the time of communication to sixty hours. Another bookseller, James Chalmers of Dundee, worked on the concept of an adhesive postage stamp. When the subject of a standard British postal rate was raised in Parliament in 1839, Chalmers submitted his scheme, but Rowland Hill was formally credited with the invention of Britain's pre-paid postal service and the first British stamp, the Penny Black.

James Watt was born in Greenock in 1736. The sole survivor of five children of a Scottish builder, Watt throughout his life was plagued with migraines. While working as an instrument maker at Glasgow University he was asked to repair a demonstration model of a Newcomen steam-engine and in so doing built a new machine that was more efficient. He devised his separate condenser in 1765 and introduced his system of a flywheel and a governor. By 1800 Watt's steam engine designed to drive a rotating shaft, manufactured in England, was a mainstay of British industry.

During the late eighteenth and early nineteenth centuries, the Kirk served industrialized capitalism well. The Calvinist theology was of hard work and social obedience, and the school system was designed not as a liberating force but as a way of producing a disciplined mass and logical, ambitious individuals. The Kirk itself, however, by the middle of the eighteenth century, was fraught with dissension. At the root lay the Patronage Act of 1712, by which lairds, not congregations, chose ministers. In the previous year, the congregation of the West Kirk in Stirling had chosen

Ebenezer Erskine (1680–1754). *(CAC)*

The General Assembly of the Kirk of Scotland 1783, drawn by David Allan (1744–96). (NGS)

Ebenezer Erskine as their minister. The local patron set him aside and Erskine protested. The Kirk disciplined him. Matters came to a head in 1732, when the General Assembly passed an Act which effectively put the right to call ministers entirely in the hands of patrons and in response Erskine left the established Church of Scotland in what came to be known as the Original Secession of 1733. The protest was popular. By 1819, forty per cent of the population of Glasgow and the west were seceders of one kind or another. A Second Secession took place in 1761. Thomas Gillespie, the minister of Carnock parish, openly opposed the existing church-state relationship and in 1752 was deposed by his patron. With two other ministers, Gillespie formed a presbytery 'for the relief of Christians oppressed in their Christian privileges', commonly called the Relief church. The Kirk made strenuous efforts to reconcile the seceders and they were left in full possession of their parishes and stipends until 1740, but still the movement grew.

Norman MacLeod of Assynt in Sutherland was another who was unable to conform with the dictates of the established Kirk. The son of a poor fisherman, he went to Aberdeen University and took a degree in Moral Philosophy at Edinburgh, where he criticized his professor of divinity for 'loose living' and was dismissed. At the age of thirty-four and barred from preaching by the established Church, MacLeod became a teacher at a salary of £8 a year in Ullapool. He also became an informal preacher and, a man of courage, carried his first child fifty miles to be baptized when his parish minister Dr Ross refused to officiate. Very soon he had created a minor

Norman MacLeod (1780–1866), founder of religious communities in Nova Scotia and New Zealand. (CBC)

Thomas Chalmers (1780–1847).
(*SNPG*)

Church of his own anticipating the Disruption of 1843. Dr Ross had MacLeod summoned before the local Kirk Session who gave him an ultimatum: either cease preaching or be dismissed as schoolmaster. When MacLeod would not relent Dr Ross locked the school and pocketed the key. The following year, 1817, Norman, his wife and child sailed for Canada. Within ten years, MacLeod had 500 followers from Scotland at St Ann's Bay, Cape Breton. His own family grew – his first-born joined by five brothers and two sisters – and a new church that could house 1200 was built for his swelling congregation.

In Scotland, meanwhile, dissension continued to split the Kirk. After the Reform Act of 1832, there were fears that the mood of political radicalism might bring about the creation of a secular state and many who genuinely believed the Kirk to be of Divine origin demanded that the Church be disestablished to preserve its spiritual independence and integrity. These dissenters called themselves 'voluntaries'. By 1832, Voluntary Associations had sprung up all over Scotland and in the following year there was open strife in the General Assembly between the Voluntaries and another group called 'evangelicals'. Led by Thomas Chalmers, the Evangelicals advocated the expansion of the Kirk's work in missions at home and abroad.

In 1814 Chalmers became minister of the Tron Kirk in Glasgow. There Lord Cockburn heard him preach with peculiar power:

> The magic lies in the concentrated intensity which agitates every fibre of the man, and brings out his meaning by words and emphasis of significant force, and rolls his magnificent periods clearly and irresistibly along, and kindles the whole composition with living fire.

At St John's Parish in Glasgow over a period of four years, Chalmers reduced the expenditure on the poor from £1400 to £280 and reduced the incidence of drunkenness. Chalmers toured England to examine how the English Poor Law worked and preached in London. Despite his Scottish accent, crowds flocked to hear him, including George Canning, the Whig MP, who is said to have whispered with a tear in his eye, 'This is indeed true eloquence. The tartan beats us all.'

With many paupers in his Glasgow parish, Chalmers was convinced that Christian charity, not poor rates, was the solution to the social evils of industrialization. Like the Reformers he above all believed in education. 'The true secret for managing people,' he remarked in 1819, 'is not so much to curb, as to enlighten them.'

Chalmers, Thomas Carlyle remarked, became 'intrinsically the chief Scotsman of his time'. He was a curiously attractive man. As his friend Lord Cockburn wrote:

> In point of mere feature, it would not be difficult to find him ugly. But he is saved from this, and made interesting and loveable, by singular modesty, kindness and simplicity of manner, a strong expression of calm thought and benevolence, a forehead so broad that it seems to proclaim itself the seat of great intellect, a love of humour, and an indescribable love of drollery when anything ludicrous comes over him.

In 1823, Chalmers went back to the academic life. He was appointed Professor of Moral Philosophy at St Andrews and five years later became Professor of Divinity at Edinburgh. He believed that spiritual independence, guaranteed the Kirk since the time of the Reformation and embodied in the Treaty of Union of 1707, had been abused by government and ignored by a ministry appointed under the patronage system.

In 1833, the General Assembly of the Church of Scotland discussed legislation later known as the Veto Act, which permitted a majority of male heads of families in a congregation to reject the patron's choice of minister. The Act was passed by the Assembly in 1834 and approved by the Lord Advocate and the Lord Chancellor. John Hope, Dean of the Faculty of Advocates, fiercely opposed its passage on the grounds that it interfered with the rule of state law, and legal disputes tore the Kirk apart for a decade as Hope brought test cases to court.

In 1834, Robert Young was presented to the parish of Auchterarder but rejected almost unanimously by the 300 heads of families. Young took his case to the Court of Session, where the judges, bitterly divided, took four years before finding in his favour. The Evangelicals were horrified by this decision, for it meant that church courts appeared to have no power beyond that specifically given by Acts of Parliament. When the General Assembly appealed to the House of Lords, the peers decided in May 1839 that the Assembly had no right to alter the 1712 Patronage Act.

David Welsh (1793–1845). (*HA*)

By 1842, an impasse had been reached. The General Assembly drew up a Claim of Right which was presented to the British government. The Kirk, according to the Claim, had complete spiritual independence and the state no right to interfere in religious matters. The government refused to accept the Claim: Robert Peel, the Tory Prime Minister believed the General Assembly was trying to put itself above the law of the land. In the spring of 1843, the Law Courts threw out the General Assembly's Chapel Act which had allowed Chapel ministers the right to sit in church courts. When the General Assembly met that year the politicians were given a shock. The Disruption, as it was called, was witnessed by Henry, Lord Cockburn. 'First the Moderator, Dr Welsh . . .

> . . . rose and announced that he and others who had been returned as members held this not to be a free Assembly – that, therefore, they declined to acknowledge it as a Court of the Church – that they meant to leave the very place, and, as a consequence of this, to abandon the Establishment. In explanation of the grounds of this step he then read a full and clear protest. It was read as impressively as a weak voice would allow.
>
> As soon as it was read, Dr Welsh handed the paper to the clerk, quitted the chair, and walked away. Instantly, what appeared to be the whole left side of the house rose to follow . . .
>
> They walked in procession down Hanover Street to Canonmills, where they had secured an excellent hall, through an unbroken mass of cheering people, and beneath innumerable handkerchiefs waving from the windows.
>
> But . . . no thinking man could look on the unexampled scene and behold that the temple was rent, without pain and sad forebodings. No spectacle since the Revolution reminded one so forcibly of the Covenanters.

Hugh Miller the noted geologist, who went on to edit the Free Church magazine *The Witness*, remarked as he looked down from the Gallery upon those who remained that they reminded him of:

> . . . a bed of full blown peony-roses glistening after a shower; and could
> one have substituted among them a monk's frock for the modern
> dress-coat, and given to each crown a shaven tonsure, they would have
> passed admirably for a conclave of monks met to determine some
> weighty point of abbey-income or right of forestry.

Miller regarded the Moderates as, like the Roman Church of the early sixteenth century, more concerned with their stipends than with things of the spirit.

Four hundred and seventy ministers quit the Kirk in the Disruption. They took with them almost as many elders, numerous teachers, most of the Church's overseas missions and nearly forty per cent of the Church of Scotland's communicants. The Free Church of Scotland was born on 18 May 1843 and held its first General Assembly at Tanfield Hall in Edinburgh, where Thomas Chalmers was elected Moderator. It was the most momentous single event in nineteenth-century Scottish history. Scotland was now a land of not one church but two and an Act of Parliament in 1845 deprived the established Church of Scotland of its power to administer poor relief. Parochial boards were set up to see to the needs of the poor.

The Disruption also affected education. Four hundred teachers had quit the Kirk and by 1851 the Free Church had built over 700 schools of its own and brought about a huge extension of education. After 1847, state aid had to be given to the Free as well as to established Church schools, and in 1861 the established Church lost its legal powers over Scotland's parish school system. This prepared the ground for the Education Act of 1872 which set up a national system under a Scottish Education Department.

Many Free churchmen became pioneers in education. Thomas Guthrie after the Disruption formed Free St John's Church at Castlehill and took a special interest in Edinburgh's pauper children. In 1847 he wrote his famous *Plea for Ragged Schools* and became a recognized authority in Britain on the care of destitute and criminal children. Guthrie realized that no church could solve the problem on its own and that the state would have to help. Another Free churchman, David Stow, established evening Sunday schools for general instruction. Born in Paisley, Stow was also responsible for founding the Free Church College for training teachers. The Disruption also had far-reaching consequences for Scottish politics. After 1843, the Free Church vote tended strongly towards the Liberal Party and made that party's position impregnable in Scotland's burghs. Whig landlords benefited from granting the Free Church facilities. After 1847, however, only the county of Inverness in the Highlands stood by the Conservative Party.

In the Highlands, Conservative lairds harried and persecuted the Free Church. They denied building sites, forcing Free Church followers to worship in the open. At Strontian in Argyll the laird, Sir James Riddle, forced the Free Church congregation to have a boat built in Glasgow which they towed to their village and used as their only church for many years.

The new Church's major problem was financial. How were its ministers to live? Chalmers came up with a simple solution. If each member of the Free Church contributed a penny a week, a living of £150 a year could be provided for 500 ministers. The Sustentation Fund, as it was called, worked. In three years over two million pounds was raised. Money was also raised in the colonies. Three ministers, Dr Steel, Dr Begg and Dr Robb, were sent

Thomas Guthrie (1803–73). (*SNPG*)

Captain William Cargill (1784–1860). (*OESA*)

abroad to promote the new Church and many Presbyterian Churches abroad divided as they had done in the homeland.

The Lay Association of the Free Church also became colonizers. In August 1842, George Rennie, the brother of the civil engineer, wrote an article for the *Colonial Gazette* on the desirability of founding a colony in New Zealand to relieve 'the unemployed and destitute masses' of his native Scotland. He wrote to the New Zealand Company and the Colonial Office and his scheme was boosted when the new Free Church of Scotland decided to create a colony. The Lay Association, a group of fifty prominent members, agreed to promote Rennie's project in conjunction with the New Zealand Company. In February 1846, Charles Kettle surveyed Otago and drew up plans for a settlement at Port Chalmers and Dunedin, the anglicised form of the old Gaelic name for Edinburgh.

The colony was to be settled on 144,600 acres of land divided into 2400 properties, consisting of a town section of a quarter of an acre, a suburban allotment of ten acres and a rural allotment of fifty acres, at the very reasonable price of forty shillings an acre. It was to be a thoroughly religious settlement, a Calvinist version of St Augustine's City of God.

William Cargill was one of those chosen to lead the expedition. Born in Edinburgh on 17 August 1784, he claimed to be directly descended from Donald Cargill the Scottish Covenanter who had been executed in 1681.

Two ships with 344 pioneers sailed for Otago in 1848. Cargill was sixty-three when he boarded the *John Wickliffe* and on the long voyage, as his companion Thomas Arnold observed:

> His glass of toddy sometimes elevated him considerably, and on such occasions he would walk about the cuddy, trolling out with flushed features the burden of some old Scottish song. At other times he would hold forth interminably on the distinction between Church and State . . . a distinction which he used to say, an Englishman could never comprehend.

The Reverend Thomas Burns was the other leader of the party. Born on 10 April 1796 at Mossgiel in Ayrshire, he was the third son of Gilbert Burns, the brother of the poet Robert.

The *John Wickliffe* dropped anchor at Port Chalmers on 23 March 1848. Three weeks later the *Philip Laing* reached New Zealand with 247 passengers. At first the women and children stayed on board while two long barracks, one for the English settlers, the other for the Scots, were built. In both the young men were put at one end, the single women at the other, with married couples occupying the middle.

The frame of the house occupied by the Reverend Thomas Burns was quickly erected on a prominent site, as was the building which served as both school and church. By December 1848, the *Otago News*, the settlers' newspaper, noted:

> . . . the eye is gladdened with a goodly sprinkling of houses, some of wood, others of mud and grass; whilst numerous gardens, well fenced and cleared, and one street, at least, showing a broad track from end to end of the future town, gives evidence of the progress we have made. We have two hotels, a church, a school, a wharf, small though it be. We have butchers, bakers and stores of all descriptions . . . and every outward sign of commercial activity and enterprise. ·

The Reverend Thomas Burns (1796–1871).   (*OESA*)

The monument at Waipu, New Zealand, commemorating the early pioneers.   (*Author*)

By the end of the first year, the population of Dunedin had reached 745.

North Island, New Zealand, also attracted a religious colony of Scots descent. By 1850, Norman MacLeod had grown weary of Nova Scotia and sought a new land for his people. At St Ann's in Nova Scotia, his community had suffered some bad winters and the fishing had deteriorated. On 28 October 1851 he sailed for Australia with 136 followers in two ships, the *Margaret* and the *Highland Lass*, they had built themselves. MacLeod, however, took an instant dislike to Adelaide and Melbourne, where his party contracted dysentery. Within six weeks three of his own children were dead and the old man decided to move on.

By 1860 five ships from Nova Scotia, carrying 883 people, had reached Waipu in North Island. MacLeod's new parish was ten miles by thirty and he travelled round it every Sunday by sea, horse and foot, preaching four times a day, twice in English, twice in Gaelic. When he died at the age of eighty-five his disciples quarrelled over the right to carry his coffin and no man was thought worthy to fill his pulpit, which remained empty for years.

The nineteenth century in Scotland had been one of resounding change. A people who had once almost exclusively made a living from the land was now in large part concentrated in the Lowlands, huddled in industrial towns. Queen Victoria for much of the century gave regal stability to an age that otherwise was one of social turmoil. She ruled an Empire that encompassed a quarter of the world, yet there was no part of it she loved more than the land of the Scots.

A group of early Otago settlers, *c.* 1880s. (*OESA*)

Curling in New Zealand, *c.* 1880s. (*OESA*)

A group of Presbyterians at Whycocomagh, Nova Scotia, who became members of the Free Church after the Disruption in 1843. (*CBC*)

18

The Age of Victoria

Queen Victoria (1819–1901), who ruled longer than any other British monarch. (*SNPG*)

ON 22 JUNE 1897 Queen Victoria celebrated her Diamond Jubilee. Australians, New Zealanders, Africans, Canadians and men from India and the East paraded in London to honour her. The Scots also celebrated the day with good reason. In 1869 Victoria wrote that Scotland was 'the proudest, finest country in the world'. More than any other British monarch, Victoria had taken the Scottish people to heart and her reign had put the royal seal of approval on a culture called Scottish. Her image of Scotland, however, was a manufactured one, the acceptable twilight of the proud but pacified Celt, a view that plagues the nation to this day.

Queen Victoria first visited Scotland by accident. In 1842 she planned to go to Brussels; but when her visit was postponed due to illness, it was suggested to the young Queen that Scotland might afford an alternative summer break. She was captivated on arrival and wrote in her diary: 'Edinburgh is quite beautiful – totally unlike anything else I have ever seen.' After a brief stay in the capital, on 5 September the royal party set off for the Highlands and the Queen fell in love.

Balmoral was first suggested by the Queen's Scottish physician, Sir James Clark. His son had recuperated on Upper Deeside at the home of Sir Robert Gordon, brother of Lord Aberdeen, and as both Victoria and Albert suffered from rheumatism, he recommended the climate. When Sir Robert Gordon died on 8 October 1847 his estate, including the lease on Balmoral, passed to the Earl of Aberdeen, who suggested Victoria might like to take over the unexpired twenty-seven years. In September 1848, she wrote of Balmoral: 'All seemed to breathe freedom and peace and to make one forget the world and its sad turmoils.'

The castle was small but distant from London, which appealed to the Queen. Victoria liked her pleasures simple and life at Balmoral was free from protocol and court etiquette. She favoured Deeside for the rides and walks the estate afforded, Albert because it reminded him of his native Thuringia in Germany and he loved to stalk deer. But the old building was hardly suitable for royalty. As the Earl of Malmesbury pointed out:

> . . . an old country house in bad repair and totally unfit for Royal personages. We played at billiards every evening, the Queen and the Duchess [her mother] being constantly obliged to get up from their chairs to be out of the way of the cues.

In 1852, the Queen bought the old house and the estate for £31,500 and planned to remodel both. The royal family, however, were not particularly wealthy, and the bequest of an eccentric barrister John Camden Neild was responsible for the present castle. His entire fortune of over half a million pounds was left his Queen 'for her sole use and benefit'. Designed by an Aberdeen architect, William Smith, and Prince Albert, and built of local granite, the new Balmoral Castle took two years to construct. From the beginning, Albert gave the place a definite Scottish air. In 1856 Lord Clarendon noted that:

> The curtains, the furniture, the carpets, the furniture [coverings] are all of different plaids, and the thistles are in such abundance that they would rejoice the heart of a donkey if they happened to look like his favourite repast, which they don't.

The Royal Pavilion at the Braemar Gathering, c 1880s.   (AU)

Until the railway came from Aberdeen to Ballater, the royal party made the journey by coach from Perth. Family gatherings were large, highly organized affairs; but Victoria also went out of her way to make contact with the local residents, visiting them in their homes and befriending their children. The Queen regularly donned a tartan plaid or sash and Albert and the royal children wore the kilt. The Consort designed a tartan for his family which to this day is for the exclusive use of British royalty. Visiting royals from abroad were also expected to dress accordingly and the children learnt Highland dancing. From a royal obsession sprang Balmorality as Britain's upper class emulated the royal example.

From 1848, the Queen annually attended the Braemar Gathering. One of the first Highland games, Braemar was established in 1817 by officers and men who had fought at Waterloo. Putting the shot, cross country races and tossing the caber were included as competitive sports from the start and pipers from all over Scotland went to Braemar to contest their skills.

In December 1861, Prince Albert died of typhoid. His Queen was grief-stricken and thereafter led a secluded life. Even after the Consort's death, Balmoral honoured his birthday. Prayers were said by the estate workers before his statue and whisky was sent out by the Queen, who noted in her diary:

The result was that the whole community was three parts intoxicated and when we went for a walk in the afternoon it was no uncommon sight to find a man in a top hat and frock coat fast asleep in the woods.

John Brown became the trusted friend and adviser to the widowed Queen. The son of a local Aberdeenshire farmer, Brown was seven years younger than Victoria and the press lampooned the relationship, wickedly referring to the Queen as 'Mrs Brown'. But the friendship was a reflection of her genuine love of the people of Deeside and such was his companionship that Victoria set aside a house for him near Balmoral for his retirement. In 1883, however, Brown fell ill with erysipelas and was dead within weeks. Victoria mourned.

Tartan became the most fashionable cloth of the Victorian age. The first book on tartans was published in 1832 and within twenty years six more had appeared, including the *Vestiarium Scoticum* written by the Sobieski brothers. John Sobieski Stuart and his brother Charles claimed to be descendants of the Young Pretender. They produced coloured drawings of over fifty tartans, many of them previously unheard of: the Sobieski tartans, in fact, were fakes. So too were those claimed to be worn in Scotland since the mists of time that Mr Hunting produced for Sir Walter Scott, the so-called Hunting tartans. Fake too were those shown in the romantic prints produced by Robert Ronald MacIan.

MacIan was a young Scots actor who had made his name playing Sir Walter Scott's romantic characters on the London stage. At the age of thirty-six, he co-operated with James Logan in publishing the *Clans of the Scottish Highlands*. The book was a huge success and in 1848, MacIan and Logan followed up with *Gaelic Gatherings* which depicted Highlanders 'in their pastoral, agricultural, piscatorial and hunting occupations'. MacIan's illustrations oozed nostalgia: sad representations of the interest that swept over the Scottish Lowlands and England as the Highlands were 'discovered'. He also published thousands of postcards and engravings of his 'veritable Highlander', dressed, as he claimed, in tartans of the 'latest patterns'.

Sir Edwin Landseer captured the Highlands of Victoria and proved himself one of Britain's greatest painters. He first visited Scotland in 1824 at the age of twenty-one and the country made a deep impression on the highly-strung English youth. He travelled Scotland widely and although a court painter depicted the life of the ordinary Highlander with sympathy and understanding. Landseer did for Scotland in his painting what Sir Walter Scott had done by his writing.

The invented dress of the Highlander became fashionable. Long hairy sporrans hung below the knees and were worn with finely fashioned pistols, dirks and a profusion of Celtic jewellery. A jacket to go with the kilt was created, with double cuffs, shoulder straps and braided pockets. Invented too were rules: shoes had to be black and no Highlander, it was said, wore the kilt south of the Highland Line. The traditional Lowland shepherd's crook was essential for long walks, despite the fact that no indigenous Highlander would have wished to associate himself with the animal that had displaced so many of his kith and kin.

Clanship was 'discovered'. In the 1890s no fewer than eighteen separate clan societies were founded. Victorian Scotland also invented a mythology of piping. In 1838, Angus MacKay published his *Collection of Ancient Piobaireachad or Highland Pipe Music*. MacKay claimed his father had been

John Brown (1826–83), personal servant to Queen Victoria. He is first mentioned in the Queen's *Journal* in 1849. (*AAG*)

trained by the last of the great MacCrimmon teachers. Between 1500 and 1800, said MacKay, a piping Camelot existed in Skye which was run by the MacCrimmon family. The school was supposedly at Boreraig, near Dunvegan and sadly came to an end as a result of Prince Charles Edward's defeat at Culloden. Much of the evidence in support of a school of piping has leant on the indenture of 1743 whereby the Jacobite Lord Lovat agreed to send his servant, David Fraser, 'To the Isle of Skye in order to have him perfected as a Highland Pyper by the famous Malcolm MacCrimmon.' But no other document has been found to prove the existence of the MacCrimmon school of piping and MacKay's claim was probably a hoax. Members of the Highland gentry, however, helped to pay for the publication of his book, in an attempt, perhaps, to cover up the part their ancestors had played in bringing about the destruction of Highland culture after the Forty-Five.

MacKay was personal piper to Queen Victoria and his personal life was as bizarre as his fictional school of piping. He suffered a mental collapse brought about by cerebral syphilis and became a great embarrassment, claiming he was secretly married to Queen Victoria and accusing Albert of interfering with his marital rights. In 1854, MacKay had to be hauled off to the madhouse at Windsor. Eventually shipped back to his native Scotland, Angus MacKay drowned himself in the River Nith after escaping from the lunatic asylum at Dumfries.

Gaelic song harmony was also an invention, first performed in 1875 by the Glasgow St Columba Church choir. In 1872 the Lorne Ossianic Society was founded in Oban by Professor John Stuart Blackie of Edinburgh University and others to help stimulate Gaelic literary and vocal competition. By the 1880s, the society had foundered and some of its surviving members in 1891 helped create An Comunn Gaidhealach, the Highland Society which aimed to start a Highland Eisteddfod similar to that held in Wales. Under the Education Act of 1872, Gaelic was discouraged. An Comunn Gaidhealach hoped to promote the language of some seven per cent of Scotland's people. The first Mod, yet to be known as the National Mod, took place in Oban on 13 September 1892. The proceedings began at eleven in the morning and for four hours forty competitors contested fewer than a dozen awards. Nobody took much interest and a man was put on the door to encourage passers-by to come in.

John Stuart Blackie (1809–95). (HA)

As the culture of the Gael began to interest Victorian Britain the economic condition of Highland Scotland continued to deteriorate. Many traditional Scottish lairds, whose tenants rarely managed to meet their rents, found themselves impoverished. Owners found the good life of London to their liking and their estates were frequently mismanaged by their factors. Many found eager buyers south of the border, where English entrepreneurs, rich on the spoils of Victorian industry, were eager to gain social status. In Highland Scotland, industrial brass could be turned into social class by the purchase of a large country estate.

The 2nd Duke of Sutherland continued his father's work of improvement, but with little success. By 1833, the Sutherland family had invested nearly half a million pounds in the county and continued to spend more. The age-old problems thwarted well-meaning schemes. In 1832, an epidemic of cholera ravaged Sutherland. In the 1840s, blight destroyed the potato crop as it did in Ireland and Belgium year after year. The people of the north-west suffered most. In December 1846, the Reverend Norman Mackinnon wrote that the people of Bracadale in Skye were:

> . . . now in actual want of everything in the shape of food; some of them days past told me that they had not eaten anything for two days but a salt herring which they said 'kept them in good heart'. This day a great number of them came to my house, who said that they had not a bite and the meal store was run out.

MacLeod of MacLeod almost went bankrupt trying to save his tenants on Skye from starving to death, and Highlanders who had migrated to Glasgow gave generously to help those they had left behind in the glens. The Minister of Glasgow's Gaelic Church, Norman MacLeod, earned the nickname, 'The Friend of the Gael' when he raised £250,000 in six months towards famine relief.

Despite everything, the population of Sutherland continued to grow and reached its peak in 1851. The Duke used the profits from his English coal mines to finance his northern estate and bought out lesser landowners in the area when they could no longer afford to support their tenants. Deer were introduced and proved fairly successful. When the Corn Laws were repealed in 1846, the importation of cheap grain from North America made the growing of cereals in much of Scotland uneconomic and the import of cheap wool from Australia likewise put paid to the boom years that had stimulated Highland improvement.

For thousands emigration was the only hope. In 1850 alone, 10,000 left Carsethorn pier in Kirkcudbright for Canada, 7000 took boat for Australia and 4000 emigrated to New Zealand. John McKenzie was born on 18 October 1838 at Ardross in Ross-shire. As a boy, he worked as a shepherd and witnessed the evictions at Glen Calvie, when some thirty families, forced off their land, pitched tents in the cemetery of Croick church. He quit Scotland at the age of sixteen for New Zealand. Five years after he had arrived at Otago, McKenzie purchased a farm in the Palmerston district and he represented the area in Parliament for nineteen years. As Minister of Lands, McKenzie pushed through legislation to ensure that New Zealand would not become the private property of a handful of landowners. Between 1891 to 1900, legislation was passed whereby those who wished to farm were given leases of 999 years at a reasonable price. In 1892, McKenzie told the New Zealand House of Representatives:

> The Minister of Lands, Sir, got his ideas as a boy when he saw the poor people evicted from their houses in the most cruel manner and unable to get a place for their feet to stand upon except they went to the cemeteries.

Sir John McKenzie (1838–1901). (*HLD*)

The Crimean War, which began in 1854, gave the men of the glens work, as had Britain's imperial wars a century before. But the 'thin Red Line' that fought with courage at Balaclava in October 1854 was raised with difficulty. The Duke of Sutherland was told by an elderly tenant:

> I am sorry for the response your Grace's proposals are meeting here today, so near to the spot where your maternal grandmother by giving some forty-eight hours' notice marshalled fifteen hundred men to pick out the eight hundred she required, but there is a cause for it and a genuine cause . . . These lands are now devoted to rear dumb animals

which your parents considered of far more value than men. I do assure your Grace that it is the prevailing opinion of this county, that should the Czar of Russia take possession of Dunrobin Castle and Stafford house next term that we could not expect worse treatment at his hands than we have experienced at the hands of your family for the past fifty years.

Highland troops, however, continued to help Britain hold her Empire. The Seaforth Highlanders fought at Omdurman in 1898 and helped reconquer the Sudan. By 1899, Britain was again at war with the Boers in South Africa and so great was the loss of men that a school was founded for the orphaned sons of Scottish soldiers. Contributions from all over Scotland built the Queen Victoria School at Dunblane in Perthshire. Education, clothing and board were to be provided free of charge to boys between the ages of ten and eighteen who were the sons of non-commissioned officers killed in action.

When there was peace, Victorian Highlanders returned to the glens that had become playgrounds of the rich. Baronial mansions sprang up everywhere. Sir Dudley Couttes Marjoribanks built a home at Tomich which was typical of the grotesque gothic architecture then so fashionable. Complete with pepperpot towers and battlements, these monstrosities frequently reflected the Englishman's view of a Scotland that never was.

But the building boom brought work. Labour was cheap and available and the stonemason's job became one of the commonest Highland occupations. As new estates were formed, there were country homes to be built and walls and villages. Marjoribanks built the village of Tomich, just large enough to house the employees of his estate and no more, to serve him and his cronies during the summer and autumn months while they fished for salmon and stalked the deer.

Hunting and shooting became obsessions. In 1845, Charles St John wrote a lavishly illustrated book, *Wild Sports and Natural History of the Highlands*. Nine editions were printed before the end of the nineteenth century. Others praised the wildlife that Scotland's remote areas had to offer the keen killer. When the breech-loading shotgun was invented in 1860, shooting was made easy for the urban rich to learn. Vast parties came north to

Soldiers of the 42nd Royal Highlanders at the time of the Crimean War (1854–6).   (*IWM*)

'The Chiefs' return from Deerstalking'.   (*CL*)

slaughter anything that moved, deer, ptarmigan, grouse and pheasant. The moors of Scotland were strenuously keepered; eagles, hawks, wild cats and foxes were trapped and shot to preserve the edible game. Deer replaced sheep in many parts of the Highlands and provided even less work for the local inhabitants, as a Highland shepherd complained in 1883:

> I am able to prove that the Lochalsh forest is laboured by one game-keeper, and when under sheep there were four shepherds, three wintering shepherds, and several helpers, besides clipping and smear-ing. And then how can any man tell me that there is as much labour attached to deer forests as sheep walks?

The Victorian deer-stalking fraternity produced monsters. By the 1880s William Louis Winans, an American millionaire, held the shooting rights to 200,000 acres between Kintail and Beauly and tried every method possible to evict crofters so that game could not be disturbed. Winans cared not for stalking; he had his ghillies herd the deer into a confined space where he could blast off at will.

The Highland inn catered for the needs of southern sportsmen. The owners usually held the rights to fishing and shooting and those who could not afford to own an estate could at least, on payment of a modest sum, lead the life of a country gentleman.

The Hebrides also suffered. Many of Scotland's islands became personal empires. Until the middle of the nineteenth century, the island of Rum had been owned by the chief of the MacLeans of Coll and at one time boasted a population of over 400, making a reasonable livelihood raising cattle for export. In 1828, the chief helped the entire community to emigrate to Canada, hoping, like others, that sheep would be more profitable. MacLean, however, found that this wholesale evacuation was an inconvenience and was forced to import crofters from Skye. But with or without people, sheep proved to be of little profit. In 1845, MacLean sold Rum to the Marquis of Salisbury, the father of the Victorian Prime Minister, who introduced deer. Rum became a place to ease the pressing worries of high Tory politics and the social whirl of London. The island changed hands once again before it was bought by its most famous owner, John Bullough, who amongst other things insisted on spelling his possession with an 'h' – Rhum.

A Lancashire industrialist, he had made his fortune out of iron. He already owned Meggernie Castle in Perthshire and resolved to make Rum his sporting playground. When his son George inherited the island in 1891 at the age of twenty-one he had already done the Grand Tour of the world and he built on Rum a castle to house his treasures from China, Japan and Russia. In Kinloch Castle one of the first inter-room telephone systems in Britain was installed, as was electricity. There was a ballroom, a billiard room and bathrooms that boasted the very best Edwardian plumbing. In the corridor, he installed a vast organ complete with drums, bells and trumpets that cost £2000 and was one of only two ever made.

Bullough employed a vast staff. There were forty gardeners to manicure the gardens. On the island were built new well-appointed shooting lodges, where parties could rest and refresh themselves, and a mausoleum to honour the Bullough achievement in death.

But the presence of English overlords in the Highlands and islands was

A Highland deerstalker.
(*HA*)

as resented in the nineteenth century as it had been in the days of Wallace and Bruce.

Not all Victorians came to the Highlands to kill. In 1815, the Highland Mountain Club of Lochgoilhead was founded and by 1889 the famous Cairngorm Club was bringing enthusiasts together. Britain's first schools of mountaineering were all Scottish and in honour of Sir Hugh Munro, a stalwart pioneer of the new sport, all peaks over three thousand feet in Scotland are still called 'Munro's'.

Tourism became a major employer. Former tenants degenerated into paid employees – ghillies, gamekeepers, gardeners and foresters. During the season the women of the glens became cooks and chambermaids. From 1820 spas like Ballater and Strathpeffer flourished as the regular haunts of Scotland's urban middle-class; but Highland Scotland was unknown to the mass of Lowlanders, let alone the English.

Thomas Cook was a Baptist, deeply interested in the temperance movement. His first tour was a day trip he organized for 570 of his urban followers from his native Leicester to Loughborough. He progressed by organizing tours farther afield and, as he wrote in his diary in 1845, 'From the heights of Snowdon my thoughts took flight to Ben Lomond, and I determined to try to get to Scotland.'

Accordingly in 1846, Thomas Cook organized his first Scottish tour. At a total cost of a guinea, the people of Leicester were offered an 800-mile tour to the Lowlands, travelling to Fleetwood by rail and then by steamer to Ardrossan, where trains were waiting to take them to Glasgow and Edinburgh. Three hundred took advantage of Thomas Cook's first tour and in Glasgow guns saluted as their train entered the station and bands played. A celebratory meeting was held in one of the city's halls where for hours the virtues of temperance were extolled, and the tour was similarly fêted in Edinburgh.

Thomas Cook (d. 1892) stimulated interest in Scotland's scenery. By the 1880s more independent tours were visiting St Kilda (*left*), Scotland's most isolated isle.   (*GH*)   (*Author, left*)

By 1866, Cook estimated that he had brought 40,000 tourists to Scotland. Four thousand of them had taken to boats and toured the Western Isles, visiting Iona and Fingal's Cave made famous by Mendelssohn. Ten thousand at least had promenaded the decks of the steamers on Loch Lomond; under Cook Scottish tourism was firmly established. His only concern was the quality of Scottish hotels:

The Forth Rail Bridge under construction, seen from the south. (*AU*)

We had always a difficulty in Scotland in making hotel arrangements of a satisfactory character. This was in great measure owing to the inveterate love of whisky which has been the drink and the curse of that country.

In the Highlands tourism, of course, depended upon the north's being made accessible, and Scotland's railway system, although late, was a triumph of Victorian engineering. By 1863 a railway line from Perth to Inverness had been completed, a route that not only brought travellers north but also enabled the Scottish fish industry to prosper. By 1874 herring from Wick could readily be transported to the southern urban markets, and during the boom years over a thousand boats operated out of Wick alone.

The West Highland Railway reached Strome, opposite the island of Skye, in 1870, and the village became one of the most important ports on the west coast. A large pierhead was built and trainloads of sheep, cattle and fish from Scotland's islands were regularly transported south. But it was not until 1894 that the track crossed Rannoch Moor to Fort William. Alongside Loch Shiel, the viaduct to carry the line was a prodigious feat of engineering. The North British was the largest railway company in Scotland. At their workshops in Cowlairs, they built the first sleeping coaches in 1873, as the opening up of Scotland's hinterland made journeys longer. They were also responsible for the great bridges that took their tracks across the Firth of Forth and the River Tay, and by the turn of the century Scotland had a proper and efficient system of communication for the first time.

In 1852, Aberdeen Angus cattle caused a sensation at the Royal Highland Show. 'Old Jock', the number one bull in the Aberdeen Angus Cattle Society's Herd Book, was awarded the Sweepstakes for Bulls when he was eleven years old. William McCombie of Tillyfour dominated the fatstock shows. In 1867, his 'Black Prince' won the championship at

London's Smithfield and so impressed was Queen Victoria that she demanded that his bull be brought to Windsor so that she could examine the beast. Careful breeding by Sir George Macpherson Grant brought the Aberdeen Angus strain to perfection, and when the railways began to cross the mid-west of the United States, Aberdeen Angus became one of America's most popular breeds.

The distillation of whisky had been a cottage industry in Scotland since the sixteenth century, and when Britain's war with France put paid to the import of brandy, as General Stewart explained in 1822 in his *Sketches of the Highlanders in Scotland*, ' – the traffic spread rapidly, and, in many districts, became the principal source from which the rents were paid.' John Stuart Fraser was one of the last big-time distiller-smugglers. By the 1820s he was turning out thirty gallons of malt whisky a week from the Conven in Glenlivet, often smuggling his brew south in coffins. In the area round about there were over 200 stills, producing almost half the whisky made in Scotland.

'Tussle with a Highland Smuggler', by John Pettie (1839–93).   (*AAG*)

The Duke of Gordon, one of Scotland's largest landowners, informed Westminster that the illicit industry could only be stopped if the government made it possible to produce legal whisky just as good. Given the Duke's guarantee that he and fellow landlords would do their best to stamp out smuggling, an Act was passed in 1823 which reduced the duty to two shillings and threepence per proof gallon, and henceforth whisky was to be stored in warehouses, duty paid only when it was sold. The Duke and his fellow lairds kept to their word: in 1823 alone 1400 illicit stills were seized.

Whisky production became big business, centred not in the north of Scotland but in the Lowlands. At Kirkliston, Robert Stein invented a steam-heated still which enabled the spirit to be manufactured in one continuous operation. In 1831, Aeneas Coffey invented his 'patent still' which could distill quickly and cheaply and made large-scale production possible. At 12 Torpichen Street in Edinburgh, six Lowland distillers of grain whisky agreed in 1877 to form The Distillers Company, with a nominal capital of £2,000,000. They were soon producing vast quantities of spirit which they sold in bulk to publicans who then drew the whisky from barrels and diluted it for sale. William Usher of Edinburgh pioneered whisky blending in 1865 and was the first to sell the drink under a 'proprietary' label which guaranteed its quality.

The 1870s were good years for the industry. As the iron and steel factories of the Lowlands boomed during the Franco-Prussian War their workers and Scotland's coal miners enjoyed high wages and a good drink. The minister of the parish of Liberton noted for the *New Statistical Account*:

> There are thirty-two shops for the sale of spirits in this parish, which is just thirty too many ... One man is paid for teaching sobriety, but thirty-two have an interest in defeating his efforts, and human nature is on their side.

Until the 1860s brandy was the main spirit consumed in England, but thanks to an aphid, *Phylloxera vastatrix*, which ravaged the vineyards of France, brandy became scarce, often unobtainable. Scots of extraordinary commercial ability helped to swing public taste away from the grape to the grain. Within decades whisky had taken over from brandy as the drink of the middle and upper classes.

In 1880, Alexander Walker of Kilmarnock established a London office and four years later Thomas Dewar of Perth followed suit. The Scottish whisky industry changed out of all recognition as the grain distillery giants of the Lowlands bought out the small Highland malt distilleries and made fortunes out of blending the products of both. Output doubled, then trebled. By 1898 there were 161 distilleries in Scotland.

Once the English market was established Scottish distillers looked overseas. In 1890 Alexander Walker opened an agency in Sydney, Australia. In 1892 Thomas Dewar began a two-year journey round the world to promote his product. He appointed thirty-two agents in twenty-six countries and went on to make the first promotional film for whisky in 1899. Within decades, America, Australia and New Zealand were taking the bulk of whisky exported from Scotland.

Whisky gave work to few in the Highlands. Distilleries employed a handful of men and the more labour-intensive blending and bottling plants were all Lowland based. The profits made went south as well; but by the second half of the century, the money economy was replacing barter in Highland Scotland. Ghillies and chambermaids were paid in pound notes and sons and daughters migrated to help bring in the grain harvests of the rich Lowlands. Others gutted fish during the herring season at Lowestoft. When, however, the harvests were in there was nothing to do but return to the glens.

The Highland croft was a nineteenth-century invention. These individual holdings of land were deliberately kept small so that their occupants would be forced to take up other employment in order to pay the rent and make ends meet. At best the croft, with its few acres of arable land and rights to common grazing, gave families a subsistence living; but as families increased, children demanded land for themselves and their families and crofts were divided, sub-divided and ultimately fragmented. The croft often suffered when the young went south in search of paid employment, and there was little incentive for improvements which, if undertaken, frequently

Planting potatoes in Skye with the cashrom. (*AU*)

resulted in increased rent. Also, as a Skye crofter told a government inquiry:

> The smallness of the crofts render it imperative on us to till the whole of our ground from year to year, and by so doing the land is growing inferior and less productive.

Crofters made do with what was to hand. Their homes were lit by candles made from the fat of their own sheep or fish livers boiled down. Knives, forks and crockery were uncommon; most ate with their hands. Spoons were bought off travelling tinkers who fashioned them out of horn. Flax was often

grown, carded and spun and made into rough linen. Few crofters could boast a horse and cart; sledges were used to move peats from the bogs and carry manure to the fields. Small hand ploughs and the *cashrom*, the foot plough, broke the stony soil.

A crofter's house, 1889.   (*SSS*)

The crofter's diet was healthy enough. Herring in coastal settlements were plentiful and deer and mutton tongues were preserved by smoking or salting for winter use. Potatoes, as in Ireland, were grown in quantity, but when the crop failed there was often hardship. Throughout the century emigration was still seen as the permanent solution to the Highland problem.

Many Scots followed the Earl of Selkirk's pioneering example and tried to make emigration easier for their kinsmen. John Galt, born in Irvine in 1779, probably did most to colonize Canada. In 1824 he founded the Canada Company to establish independent well-educated settlers in Guelph and Goderich, Ontario. When he died a pauper in 1839 in Greenock, his son Alexander went on to make a fortune in Canada out of coalmines.

In 1852, the trustees of Aeneas MacDonnell attempted to raise sheep in

Knoydart. Over 400 families were forcibly evicted from Airor, Doune, Inverie and Sandaig. Three hundred people were transported to Canada and their houses promptly demolished. Those who did not emigrate hid in caves and hovels and when they tried to rebuild their homes these too were destroyed by the estate.

The isle of Skye also witnessed evictions in the middle of the century. Thomas Fraser, the island's Sheriff-Substitute, was so concerned that in 1851 he formed the Highlands and Islands Emigration Society. The following year, the society moved its headquarters to London where Prince Albert was made patron and Sir Charles Trevelyan, the Assistant Secretary to the Treasury, appointed Chairman. In seven years, the society helped over 5000 Highlanders emigrate, mainly to Australia. The problem of land shortage, however, remained for those who stayed behind.

In 1873, *The Highlander* newspaper was started in an attempt to voice the grievances of crofters. Its publisher, John Murdoch of Inverness, won sympathy from many in the Lowlands who were drawn into the cause. Funds were raised, mass meetings were held to put pressure on the government and circulars in Gaelic as well as English were printed to keep crofting communities informed. Matters came to a head in 1881 in Skye. On that island alone between 1840 and 1880 more than 40,000 eviction notices had been served. The landlord, Lord MacDonald, owned 10,000 acres of deer forest and was long accustomed to doing what he chose. In the 1860s he summarily deprived the tenants of the Braes of their hill-grazing on Ben Lee and when in the autumn of 1881 the crofters asked for it back their plea was rejected. As Angus Stewart, one of MacDonald's crofters explained:

> The smallness of our holdings is what has caused our poverty, and the way in which the poor crofters are huddled together and the best part of the land devoted to deer-forests and big farms. I cannot bear evidence to the distress of my people without hearing evidence to the oppression and high-handedness of the landlord and his factor.

John Murdoch, publisher of *The Highlander*. A photograph taken *c* 1873. (*SNPG*)

The tenants of the Braes marched on Portree to declare their refusal to pay their rents. The land rights movement had crossed the Irish Sea and the landlords were fearful. In swift reaction MacDonald had a sheriff officer serve eviction orders on twelve of his tenants in April 1882. The officer was accosted by a crowd of 150 crofters and his summonses were burned. On 19 April 1882 William Ivory, Sheriff of Inverness-shire, landed a force at midnight at Portree and, with sixty men, marched to meet the rebellious crofters. A famous 'battle' was fought at the Braes, as a Lowland newspaper reported:

> Huge boulders darkened the horizon as they sped from the hands of infuriated men and women. Large sticks and flails were brandished and brought down with crushing force upon the police.

The attention of the public had been focused on the problem and by December Lord MacDonald was forced to lease Ben Lee to his crofters for grazing again. Almost as a symbol of the crofters' struggle Professor Donald MacKinnon from Colonsay was appointed to the first Scottish chair of Celtic studies at Edinburgh in 1882. Many crofters and workers' organizations in Scotland's towns contributed to its endowment.

Scottish crofters had looked to Ireland as an example of how they should

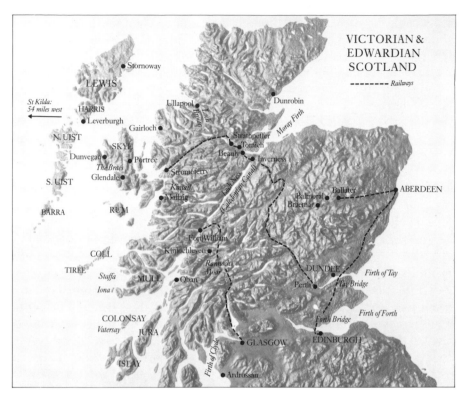

VICTORIAN &
EDWARDIAN
SCOTLAND

------- *Railways*

go about obtaining proper rights. The Irish Land League was campaigning to obtain security of tenure, fair rents and a legal guarantee against arbitrary eviction, and in April 1882, a Highland Land League was formed. Rebuffed by the British Liberal Party, the League later successfully exploited the Third Reform Act of 1884 which extended the franchise. In the General Election of 1885 the League put up six candidates and four won seats. Its remarkable success paved the way for later political organizations, like the Labour Party, that were to grow out of Scotland's towns.

After the Braes there was agitation in Lewis and again in Skye, where at Glendale crofters beat up officials who tried to serve summonses for non-payment of rent and marched on Dunvegan. The government took swift and stern action. Troops were sent in and, on 15 March 1883, five crofters were tried in Edinburgh. Sent to prison for two months, their valid cause was investigated by a Royal Commission under the chairmanship of Lord Napier.

On 8 May 1883, the Commission started to take evidence at the Braes but the crofters, fearful of eviction, were hesitant to voice their grievances. Napier's commission sat for three years, and meanwhile rebellion continued. In Skye, fences were pulled down, hay ricks set on fire and sheep driven from pastures which the crofters regarded as theirs. In November 1884, the British government sent a gunboat to the island with 300 Marines on board. A steamer, to be used as a mobile police station, was anchored off Staffin. The further collapse in wool prices in 1885 forced the landlords to give way. Now they needed their tenants' rents; grudgingly they accepted the Crofters' Holdings (Scotland) Act passed by Westminster in June 1886. The result of Lord Napier's findings, the Act was a breakthrough in terms of crofters' rights. For the first time they were to be given security of tenure and

Working the land, Isle of Skye, 1880s. (*AU*)

crofts could be passed down through the family. When they improved the land, crofters would henceforth be compensated, and a Crofters' Commission would fix fair rents and supervise the new legislation.

But the Act had not made any new land available. When the Crofters' Commission visited Lewis in 1888, they found widespread poverty despite the fact that arrears in rent had been cancelled. Among over 600 crofters for whom fair rents had been fixed, there were only a dozen who had not received 'destitution' meal or relief of some form. Lewis had some thousand cottars, people forced to squat on lands to which they were not entitled. About 200 people annually were quitting for Canada or Australia but the birth rate was four times the rate of emigration and the pressure on the land was high.

The Highland Land League continued to press the crofters' case while the government clamped down on tenants who rebelled. In July 1886, 750 police and 250 marines were sent to Tiree to bring order to an island in revolt. Eight crofters were arrested, five of their number sent to prison.

On 22 November 1887 200 crofters marched on the deer forest of Park in south-eastern Lewis. Their aim was to slaughter their landlord's deer to help feed their families and also to protest against so much land being devoted to sport. A gunboat and 100 troops were sent to counter the revolt. Park was in many ways typical. From the 1820s scores of families had been evicted to make way for sheep-runs on Lewis; then, by the 1880s, upwards of 10,000 sheep made way for a deer forest which created employment of a peculiarly servile and somewhat unpleasant type. When deer forests were the rage, they were often advertised in England's sporting press with the phrase 'No Crofters' as the most significant single selling-point.

In 1897, new legislation brought about the Congested Districts Board. Public works were to give the people paid employment and funds were made available by central government to build new roads and bridges, develop cottage industries and fishing, assist those who wanted to improve croft land. The Board's attempt to solve the economic problems of Highland Scotland was as genuine as it was unacceptable to the mass of stubborn crofters who craved land. Before central government, private landlords had equally seen industry as a panacea and been disillusioned. In truth, the Highlander was resistant to change.

In 1844, Sir James Matheson, who had made his fortune as a partner in the great Far East trading company, Jardine Matheson, had bought the island of Lewis. At his own expense, he provided the islanders with a regular boat service and built new roads across Lewis to ease communication. He tried to reclaim the peat bogs and convert them into arable land. Matheson bought his Lewis estate for £190,000; when he died in 1878, he had spent over half a million pounds of his personal fortune trying to make the community viable. He built a brick works and a fish-curing plant and encouraged local boat-building. He even attempted to turn peat into oil with some success. Chemists from London were brought north and an oil industry flourished for ten years. The discovery of oil in America in the 1870s, however, made Matheson's plant uneconomic and his chemical works were forced to close down. But the passion for land, for a croft of one's own, had made Matheson's far-seeing schemes unacceptable to many Lewismen.

A crofter's house, Stornoway, Isle of Lewis, c 1880s. (SSS)

Spinning wool in Skye and sorting wool before dyeing (*above left*) in Harris, *c* 1900. (*AU*)   (*SSS, above*)

Elsewhere in the Western Isles, crofters without land began taking the law into their own hands. In February 1906, men from the island of Colonsay landed on the nearby island of Vatersay. Having ferried over their sheep, cattle and belongings, they illegally set about building new homes for themselves and their families. Two years later ten were arrested and sent to prison. The Congested Districts Board, however, sympathetic to their plight, bought Vatersay in 1908 and gave some of the raiders a legal claim to their holdings.

By 1911, the Small Landholders (Scotland) Act had transformed the Crofters' Commission into the Scottish Land Court. Appeals could then be made by crofters or landowners who felt that justice had not been done and the court has since proved to be one of the most successful public bodies to operate in the Highlands, although its attempts to encourage smallholding came to little in practice. In 1911, the Congested Districts Board became the Board of Agriculture for Scotland, with powers to settle people on land and compensate the previous owners, and later the Board was given the power to purchase land compulsorily and give crofters loans. But land continued in short supply, and work remained scarce despite the efforts of hard-headed businessmen from the south.

Aluminium was discovered in 1825 but could not be produced until 1886 when the electrolytic reduction process made large-scale works feasible. The British Aluminium Company was formed with the enthusiastic support of Lord Kelvin, who himself had made outstanding discoveries in the field of electricity. By June 1896 a factory was producing aluminium from imported

Weaving in Harris, 1910.
(*SSS*)

ore at Foyers on Loch Ness. The major difficulty, however, was in persuading manufacturers to make use of the metal. For nearly a decade British Aluminium went on producing without a sale and a large stockpile developed. With great foresight, the company planned another plant at Kinlochleven. The factory involved the construction of the Blackwater Dam, over 3000 feet long in rugged and inaccessible terrain; it took four years to build. On Hogmanay 1907 the first metal was produced at Kinlochleven, powered by Britain's first large-scale hydro-electric development; but the price of aluminium had fallen by two-thirds to the point where it barely covered the cost of production. It was an economic situation that later bedevilled the modern plant at Invergordon in 1981.

More traditional Highland skills, however, had proved profitable. In 1844, the Earl of Dunmore asked weavers of Harris to make a copy of the Murray tartan and the Victorian obsession with hunting and shooting stimulated others to follow. Hard-wearing and available in a variety of sombre country colours, Harris tweed was ideal for sporting clothes. In 1857, an Edinburgh lady began to take orders and by 1888 her business had grown so large that she moved her headquarters to London.

To begin with, all the processes were performed by hand. The wool was washed and dyed out of doors and the carding, spinning and weaving was done in the Black House by the women of Harris. Payment for manufactured cloth was in kind: webs were bartered for peats and potatoes. When, however, the Congested Districts Board took an interest instructors were sent to Harris and Lewis to teach the people better design and show them how to use the flying shuttle. Weaving thereafter became a full-time occupation for the men and a Harris Tweed Association was formed to standardize quality and guarantee the cloth.

By the outbreak of the First World War, much had been tried in the Highlands and islands to make the lot of the people better. Work for most, however, was found away from home. It was an almost insoluble problem. As Joseph Chamberlain told the people of Inverness in 1885:

> The history of the Highland Clearances is a black page in the account with private ownership in land . . . Thousands . . . suffered unbearably; very many died. However, as time went on the descendants of those who did survive have contributed in no mean degree to the prosperity of the countries in which they finally settled. The Highland countryside was depopulated by those clearances. The general condition of the people left behind suffered and it has gone on deteriorating until it has become at last a matter of national concern. I ask you whether it is not time that we should submit to careful examination and review a system which places such vast powers for evil in the hands of irresponsible individuals and which makes the possession of land not a trust but a means of extortion and exaction?

Within thirty years of Chamberlain's speech the world was at war. Thousands of Highlanders would not return from Britain's struggle to save an Empire Scots from the Lowlands as well as the Highlands had in large part created.

19

The Scots Empire

BY 1897 BRITAIN HAD AN EMPIRE that covered ten million square miles of the earth's surface, an empire of nearly four hundred million people. Trade was at the root of what was originally a creation of English adventurers, and the flag had followed. Perhaps because Scotland was a small and historically individualistic nation, she produced men of strong character and entrepreneurial spirit, whether as missionaries, educationalists, explorers or businessmen, who were keen to capitalize on what was first England's and then Britain's world empire. Until 1707, the Scots played little part. Excluded from trading directly with England's colonies by acts of the English Parliament, they had concentrated on Europe.

A portrait of Queen Victoria painted two years after her Diamond Jubilee of 1897. Her reign was the heyday of British overseas power. (*NPG*)

Scottish soldiers, scholars, settlers and traders had been more active on the Continent. During the Auld Alliance from 1295 until 1560 many looked to France, where Scots had citizenship. Until Scotland's own universities were founded in the fifteenth century, Scots in search of higher education went abroad and the Abbey of St James at Ratisbon in France by the beginning of the seventeenth century was a purely Scottish community. Others went further afield; when James VI became King of England he was petitioned not to allow Scots to settle in Poland, so great was the influence of the large community already established. By the beginning of the eighteenth century there was a thousand-strong Scottish community at Rotterdam. Scots in their thousands had also, before the Union, fought in the armies of countries often at loggerheads with England.

The Scots had learnt from the Continent and were perhaps more outward-looking and open-minded than their southern neighbours. When Scots returned home, they brought new knowledge to bear upon the institutions of their own country. The development of Scotland's education and legal systems were greatly influenced by the European connection.

The Scottish contribution to Europe was to continue well after the Union of 1707. Examples are legion. Louis XIV's Scottish gardener, for instance, gave the French language a new word, *étiquette*, derived from the tickets he placed at Versailles reminding courtiers to keep to the paths. George Learmonth of Dairsie in Fife served as a soldier with the Poles then the Russians. His great-grandson was the poet Lermontov. Peter the Great's adviser, Patrick Gordon, hailed from Aberdeen and Samuel Greig from Inverkeithing created the Russian Navy, which had mainly Scottish officers.

Gilbert Elliot, 1st Earl of Minto
(1751–1814). (*SNPG*)

James Andrew Broun, 10th Earl of
Dalhousie (1812–60). (*NPG*)

During the Russian-Turkish war of 1768 to 1784, Greig took a fleet from the Baltic to the Mediterranean and destroyed the Turks. Charles Cameron from Aberdeen lived in Russia for twenty years and planned many of Leningrad's chief buildings for Catherine the Great.

After 1707, however, it was the contribution made by Scotland to Britain's influence abroad that was out of all proportion to the size of the country. Much was due to patronage; but the Scots were quick to prove themselves well-suited to serving abroad. One in seven of all diplomatic appointments went to Scotsmen, who readily adjusted to strange conditions and were prepared to live for years on end in remote capitals. From 1763 onwards, there was nearly always a Scot in charge of Britain's embassies in Austria, Prussia, Poland, Sweden and Russia.

By the 1700s, the English East India Company had trading factories in Madras, Bengal and Bombay; but as the Company expanded many became critical of its management and a government Board of Control for India was set up by William Pitt in 1784. For eight years Henry Dundas was head of the Board and, as Pitt created the foundations of Britain's empire, Dundas made sure that able Scots would help manage it. India became what Sir Walter Scott called 'the corn chest of Scotland'. In 1795 Dundas, together with a fellow Scot, Hugh Cleghorn, engineered the defection of the mercenaries who garrisoned Ceylon for the Dutch and made the island British.

The Scots who served in India were often the sons of less well-off lairds or of more humble background. The sons born to George Malcolm, the minister of Burnfoot in Dumfriesshire, were knighted by a Crown grateful for their service to the Empire and became known as the 'Knights of Eskdale'. The family had been impoverished by speculation and a post was sought for John Malcolm with the East India Company at the age of twelve. Within two years he found himself in command of two companies of Indian sepoys. At nineteen he became a diplomat acting for the East India Company in Persia and subsequently he was Governor of Bombay. Mountstuart Elphinstone, the son of a Scots peer, began his career as a Clerk in the East India Company in 1795. Governor of Bombay from 1819 to 1827, Mountstuart founded the Elphinstone Institute which became part of Bombay University in 1857 during the governorship of his nephew, Lord Elphinstone. Thomas Munro also began as a junior official in the East India Company. As a Major-General, Munro fought against Hyder Ali between 1780 and 1784 and was Governor of Madras.

In 1807, Gilbert Elliott, later 1st Earl of Minto, became the first of many Scots to hold the highest office India had to offer – Governor-General. In a series of campaigns, Minto forced the French out of the sub-continent. In 1810 he wrote:

> I am just sending an expedition to make the conquest of the Isle of Bourbon. I propose to follow up the blow by attacking the Mauritius, generally called the Isle of France. These two acquisitions will be of extreme importance; they are the only French possessions east of the Cape, and furnish the only means our arch-enemy can command for annoying us in this quarter of the world.

Scots were rarely humble servants of the British government. When General Charles Napier, against orders, annexed Hyderabad, capital of Sindh, he sent a terse message to his superiors in Delhi: '*Peccavi*' (I have sinned).

James Ramsay, the 1st Marquess of Dalhousie, was Governor-General of India from 1847 to 1856. In nine years Dalhousie annexed eight Indian states, including the Punjab. Apart from creating most of what came to be British India, Dalhousie carried out a vast programme of public works. He extended India's road system and supervised the construction of canals and railways as well as the introduction of the telegraph. As he said himself,

> There can only be one master in all India, and while I am in India, I have no mind that it should be anybody else than the Governor-General in Council.

In 1857, a year after Dalhousie retired to Scotland, Indian sepoys who helped the East India Company control the country rebelled. The Mutiny took fourteen months to crush and the most famous of the commanders, who won back the cities of Lucknow and Cawnpore, was Sir Colin Campbell, the son of a Glasgow carpenter who had joined the army at fifteen. Before he served in India he had commanded the 93rd, the Thin Red Line that beat off the Russian threat at Balaclava in the Crimean War. At Lucknow, in March 1858, Campbell put 20,000 men and 180 guns into the field, the largest army India had ever seen. In the Mutiny 11,000 troops were killed, all but a quarter of them dying from heat-stroke and disease. British public opinion was outraged by the Mutiny, and in November 1858 the British Crown took over from the East India Company.

Sir Colin Campbell, Lord Clyde (1792–1863).   (*IWM*)

The Bruce family, which had given Scotland kings, made a unique contribution to British diplomacy in the nineteenth century. The 7th Earl of Elgin served at the Court of Emperor Leopold in 1790 and was later British Ambassador in Brussels and Berlin. In 1816 he brought the Elgin Marbles from Greece. Both his sons became distinguished diplomats, the 8th Earl serving the Empire for twenty years as Governor of Jamaica, Governor-General of Canada and finally Viceroy of India, where he died in 1863. In 1857 Elgin was sent to deal with the troublesome Emperor of China. After four years of negotiation he persuaded him to cede Kowloon to Britain and left his brother Sir Frederick Bruce behind in Peking to ensure the Emperor kept his word.

The 9th Earl of Elgin also became Viceroy of India, much against his will. More interested in domestic politics, he was finally persuaded to accept the overseas post in 1894. However, he refused to be denied all his pleasures. At the Vice-Regal Lodge at Simla he had the ballroom floor polished so that he could curl with his friends. By 1900 the Indian Civil Service at every level was staffed by a disproportionate number of Scotsmen, and as engineers and surveyors they helped build India's canals, railways and telegraph. They played a part, too, in the development of Indian agriculture and in providing medical care and education. In 1829 the Church of Scotland sent Alexander Duff from Perthshire to act as minister in Calcutta. He was instrumental in bringing about the establishment of universities in Calcutta, Bombay and Madras and schools supported by government grants. Duff fervently believed that education was 'the panacea for the regeneration of India', and wrote:

James Bruce, 8th Earl of Elgin and Kincardine (1811–63).   (*LE*)

> Let us awake, arise and rescue unhappy India from its present and impending horrors. Let us arise and revive the genius of olden time: let us revive the spirit of our forefathers. Like them let us enter into a

Sir Thomas Lipton (1850–1931). (*GAG*)

The headquarters in Hong Kong of the Jardine Matheson Company. The gun, fired by the Company at noon, was immortalized in Noel Coward's song 'Mad Dogs and Englishmen'. (*Author*)

Solemn League and Covenant before our God, on behalf of that benighted land, that we will not rest, till the voice of praise and thanksgiving arise, in daily orisons, from its coral strands, roll over its fertile plains, resound from its smiling valleys, and re-echo from its everlasting hills.

The Scots in India were also great traders. By 1813, there were thirty-eight trading companies in Calcutta, fourteen of which were run by Scots. Scots were also responsible for the first jute mill at Barangar, and by 1885 Dundee had supplied twenty-four factories in Calcutta alone with power-driven looms to make sacking. Together the factories employed more than 50,000, managed totally by expatriate Scots. During the First World War the mills of Calcutta were to manufacture eight million sandbags a month for the British War Office. Such was the wealth made that when the armistice came, the Scots of Calcutta called the day Black Friday.

Thomas Lipton was the youngest of five children born to an Irish-Scottish family, and the only one to reach adulthood. In 1870, at the age of twenty, he opened his first shop in Stobcross Street in Glasgow. By 1885 his business had grown into Liptons Limited, a vast company of over 600 shops whose fortunes were based on tea. To eliminate the middle-man Lipton bought vast plantations in Ceylon, and he packaged his tea in eye-catching yellow packets. A tremendous showman, Thomas Lipton hired sandwich men and organized parades to promote his product. When he had captured the British market, Lipton looked elsewhere. Within years, Lipton's Tea was drunk all over the world and Thomas was a multi-millionaire.

Almost a century before, another Scottish company had begun trading in tea – Jardine Matheson. William Jardine was born in 1784 in Dumfriesshire. He became a surgeon on an East Indiaman and in 1822 joined a European trading agency in Canton. Already established there was James Matheson from Lairg in Sutherland. When the East India Company lost its monopoly in the China trade, Matheson and William Jardine formed a partnership in 1832.

Before tea was grown in India and Ceylon, China supplied the world and Jardine and Matheson organized its shipment to Europe. But the men of the East were little interested in British manufactures, so to avoid a balance of payments problem, opium from the factories of India was illegally sold to

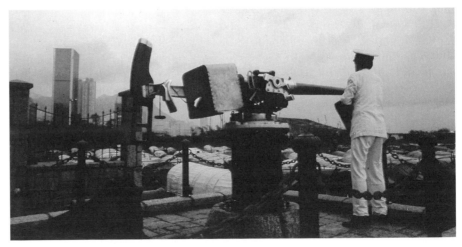

China in exchange for silver, which could then be used to pay the tea producers.

In 1844, the company opened offices in Hong Kong, ceded to Britain four years before, and later diversified into insurance, banking and land. By 1865, from their Hong Kong base, Jardine Matheson had established twenty offices in China, Japan, the United States and Britain and had helped break down the barriers between East and West. Today, the company is involved in every aspect of the life of Hong Kong with an annual world turnover of over £800,000,000. In March 1984 Jardine Matheson announced they were to move their headquarters to Bermuda in advance of Britain's handing back the New Territories to the Republic of China; but they will continue proudly to display the company's emblem – the Scottish thistle – in over twenty countries. From the outset family connection was Jardine Matheson's 'steel frame' and thirty senior partners of the company have come from the rolling hills of Dumfriesshire. Neither of the founders had children but they made sure that their nephews who succeeded them were properly educated. Many Scots serving abroad have done the same. In 1818, Dollar Academy was founded with a bequest left to the town by John McNab, a local sea captain who died rich. Many of the school's first pupils went on to serve in India and Hong Kong, and Scots serving abroad still send their children back, generation after generation, to receive the same education that had stood them in such good stead.

Britain's vast, scattered Empire needed ships and Scots created the great Victorian shipping fleets. Alexander and William Thomson, sons of an Edinburgh builder, acquired their first ship in 1839. Originally Thomson ships carried Alloa coal to Canada and brought back valuable timber which was auctioned by William Thomson himself. When the Canadian trade began to dwindle in the 1850s the Thomsons cast a wider net. Passengers and cargoes were regularly transported to and from India and Australia and, as trade grew with the East, ships of the Thomsons' Ben Line sailed to Colombo, Bangkok, Japan, North Borneo and Hong Kong.

Arthur Anderson was born in Shetland in 1792, so poor that as a child he worked on the beach at Lerwick, cleaning fish and laying them out on the pebbles to dry. When he was sixteen Arthur joined the Navy and sailed the Baltic. In 1815 he went to work for Brodie McGhie Willcox, a London shipowner, and with him formed the Peninsular Steam Company which won a government contract to take mails from Falmouth to Gibraltar. In 1840 the company expanded into the Peninsular and Oriental Company, the first in the field in the lucrative trade with the Far East. Anderson amassed a fortune but he did not forget his roots. In 1836, he funded Lerwick's first newspaper, *The Shetland Journal*, which was printed in London and shipped north. He also financed the Anderson Education Institute in an attempt to dispel what he regarded as the curse of the community – illiteracy.

After union with England, Scots, it seems, developed a wanderlust that was epitomized by Alexander Selkirk, born in Largo in Fife in 1676. While he was sailing master of the *Cinque Ports*, Selkirk fell out with his officers and was marooned on the island of Juan Fernandez in the Pacific for four years. His account of his adventures inspired Daniel Defoe's *Robinson Crusoe*.

Scottish sailors, and those of Scottish parentage like Captain James Cook, roamed the world's seas. It is perhaps not surprising that a nation that

Dr William Jardine (1784–1843). (*JM*)

James Matheson (1796–1878). (*SNPG*)

John Galt (1779–1839), founder of the Canada company. (*SNPG*)

Mungo Park (1771–1806). (*NPG*)

Hugh Clapperton (1788–1827). (*SNPG*)

could boast over two hundred inhabited islands produced intrepid sailors who had an inborn respect for isolated communities. They gave islands they discovered Scottish names like New Caledonia and the New Hebrides. In 1816, a British garrison was sent to Tristan da Cunha in the South Atlantic and William Glass, a Scot, decided to stay on when the troops were recalled. He and his wife raised sixteen children, the nucleus of the colony's present population. The Cocos Islands in the Indian Ocean attracted another Scot, John Clunies-Ross from Yell in Shetland. In 1827, he resolved to settle a community there that would prosper by trading in pepper and spices from the East. Thirty years later, the Cocos became part of the Empire and the Clunies-Ross family were granted their lands in perpetuity by Queen Victoria.

By the nineteenth century the continent of Africa presented the last great challenge to Europeans. What little was known came in large part from the work of early Scottish explorers like James Bruce, born in Stirlingshire in 1730. British consul in Algiers from 1763, Bruce set out in 1768 to explore. He reached what is now Abyssinia and discovered the source of the Blue Nile. He returned to Britain in 1774 and set about recording his travels. When the five volumes were published in 1790 he was accused of writing fiction, but his adventures inspired others.

Mungo Park from Yarrow near Selkirk qualified as a physician. At the age of twenty-four he set off for Africa and in 1795 travelled from Senegal to the Niger. Of his first sight of the great river, one of the great moments of African exploration, Park wrote:

> Looking forwards I saw with infinite pleasure the great object of my mission – the long sought for majestic Niger, glittering in the morning sun, as broad as the Thames at Westminster, and flowing to the eastwards. I hastened to the brink, and, having drank of the water, lifted up my fervent thanks in prayer to the great Ruler of all things, for having thus far crowned my endeavours with success.

On his return to Africa in 1805, Park travelled from Gambia to the Niger, where he was drowned during a native attack.

Hugh Clapperton from Annan was pressed into the British Navy and became a captain. Between 1822 and 1827 he led several expeditions from Tripoli across the Sahara to the Niger and was the first European to see Lake Chad. Clapperton's journeys helped open up trade in African palm oil which was used in Europe to manufacture soap and candles. Major Gordon Laing, another Scot, with the self-confessed ambition of saving his name from oblivion, was the first European to cross the Sahara from north to south, a journey of over 2500 miles. It took Laing and his small party thirteen months to reach Timbuktu where he was murdered by the natives.

In May 1796, the General Assembly of the Church of Scotland had declared:

> To spread abroad among barbarians and heathen natives the knowledge of the Gospel seems to be highly preposterous, in so far as it anticipates, nay reverses, the order of Nature.

Yet Scotland was to give the world, especially Africa, more Protestant missionaries than any other European country. Given the established Kirk's antagonism, Scots could travel only under the auspices of the London

Missionary Society, who sent John Philip from Aberdeen to South Africa to act as superintendent in 1820. He was largely responsible for the Fiftieth Ordinance which recognized the equality of all races in Africa before the law, and his revelations about the slave trade horrified the British public. A missionary for thirty years, he was known as the Elijah of South Africa.

Robert Moffat was born in Ormiston in 1795. A gardener by trade, he spent fifty-four years in Bechuanaland. At Kuruman, he built his mission church with his own hands and practised his concept of 'the Bible and the plough'. He was the first to give the natives of Africa a written language and he translated the Bible into their own tongue. Moffat's great and lasting achievement in Africa was overshadowed only by that of his son-in-law, David Livingstone.

Born on 29 March 1813, David Livingstone personified the story of Scotland. His great-grandfather, a Jacobite, had died at Culloden in 1746. His grandfather had been forced to quit his island home on Ulva and go to the mainland in search of work. David's father worked in the cotton mill at Blantyre and he himself was a child of Scotland's industrial revolution:

Dr Robert Moffat (1795–1883). (*SNPG*)

> The earliest recollection of my mother recalls a picture so often seen among the Scottish poor – that of the anxious housewife striving to make both ends meet. At the age of ten I was put into the factory as a 'piercer', to aid by my earnings in lessening her anxiety . . .
>
> My reading while at work was carried on by placing the book on a portion of the spinning jenny, so that I could catch sentence after sentence as I passed . . . The toil of cotton-spinning, to which I was promoted in my nineteenth year, was excessively severe on a slim loose-jointed lad, but it was well paid for; and it enabled me to support myself while attending medical and Greek classes in Glasgow in winter, as also the divinity lectures of Dr Wardlaw, by working with my hands in summer. I never received a farthing of aid from any one.

Scots missionaries, like many who served the Empire, were of humble background. They were products of a country with a long history of poverty and injustice, and were eager to rectify both in other parts of the world. David Livingstone was determined to become a doctor and to do missionary work in China. The London Missionary Society, however, had other plans. They sent him to Africa where he crossed the Kalahari Desert, went up the Zambesi River and discovered for the Western world Lakes Nyasa, Mweru and Bangweolu as well as the Victoria Falls. Livingstone's ambition was that his explorations would open up Africa and give traders an alternative to selling slaves. The word of God would be followed by freedom for the blacks and an improved standard of living. In 1857, he told a meeting of undergraduates in Cambridge:

David Livingstone (1813–73). (*SNPG*)

> I go back to Africa to make an open path for commerce and Christianity; do you carry out the work which I have begun.

Livingstone believed in advancing the kingdom of God by honest trade and believed the Scots well equipped for the task:

> I think a mission of our own honest Scottish poor will do more in this country than any other measure. There is room enough to spare and they would shine as lights in the world and hold up their pastors hands when all the heathen are against him.

Mary Slessor (1848–1915). (*DCAG*)

In 1865 Livingstone, like other Scots before him, went in search of the sources of the Nile. Nothing was heard of him for over five years. Then in October 1871, he was found by a Welsh-born American newspaper correspondent, Henry Morton Stanley at Ujiju on Lake Tanganyika. When he died at Ilala in Northern Rhodesia in May 1873 the nation mourned. Two years later the Free Church founded Livingstonia on the shores of Lake Nyasa as a centre of commerce and Christianity. The Church of Scotland, not to be outdone, founded Blantyre and, in 1878, a group of Glasgow businessmen formed the African Lakes Company which laid out tobacco and tea plantations and ultimately forced the British government to take responsibility for the area now known as Malawi. Livingstone's death inspired Scotland's most famous woman missionary.

As a child, Mary Slessor worked in a Dundee weaving shed. Her father was a drunkard, her home a slum. From six in the morning until six at night she worked. In 1876, at the age of twenty-eight she took herself off to Calabar in Nigeria. As a missionary her life was fraught with danger; but from the beginning she ate native food and learnt their language. She constantly scolded the natives and confiscated their drink and firearms. With great courage she forced them to abandon tribal customs such as murdering twins, flogging women, practising human sacrifice and trial by poison. She won their respect and was nicknamed 'Ma'. When Mary Slessor died in January 1915, she was buried in Calabar and her worldly possessions were sent back to Scotland: a few clothes, some Bibles, her mother's pebble brooch, a bracelet, a fountain pen, a compass and a thick bundle of letters. Mary Slessor and her Scottish predecessors had opened up a continent; in their wake came trade, British rule, and yet more Scots.

In Africa as in India the greatest and most lasting contribution made by the Church of Scotland and the Free Church after 1843 was in the fields of education and medicine. Schools like that at Lovedale in the Cape Colony brought literacy and Christianity. Founded in 1824, Lovedale offered an education in English to racially integrated classes, much to the dislike of the Boers. Until the 1950s Scottish missions dominated education, producing among others Kenneth Kaunda of Zambia and Julius Nyerere of Tanzania.

Camden Park Farm, New South Wales. John Macarthur (1767–1834) and his wife Elizabeth (1790–1850), who were largely responsible for founding Australian agriculture. (*Author*) (*NSWL, right*)

In the vast continent of Australasia Scots were active too. In 1790 John Macarthur, whose grandfather had been a Jacobite at Culloden, became a lieutenant in the New South Wales Corps responsible for keeping the peace in Britain's convict colony of Botany Bay. Having made a fortune out of the illicit sale of rum, Macarthur turned his mind to farming. He raised sheep for mutton at Elizabeth Farm and became the largest sheep owner in New South Wales. In 1803, he was granted a new estate of 5000 acres at Camden Park outside modern Sydney, and based his flock on five Spanish merino rams he purchased from the Royal Stud at Kew in London. By the time of his death, he owned a million acres and his wife Elizabeth, who survived him by fifteen years, carried on his work with the help of their sons James and William. The wealth of the Macarthur family grew. They not only raised sheep for meat and wool but were also silk farmers with huge mulberry plantations, and exporters of wine which won gold medals even in France.

Lachlan MacQuarie (c 1761–1824). (NSWL)

In 1809 Lachlan MacQuarie was sent out by the British government to govern the 10,000 criminals and colonists of New South Wales. Born around 1761 on the island of Ulva off Mull, MacQuarie joined the army at the age of sixteen and became a major-general. As Governor of the colony for twelve years, he set about planning a new town to replace the convict shacks. Decent barracks were built for the increasing numbers sent out by Britain, and St James's Church and a new Court House were among the buildings commissioned. MacQuarie also built roads and hospitals and, like Macarthur, encouraged agricultural improvement. He allowed convicts who had served their time to be admitted to public office and treated as equals, preparing the ground for the colony to prosper once it ceased to be a dumping ground for British dissidents.

In 1821, MacQuarie, accused of extravagance and criticized for his enlightened views, was replaced as Governor by another Scot, Sir Thomas Brisbane from Ayrshire. MacQuarie, the 'Father of Australia', was buried on Mull in 1824; his mausoleum is now a shrine for Australian tourists, yet few Scots are aware of his achievement.

Other Scotsmen helped to open up Australia's vast hinterland. John McDouall Stuart, the son of a customs officer, was born in Dysart in Fife on 7 September 1815. He was orphaned at the age of ten; but his parents had made provision for his education and at Edinburgh University he qualified as a civil engineer. In 1838 at the age of twenty-three Stuart left for Southern Australia. Five years later he embarked upon the first of six expeditions into unknown territory at the centre of Australia, naming one mountain Central Mount Sturt after the explorer Charles Sturt whom he had once served under – although it is now named after Stuart himself. In 1860, he was awarded the Gold Medal of the Royal Geographical Society for his discovery of the centre of Australia. Three years later he won the £2000 prize offered by the South Australian government to the first person to cross the continent through the middle, a journey of 2000 miles. But he scarcely survived the expedition and in April 1864 he set sail for Britain. Within ten years of his famous crossing a telegraph line following his route linked Australia and a highway and settlers followed.

John McDouall Stuart (1815–66). (KMAG)

The Scots played a disproportionate part in exploring a world unknown to Western man. Alexander Mackenzie, born in Stornoway in 1763, sailed

Sir John Alexander MacDonald (1815–91).   (*PAC*)

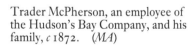

Trader McPherson, an employee of the Hudson's Bay Company, and his family, *c* 1872.   (*MA*)

Old Sydney Town at Somersby in New South Wales was begun in 1969 and is an attempt to construct a living historical model of the birthplace of Australia. It was to the convict colony at Botany Bay that Scottish political dissidents were sent from the end of the eighteenth century. The Old Government House at Parramatta was largely rebuilt by the Scottish Governor of New South Wales, Lachlan MacQuarie, who was succeeded by another Scot, Thomas Brisbane (1733–1860).   (*Author*)

for Canada at the age of sixteen. In June 1789, he was made a senior partner in the North-West Company and decided to explore Canada's great unknown territories to the west and north. He followed the river that flowed from the Great Slave Lake a thousand miles until he saw the ice flow of the Arctic Ocean.

A quarter of a century later, John Ross, who had served in the British Navy during the French wars, began exploring for the North-West Passage and crossed Baffin Bay. In 1850 he led an expedition to search for Sir John Franklin, whose expedition had gone missing in the Arctic wastes. Today in his memory are Ross Island, a Ross ice shelf and a Ross Sea lying almost due south of New Zealand.

Scots who settled in Canada carved themselves a place in history as inventors, engineers and educators. James McGill, a Glasgow fur trader,

gave his name to the University his bequest founded in Montreal in 1821. James Ross, born in Cromarty in 1848, financed and partially built street car systems for Toronto and Montreal. Alexander Graham Bell, born in Edinburgh in 1847, emigrated to Canada and is remembered round the world as the inventor of the telephone. Scots were also among the country's leading politicians.

Sir John Alexander MacDonald, born in Glasgow of parents evicted from their croft in Sutherland, masterminded the confederation in 1867 and was Prime Minister for nineteen years. From 1873 to 1878 Alexander Mackenzie from Logierait near Dunkeld headed Canada's first Liberal administration. William Lyon Mackenzie was Prime Minister for twenty-two years. Even the present Prime Minister, Pierre Trudeau, claims a Scottish grandmother, an Elliot, and his Deputy, Alan MacEachan, has origins in the Gaelic-speaking Western Isles.

Scots had settled in Britain's American colonies long before the Revolution. Many, especially Highlanders like Allan MacDonald of Kingsburgh, were Loyalists and fought in the armies of King George III. Others were ardent revolutionaries. John Witherspoon, born in Gifford near Haddington in 1723, signed the Declaration of Independence in 1776. The time to break away from Britain was not only ripe but rotting, he declared. During the American Revolution nine of George Washington's twenty-two brigadier-generals were of Scots descent. One was James Robertson, who after the war moved west to settle Tennessee and help found the present town of Nashville. In a letter now deposited in the Library of Congress, Robertson proclaimed in 1783: 'We are the advance guard of western civilization and our way is across the continent.' His nephew, Sterling Robertson, was a major in the war of 1812, and when peace came decided to move farther west. With a group of like-minded Nashville townsfolk he secured a grant of land from Mexico which then owned all of Texas. To encourage settlers he gave free land and out of the Robertson colony thirty counties of present-day

Reverend John Witherspoon (1723–94). The President of Princeton College, New Jersey, he helped to frame the American Declaration of Independence. (*SNPG*)

Scottish immigrants waiting to go ashore at Quebec, *c* 1911. (*PAC*)

The grave of William Cargill overlooks Otago Bay, New Zealand. Cargill, who died in 1860, had been an officer in the 74th Highlanders before helping to found the Free Church of Scotland's colony in South Island. The monument to Cargill at Dunedin was modelled on that raised in Edinburgh to Sir Walter Scott.
To the Scots education was all important. The University of Otago, dating from 1869, was the first university in the country. The 1878 complex is based on Sir George Gilbert Scott's plan for Glasgow University in 1870. (*Author*)

central Texas were formed. Ninety per cent of Robertson's colonists had Scottish names. Robertson's son, Sterling Clack Robertson later helped write the constitution of Texas.

The list of Scottish successes in America is as long as it is varied. John McLaren created San Francisco's Golden Gate Park out of shifting sand dunes. John Muir, born in Dunbar in 1838, emigrated with his family to America at the age of eleven and was largely responsible for creating what became America's first national park, Yosemite, established by Act of Congress in 1890. Many emigrant Scots led the field in journalism. John Campbell in 1704 started *The Boston Newsletter*, the first newspaper printed

Major Sterling Clack Robertson (1785–1842).   (*TS*)

Before and after the First World War, Scotland's greatest loss was her people, like these young emigrants to Canada, *c* 1911.   (*PAC*)

in North America. James Gordon Bennett founded the *New York Herald*. Others were active in religion: Mary Baker Eddy, the founder of Christian Science, claimed Scottish ancestry, as did David Oman McKay, leader of the Church of Jesus Christ of Latter Day Saints, the Mormons. Five thousand Scots, mostly from the Lowlands, took part in the original trek that culminated in the founding of the Mormon city at Salt Lake.

Scots wheat and cattle experts went to Oregon and money from Scottish-based institutions helped build the state. In 1883, Scottish investors bought the Swan Land and Cattle Company which occupied an area of Wyoming larger than the state of Connecticut. Based at 16 Castle Street, Edinburgh, the new owners paid over a million pounds to buy out the former American company. Within a year, the Scots owned over three and a quarter million acres and dividends frequently exceeded twenty per cent. For the benefit of Scottish visitors, Alec Swan, the manager, staged rodeos and one of his cowboys, Butch Cassidy, entertained the guests with some fancy pistol shooting. But Swan's phoney book-keeping led to a financial collapse that shook both Wall Street and Edinburgh in 1889 and Finlay Dun was sent out from Scotland to manage the shaken empire.

Of the Scots Theodore Roosevelt said:

> They became the vanguard of our civilization. These were the men who first declared for American independence. For generations their whole ecclesiastical and scholastic systems had been fundamentally democratic.

Few Scots influenced the history of modern America more than Andrew Carnegie. Born in Dunfermline in 1835, Carnegie emigrated with his parents to Pittsburg at the age of thirteen. To pay their passages the family had to sell their loom, take out a small deposit they had made in a local friendly society, borrow a further £20 from a friend and £2 10s from an aunt. Andrew started work in a cotton factory in Pennsylvania, educating himself in his spare time. He got his first job with the Pennsylvania Railroad and ultimately became an iron manufacturer. By the age of sixty-seven Andrew Carnegie was one of the world's richest men and lived in what he called 'the modest, plainest' house on New York's Fifth Avenue. Railroads, iron, coal and steel were the cornerstones of his vast industrial empire. Carnegie was in Scotland at Skibo Castle when, in 1892, a great and ultimately bloody strike broke out at his Homestead steelworks outside Pittsburg. The strikers were treated harshly, damaging Carnegie's reputation. When he sold out to the United States Steel Corporation in 1901, Carnegie gave away 350 million dollars, much of it to his home town of Dunfermline and to libraries and universities throughout the world. The archetypal capitalist, Carnegie is remembered in Scotland for his philanthropy, his success in the New World an inspiration to his countrymen.

Between 1871 and 1901, a quarter of Scotland's natural increase in population – 483,000 – emigrated. Her people, scattered throughout the world, were Scotland's best and most lasting export.

Andrew Carnegie (1835–1919). (*SNPG*)

Advertising trailers were used by the Canadian government to encourage Scots to emigrate. (*PAC*)

YOU NEED CANADA NEEDS YOU

20

A Generation Lost

The women of Calton, Glasgow,
c 1910. (*PP*)

WITHIN THE BATTLEMENTS of Edinburgh Castle stands Scotland's National War Memorial. When opened on 14 July 1927 the Memorial aroused such interest that the public queued for months to pay homage to the Scots who had died in the Great War. Unlike any other war memorial in the world, Scotland's commemorates civilians as well as those who fell in battle. During the First World War, 147,609 Scots lost their lives. A wrought-iron casket set on the Castle's highest pinnacle of rock houses the rolls of honour.

Some of Scotland's most talented artists were employed. Sir Robert Lorimer designed the building. The stained-glass windows were by Douglas Strachan, who depicted war as one of the mysteries of man's destiny. The paintings by Maurice Meredith Williams that show the wounded, the blinded and the weak, were drawn from life. But in all the tableaux the word 'victory' is used but once and Field Marshal Douglas Haig, the Scots-born commander of Britain's forces during the First World War, is the only individual commemorated. Still visited by nearly a million people every year, Scotland's National War Memorial is a shrine to sacrifice, a coronach in stone.

Britain did not declare war on Germany until 4 August 1914; but the years preceding the outbreak of hostilities had been busy ones for Scottish industry as naval rivalry between Britain and Germany stimulated the heavy industries of the Clyde. Skilled men in the shipyards and engineering shops were again in work and the defects of Scottish industry were put to one side.

Before the war, only a few Scottish employers had seen new technology and what was termed 'scientific management' as a way of cushioning the worst effects of the slumps that had bedevilled Scottish heavy industry in the last quarter of the nineteenth century. William Weir, the managing director of G. and J. Weir Pumps of Cathcart, had pioneered the new American ideas of production in his engineering works. In 1900, Weir introduced a productivity-related payment system and modern cost accounting and met with little resistance.

From the very outset of the Scottish industrial revolution, workers had been slow to react to the ever-present threat of unemployment and poverty. Strikes were ill-led and ill-organized and men often crawled back to their jobs. Yet despite the harsh action taken by the government in the years leading up to the so-called Scottish Insurrection of 1820, during the

Britains Glory
LIVE and LET LIVE
UNITED we Stand
DIVIDED we fall

Success to the COTTON Tree

Success to Commerce.

Success to the Friendly Association of Cotton SPINNERS

The ceremonial banner of Glasgow's Friendly Association of Cotton Spinners.   (*PP*)

nineteenth century trade unionism had taken root. Most were craft unions – combinations of printers, tailors and shoemakers – out to protect themselves in the face of increasing industrialization. When the cotton industry came to Scotland the Glasgow Association of Operative Cotton Spinners was formed; but like the old craft unions the spinners were defensive, more anxious to keep new workers out of the union than to obtain more members.

From the middle of the nineteenth century, attempts were made to create national unions in Scotland, federated in structure, with power and funds kept firmly in local hands. In 1855 the United Coal and Iron Miners' Association of Scotland was founded in large part due to the efforts of Alexander Macdonald, who was to prove to be one of the most important trade union leaders of his age. The son of a miner and the grandson of a Jacobite who as a boy had been at Culloden, Macdonald went to work in an ironstone mine near Airdrie in 1830. Walking four miles each day to evening classes he learnt Latin and Greek and at the age of twenty-five went to Glasgow University. In 1874 Macdonald was one of the first trade union leaders to be elected as a Liberal MP. He helped bring about the Mines Act of 1850 which enabled the miners themselves to check how much coal they had produced and from 1863, he was president of the Miners' National Association, the forerunner of the National Union of Mineworkers.

In 1858 the Glasgow United Trades Council was formed, to discuss matters that affected the working class generally, and within a decade similar organizations existed in Aberdeen and Dundee. In Scotland trades councils were in fact to exert more pressure than individual unions. But the majority of workers took little interest. By 1892 less than four per cent of the population belonged to a union. As a result, unions were able to do little to improve working conditions and Scottish industrial workers were regularly paid below the rate of their English counterparts. By the late nineteenth

A carpenter in a Clydebank woodworking shop, 1901.   (*NMM*)

century, however, the trades councils had become talking shops for socialist ideas. In Glasgow and other cities the councils began to put up candidates in local and general elections and campaigned on issues such as housing and rents. Under the initiative of the trades councils, a Scottish Trades Union Congress was formed in 1897. At the first meeting some fifty-five organizations with over 40,000 members were represented. The decades before the First World War were the seed-time for Scottish socialism.

One of the first to realize the need for workers to be organized was James Keir Hardie. He was born near Holytown in Lanarkshire in August 1856. His stepfather was a carpenter who earned 14s a week in a Govan shipyard. When he was badly injured at work, the family lived off bread and tea, and when he was well enough to return he found another man in his job.

At the age of ten James also lost his first job, when he was summarily dismissed from his bread delivery round for being fifteen minutes late. The following year, the boy became a trapper in a coal mine. From six in the morning until five o'clock at night, James sat opening and shutting the ventilation trap that provided the men in the pit with air. Forty years later James Keir Hardie looked back on his childhood with bitterness:

> I am younger in spirit at fifty than I can ever remember to have been. I am of the unfortunate class who never knew what it was to be a child – in spirit, I mean. Even the memories of boyhood and young manhood are gloomy. Under no circumstances, given freedom of choice, would I live that part of my life over again.

James Keir Hardie (1856–1915). (*SNPG*)

At Holytown he went to a night school run by a local schoolmaster and made friendships that lasted a lifetime. Bob Smillie, later a national leader of the coalminers, and Andrew Fisher, a future Prime Minister of Australia, were among those who shared his evening classes.

Hardie took to journalism and held public meetings advocating that only trade unionism would improve the lot of Scotland's miners. When he organized the Ayrshire Miners Union he was refused employment by pit owners. He went on to join the Ayrshire miners with those of Lanarkshire, Fife and the Lothians in the Scottish Miners Federation. In 1888 the miners of mid-Lanark invited Hardie to stand as a parliamentary candidate. The Scotland of Hardie's youth was the bastion of the Liberal Party. Only Glasgow, with its militant Ulster Orangemen and its wealthy industrialists bent on maintaining the status quo gave the Conservative Party any cheer. Turned down by the Liberal Party, Hardie was forced to stand as an Independent.

A poster in support of the 3rd Reform Bill. This Bill enlarged the electorate and was passed in 1884 by the Scottish Prime Minister, William Ewart Gladstone. (*SLHS*)

In defeat Hardie founded the Scottish Labour Party, a coalition of small labour and socialist groups that was to be short-lived but revolutionary, introducing for the first time the idea of workers paying for their own politics. Then he took himself off to London and in 1892, in South West Ham, became the first Labour MP. He subsequently sat as a Welsh member, but never, despite the fact he had Scottish Home Rule on his programme, was elected to serve a Scottish constituency. Hardie used Parliament as Charles Stewart Parnell had done for Ireland. Believing that parliamentary representation was more important than doctrinaire socialism, by brilliant speeches he promoted the cause of the working class. Although an atheist, he believed that socialism embodied in the industrial sphere much of what Christianity preached.

Hardie's socialism stemmed from the heart and the gut. He was neither a great theoretical nor doctrinaire politician but in the House of Commons he became a passionate advocate of the dignity of the working man. In 1893, largely through his influence, the Independent Labour Party was formed in Bradford. The Scottish Workers' Parliamentary Election Committee, set up by the Independent Labour Party and the Scottish TUC, were among those who in 1900 merged to form the Labour Representation Committee, pledged to return MPs who supported working-class policies. The Labour Committee's first secretary was Ramsay MacDonald, a young journalist from Lossiemouth. The nucleus of the Labour Party had been formed.

In the General Election of 1906, the ILP won nine seats. In Scotland, due to a split in the Irish vote, the party had two candidates elected, for Glasgow Gorbals and Dundee. The Liberal Party formed the government. With a large majority, the quiet but ailing Scot, Sir Henry Campbell-Bannerman became Prime Minister. Before his death in 1908, Campbell-Bannerman gave his party a new sense of purpose. With the help of the nine ILP members elected in 1906, the Liberals pushed through a programme of radical social reform. Old age pensions were introduced as were free school meals and compensation for injuries at work.

For Keir Hardie alcohol was the great evil of the age. In his native Scotland heavy drinking amongst the working class was an accepted part of life, as O'Connor Kessack noted in 1907:

A Glasgow Temperance poster, c 1895. (*PP*)

> If we look along the streets of our cities on a Saturday night we will witness many a scene of human wretchedness and depravity. Men and women are to be met in all stages of drunkenness; some cursing and swearing and shouting the most shocking obscenities, others helplessly and painfully depositing the contents of their stomach on the pavement . . . And if we go into the slummiest districts, the horrors of excessive drinking baffle description. Debauchery, immorality and crime have simply run amok among the denizens of the slums . . . Men fight and women shriek and children cry bitterly. The slum scene on Saturday night is an infernal pandemonium.

To Keir Hardie, drunkenness was an obstacle to socialism:

> The man who can take a glass or leave it alone is under moral obligation for the sake of the weaker brother who cannot do so, to leave it alone . . . The moral force of the movement would be perceptibly increased were this done, and it is the moral force which carries a movement forward.

In 1829, John Dunlop, a Greenock lawyer had established Glasgow's first major temperance societies. William Collins the publisher was attracted to the movement and by 1830 was printing over half a million temperance pamphlets a year. In 1869, the Independent Order of Good Templars had been established in Scotland by a Scot living in America. Within months forty-three lodges had been founded in Glasgow alone. By 1876 there were over 1100 in Scotland with a total membership of nearly 84,000. In 1897, the Good Templars marched on Bannockburn, claiming that drink was:

John Dunlop (1789–1868).   (*PP*)

> More to be feared by the Scottish people than the enemy faced by our forefathers in 1314.

But such appeals usually failed. By 1875, 300 people a month were being jailed for drink offences in Glasgow alone. In the preceding three years over

The founding fathers of the Independent Order of Good Templars in Scotland in 1869. (*PP*)

125,000 arrests were made in Scotland for being drunk and incapable.

The Glasgow Evangelical Association had been set up in 1874 to encourage and co-ordinate philanthropic work. From a tent on Glasgow Green the Association organized large open-air meetings which reached thousands of Glasgow citizens who had never seen the inside of a church. In 1875 Tent Hall was built to carry on the work on a permanent basis and continued to look after the socially fallen until after the Second World War. In 1879, the Salvation Army, founded by William Booth in Whitechapel, London, crossed the border and conquered Scotland with its own brand of militant teetotalism.

In the search for alternatives to the public house, the temperance movement nourished generations of Scottish entertainers. Many who became Scotland's best-loved stars were given their first break at the cheap concerts, called 'bursts', organized by the temperance societies.

In Glasgow the Temperance Party on the Town Council became a force to be reckoned with. In the municipal elections of 1892, fifteen of the twenty-six councillors elected were advocates of restricted sale of drink. In the space of thirty years, three of Glasgow's Provosts – Sir William Collins, Sir Samuel Chisholm and Sir Daniel Macaulay Stevenson – were notable temperance men.

Temperance also meant holding the Sabbath holy. In 1900 the British Women's Temperance Association petitioned the Glasgow Council to ban the opening of ice-cream shops on Sundays. Representatives of the Scottish burghs also called for legislation to end the Sunday sale of 'ice-cream' and Provost Black of Greenock declared:

> Ice-cream shops are just houffs for persons entering and enjoying themselves in a manner which was not proper.

The co-operative movement in Scotland was also staunchly teetotal. When the Scottish Co-operative Wholesale Society was founded in 1868 its members were banned from retailing alcohol, a ban that was not lifted until 1958.

A temperance demonstration on Glasgow Green.   (*PP*)

In an attempt to keep youth off the streets and out of the public house, Sir William Alexander Smith had founded the Boys Brigade on 4 October 1883. Smith was secretary of a Sunday School of the Free College Church mission in Glasgow. His first group of thirty boys, like the thousands that were to be part of a world-wide organization, met weekly for drill and attended Bible classes on Sunday.

The temperance movement in Scotland achieved much. Many within its ranks were trained as organizers, journalists and politicians. Keir Hardie was a Good Templar as were Willie Gallacher, the Communist, and David Kirkwood, the Clydeside workers' leader. Tom Johnston, later to be Secretary of State for Scotland during the Second World War, was in the Band of Hope and John MacLean, the most famous of all the 'Red Clyde-siders', was a lifelong abstainer. Tom Honeyman, who started life as a railwayman, became the International Secretary of the Good Templars and edited their magazine for twenty years. His son, who was in the Band of Hope, became Director of Glasgow's Art Galleries and Rector of the city's university.

Flora Drummond (1879–1949), the suffragette who in August 1914 supported the war effort. (*PP*)

The Scottish Labour Party, however, had as the first item on its programme the establishment of universal adult suffrage. Keir Hardie was a moving spirit behind the Women's Social and Political Union founded by the Pankhurst family in 1903. On 11 January 1908, the Union opened its Scottish Headquarters in Bath Street in Glasgow. The organizers were ladies of spirit. Helen Crawford, later a founder member of the Communist Party of Great Britain, and Janie Allan, daughter of the shipping magnates, the Allan Line, spread the word in a country where women had long been designated second-class citizens. In London Flora Drummond became a pillar of the movement. Dressed in quasi-military uniform, she organized all the movement's processions and was nicknamed 'Bluebell' by the London crowds, who regarded her as a match for any politician.

In the spring of 1908, the death of four Liberal MPs prompted the suffragettes to campaign to 'Keep the Liberals Out'. Their main target was Winston Churchill, the Party's candidate in Dundee. The women hired the Gaiety Theatre, the Kinnaird Hall and the Dundee Drill Hall and held mass meetings. They failed to stop Churchill from being elected but reduced the Liberal majority by 2000.

A suffragette badge, 1909. (*PP*)

The Glasgow School of Art was a hotbed of the women's movement. Between classes women students sewed their banners. The first two Scots arrested for furthering the cause of women's suffrage were both actresses, Annie Fraser and Maggie Moffat, whose husband Graham helped found the West of Scotland's Men's League for Women's Suffrage.

In October 1909, Scotland's women staged an historical pageant in Edinburgh to demand the vote. In the years that followed both the Kirk and local government were won round. Between 1910 and 1913, thirty-five Scottish burghs passed resolutions supporting votes for women, and in July 1912, the Scottish Churches League for Women's Suffrage was founded. Over seventy male organizations from the Inverness Town Council to the Fife and Kinross Mineworkers offered to send a delegate each to the great deputation that was to petition the Prime Minister. When Asquith refused to see them, the delegates took part in a demonstration in the Albert Hall.

When the government stubbornly refused to legislate, the movement

Margaret Moffat (*d.* 1943), actress. (*SNPG*)

The House of Commons, 1914. (*PW*)

became violent. In February 1913, Jessie Stephen and her Domestic Workers Union began a campaign of dropping bottles of acid into Glasgow's letter boxes. In May of the same year, Farrington Hall in Dundee was bombed and burned by suffragettes. The following month the Gatty Marine Laboratory in St Andrews was set on fire and the railway station at Leuchars burnt to the ground. In December, Kelly house at Wemyss Bay was also fired, but the Scottish Outrages, as they were called, made little impression on the male minds of a government preoccupied with thoughts of war.

The war with Germany declared in 1914 split the ranks of both the women's movement and the Labour Party. Keir Hardie had opposed the Boer War and advocated a general strike in protest against war with Germany. Some suffragettes saw war as a way of working for the vote, others advocated that women should stay at home and try to stop the war from happening. In Scotland and elsewhere, the Labour Party fell hostage to the labour movement. The party was forced along the line of pacifism by the shop steward movement in Glasgow, and to a lesser extent in Belfast, Newcastle and Sheffield.

Yet in Scotland, soldiering had long been an honourable occupation. Samuel Smiles, the author of *Self Help* published in 1859, saw service as complementing his views of how the industrialized working man could improve his lot. He waxed lyrical about the volunteer movement, the forerunner of Haldane's Territorial Army:

> Wonderful is the magic of drill! Drill means discipline, training, education. These soldiers who are ready to march steady against volleyed fire, against belching cannon, or to beat their heads against bristling bayonets were once tailors, shoemakers, mechanics, weavers, and ploughmen; with mouths gaping, shoulders stooping, feet straggling, arms and hands like great fins hanging by their sides; but now their gait is firm and martial, their figures are erect, and they march along to the sound of music, with a tread that makes the earth shake.

When war broke out in August 1914, the London Scottish were the first territorial battalion to join the British Expeditionary force, and Scots volunteered in their thousands. John Welsh was a clerk in the Stock Exchange in Edinburgh and had served with the territorials for six years. When he went to enlist, he was disappointed:

> ... there was such a rush of volunteers when I went down to the recruiting office they told me to come back in a month, that they had not the staff to cope with what was going on.

Field-Marshal Earl Haig (1861–1928), born in Edinburgh, commanded the Western Front between 1915 and 1918. (*NPG*)

He was finally accepted later in the year at the age of twenty-two and sent to train at Aldershot and Wellington Barracks. As rifles were scarce, they trained with broom handles. In October 1915, Welsh finally saw action. Joffre, the French General, had chosen Loos for the first British attack of the war without really considering whether it was suitable. Sir John French objected but Kitchener ordered him to follow the French commander. Haig was confident of victory as gas was to be used. On the day of the battle the wind was in the wrong direction and one British commander who insisted on releasing the gas, gassed his own men. The British lost over 50,000 against 20,000 Germans. No strategic gains were made but the generals remained confident; the Germans, they claimed, were being worn down.

John Welsh's lasting memory of the battle of Loos, which went on for three days, is what a shambles it all was:

> In my own case we were getting ready for the takeover, a matter of an hour or so beforehand. We all knew the time and the lieutenant in charge of this little platoon I was with was very anxious about it and he put his head over the parapet to have a look-see and he was shot right through the head, right through the top part so he was out and we lost our officer right away to begin with.
>
> The other thing was that at that time we had no gas-masks or anything, all we used really was our handkerchiefs and urine and covered our nose and mouth as best we could.
>
> We were never trained somehow to protect ourselves. Machine gun emplacements were all around and these machine guns were going off and you didn't think of getting on your tummy and crawling along. You marched along practically in formation. The same thing happened with Germans when we caught them on the hop. They were coming along in the same reckless fashion of walking upright with their rifles and equipment. The machine guns just ploughed into them. This is not book reading or anything. It is just my personal thoughts afterwards of the thing, that it was a very haphazard way somehow to conduct a war.

British troops returning from the line after the Battle of Loos, September–October 1915.   (*IWM*)

Injured at Loos, Welsh was taken to a Canadian field hospital, where the surgeon explained how men reacted differently to the horror of the Front:

> He illustrated how an awful lot depended on the nature of the patient as to whether he would recover or not and he pointed out a small Glasgow boy and said, 'By all the laws of the game, that boy should be dead. He's lost an arm, he's lost part of his leg and he's been mauled unmercifully but he'll live.' He said, 'There's another one along there with very little the matter with him but he's turning his face to the wall and there's nothing I or any doctor can do.'

Within a year of the declaration of war over a quarter of Scotland's coalminers had enlisted, and the government, afraid that coal production would suffer, had to ban them from joining up.

The islands of Scotland also gave their men. On Lewis, many were in the Royal Naval Reserve as well as the territorials. Murdo Macfarlane, in his nineties, recalls how the island was stripped of its young men:

> Many of these lads off they went in August 1914, and I need not tell you after that, mothers were scared of the postman – longing for the postman to come and yet scared of the postman coming because the postman then was the carrier of bad news. Students were all in the territorials and they were practically all officers. Very few of them ever survived.

Orderlies of the 17th Highland Light Infantry in camp.   (*GCC*)

Glasgow, Scotland's largest city, supplied enough able-bodied men to form twenty-six battalions. Twenty-four out of every thousand of the city's population joined up, a higher proportion than in any other British city. James Dalrymple, the manager of the Glasgow Corporation Tramways Department, persuaded 1110 employees to enlist in just sixteen hours. Formed in September 1914, the 15th Highland Light Infantry were nicknamed the Tramway Battalion.

Glasgow University and Technical College, together with the city's Chamber of Commerce, were the source of the 17th Battalion of the HLI. The Chamber of Commerce Battalion, as it was called, went to Troon for training. Housed in the town's seaside villas, the recruits were called 'featherbeds' because of their lavish accommodation. On 22 November 1915 the 17th Battalion HLI went to France. At Étaples, near Le Havre, John Hardie, now aged 91, began to realize what war was about:

> I saw troops from the regular army and the expeditionary forces and thousands of territorials coming back on stretchers, maimed with faces of torture and agony on them. One began to realize that these people were returning from the front trenches and that they were in the state of utter injury and collapse. I think that that was the moment that one realized that whenever one got pushed up to the front line that was possibly the fate that one might have. It didn't scare because one would really need to be a coward to be scared because you have the gregarious instinct in you makes you feel that you are just one with a big number that are doing the same thing and are subject to the same risks. Consequently there was no kind of fear running through the troops.

The 17th HLI in the trenches of France, June 1916.   (*GCC*)

Winter in the trenches was grim. Men greased their feet to prevent frostbite. In the summer of 1916, the men of the 17th Battalion went into action at the Somme. A major British offensive had been demanded by the French who hoped it would distract the Germans from Verdun. Despite the fact that by June 1916 the German attack at Verdun was petering out and contrary to the advice of his leading commanders, Haig pressed ahead.

On 24 June 1916, the British began to bombard the German lines at the Somme. For seven days, the guns raged, the longest artillery offensive of the war up to then. The French were supposed to put 40 divisions into the field and Haig 25 but by 1 July only 14 French divisions were at hand. The British forces were led largely by inexperienced officers trained by generals steeped in the heroic exploits of the Duke of Wellington. The Germans occupied the crests of the hills; the attackers would have to fight their way upwards against a concealed enemy armed with machine guns.

But Haig had convinced himself that a powerful offensive on the Somme would win the war. On the eve of battle he wrote:

> I feel that every step in my plan has been taken with the Divine help.

The 17th Battalion, together with the 16th HLI, were to assault the Leipzig Redoubt. The two battalions massed in the assembly trenches forty minutes before zero. Just after 7.20 the first four platoon commanders of the 17th HLI stepped up to the parapet and began to crawl forward into the close craters in No Man's Land. By 7.30 the two leading companies had joined them. The advanced British line was now less than forty yards from the German trenches.

The men waited, weighed down by sixty-six-pound packs, field telephones, picks, shovels and even carrier pigeons. With a shout they sprang into action. Bagpipes skirled, the men cheered and all seemed well. Whistles blew to order them over the top. Spaced regularly apart, with not more than 'two or three paces interval', they advanced across No Man's Land. I can do no better than allow John Hardie to recall his experiences, which since July 1916 have been engraved on his mind:

John Hardie (1893–) and Duncan Paterson (1894–). (*STV*)

> It was a glorious summer day, one of the finest days that ever we had in France so far as weather was concerned. The balloons, the observation balloons were above us. The artillery barrage was already proceeding and smashing up the first German trench, and besides the machine guns and trench mortars were spitting over the whole ground. Before we went over the top each individual soldier knew that our objective on that day was a place called Mouquet farm which was a German machine gun emplacement, with light artillery. Now we knew that was the objective. It could be seen from our trenches. It stood on a hillock, less than a mile from our front trench. It was supposed to be taken by three o'clock that afternoon.

The Germans held a most perfectly defended position, and their machine guns mowed down the advancing troops. As the men fell like rows of dominoes, others came over the top, advancing at regular hundred-yard intervals – four lines of British troops in all. The Germans found their courage almost unbelievable. The loss of life at the Somme on 1 July 1916 was the greatest suffered by any army in the First World War. By evening, Haig had lost nearly 60,000 men, 20,000 of them dead. Those who were to survive the day, like John Hardie, had taken what shelter they could in the graveyard of No Man's Land:

A drawing made by a member of the 17th HLI with the caption: 'One year has gone and I am still at your service', referring to the fact that over a year had elapsed between formation and the Battle of the Somme. (*GCC*)

> I lay down because lying down was the safest position against the enemy machine gun fire and those who survived could only have survived either by luck or by lying down. In the early afternoon I was tired, not by physical exhaustion but sheer mental tension, emotional tension that had built up during these hours that it exhausted far, far more deeply than ever physical fatigue could do. The result was that I began looking about, having no one to command me, having no idea except that the objective lay in front of me, having only that in my mind I lay about, looking around to see what would be the best form of shelter.
>
> All the German trenches were smashed. There was no use looking for a dugout in their trenches. I was now near the second German trench. The firing was still going on. The casualties were still mounting up through the barrage of their artillery.
>
> The whole atmosphere was misty, grey, dull, in spite of the glorious sun and I found a fairly deep shell hole, about four feet deep, and I lay down there and surprising as it may seem, I fell fast asleep.
>
> I woke up, I remember, round about 7 o'clock at night. I felt peculiarly wet at the collar but it was only a graze of shrapnel, nothing at all mortal.

Lieutenant Colonel David Morton, Commanding Officer of the 17th HLI Battalion, who in civilian life was a paint manufacturer.   (*GCC*)

However I just lay there and mopped it up as best I could. I took a dog biscuit and a drink of water and continued to lie in the shell hole until evening fell and then I knew better my way back than any way forward and I had no command so I went back to my trenches, crawled back. And I came into our communication trench and I so proceeded down to a place where we had often billeted, two miles behind the line which was distinguished by a great crucifix of the Virgin Mary and I lay down in front of the crucifix and I waited for whatever would befall me.

The next morning the Colonel who mercifully was all right and his Adjutant, called a parade and out of the eleven hundred men only some four, three to four platoons were hastily formed, stood up to be counted. It was too much for Colonel Morton. He wept in front of us. He was taken home. He did eventually come out again but never to trench warfare.

Duncan Paterson, like Hardie, went over the top on 1 July 1916. His memory of that day is still strong:

To inexperienced people like us it was a nerve shattering business, that First of July. I think the men who were spared to come home, they never got over it. It's in your mind whether it's a good bit or a bad bit. There's a corner of your mind which you cannot erase. You can't put it out no matter what you do or try. Even yet I get it. We weren't mentally trained to stand up to that kind of thing. Our senses were numb.

In the battle of the Somme the 17th Battalion of the HLI lost 22 officers and 447 other ranks in a single day. Duncan Paterson's parents waited for news:

The strain on them was far worse than it was on us because we had the excitement of being alive, or being wounded or getting out of it but they had nothing but the paper to look and see if they were going to be happy or unhappy.

The send-off meeting of the 17th HLI that took place in the Examination Hall of the Technical College before they left Glasgow.   (*GCC*)

July 1 was followed by 140 days of battle on the Somme. British, Australians, South Africans and Newfoundlanders were poured over the trenches in their thousands, and it was not until 18 November that the offensive was closed down. The Somme was the graveyard of Kitchener's army. When it tailed off in November 1916, 420,000 British troops had been killed; three British soldiers dead for every two German.

The Somme soured the idealism of those who had so swiftly enlisted and made a lasting impression on the nation's memory. Nothing in Britain's experience of war had led to such great loss of human life, deaths made the more hurtful by the fact that it was eager civilians, volunteers who took the brunt, not the professional army.

In all some twenty-six HLI battalions were raised during the First World War. Eleven thousand officers and men were killed in action. In silence, the cinemas of Scotland continued to proclaim to audiences:

> Where Scotland's thistle sways on High,
> And foeman meet here knee to knee,
> Blow up the pipes and then ye'll see,
> Her courage wake,
> And learn how Scotland's sons can die for
> Empire sake.

When the war broke out, Scotland's population was a tenth of England's, yet Scottish regiments made up a seventh of Britain's army.

The Lowland regiments, the Royal Scots, the King's Own Scottish Borderers and the Royal Scots Fusiliers, together with the Scots Guards, fielded over 70,000 men between 1914 and 1918. Thirty-five battalions of Royal Scots were raised. Between them, they won 71 battle honours and 6 Victoria Crosses, the highest award for bravery.

The Cameronians, the Covenanter regiment, raised 27 battalions and fought in France, Flanders, Macedonia, Egypt and Palestine. The 7th battalion were the last to leave the shores of Gallipoli.

Twenty-one battalions of Gordon Highlanders were raised. In the Great War they gained 65 battle honours and 4 VCs. Nineteen battalions of Seaforth Highlanders and 13 battalions of Cameron Highlanders were also recruited. The Argyll and Sutherland Highlanders, the victors of Waterloo and Balaclava, won 79 battle honours. Some 30,000 joined the Black Watch, since the eighteenth century the British government's Highland stalwart. Nearly 8,000 were killed and 20,000 came home wounded or maimed.

In an attempt to bring medical care to the Front, Dr Elsie Inglis, the Secretary of the National Union of Women's Suffrage Societies, started the Scottish Women's Hospitals for Foreign Service at the outbreak of the war. By the end of 1915, Dr Inglis had hospitals in France and Serbia and was providing over thirteen hundred beds for the wounded. Dr Inglis died in 1917 at the age of fifty-three, having literally worked herself to death.

David Lloyd George, 1st Earl Lloyd-George of Dwyfor (1863–1945). (*SNPG*)

An army six times greater in size than Britain had ever before put into battle had to be supplied, and in 1915 Lloyd George was made Minister of Munitions to ensure the demands of war were met. In Scotland, William Weir was put in charge of production. His radical proposals to deal with the scandalous shortage of shells and other problems of supply were incorporated in the Munitions of War Act which subjected industrial workers to near-military discipline. For Weir the national interest transcended individual rights, and he was a dynamic organizer. By August 1915 he had got the production of shells up to 28,500 a week.

Skilled workers who felt that their status was being eroded by increased rents and rising prices formed the Clyde Workers Committee. The actual conflicts were few, but in February 1915, the Amalgamated Society of Engineers, who controlled the most skilled men on the Clyde, struck for 'Tuppence an Hour'. In August of the same year, the men walked out of Fairfields shipyard and in October and November the rent strike took place, when over 25,000 stopped work in support of their demand that rents be frozen. As a result the government set up the Clyde Armaments Output Committee on which an equal number of union representatives and managers sat. Weir scrapped the Committee and replaced it with a board dominated by management.

An already delicate industrial situation was aggravated when Weir brought in American workers at higher wages. When the unions called for industrial action they were accused of stabbing Scotland's soldiers in the back. In a sense, the war was an irrelevance for many of the leaders, who saw the real struggle was against capitalism.

In an attempt to rally Glasgow's workers Lloyd George visited Parkhead in December 1915, only to be shouted down. The Prime Minister returned to be made a freeman of Glasgow in June 1916 and again met hostility. As Lloyd George reviewed the troops outside St Andrews Halls, the Red Flag

Women at work in a Scottish
shipbuilding yard during the
First World War.   (*IWM*)

flew from a tenement opposite. The press were banned from reporting the incident.

From January 1916, women were employed in munitions factories. The strike that followed led to the deportation and imprisonment of shop stewards. An impatient government bullied the unions into accepting dilution of labour but paid little heed to the genuine call for wages that took into account raging wartime inflation.

The Red Clydesiders, as they were called, were suppressed. When David Kirkwood printed what was regarded as seditious material in the *Forward*, the paper was banned, as was the Clyde Workers Committee's weekly *Worker*. In March 1916, the leaders of a strike at Beardmores, including David Kirkwood, were deported. Others, like Walter Bell, Willie Gallacher and John MacLean, were put in prison. During and after the war, MacLean was sent to jail five times and Gallacher received four sentences; but government repression only helped enhance the prestige of the left-wing Clyde Workers Committee. Heroes were created.

John MacLean was born in 1879 of Highland parents who had settled in Glasgow. He was the sixth of seven children, four of whom died of silicosis. By 1900 MacLean was teaching children by day and workers Marxist economics at night. James Maxton, a school teacher was converted to socialism by MacLean, who captured the minds and hearts of Glasgow's working class when he was imprisoned in 1916 for calling a General Strike on the Clyde. After the Russian Revolution MacLean's reputation as a folk hero was enhanced; but it is often forgotten that when the Communists seized power in October 1917, Scottish socialists like Willie Gallacher and David Kirkwood did not take to the streets of Glasgow but were actually leading shop floor collaboration on the Clyde. For three of the four years Britain was at war with Germany the men of the Clyde took no industrial action at all, and Glasgow, in fact, was quieter than other parts of the country where munitions were made.

By 1917, a quarter of a million Scots were making munitions. The Clyde

The aeroplane department of Dennys
of Dumbarton.   (*IWM*)

Valley had become the biggest concentration of production in Britain, producing tanks, battleships, guns and shells, boots and clothing for the men in the trenches. James Templeton converted their carpet looms to weave blankets for the troops and their machines ran continuously night and day. The company made four million blankets, more than any other British factory. The investment in munitions was huge. Eleven million pounds was spent setting up new factories of war, like the vast explosives works at Gretna in Dumfriesshire.

From 1915, the Admiralty took over the shipyards of the Clyde. Over half a million tons of shipping a year were launched. In December 1918, the *Glasgow Herald* proudly honoured the men of the Clyde by publishing a special supplement. Fairfield's yard had built the cruisers *Valiant* and *Renown*. William Beardmore's had constructed the battleships *Benbow* and *Ramillies*. John Brown's yard had launched the battleship *Barham* and the battle cruisers *Tiger*, *Repulse*, and *Hood*; and apart from the capital ships dozens of minesweepers and other craft were constructed and repaired.

The war came to an end as abruptly as it had begun. An armistice with Germany was signed on 11 November 1918. In Scotland the day was St Martin's Day, the old festival when the ghosts of the dead were said to return to earth. The aftermath of war was to prove devastating. John Hardie, one of the few survivors of the Glasgow Chamber of Commerce Battalion, recalls:

> Apart from the general impoverishment of human life there was created a generation gap which of course can never be replaced. In particular the Glasgow Chamber of Commerce Battalion had in its 'A' Company mostly men who had a diploma or were studying for a diploma at the Royal Technical College in Glasgow. In 'B' Company they had mostly graduates and undergraduates of Glasgow University. Now these I think you would agree are potential leaders of any society.

In 1920, a government White Paper estimated that Scottish losses accounted for at least a fifth of Britain's dead. The effort and tragedy of the Great War was the great watershed in the history of modern Scotland. Within the experience lie the roots of economic and social problems that to a large extent plague Scotland to this day.

A woman controller of Glasgow's Tramways Department.   (*IWM*)

Destroyers on the stocks in Clydebank during the First World War.   (*IWM*)

The remnants of the London Scottish after the Battle of Messines, 31 October 1914, when it is claimed that only two dozen survived out of over a thousand men.   (*IWM*)

21

Lean Years

The 'Red Clydesiders'. This Bailie cartoon shows four of the ten Socialists elected in 1923: (*from the left*) James Maxton, George Buchanan, John Wheatley and Campbell Stephen. (*GCC*)

IN MAY 1938 GLASGOW played host to the world. At Bellahouston Park was held the great Empire Exhibition, a celebration of Britain's past. In the stadium Scottish veterans marched in pride and an historical pageant recalled the role the Scots had played in building the greatest empire the modern world has seen.

The Empire Exhibition that cost £11 million to mount was planned to do the Scots a good turn. The twenty years that followed the Great War had highlighted the social and economic consequences of the country's narrow and limited industrial base. The world had suffered a Great Depression; for the men of the Clyde the effects had been nearly fatal. Most Glaswegians who flocked in their thousands to view the exhibits in 1938 knew that their city's place – Second City of the Empire – that their Victorian and Edwardian forefathers had thought would last for ever, had gone. The lean years of the 1920s and 1930s had seen to that.

After the Armistice with Germany was signed in November 1918, the troops came home. They had been promised by Lloyd George that they would return to a land fit for heroes; but as Britain's vast army demobilized in 1919, it was soon apparent that the Welsh Wizard's promise was hollow. Hopes of better housing and steady wages in the wake of victory were dashed by the reality of mass unemployment. Even Sir Edward Carson, the Conservative MP who had served in the wartime Cabinet, rounded on Lloyd George for failing to provide even decent civilian clothing for the demobbed.

On 14 March 1918 the Scottish Trades Union Congress had called upon the government to introduce a forty-hour week to prevent mass unemployment when peace came. The Clyde Workers Committee, however, felt that a thirty-hour week would be needed to absorb the survivors of the trenches into the workforce. The Committee approached the Glasgow Trades Council, whose chairman, Emanuel Shinwell, persuaded them to accept the STUC recommendation on the grounds that their claim, at a time when a sixty-hour week was not uncommon, would not be seriously considered. A joint committee was set up to press the claim in Glasgow and a mass demonstration planned to bring the matter to the attention of both government and the city's leaders.

On 27 January 1919, 40,000 Glasgow workers went on strike in support of the demand. By the following day the number had doubled. Paranoid

The Red Flag flies in George Square, Glasgow, 1919. (*MG*)

To those who rallied in George Square, 1 February 1919 was known as 'Bloody Friday'. (*PP*)

about the events in Russia of the past fifteen months, Robert Munro, the Secretary of State for Scotland, believed the strike to be a preamble to a Bolshevik rising and asked Lloyd George for help. Twelve thousand troops, a hundred army lorries and six tanks appeared in the streets of Glasgow. But revolution, despite the raising of the occasional Red Flag, was hardly in the minds of strike leaders like Emanuel Shinwell.

On Friday 1 February another huge crowd rallied in George Square. While David Kirkwood and Shinwell were in the City Chambers trying to persuade the Provost to support the claim, there was a scuffle involving a

John MacLean (*d.* 1923), and his family.   (*PP*)

tram car, and rumours that the crowd intended to break into the post office. Police with batons began to clear the square. They arrested Gallacher and Kirkwood and at night ten detectives went to Govan and took Shinwell away to the police station where he was put into a cell. He was held in Duke Street prison for six weeks before being granted bail, while the strike spread to Sheffield and Belfast. Twelve of the leaders of the Glasgow demonstration were tried. All were acquitted except Gallacher and Shinwell, who were sent to prison for three and five months apiece, just enough, according to Lord Shinwell, to satisfy Lloyd George, who had been laughed at when he came to St Andrews Hall a few years before. 'If only,' Lord Shinwell claims, 'Lloyd George had recognized the force of opinion that prevailed at the time and the despair of the unemployed and, particularly, the sacrifices so many had made during the war and had done something to help . . .'

To the people of Glasgow John MacLean was a symbol of integrity, a legend in his own lifetime; to the government in Westminster he epitomized the fear of the time that Bolshevism would engulf Britain. In 1918 he tried to turn the city's Trades Council into a Scottish soviet. When the Russian Bolsheviks appointed him their consul in Britain, he was promptly arrested in April 1918, and sent to prison for five years. But he was released at the end of the war and, despite bad health, spent his last years with the Scottish Workers Republican Party, which blended Marxism with the ideas of Ireland's Sinn Fein.

He refused to join the British Communist Party, on the grounds that its centralized and authoritarian structure was alien to the Scottish tradition, and in the autumn of 1920 founded the unemployed workers movement. By January the following year, he could write to Lenin:

> Three thousand five hundred unemployed meet twice a week in the City Hall, so that we may discuss principles and tactics applied to the present situation from a Marxian point of view.

Out of MacLean's Glasgow organization grew the National Unemployed Workers Movement; but he was sent to prison in 1921, in part for his work among the unemployed, and was locked up in Barlinnie Jail until the end of 1922. When he died in the following year, 5000 attended his funeral.

John MacLean's funeral, 1923.   (*PP*)

The Great War made the economy of Scotland virtually its own executioner. By 1916, Scottish exports of heavy industrial goods to the Empire and the rest of the world had almost ceased. The needs of war and German U-boats had seen to that. After the war Scotland's coal industry fell on evil days. In 1921 there was a long and bitter strike when coalowners demanded longer hours for reduced wages. Many of Scotland's once rich seams had been exhausted and others needed capital investment if they were to be profitable. In 1913, Scotland's coalfields had produced forty-two million tons; within twenty years output was to fall by a quarter. Pig-iron, pre-war, had been a major Scottish export; but by 1931 output had fallen to less than a quarter of what it had been in 1920.

Shipbuilding, the lifeblood of the Clyde since the age of Victoria, was damaged by the post-war policy of 'squeezing Germany till the pips squeaked' as confiscated shipping was sold at knockdown prices. In the east of Scotland the trenches had brought work to the jute industry. Peace almost brought disaster, for the mills had expanded out of all proportion to make sandbags and sacking, basic goods outside the normal peacetime pattern of trade.

Few Scots looked to trade unionism for a way out of their nation's economic ills. In 1924, the Scottish TUC estimated that only 536,000 Scots belonged to a union, eleven per cent of the population and a lower proportion than elsewhere in the United Kingdom. During the Depression the unions offered little in the way of remedies.

Nor could Scots look to their industrialists. After the war, William Weir's pioneering ideas of scientific management and production were not taken up. Only Sir John Craig, head of Colvilles, successfully rationalized Scotland's steel industry. By 1937, his firm had brought most of Scotland's steel-making and heavy rolling capacity under its control. Management and men by and large went back to their old ways, took what comfort they could from peacetime production.

The war effort had brought about a greater centralization of British industry. Manchester and the English Midlands became the major centres of production. Birmingham, close to London, with its sober population that had little history of union activism, became the home of the new light industries in the wake of war. Scottish management had lacked foresight; the products of the future were put out of mind while there were ample industries of old from which to make profit. Much of Scotland's post-war industry was to hinge round the Clyde: a narrow shipbuilding base susceptible to market forces. Scotland otherwise became a branch factory.

Rural Scotland also lacked work after the Great War. Crofting as a way of life was in the doldrums. A Royal Commission in 1892 had found land that could form new crofts or extend existing townships. There was considerable expansion and by 1939 over 2600 new crofts had been created, over 5000 enlarged and more pastoral land made available. Much of the land lost to small tenants during the nineteenth century was thus returned; but there was still not enough to make crofting a viable way of life.

In the north-east, a severe blow was dealt to the Scottish whisky industry by American Prohibition. Fishing had been expanded during the war when the nation's need was for self-sufficiency but in peacetime the market for fish was not so great. Cash returns were poor and export markets, cut off by war, had begun to organize their own fleets.

King George V launching a warship on the Clyde in September 1917, a boom year for shipbuilding. (*IWM*)

In the Western Isles, men returned from war proud of their fighting record and hungry for land. Lewismen had fought in the Seaforth Highlanders and the Ross Mountain Battery at Gallipoli. Lewis fishermen had also enhanced the fighting effort of the Royal Navy. With fewer than 30,000 inhabitants, the island had provided nearly 2500 men for the Royal Naval Reserve alone. Peace was marred by tragedy.

On the last day of 1918, the *Iolaire*, bringing men back from the war, was wrecked on the rocks outside Stornoway. Two hundred and five men drowned within sight of their native land. Families had welcoming meals prepared; on hearing the news they rushed to the beach to identify the washed-up dead. A government inquiry found that the officers in charge were to blame; no orders had been given with a view to saving life.

Land-hunger in Lewis was acute. The population of the island was rising and there was less useful land to support people than elsewhere in the Highlands and islands. Those who returned home from the war had been promised crofts by Robert Munro, the Secretary of State for Scotland. When the promise was unfulfilled, they took land for themselves, became 'raiders', squatting on the estate that had been bought by Lord Leverhulme, the English soap magnate, in 1918.

Leverhulme rightly argued that the sea around Lewis was richer than the land. Fishing, he believed, should become the community's primary occupation and he purchased deep-sea trawlers and a chain of retail fish shops on the mainland, MacFisheries, to sell what the Lewismen could catch. Stornoway was to become one of Britain's leading fishing ports. The people of Lewis, however, wanted to be crofters and he was forced to abandon his grand scheme. When he took his leave of the island, Leverhulme gave the crofters their land as a gift and Lews Castle and all his property were given to the town of Stornoway. At Obbe, in Harris, Leverhulme began again. New quays were constructed together with kippering sheds; but when Lord Leverhulme died in 1925, so too did his dream. His new town, Leverburgh, became a concrete memorial to a stubborn people.

Emigration was again the panacea. In 1923 three ships called at Stornoway to take the young to Canada. But the New World, like the Old, was gripped by Depression and most of those who left Lewis, if employed at all, became cheap farm labour.

In 1921 ex-Servicemen raided Raasay near Skye. Grants of land under the 1919 Land Settlement Act had been delayed by the owners of the Raasay estate, the Glasgow ironmasters, William Baird and Company. Seven men, therefore, decided to seize plots on the island and build makeshift homes. In a midnight swoop the men were arrested by police from Portree. On 8 September 1921, the *Glasgow Herald* reported:

> The incidents connected with this revolt of the landless Highlanders have served to set forth in lurid relief the cynical contempt of the government for the men who fought for their country in the Great War and returned to their native straths and glens buoyed up by the hope that something would really be done to make Scotland a land fit for heroes to dwell in.

The men were dragged from their wives and children and sentenced to six weeks' imprisonment. Pleas to government and a petition from the prisoners' wives to the Queen failed to secure clemency. By the end of 1921, the

A crofter family at Poolewe in Wester Ross in 1890. At the end of the Great War the problem of rural poverty was as real in the Highlands as it had ever been. (*SSS*)

Board of Agriculture for Scotland finally reached a compromise with Bairds over Raasay when the company offered rent-free homes elsewhere until the handover on Raasay could be negotiated.

After the Great War tourism was again one of the industries of the Scottish Highlands and islands that enjoyed better days. Even St Kilda, the most remote of the Western Isles, became an attraction for the middle class. Tourists were seasonal but gave Highlanders a chance to sell craftwork and, in their words, 'turn a penny'.

More traditional Highland enterprises, disrupted by four long years of war, found it hard to survive the economic constraints of the Depression. Imports of wool and mutton from Australia and New Zealand brought about a slump in Scottish sheep farming and those who raised cattle found it hard to compete with cheaper imports from South America. Coupled with high taxation, the decline in profits forced many landowners to cut back on the staff they employed on their estates. Many lairds were forced to sell up completely and some of Scotland's traditional land-owning families were replaced by foreigners and British companies eager to invest in sporting estates.

The giant aluminium works at Kinlochleven, which went into production in 1907. (*GH*)

In 1924, the North British Aluminium Company was formed with government support. Smelting, between the wars, was to be the only large-scale industrial development in the Highlands of Scotland, although the Forestry Commission was also set up in 1924 by a government anxious to ensure that Britain would be self-sufficient in timber. Planting and tending the new forests, however, gave work to but a few and for small wages, and many in the north, as before, were forced south in search of work. Girls from the Highlands and the north-east went to England to gut and pack the summer herring and men moved to the towns to find work where they could.

After 1918 British industry slowly turned to mass production and the manufacture of consumer goods. In 1900, the Argyll Motor Company of Scotland had built its first car, the Voiturette, which, with a top speed of eighteen miles an hour, cost £155. Between 1905 and 1907, the Argyll Company claimed to be the largest producer of private cars in Europe. The Arrol-Johnston Company, William Beardmore's, and Albion Motors also gained the reputation of producing some of Britain's best cars. But the Scottish companies built for a landed and sporting clientèle and were famous for the 'heavy car'. The Argyll or Arrol-Johnston cars weighed up to three tons and were fitted with thirty horsepower engines. Albion Motors had the sense to convert their machines into lorries and survived. When Argyll Motors attempted to mass produce they ran into technical and legal difficulties which virtually ruined the firm before the First World War.

Many of Scotland's industrialists had made fortunes during the war. By 1916, the profit margin on completed shell forgings was estimated at forty per cent. Despite government control on profits, by 1919 the Scottish banks were glutted with the spoils of war but little profit was reinvested at home when peace came. Many sold their shares to buy land or invest overseas. In the face of high unemployment and inflation, the unions of the Clyde stood by the rulebook although they had allowed many concessions on manning and work practices during the years of war. By 1922 there were over 80,000 unemployed in Glasgow alone.

The Labour Party in Scotland shrewdly exploited the economic situation. In Glasgow, in particular, the party's candidates in the General Election of that year made great play of local problems. During the war John Wheatley had supported the 1915 rent strike in Shettleston and was a hero in his constituency, even though he had opposed the war itself. In 1922 he was the victorious Labour candidate in a campaign which, he claimed, 'talked local politics, advocating the claims of the Far East of Glasgow rather than the Near East of Europe'. Catholic support for the Independent Labour Party in Glasgow was due in large part to the city's large Irish vote and the consequences of the 1918 Representation of the People Act which tripled the size of the electorate. In 23 Scottish seats Catholics accounted for twenty per cent or more of the vote.

Forty of Labour's 43 candidates in the 1922 election were ILP. Three years later the ILP was to reach its peak when it could claim to have 307 branches in Scotland out of a total of just over a thousand in the United Kingdom as a whole. From the ILP, the socialist movement drew its stamina and moral idealism. MPs like Jimmy Maxton and John Wheatley were the political saints of inter-war British politics, and the Scottish electorate believed in them and fought hard to have them elected. Tom Johnston, the editor of the Labour paper *Forward*, wrote of his own victory in West Stirlingshire in the 1922 election:

> They hustled the indifferent to the booths: they lent shawls and held babies; they carried the sick and dying to the polls on mattresses – and they won. May black shame fall upon the individual or the party who, having the trust of these women, ever betrays it.

James Maxton (1885–1946). (*SNPG*)

Although the Conservative Party swept England in the General Election, Scotland returned 29 Labour MPs and 1 Communist. In Glasgow the party took 10 of the city's 15 seats.

In the House of Commons, the new Scottish MPs scorned tradition and ceremony. Many were to be suspended by the Speaker for their outspokenness. On 27 June 1923, Jimmy Maxton was told to leave the House when he described a Conservative who supported the cutting of child welfare as a murderer. When Wheatley and Campbell Stephen repeated the accusation they too were suspended. In the rumpus, Emanuel Shinwell was called a Jew and George Buchanan, who came to his aid, was suspended when he questioned the impartiality of the Speaker. In the Commons, the hard-faced pin-striped gentlemen of the Conservative benches went out of their way to goad whenever they could what they thought were uncouth Clydesiders.

In 1923 there was another General Election. In Scotland the Labour Party won 35 seats and, with the support of the Liberal Party, Ramsay MacDonald formed the first Labour government. Those who had voted for the party expected a social revolution but Ramsay MacDonald depended upon the Liberal leader Sir Herbert Samuel, and the Conservatives under Stanley Baldwin were eager to bring Labour down at the first opportunity. The Scots soon called MacDonald's administration 'a bloody lum hat government like a' the rest'.

Although many Scots were now playing a leading role in British politics, few felt strongly about their native land. The more left-wing the Scottish Labour MPs, the less nationalist they were in outlook. Most viewed Westminster as a thankful deliverance from the kailyard. Although there was

John Wheatley (1869–1930). (*PP*)

much talk about changing the face of society little had been done to plan how to achieve change. John Wheatley, a self-taught miner from Lanarkshire, was one of the few successes.

Born in 1869, Wheatley was the most outstanding socialist Glasgow produced. His Housing Act of 1924 was politically sound, one of the few successful measures taken by the first Labour government that dealt with one of Scotland's greatest problems. Under his scheme the government paid a subsidy of £9 per house per year to the local authority, which cut weekly rents by up to a third. Unfortunately the Act was curtailed in 1926 and never ran its course.

In 1920 the Communist Party of Great Britain had been founded with considerable Scots help. Although electorally it was weak, with only one MP, Walton Newbold the Member for Motherwell, other Communists, such as Willie Gallacher from Fife, were bent on infiltrating the Labour movement and undermining Parliament from within. The Labour Party refused to allow the Communist Party affiliation, but individual members could still belong to the party and even become Labour MPs. In 1924 the Conservatives and their allies in the media raised the old Bolshevik bogey to help bring MacDonald down. John R. Campbell, the Scots-born temporary editor of the Communist *Worker's Weekly*, was accused of printing a seditious article. Campbell had fought in the Great War and been wounded; but now he was said to be encouraging the British army to mutiny. Mutinies there were in Scotland and in south-east Kent, by men bored by the conditions of army life; but the incidents had no connection whatsoever with Campbell.

James Ramsay MacDonald (1866–1937). (*SNPG*)

The embarrassment caused by the case, however, inspired another Bolshevik scare, the Zinoviev Letter. Purportedly written by Gregori Zinoviev, the Head of the Russian Comintern, to Arthur Macmannus, a Clydesider who was President of the Communist Party of Great Britain, the letter was published by the *Daily Mail* on 25 October 1924, four days before a General Election, and played a considerable part in the defeat of the Labour government. According to the document, British Communists were to carry out a policy of subversion, using the Labour Party as a dupe. Then and since the Zinoviev Letter has been considered by many to have been a fake; but it successfully scared the British electorate.

In October 1924, the Conservative Party swept to power. Their leader, Stanley Baldwin, however, had few solutions to the problems of unemployment and world depression. In Scotland, as elsewhere in Britain, the coal industry after the war had been run by second-rate management, and strife led to Britain's Trades Union Congress calling a General Strike in 1926. The following year there was open hostility between the ILP and the Labour Party when the Conservatives introduced their Trade Union Act of 1927. This outlawed general strikes and obliged trade unionists to 'opt in' rather than 'opt out' of funding the Labour Party, whose opposition to the Act was weak.

In 1929, Britain again went to the polls. When Ramsay MacDonald formed Labour's second government he felt strong enough to exclude the Independent Labour Party from high office except for Emanuel Shinwell and Tom Johnston. In March the following year there was a National Hunger March to bring the plight of the unemployed to the government's attention. In London there was a vast rally on May Day and the same month the Independent Labour Party MPs decided to form a separate group at Westminster, angered by MacDonald's lack of initiative to put the economy to rights. The hostility of ILP members and the worsening economic depression forced MacDonald to resign in April 1931 and form a National Government with the Conservative Baldwin and Sir Herbert Samuel of the Liberal Party.

By the summer of 1931, however, MacDonald's political manoeuvres had done little to bring about a recovery and in November he was forced to go to the country and seek a vote of confidence in his National Government. Throughout the campaign, ILP candidates in Scotland like Jimmy Maxton spoke out against MacDonald and his policies to little effect. The National Government swept to power in the greatest election victory ever recorded in British politics.

Reconciliation between Maxton's ILP and the Labour Party proved impossible and from 1932 they went their separate ways while the Depression deepened. In Dundee, where the majority of the workforce were employed by a single industry – jute – the 1930s put paid to the town's economy. Shipbuilding on the Clyde had virtually come to a standstill. In the year before the outbreak of the First World War, three-quarters of a million tons had been launched on the Clyde. Within twenty years, the annual tonnage launched had dropped to 56,000. For the workers and their families, life became desperate. Many saw no future in Scotland at all.

Between 1921 and 1931, 400,000 Scots emigrated. They left from the industrial Lowlands and from the Highlands and islands and with her people went much of the nation's skill and self-confidence. Between 1871 and 1901, there had been a net loss of 483,000 Scots. Between 1901 and 1961, 1,388,000 Scots were to leave their native land, equivalent to about two-thirds of the natural increase in population over the same period. No country in Europe has ever in history lost such a high proportion of her people.

For those who remained to weather the storm, the unemployed received insurance benefit for the first few months then had to live off unemployment assistance, for which they had to report to the Labour Exchange twice a week. In 1920 a man received fifteen shillings a week, a woman twelve shillings. Boys were entitled to seven shillings and sixpence, girls a shilling less. For children still at school the unemployed man was given an additional shilling. A couple with one child had to live off twenty-eight shillings a week and, given rent, rates and heating, could ill afford to spend much on food. In the early 1930s, according to John Boyd Orr, the noted Scottish nutrition expert, half the population of Britain lived off less than a pound per head per week and less than half of that sum was spent on food.

In 1931, there was a cut in unemployment benefit. Foreign bankers demanded MacDonald cut public expenditure before agreeing to grant a loan and the hated Means Test was introduced. On the Clyde young skilled and semi-skilled men received a shilling a week from the 'Burroo' when work could not be found. David Stephen, who worked as an inspector of the poor in Airdrie, recalled the 1930s in *The Scotsman* in 1981:

> There were the means test butchers, who specialized in the cheapest cuts of meat, and the lousiest sausages. They had queues at their door every day. The orders were huge: 2 oz of this and 4 oz of that, and the inevitable dripping.

Scottish immigrants on board a Canadian train, 1911. (*PAC*)

When a family had been a certain time on poor relief, a clothing issue was granted (in the jargon of the time). The amounts, in cash, were fixed, but there was a little elbow room for choice of articles. There were also strict rules: wool was for nursing mothers, fine boots only for men over 70.

The means test was iniquitous and a shatterer of homes. It broke up families, it penalized the tryers, it starved children, it drove people to suicide and insanity.

Even when there was work, men again put up with low wages and intolerable working conditions. Ships were built in the open in all weathers. If conditions got too bad, they were sent home and not paid for the hours lost. During the Glasgow Trades fortnight, when men were supposed to take a holiday with their families, shipyards locked them out for ten days and no wages were paid. There were no canteens and men were allowed seven minutes to visit the archaic toilet facilities.

Men in work lived miserably. Bread, jam and tea was their staple diet; eggs, sausages and meat rare luxuries. But in the 1930s the men of the Clyde had their moment of glory – the *Queen Mary*. The Cunard Line asked John Brown's to plan for two ships which could ply the Atlantic on a regular basis. The price agreed for the largest ships that the world had ever seen was £3,990,000, and the formal contract was signed on 1 December 1930. To the men of Clydebank, Job Number 534, the first thousand-foot liner in the world, would mean steady work and good wages. The hull plate was quickly laid and three shifts of workmen toiled night and day on the vessel.

By late spring the following year the skeleton of the hull was complete. Cunard, in November 1931, had spent a million and a half pounds on the ship when they ran out of money. On Friday, 11 December 1931 the workforce was sacked and John Brown's shares dropped to fourpence each. Not only were the men of the Clyde without work, 10,000 men and women throughout Britain, in rolling-mills, foundries, and factories making crockery, cutlery, glassware and furniture, were made jobless. The public re-

The *Queen Mary* almost ready for launching. (*FP*)

sponse was unforeseen. The Cunard Company was inundated with offers of financial help from people all over Britain.

In Clydebank alone 3,200 men were out of work. Families were forced to ration their food. Mothers took their children to the local cinemas in the afternoon to keep them warm. Clydebank was unemployed for eighteen months, but the men never lost their sense of humour as William Black, who worked on the ship, recalls:

> Some Americans came over and they were taking photos of the shell and they said, 'Oh look at the rust on the shell,' and a riveter said, 'You should come up and see my frying pan!'

David Kirkwood, the socialist MP for Clydebank, persuaded the Prince of Wales to visit Glasgow and see for himself the effect of the loss of the ship. In the spring of 1933 the Prince witnessed idle men passing the time playing cricket and working allotments to grow food for their families. In the cinemas of Glasgow, Ramsay MacDonald's New Year message for 1934 fell on deaf ears, as he proudly announced in a Movietone newsreel that the unemployment figure was going down.

The dead ship became an obsession for Kirkwood and he was to claim responsibility for getting work restarted, although others played a more significant part. Lord Weir was among those who recommended that public funds should be used to bale out Cunard. On 27 March 1934, the Bill that allowed Cunard nine and a half million pounds to complete the *Queen Mary*, build her sister ship and construct a massive dry dock at Southampton, passed through both Houses of Parliament.

Many Scottish MPs opposed the decision. A Glasgow MP suggested that the money would be put to better use if it was divided out among the unemployed rather than wasted on a rich man's luxury liner. David Kirkwood, however, in one of the most famous speeches ever delivered in the House of Commons, defended the government's decision:

> I welcome this new ship, not only for the good which it will bring to my own constituency but for what I really believe it means to the shipbuilding and engineering industry of this country. I believe that as long as this ship, known as 534, lies like a skeleton in my constituency so long will depression last in this country, because as it lies there in Brown's yard, it seems to me to shout 'failure, failure' to the whole of Britain.

On 3 April 1934, the gates of John Brown's yard were reopened. The men returned to work triumphantly led by the Dalmuir Pipe Band. The first task was to remove 130 tons of rust from the ship's frame but in less than six months the giant vessel was ready for launching. On 26 September 1934, a quarter of a million people stood in the rain to watch her slip across the Clyde into the River Cart. The *Queen Mary* was a floating monument to the skill and craftsmanship of Clydebank and the excitement of the launch veiled the reality of the future for Glasgow's traditional industries. Capitalists were already wary of investing in Scotland's heavy industries. British taxpayers had built the *Queen Mary* and financed her sister ship, the *Queen Elizabeth*. In the 1930s emerged a formula for the salvation of the economy of Scotland that future governments would adopt.

By 1932 the unemployment rate in Scotland had risen to almost twenty-eight per cent. The Scottish Office warned Whitehall that the

David Kirkwood (1872–1955). (*GH*)

A band of pipers led the men into John Brown's yard when work resumed on the *Queen Mary*. (*KP*)

Walter Elliot (1888–1958), Secretary of State for Scotland. (*GH*)

situation was potentially dangerous, reviving nationalist sentiments. Whitehall paid no attention. Sir Godfrey Collins, Walter Elliot and Colonel John Colville all in turn urged for an extension in powers for the Scottish Office to allow inducements to be offered to attract firms to Scotland. A few trading estates and factory units were built in the hope that some industrialist might be wooed north, but little else. After 1935, when the rearmament programme increased the level of industrial activity, the Treasury argued that Scotland was better off than many parts of England. But as late as 1938, Elliot wrote to the Chancellor of the Exchequer:

> There is not south of the Border a general state of affairs so unsatisfactory as we find all over Scotland.

Between 1932 and 1938, 146 new factories were opened in Scotland and forty-three were enlarged. One hundred and fifty other firms, however, closed their doors for good. By the end of 1938 nearly £5 million had been spent by the Commissioners for the Special Areas in Scotland but little of the investment was planned. In *Scotland's Industrial Future*, published in 1937, the Scottish Economic Committee warned the government of an '. . . undue concentration of modern industries in certain Southern areas, involving dangerous social and strategic consequences'.

In truth, unemployment did fall and the rise in real income though hardly spectacular was encouraging. But the condition of Scotland's working-class continued to deteriorate. By the late 1930s the country had one of the highest infant mortality rates in Europe and housing in Glasgow and other cities was intolerable. Judged by the standards of the Housing (Scotland) Act of 1934, overcrowding in Scotland was six times higher than in England and Wales and by 1937 stood at 22.6 per cent. In Lanarkshire the percentage was even higher, 36.8 per cent. Over a third of Scotland's homes lacked the basic amenities such as a water closet or bath. In 1937 1 in 40 in England and

Wales were receiving poor relief. In Scotland as a whole the figure was nearly 1 in 20, in Glasgow 1 in 12. While the Glasgow area accounted for nearly a quarter of Scotland's total population, it was also responsible for 42 per cent of those dependent upon poor relief.

The 1930s disillusioned a generation of Scots for life. The educated suffered with the unskilled. In some Scottish towns that depended upon single industries two-thirds unemployment was not uncommon. Half of Glasgow's population had to make do on less than a pound a week and only football, which drew huge crowds, brought relief to a life of despair.

By 1900 football had already become part of Glasgow's way of life. Queen's Park, the city's oldest club, was instrumental in founding the Scottish Football Association in 1873. Rangers was founded the year before the SFA and Celtic Football Club was started in 1879 by Brother Walfrid, a member of the teaching institute of the Manst Brothers in the Catholic East End of the city. The club originally was a charitable affair, the profits going to provide free food for poor children. It was modelled on another Irish-Scottish club, Edinburgh Hibernian, founded in 1872. When Celtic was formed they employed four of Hibernian's best players and the club was going to be called Glasgow Hibernian, until the organizers changed their minds after Edinburgh fans invaded the pitch three times at their first match to protest about the Glasgow team poaching the name, let alone some of the talent, of their Edinburgh club.

There was little hostility between Rangers and Celtic until a Belfast shipbuilding firm opened a yard in Govan. A large number of Orangemen were brought over from Ulster and, as Rangers were their nearest club, they became fanatical supporters. Before the Second World War, however, football had already become a way of breaking out of the slum. Players, although meanly paid, were the aristocrats of the working-class.

During the Depression, the children of the unemployed suffered most, crowded in tenements and rarely given proper food. Childhood for most was a nightmare that was to haunt them in adult life. So concerned were some about the health of Scotland's children that Necessitous Children's Camps were set up. In 1936 it was estimated that 36,000 Glasgow children were in medical need of extra food and fresh air and each year upwards of 6000 of the city's children were sent to Scotland's east coast and elsewhere to live under canvas and receive proper food and exercise.

Malnutrition and poverty took their toll of adults as well. The National Fitness Council for Scotland was set up to encourage Scots to exercise and boasted that for two shillings and sixpence a day Scots could enjoy the benefits of a holiday in Youth Hostels. The people of Glasgow also joined in the popular craze for dance; the city boasted fifty ballrooms between the wars. Alcohol was banned in the halls, and for sixpence, serious dancing could be enjoyed for six hours each night. In the 1930s, the craze was the cinema. The old picture houses were replaced by palatial buildings like Green's Playhouse, which, with nearly 4500 seats was the largest cinema in Europe. Glasgow's interest in the art of cinematography was profound. One of the city's solicitors, John Maxwell, gave up the law to pioneer the production of British talking pictures at Elstree Studios, and in John Grierson the city fathered British documentary film-making.

The Great War diminished the strength of the temperance movement;

The crests of Rangers (*top*) and Celtic Football Clubs.   (*GH*)

but some continued the fight. Edwin Scrymgeour, a former member of the ILP, campaigned for total prohibition. In 1922, he unseated Winston Churchill as MP for Dundee and became Britain's first and only Prohibitionist MP. The following year he introduced a Bill to ban drink. Although supported by the Reverend James Barr, Labour MP for Motherwell, and Jimmy Maxton, MP for Bridgend, Scrymgeour's Bill failed on its second reading, defeated by 235 votes to 14. As the crime caused by prohibition in America became clear, passions against drink weakened. Scrymgeour lost his parliamentary seat in 1931.

Edwin Scrymgeour (1866–1947). (*GH*)

Between the wars the Scots became more secular, beginning to resent the sabbatarianism of previous generations. Presbyterianism was seen to offer little to the hungry and the unemployed. Aware of its weaknesses, Scotland's churches sought unity. In 1900 the Free Church and the United Presbyterian Church formed the United Free Church, and made peace with the Church of Scotland in 1929.

By 1937 Clydebank was hard at work on Ship Number 552, the *Queen Elizabeth*, and as prosperity returned, regular visits to the pawn shop became a thing of the past. In November the same year Ramsay MacDonald died. Scotland had given Britain her first Labour Prime Minister but had little to thank him for. He had spent much of his life trying to keep the fragile peace of Europe. The war to end wars had solved nothing and a spiteful peace and world depression had brought the dictators of Europe to power. By the end of 1938, another war with Germany seemed certain.   •

Fascism found no foothold in Scotland. Enough of Calvinism remained to ensure that the Jews, 'The People of the Book', as they were called, were not made scapegoats for economic ills and there were no street battles as in England. By the middle of the 1920s there were 20,000 Jews in Glasgow, hard-working and respected people, and the fight against Hitler was thought by most Scots to be a crusade against intolerance.

On 1 November 1938, Glasgow's Empire Exhibition closed. More than thirteen and a half million people had visited the showground and on the last night massed military bands played while searchlights picked out aircraft overhead. Three hundred and sixty-four thousand attended the last parade in the exhibition stadium, the largest public attendance at any function ever held in Britain. Amid the euphoria of the grand finale was the sound and smell of war. Adolf Hitler would soon have his own solution to the Depression and again Scots would be called upon to help lick Germany. Once again there would be work in the shipyards and the engineering shops of the Clyde. But for a time only.

22

An End to an Auld Song?

In March 1941 German bombers blitzed Glasgow. In two night raids, 439 planes of Hitler's Luftwaffe flew to the limits of their fuel to drop over 500 tons of high explosive and nearly 2500 incendiary bombs on the city. Such was the courage of Glasgow's citizens that the dead are honoured in Scotland's National War Memorial.

Upwards of 200 bombers took part in the Clydeside offensive on the night of Thursday, 13 March. The first bombs fell upon Clydebank at about half past nine and enormous fires quickly started as Singer's sixty-acre timber yard caught alight as did the Yoker distillery and the Admiralty's oil storage tanks at Dalnottar. In Clydebank alone 528 were killed. In Jellico Street all fifteen members of the Rock family died in the first attack. Nearby, the McSherry family, a widow and her seven children, were also slaughtered. The raids were an attempt to knock out the engineering shops and shipyards that had done much in the Great War to put paid to Germany's hegemonic hopes. In the Glasgow area over 1000 were killed and over 1500 injured in two nights of bombing; but the war effort went on.

At Dalnottar Cemetery they buried the dead in haste. Protestant and Catholic clergy officiated in a graveyard still littered with burnt-out incendiaries. Only seven houses in Clydebank were left undamaged and over 50,000 people were forced to seek temporary homes elsewhere. For the remainder of the Second World War, they travelled fifty or sixty miles each day to and from the factories of war.

The Singer Sewing Machine factory at Clydebank had been turned over to the manufacture of munitions when war was declared. Over a quarter of a million square feet of floor space was destroyed in the blitz, together with the Recreation Hall and the timber yard, but within six weeks production was back to normal. In the course of the war, Singer's produced 60,000 rifle components, 1,250,000 bayonets, over 250,000 sten guns, 15,000 tank tracks and 125,000,000 bullets.

Yet curiously Clydebank had been one of the last local authorities in Scotland to comply with the government's civil defence programme in the 1930s. With the support of David Kirkwood, the local MP, the council had staunchly refused to implement the order on the grounds that it was tantamount to accepting that war was inevitable. When Britain went to war with Germany in September 1939, the British government still had a

Scots helped to found an Empire and died protecting it. The scrolls within the shrine of the Scottish National War Memorial honour those who died in two World Wars. (*SWM*)
The Coldstream Guards still parade outside their old regimental headquarters in the Borders. Raised in 1660 by General Monck, they helped restore Charles II to the throne.
The Scots are proud of their soldiers and every year at the Edinburgh Military Tattoo thousands of spectators are stirred by the Massed Bands of Scotland's regiments. (*Author*)

deep-rooted fear of the apparent pacifism of Scotland's west coast, believing that the morale of the industrial workers had been endangered by the defeatist influences of their left-wing leaders. The blitz on Clydebank put paid to any such fears.

The River Clyde during the Second World War became Britain's main port. In the course of the war, 52,000,000 tons of munitions and goods were landed on the river's banks. Over 2,000,000 servicemen left its ports, and when the United States entered the war in 1941, the Gareloch was the landing port of much of America's army and equipment. The 100,000 men who worked in the thirty-seven shipyards of the Clyde also played their part as they had done twenty-five years before. The capital ships *Duke of York*, *Howe*, and the aircraft carrier *Indefatigable* were all Clyde built, and in November 1944 the battleship *Vanguard* was launched. Hundreds of smaller vessels were constructed, converted and repaired. In the first year of the war, the Clyde had also launched the *Queen Elizabeth*, which with her sister ship the *Queen Mary* were to prove invaluable in transporting troops. If the *Elizabeth* had been sunk as she was launched on 28 February 1940 she would have settled on the bed of the river and would have had to be broken up, depriving the nation not only of the ship herself but of the port of Glasgow for a year or more, with devastating effects on the convoys across the Atlantic. But although the launching was advertised the Germans did not attack.

The government opened a new steel foundry in Scotland in 1942 to make tanks for the Russian front. Winifred Kay, whose husband was in the Royal Navy, was one of many Glasgow women employed. (*CPP*)

Clydebank's greatest achievement was not a ship but the Mulberry Harbours. A hundred firms were involved in constructing and equipping the pierheads that would make possible the Allied invasion of Normandy in June 1944. To keep the workers of the yards healthy and happy, Winston Churchill, the wartime Prime Minister, demanded that the shipyard owners provide adequate canteen facilities. The management of John Brown's held out until assured by Churchill in person that the added expenditure would be tax deductible.

Almost as many Scots worked for the Ministry of Aircraft Production. Employing 25,000, the Rolls Royce factory made Merlin engines and was the largest ever built in Scotland. At Bishopton, a factory almost as large was built to manufacture explosives and fill shell and ammunition cases.

In 1939, at Churchill's insistence, Tom Johnston became Regional Commissioner for Scotland and two years later Secretary of State. Born in 1882 in Kirkintilloch, Johnston was educated at Glasgow University. In 1906, he took over a relative's printing press and started the socialist weekly *Forward* which reached about 10,000 readers. Scotland's new Secretary of State was a man of nagging prejudices. He had been excluded from membership of the exclusive Caledonian Club in London because, in his book *Our Scots Noble Families*, he lampooned the Scottish aristocracy, his pet hate. Of the Earl of Glasgow, he wrote:

> The family motto is 'Dominus providebit', 'the Lord shall Provide'. So far the task has been undertaken by the working classes of the West of Scotland.

Johnston also had a medieval Scottish distrust of the English. At meetings he often reminded his audiences that on his journeys to London he fingered the return half of his ticket like a talisman to ensure his speedy return. But he was a politician with a remarkable ability to get things done. When war broke out

At the Antigonish Highland Games in Nova Scotia, Scots Canadians celebrate their culture as seriously as the Scot at home, despite the fact that their ancestors left their native Scotland six or seven generations back. The descendants of Scottish immigrants also gather each year at Grandfather Mountain in North Carolina (*below*), at one of the largest Highland gatherings in the world. (*Author*)

A blitzed tenement on Clydebank,
March 1941. (*GH*)

The dead were buried at Dalnottar
Cemetery. (*GH*)

he and his new Scottish Advisory Council, made up of former Secretaries of State, were given a free hand – with illuminating results. The North of Scotland Hydro-Electric Board was set up in 1943, a scheme Johnston had long cherished as a vital factor in developing the Highlands, and one of the most successful government agencies ever conceived.

In 1942, Johnston had helped create the Scottish Council on Industry, to establish a practical liaison between central government and industrialists. It soon became one of the most effective pressure groups in Britain. Between 1942 and 1945 it won some 700 new enterprises or substantial extensions to Scottish industry, persuading the government to part with £12 million to build new factories and provide new plant. Of his time at St Andrew's House, Tom Johnston wrote in his memoirs:

> We had got Scotland's wishes and opinions respected and listened to as they had not been respected or listened to since the Union.

At Johnston's insistence, the Scots were the first in Britain to have tribunals to resolve the problems of rent that had so plagued the years of the First World War. Under his auspices, Scotland also pioneered what became Britain's post-war National Health Service. Using civil defence facilities, Johnston introduced a free system of medical care for workers in the Clyde Valley and by the end of the war he had extended the scheme to much of Scotland.

One of Johnston's most remarkable achievements was to help bring America into the war. In 1940, Harry Hopkins was sent over by President Roosevelt to assess whether Britain could beat Hitler on her own, but the American would give Churchill no inkling as to whether he would recommend that the US should enter the war. In the North British Hotel in George Square, Glasgow, at a dinner party held by Tom Johnston for Churchill and Hopkins, Johnston forced Hopkins to make a speech. The American explained he was glad to be in Scotland, the home of his great-great-grandmother, who had emigrated from Auchterarder and, he remarked, he was also glad to see Scots women still read the Bible, quoting the Book of Kings – 'Wheresoever thou goest we go too. Even to the very end'. Churchill. a tear in his eye, excused himself and, according to Johnston, phoned the King to say that America was about to come in on Britain's side.

The demands of war once more stretched Scotland's resources. Coal, steel and iron were again at a premium. By 1943 a quarter of all working Scots were making ships, engines and armaments. In Dundee, where the Depression had struck hard, the need for sand bags re-opened jute mills and put on full-time production those who had perilously survived the lean years. In the Borders, the woollen mills were again at full stretch, making socks and clothing for Britain's armed forces.

The Highlands of Scotland became a restricted zone. Overseas troops, from countries like Poland overrun by Hitler, were trained in the glens of the north, and when America entered the war, her commandos, like those of Britain, trained in Scotland's rugged hills. In secret, and away from causing harm, Britain's new bombs, aircraft and guns could also be tested. On Gruinard Island in Wester Ross, experiments were carried out in bacteriological warfare which make the island to this day lethal to human and animal life.

Thomas Johnston, Secretary of State for Scotland (1882–1965). (*Pictorial Press*)

Apart from the war effort there was little employment for Highlanders. The distillation of whisky was banned and it was not until 1949 that full-scale production was allowed to resume. Whisky, however, played its part in the war effort. At the outbreak of war, two million pounds' worth was sent to the United States to keep the market open and provide Britain, in need of munitions, with collateral.

Scotland's farmers were encouraged to reclaim land and put it to the plough, to cut down costly imports of food. The Scots, like the inhabitants of the rest of Britain, survived six long years of blackouts, food rationing and hard work. When peace came, 57,720 Scots had been killed in the Second World War. As a result of two wars in just thirty years, over 200,000 Scots were dead.

When the war ended Tom Johnston sadly refused to serve under Labour's Prime Minister Clement Attlee. He withdrew from active politics and devoted his life to the North of Scotland Hydro-Electricity Board.

Britain again began the long process of industrial reconstruction. In 1945 the nation's priorities were again for coal, steel and ships and little was done in Scotland to establish on a permanent basis new light industries like the aircraft and motor-car production that politicians had seen wise in time of war to site in the north. Only the Rolls Royce aero engine works at Hillington remained, and then only after a political battle. As before, men and industry from Scotland drifted south.

The Labour government abounded in White Papers of promise. Every sector of the economy was to be transformed. The eggs were to be scrambled and no one, it was thought, would be able to put them together again. Britain was to enjoy the fruits of a socialist, planned second industrial revolution. New factories were to be built in the west of Scotland and new industries encouraged north to fill them. There were to be new towns, like East Kilbride, to give people a life free from the squalor of the tenement.

The people of the Highlands were not forgotten. Crofters were to be given more aid, forestry was to be extended and new homes built. Labour's post-war vision of a brave new Scotland was intoxicating.

Little materialized. All that emerged were new towns and a few industrial estates like Newhouse near Glasgow and Kingsway near Dundee. The new industrial revolution still needed coal and steel, Scotland's old industries, but neither were particularly profitable in Scotland. The vast Lanarkshire coalfield was virtually exhausted and in many industries oil was replacing coal. The plant of Scotland's great steel industry was largely outdated. Owners of the plant, more interested in profit than the economies of scale, formed into a cartel. Few saw reason to spend money on new equipment and methods when those of old brought in handsome profit. The shortages of war had created a reprieve for heavy industry so that for a while it was quite easy to make money. With no need to do things very well indigenous industry lost the chance for the second time. Not enough was invested, there was little diversification and, above all, bad management and bad working practices were not sorted out.

For a decade the shipyards flourished. The need to replace shipping lost in the war brought a boom to Clydeside that was almost self-complacent. The workers and their unions saw no necessity to abandon old practices. Demarcation – one man one job – remained inviolate. In the 1950s,

Clement Attlee (1883–1967), Prime Minister from 1945 to 1951.   (*NPG*)

Scotland, like the rest of the country prospered by standing still. Only in the north did a new industry, born out of six years of war, come to Scotland. In 1954 the government began to build a nuclear fast-reactor at Dounreay in Caithness; but most Scots felt that the site chosen was less out of regard to Scotland's economic needs, more because the government wanted it as far away as possible from Britain's big cities.

The Labour government's commitment to nationalization served the Scots ill. Politically the voters of Scotland had agreed with the principle of public ownership; but in practice it meant that real industrial power gravitated more and more towards Westminster and Whitehall. Attlee made it clear that any form of Home Rule, for so long a plank in his party's platform, was out of the question. In 1947 he had curtly, as was his fashion, dismissed Joseph Westwood, the Secretary of State for Scotland, for being parochial; and when his successor, Arthur Woodburn, also tried to bring the Prime Minister's attention to problems peculiarly Scottish, he too preferred to resign rather than stay in the Cabinet but relieved of his Scottish Office portfolio.

Increased centralization tarnished the Labour Party's image in Scotland and in 1955 Attlee's government was given its come-uppance. In the General Election the Conservatives captured thirty-six of the seventy-one Scottish seats. For the first time – and the last – the Tories won a majority of Scottish parliamentary seats.

But under the new government heavy industry in Scotland continued to stagnate. New light industries studiously avoided the north, preferring to make their base in the more accessible Midlands and south-east of England. By the late 1950s, Scotland's shipyards had begun to feel the harsh reality of overseas competition. The devastated yards of Germany and Japan were rebuilt with modern machines and practices, while the yards of the Clyde went about their old jog trot. Hitler, in a sense, had not bombed Scottish industry enough.

Arthur Woodburn (1890–1978), Secretary of State for Scotland. (*GH*)

Unemployment rose: the rate of those out of work in Scotland was consistently double that of England as a whole. Only lower rates of pay kept many old industries alive. When, in 1959, Harold Macmillan went to the country claiming, 'You've never had it so good', Scots had reason to question his slogan and voted Labour. In British terms, however, the Conservatives were returned to power and in 1961 were responsible for the first real attempt to look at Scotland's own problems. John Toothill, the managing director of Ferranti in Edinburgh, was asked to head a committee to investigate the state of the Scottish economy and report on improvement. The Toothill Report found that unemployment in Scotland had risen steadily since 1957 and would continue to do so unless strategic restructuring of the economy took place. Scotland's industrial workers were not at the root of the problem: Scottish management – unskilled and cautious – was at fault.

Toothill's analysis of the economic state of Scotland was as tragic as it was realistic. He damned the industrial infra-structure. Communications were either bad or non-existent; in his own company, Ferranti, they had needed to invest in an aeroplane to eliminate long and tortuous road or sea journeys.

The Report's major conclusion, and one with which few Scots had

Sir John Toothill (1908–). (*GH*)

reason to disagree, was that in areas of Britain where economic growth was complicated by the problems that beset traditional heavy industry, governments were wrong to submit those areas to policies conceived to meet the needs of the booming south-east of England. The electronics industry, Toothill argued, was an industry of the future which escaped one of the bugbears of the Scottish economy, the cost of transportation. High-valued end products weighed little.

The Conservatives, however, were slow to implement Toothill's findings: the European Common Market was seen as the panacea of all Britain's economic difficulties. In 1961 the government had applied to join the EEC. Although the electorate were not consulted on the issue, the Scots, with their historic links with the continent of Europe, were probably more in favour of membership than against. When General de Gaulle rejected Britain's application, in a desperate attempt to prop up the ailing British economy the Conservatives, like the Labour government before them, turned to planning.

Michael Noble, the Conservative and Unionist MP for Argyll, became

Michael Noble (1913–84), Secretary of State for Scotland between 1962 and 1964 and Harold Macmillan (1894–), Prime Minister from 1957 to 1963.   (GH)

The giant pulp and paper mill at Corpach near Fort William.   (WT)

Secretary of State for Scotland. He had had little experience of purely Scottish affairs but with great energy he tried to encourage new light industries north. When he tried to help Wiggins Teape to site a paper pulp mill near Fort William, he found the Board of Trade in Whitehall obstructive but in the end managed to 'ditch them' because, as he says, 'they were just telling lies'.

Under the Conservatives a steel strip mill, essential if Scotland was to share in the motor industry and the manufacture of consumer goods like cookers and refrigerators, was built at Ravenscraig near Motherwell. The arm of the British Motor Corporation was twisted into setting up a truck and tractor factory at Bathgate in West Lothian and Rootes were similarly persuaded to set up shop at Linwood, near Paisley, to produce what they hoped would be a revolutionary new small car, the Hillman Imp. At long last, it seemed, Scotland was to have the industries that were making the English Midlands prosperous.

Both car factories were from the outset fraught with labour problems. Men used to building ships and turbines had to get used to making small cars on a production line. Both Rootes and BMC paid wages to their Scottish workforce below the level of their English workers, in order to offset the cost of transporting the hundreds of components required for the assembly line. Crates arrived from England marked 'Slave Labour'.

The new Scottish motor industry was a political sop. Both Rootes and BMC built only assembly plants – factories to absorb the unemployed in their hundreds but bringing little of the real work north of the Border. The wheels, seats, clocks and headlamps were all made in England and there was no plan to have them made locally. Even the increased employment prospects that factories such as these seemed to offer was more than offset by the events on the Clyde.

In the early 1960s six out of the twenty-five shipyards were forced out of business. The Conservative government stood by and when Lord Beeching was asked to rationalize Britain's loss-making railways, his recommended closures threatened to depress the north and south-west of Scotland even more. Many of his proposed cuts were only abandoned after heavy lobbying by Michael Noble, who realized that it would take time for modern roads to fill gaps created by Beeching's axe. It was only after thirty years of lobbying and negotiation, for instance, that central government finally agreed to fund road bridges to cross the rivers Forth and Tay, and a motorway between Edinburgh and Glasgow to replace one of the most dangerous roads in Britain.

When the country went to the polls in October 1964, Harold Wilson became Prime Minister. The talk was of the white heat of a technological revolution. The new Labour government, however, was formed with only a 4-seat majority in the House of Commons. While the Scots had elected 43 Labour MPs out of 71 Scottish seats, the English had voted for a change with caution. After another election Labour was returned with a majority big enough to implement the party's manifesto. Like the Conservatives, Labour had plans, some of them original and, when implemented successful.

In 1965, for instance, the Highlands and Islands Development Board was set up to create work north of the Highland Line. Its first Chairman was Professor Robert Grieve, a planner of outstanding proven ability who had done much to bring about the regeneration of Glasgow housing after the war. Under Grieve, the Board began to view Highlanders' problems through the eyes of the inhabitants rather than impose the ideas of southern civil servants. It gave grants to help stimulate the ailing fishing industry and eleven new boat-building yards were financed as well as twenty-four fish-processing plants. The Board's work was followed up by Associated Fisheries, who built a vast complex at Mallaig to make the town Europe's premier herring port, a dream since destroyed by the EEC's fishing policy. The White Fish Authority and Unilever, however, successfully developed

Professor Sir Robert Grieve (1910–). He was chief planner at the Scottish Office from 1960 to 1964, then seconded as Chairman of the Highlands and Islands Development Board from 1965 to 1970. (*STV*)

As far back as 1923, J. Inglis Kerr, a pioneer of road transport in Scotland, called for a road bridge to cross the Firth of Forth. It was not until 1955 that the Ministry of Transport announced that a bridge or tunnel would be started. The bridge took six years to build at a cost of £20,000,000, and was opened by the Queen in September 1964.   (*STB*)

The British Aluminium Company smelter at Invergordon – opened in May 1971, closed in December 1981. The excessive cost of electricity to power the plant and a fall in the world price of aluminium made 890 workers redundant.   (*BA*)

fresh- and sea-water fish farming and the HIDB have actively encouraged co-operative industrial ventures in the Highlands and islands.

At Invergordon in Easter Ross the Board planned a huge industrial complex – a vast deep water port, a grain distillery that would be the largest in Europe and an aluminium smelter that would cost the British Aluminium Company and the taxpayer £37 million.

In 1966, Labour revealed its plans for Lowland Scotland. In five years, at a cost of £2000 million, Scotland's old and ailing industries were to be streamlined and modernized. Men who lost their jobs in the process were to be retrained and given work in the new growth industries like motor cars and electronics. The whole of Scotland, apart from the City of Edinburgh, was henceforth to be treated as a development area and handsome investment grants were paid out of the public purse to encourage new industrial ventures. But the omens for the revolutionary plan were not good, as older industries, like shipbuilding and coal mining, rapidly died before new ones had been born.

By 1965, Scottish coal cost fifteen shillings a ton more to produce than English coal and most mines were running at a loss. The government demanded that the Scottish Coal Board close twenty-three of the country's seventy-one pits by 1970. In an attempt to help the Board balance its books a further ten shillings a ton was to be charged for Scottish coal. At that price few wanted to buy and Colville's the steel giant announced it would convert its plant to oil.

In October 1965, Fairfield's shipyard at Govan was on the point of collapse. A fairly modern yard, it had no orders save for a few merchant ships. Like most on the Clyde, Fairfield's had operated for years on the Micawber principle: they had put in unprofitable tenders in the hope that something bigger would turn up. Under pressure from Scottish MPs and the trade unions, the Labour government formed a consortium based on private enterprise, trade union co-operation and government financial support to save the yard. Meanwhile, a Royal Commission, under the chairmanship of Lord Geddes, was investigating Britain's shipbuilding industry as a whole.

In 1966, Geddes concluded that shipbuilding was vital to Britain and had a potential for growth. What was needed was rationalization: yards should be grouped into larger units of finance and production. On the Clyde two groups were formed out of amalgamations: Upper Clyde Shipbuilders and Lower Clyde Shipbuilders; each would specialize in different types of shipping. The plan, however, foundered almost at once. Scottish steel manufacturers, with acute financial problems of their own, were not able to sell steel to the yards at a discount as Lord Geddes had recommended.

As in the past, Scotland's economic problems were but an acute reflection of Britain's as a whole. By the middle of 1966, the Labour government was forced to deflate the economy and coerce employers and trade unions into accepting an incomes policy that neither really wanted. A bleak blast blew north from Westminster, unemployment in Scotland rose rapidly. Again a post-war government had failed to put the economy of Britain on a new and viable course. Harold Wilson, previously unimpressed by the EEC, was persuaded by the mandarins of Whitehall that Britain must join the Common Market to avoid slipping down the road to national bankruptcy. In May 1967, Britain again applied for membership of Europe's

Harold Wilson (1916–), Prime Minister from 1964 to 1970 and from 1974 to 1976. (*NPG*)

William Ross (1911–), Secretary of State for Scotland during Harold Wilson's last term of office. (*GH*)

increasingly wealthy club. The negotiations took years as Britain prepared to ditch the trading links with the remnants of her old Empire for the protectionist policies of Europe and meanwhile the government shored up Scotland's economy like some old Glasgow tenement.

In June 1970, the Conservatives were returned to power. Britain's new Prime Minister, Edward Heath, busied himself with Britain's Common Market application, believing like Harold Wilson before him that the EEC would solve all. When membership was finally accepted, Britain took her problems into the club and joined with an economy as stagnant as it had remained since the end of the Second World War. Companies continued to go out of business and in an effort to halt the decline, workers began taking over defunct factories themselves.

In the yards of Upper Clyde Shipbuilders there was staged the most eloquent 'work-in' of the 1970s. In 1971, the yards faced total extinction. The formation of UCS, which included John Brown's, Yarrow, Fairfield's, Stephen and Connell shipyards, had officially taken place on 7 February 1968, two years after the Geddes report. UCS employed 8500 men and faced receivership if the government refused an immediate loan of £6 million. Nicholas Ridley, a minister in the present Conservative government, had already given his own solution:

> Write off its debts, sell off the government's shareholdings, close one or even two of its three yards, appoint a new chairman and let it stand or fall on its own. This might cost £10 million, but it would be the end of the nightmare.

The attitude of Edward Heath's Conservative government towards Upper Clyde Shipbuilders was exploited by the SNP. (*NLS*)

But the cradle of world shipbuilding refused to die. Jimmy Reid and a fellow Communist shop steward, Jimmy Airlie, took on the might of a Conservative government bent on destroying 'lame ducks'.

The 'work-in' began on 30 July 1971: but what actually happened was a lot less dramatic than the myth. In the twelve months that followed the liquidator paid off almost 1600 men. There were never more than 390 men officially engaged in the 'work-in' and only a few reported to the yards. The shop stewards, however, raised a staggering £485,000 to use as a fighting fund and pay men who otherwise were working for nothing. John and Yoko Lennon contributed £5000 and the rest came from the public and the trade unions.

The men of the Clyde showed the world their stoic determination to work. There was, shop stewards argued, a moral issue at stake, namely the social as well as economic destruction of Clydeside. After fourteen months the 'work-in' succeeded in persuading the government to help keep the yards open. Some of the yards were subsequently sold to make oil-rig platforms but others, like Alexander Stephen of Linthouse, went out of business altogether.

Other British workers took steps to protect their jobs. In 1972, the miners struck out against what they felt was the government's determination to obliterate the coal industry. When war in the Middle East the following year dislocated oil supplies, domestic coal was at a premium. The miners were put in a more powerful position when OPEC raised the price of oil six-fold. During the winter of 1973 the miners' ban on overtime almost brought Britain to a standstill. By January 1974, much of the country was on a three-day week, and Edward Heath, the Tory Prime Minister, lost the election. The incoming Labour government placed undue faith in co-operation with the trade unions as the solution of Britain's economic problems, and in 1979 was replaced by the Conservatives.

Since the 1970s politicians of both parties have relied on a discovery made in the North Sea off Scotland's coast to finance Britain's recovery. In 1970 British Petroleum first discovered oil off Aberdeen and since the Forties Field and other wells have come onstream, revenue from oil and natural gas has helped politicians cover over the cracks in Britain's economy.

In Scotland today, there are new industries. At Glenrothes in Fife, John Toothill's dream of a Scottish electronics industry became a reality in a new town built originally for a coal mine that proved a white elephant. But the electronics factories are for the most part American owned and employ hundreds not thousands; by 1970 the electronics industry in Scotland employed only 30,000 people, a large proportion of them women. The Border towns like Galashiels have also attracted the new technology but many workers used to heavy industry have found it hard to adjust.

Under Britain's present Prime Minister, Margaret Thatcher, the revenue from oil finances monetarist policies. Oil has strengthened the pound in the world's money markets and made British exports more expensive: to sell in the world marketplace has been made more difficult. Between 1979 and 1981, Scotland witnessed an eleven per cent fall in industrial production and a twenty per cent drop in manufacturing jobs. With funds the like of which no other post-war government has had at its disposal, the Prime Minister, Margaret Thatcher, can allow what she sees as a necessary if ruthless shakeout of industrial deadwood. Companies go into liquidation, factories close and men and women are thrown out of work. Oil revenue now pays the social security of at least three and a half million British workers and their families. Most will never work again as the fate of much of Britain's traditional industry is left to the untender mercy of market forces.

Scotland's industrial belt has become a graveyard. The Singer Sewing Machine factory at Clydebank used to be the largest in the world, giving work to 23,000. After the Second World War Singer's were forced to halve their workforce, and in 1980 the micro-chip revolution closed the factory for good. New machines did not need gears and cams and the company had more modern factories to build the new machines.

On Tuesday, 3 August 1982, Carron iron works, Scotland's oldest company, called in the Receiver. The company had a market value of some £3 million with debts of over £11 million, despite a long reputation for innovation and change. They had designed the shell castings for Major General Henry Shrapnel and had pioneered modern bathroom and kitchen ware. Carron had been forced to shed manpower over the years. In 1979, Falkirk had 4000 unemployed. By 1982, the number out of work was 11,000. When, in August 1982, the recession made Carron's products unwanted, nearly 600 men were made redundant.

In Dundee and Kirkcaldy, paper sacking, the invention of vinyl for floor coverings and Third World competition have put paid to much of the jute and linoleum industry. After the Second World War, 15,000 worked in the jute mills of Dundee. Now fewer than 2000 are associated with the industry.

William Coats, the Scottish-based multinational, was forced to shed

The first oil well in Scottish waters was drilled in 1967 and three years later the Forties Field was found by British Petroleum, 100 miles east of Aberdeen. The Scottish National Party made political capital of the discovery. (*SDA*)   (*NLS, below*)

SCOTLAND'S

OIL

.... whose hands on the money?

Margaret Thatcher, who became Britain's Conservative Prime Minister in 1979, has seen her party's fortune fall in Scotland since taking power, yet she maintains her popularity in southern England. A north-south political division may yet determine Scotland's future. (*GCC*)

3000 workers in 1980 when their United Kingdom operations barely broke even. Subsidized foreign competitors in industries like steel, shipbuilding and textiles continue to make Scotland uncompetitive. When the British economy sneezes, Scotland catches a cold.

The brave attempts made by British governments since the war to revitalize Scottish industry have also failed. In 1979, Wiggins Teape closed their pulp mill at Corpach near Fort William. The plant, to produce wood pulp from locally grown trees, had given work to nearly a thousand and a village of more than 450 houses and three schools as well as shops and other amenities had been built for Corpach's workers and their families. Although Wiggins Teape still make paper at Corpach, Scottish timber is now sent to Sweden for pulping.

Scotland suffers by being distant from the marketplace. On 15 May 1981, the last car to be built at Linwood rolled off the assembly line. The plant had once been thought the £23-million showpiece of Clydeside's industrial revival. The factory, however, was initially fraught with problems. The Hillman Imp had failed to make inroads into a market dominated by the Leyland Mini and industrial unrest was never far away. At one point there had been six strikes in nine days. Peugeot-Citroën took over Linwood in 1978 from the American Chrysler Corporation whose own attempt to make the plant viable had cost the British government £162 million in 1976. At Linwood the factory employed 4500, two out of five people in the area. In Bathgate, British Leyland stopped making tractors and 900 jobs were lost. Scotland's motor industry, conceived by politicians, died in infancy.

The Ravenscraig strip mill, commissioned in 1963, was the last major capital development undertaken by private enterprise in Scotland. As a steel producing complex Ravenscraig was the most advanced in Europe; financially it proved uneconomic, and the threat of closure hangs over what is British Steel's vast nationalized mill. Fourteen thousand jobs are at risk. The steel industry is still basic to Scotland's economy; but only five per cent of the steel made in Scotland is for Scottish customers.

Industries, like dominoes, fall. At Christmas 1981, British Aluminium closed their smelter at Invergordon and nearly 900 were put out of work. They no longer make tyres at Drumchapel. They no longer make tractors or nylon at Kilmarnock. Scotland has 400,000 unemployed – one in six of the population. The nation will never be the same again. Economic pressures have made Scotland less Scottish and dealt her once proud industries a fatal blow. Now industrially, as politically in 1707, the Scots of today are witnessing 'An End to an Auld Sang'.

23

Yet Still the Blood is Strong

ABROAD THE DESCENDANTS of those who left Scotland are proud of their origins. There are 5000 Scottish societies round the world, where at least some of the 25,000,000 of Scottish extraction maintain the traditions of the land of their fathers. Every July at Linville in North Carolina, Americans meet at Grandfather Mountain to hold a Highland Gathering. Over a hundred Scottish clan societies attend each year and there is little sign of recession, unemployment and hardship among their number. Most of the 15,000 who attend the two-day event, first held in 1956, have been Americans for several generations despite their display of tartanry and their enthusiasm for the old Scottish sports. Nestor MacDonald, the Chief of the Games, is one of the few born in Scotland, leaving Armadale, Isle of Skye, with his parents shortly after his birth on 15 December 1895. During the First World War he flew Sopwith Camels with the Royal Flying Corps and was awarded the Air Force Cross and the OBE. Interest in his native land came late, when MacDonald – now a millionaire – joined the St Andrews Society of New York.

The Memorial Cairn at Grandfather Mountain, North Carolina erected in 1980 to honour the clans. (*Author*)

Founded in 1756, the New York St Andrews Society is the third oldest in America. Andrew Carnegie was once President and at least a dozen present-day members are millionaires. Each year, the Society raises over $100,000 to provide scholarships for Scots American students at Scottish universities, and over a thousand attend its exclusive annual dinner in New York's Waldorf Astoria Hotel.

The oldest Games in North America are at Antigonish in Nova Scotia, where they have met since 1861. At Antigonish they take the three-day gathering very seriously and attract as many as 1500 competitors. To the Scots of Nova Scotia, the Games are a genuine expression of their culture, despite the fact that many of Nova Scotia's inhabitants have to go back six or seven generations to find ancestors who were born in Scotland. In Nova Scotia the culture of the old country is intact.

At Iona in Nova Scotia, Scots Canadians have built a Highland village to commemorate the early settlers. The idea came after a group of Canadians visited the British Empire Exhibition in Glasgow in 1938; but it was not until 1956 that Iona was chosen and authentic reproductions of old log cabins and later types of housing were built in the wooded hills above the village. Iona's Highland Village is not a museum; but a place of living culture. There in the

A child dancer at the Antigonish Highland Games, Nova Scotia. (*Author*)

The Highland Village at Iona in
Nova Scotia.   (*Author*)

summer, the young are taught Gaelic, a language which flourished in remote
Nova Scotia until two world wars and greater social mobility put paid to it.
Until 1945 Nova Scotia published the only Gaelic newspaper outside
Europe. Alan MacEachan, the Deputy Prime Minister of Canada, is a native
of Nova Scotia and was brought up by parents who both spoke Gaelic at
home. The language was not only preserved but it was productive. Nova
Scotia had her own bards who composed some very good Gaelic songs and
poetry. Today in Nova Scotia there is a community perhaps more Scottish
than the Scots at home; but few would ever think of returning to the land of
their forefathers on a permanent basis. Instead, instructors are brought over
from Scotland to St Anne's in Cape Breton, where the Norman MacLeod
first created his religious community. A Gaelic school there runs courses in
the summer months for children from all over North America to learn to
dance and pipe.

Wherever Scots are found abroad there is the same fond pride in the old
country. Duncan MacIntyre, the Deputy Prime Minister of New Zealand,
had a father from the Highlands and a mother who was third-generation
New Zealand but whose family was originally from the Lowlands. Hugh
Templeton, whose family come from the Lowlands of Scotland, is New
Zealand's Minister for Trade and Industry. He is proud to have been
brought up in what he calls 'the Presbyterian belt' of South Island, New
Zealand, where attitudes were 'rigid but good'. Throughout the world the
Scots take just pride in what they feel has been Scotland's unique contribution to the English-speaking world. In 1979, Scots from all over the world
converged on Scotland for the first International Gathering of the Clans,
when chiefs opened up their homes and made the visitors welcome. Cynics
claimed the Gathering was a ruse got up by the Scottish Tourist Board, but
for most overseas visitors who made the journey the motive was genuine.

At home Scots are perhaps more concerned with the increasingly harsh
reality of making a living than with the romance of their past. Since the
Second World War there has been a growing national sense of disillusion-

ment and impotence. Westminster is again seen as the scapegoat and the creation of a British Parliament in 1707 as the frustrator of Scottish aspirations. Scots have come to view policies designed by an English-dominated legislature as handouts or political sops, untailored to their needs. And yet in the last hundred years Scotland has produced more than its fair share of British Prime Ministers. George Hamilton Gordon, 4th Earl of Aberdeen, was Prime Minister between 1852 and 1855. From 1868 William Ewart Gladstone formed three separate ministries and headed the British government for thirteen years. Archibald Primrose, 5th Earl of Rosebery, was Prime Minister from 1894 to 1895 and the 1st Earl of Balfour led the government between 1902 and 1905.

Sir Henry Campbell-Bannerman
(1836–1908).   (*SNPG*)

Sir Henry Campbell-Bannerman, son of a Glasgow draper, succeeded Balfour as Liberal Prime Minister in 1905. Andrew Bonar Law of an Ulster father and Scottish mother was Prime Minister from 1922 to 1923. Ramsay MacDonald from Lossiemouth became Britain's first Labour Prime Minister in 1924, and was again Prime Minister between 1929 and 1935. In more recent years, Harold Macmillan, whose grandfather had been a crofter on Arran, was Prime Minister between 1957 and 1963 and was succeeded by another Scot, Sir Alec Douglas-Home, for the next two years. Scottish Prime Ministers have sprung from all three major parties – Liberal, Conservative and Labour – and in total have held office for over forty of the last 130 years, despite the fact that the Scots account for but a tenth of England's population.

The Scots have found novel ways to protest at the way in which they feel an English-dominated Westminster has ignored them. On Christmas Day 1950 a group of Glasgow University students removed the Stone of Scone from under the Coronation Chair in Westminster Abbey. The English were horrified and newspapers described the act as 'sacrilege'. The police searched for weeks in vain for the stolen Stone and even resorted to calling in a Dutch clairvoyant to help locate it. George VI's health, meanwhile, became a matter of concern and the King had a deep-rooted suspicion that his dynasty would end if his daughter Elizabeth were not crowned on the Stone of Scone. After negotiation, the students agreed to place the Stone in Arbroath Abbey, where the local women kissed it before the police took it away.

Alec Frederick Douglas-Home,
Lord Home of the Hirsel (1903–).
(*STV*)

When it was stolen, the Stone of Scone was in two pieces. Suffragettes before the First World War had thrown a bomb into the Abbey and split it, although the public had never been told. In hiding, the thieves put the Stone together again with copper tubes, and Bertie Gray, the Assessor to the University Court of Glasgow, inserted a message. When Elizabeth was crowned Queen in June 1953, she sat on Bertie's message:

> March 1951. Stone of Destiny. This Stone belongs to Scotland. It was stolen by Edward I of England in 1296. The Church of England should be ashamed to admit that they allowed this piece of stolen property to remain in Westminster Abbey from that time. It must be returned to Scotland for the re-opening of the Scottish Parliament which was never closed but only adjourned in 1707.

On 24 June 1953, Queen Elizabeth paid a state visit to Edinburgh. At St Giles, she accepted the Honours of Scotland – the Crown, sceptre and

William Ewart Gladstone
(1808–98).   (*ACL*)

Archibald Philip Primrose, 5th Earl of
Rosebery (1847–1929).   (*NPG*)

R B Cunninghame-Grahame
(1852–1936), writer and president
of the National Party of Scotland in
1928.   (*SP*)

sword – that bestowed upon her the right to rule the Kingdom of the Scots. She did not wear royal robes for the occasion and the Scots felt slighted: the newspapers were choked with letters of protest. Such sensitivity is a relatively new phenomenon. Although the ancient Royal motto – *Nemo Me Impune Lacessit* – defies people to treat the Scot with impunity, the people of the north acquiesced for a long time after union with England. As North Britons, Scots undermined their own identity and saw their future as a deferential one.

Towards the end of the eighteenth century, however, the sound of protest was again heard. In the years of struggle that led up to the passing of the Reform Bill of 1832, the movement for extending the franchise flourished in Scotland, and was brutally put down by the British government. A Scottish MP, Lord Daer, complained to his friend Earl Grey, the man finally responsible for the 1832 Act. His letter, written on 17 January 1793, sums up the attitude of Scots not only then but now:

> Scotland has long groaned under the chains of England and knows that its connection there has been the cause of its greatest misfortunes . . . we bartered our liberty, and with it our morals, for a little wealth.

Scottish national feeling hardened in the Victorian era, as the affairs of the country were controlled increasingly from Westminster. In 1853, an Association for the Vindication of Scottish Rights was formed to campaign for a Scottish Secretary in the British government and a separate administration for Scottish affairs. On 2 November, the Association held its first public meeting in Edinburgh's Music Hall. The Tory Sheriff of Lanarkshire, Sir Archibald Alison, voiced the feelings of the majority of Scots:

> We do not wish the dissolution of the Union – we do not deny its benefits – we wish to carry out the Union in its true spirit – and we wish to obtain that justice for Scotland which the Union promised, which the English promised, but which we have not yet received.

Parliamentary reform in the 1860s increased Scottish representation at Westminster, and in William Ewart Gladstone, the Scots had one of their own as Prime Minister of Great Britain. But the Liberal Gladstone, however revered in many a Scottish home, did nothing in his first period of office to correct the glaring faults in the government of Scotland, and the 5th Lord Rosebery, later Prime Minister, wrote in anger:

> I confess I think Scotland is as usual treated abominably. Justice for Ireland means everything done for her even to the payment of the natives' debts. Justice to Scotland means insulting neglect. I leave for Scotland next week with the view of blowing up a prison or shooting a policeman.

In 1881 Gladstone made Rosebery Under Secretary of State responsible for Scottish affairs, but answerable to the British Home Secretary; Rosebery found the compromise unworkable and resigned two years later.

The General Election of 1885 brought Lord Salisbury and the Tory Party to power. A Bill was passed creating a Scottish Secretary who was soon given a permanent place in the British Cabinet, and Dover House in Whitehall became the London headquarters of the new Scottish Office. By the end of the century, the Office had powers over the Scottish county councils and burghs, law and order, the Poor Law and education, and had become the real heart of the executive government of Scotland.

In 1894, a Scottish Grand Committee was set up, comprising all the elected MPs for Scotland. In session at Westminster, the Committee had the right to discuss legislation that specifically concerned Scotland. The executive of Scottish government, however, was still London-based and it was not until the Gilmour Committee reported in 1937, that a Scottish Office was set up in Edinburgh. Yet despite having a greater say in how their own part of Britain is run, Scots in the last hundred years have made nationalism a potent political force. A Scottish Home Rule Association was formed in 1886, modelled in large part on the Irish example, and R. B. Cunninghame-Grahame, a London-born Scot and Liberal MP, became the movement's first President. But although the matter of Home Rule for Scotland was brought up in the House of Commons on thirteen separate occasions before the First World War it came to nothing every time.

During the economic depression after the War, nationalism again reared its head. In taxes, the Nationalists argued, Scots were paying out more than they received; but then, as now, with the economies of Scotland and England so intertwined, the facts were impossible to ascertain. In 1919, when a Speaker's Conference took note of pressures on parliamentary time, Home Rulers put forward the case for a federated United Kingdom: Scotland, Ireland and Wales should have their own parliaments subordinate to Westminster. The English, however, objected. Their own brand of nationalism, then as ever, verged on imperialism and would not countenance such a radical change in the British constitution.

After the Irish Treaty of 1921, however, agitation increased in Scotland for a parliament similar to that which the treaty had created for Ulster. George Buchanan, the Socialist MP for Glasgow Gorbals, introduced a Federal Home Rule Bill. He was supported by all the Scottish Labour MPs, and Ramsay MacDonald, the Prime Minister, expressed sympathy for the Bill. Even the Liberal Party promised support; but in face of opposition from the Conservatives MacDonald, the Scot, let the issue drop.

In practical terms, the case for Home Rule was strong. The English MPs at Westminster knew nothing about Scots law. In 1925, for instance, a tribunal that included English MPs was set up to inquire into a Bill to extend Glasgow's city boundaries. Scottish advocates had a field day and it was estimated that the inquiry ultimately cost the public purse over £200,000.

Nationalism, meanwhile, was fanned by a cultural revival. The Scottish literary renaissance of the years between the two World Wars stirred the soul of the nation. The poetry of Hugh MacDiarmid and the prose of Lewis Grassic Gibbon and George Douglas Brown were the re-embodiment of the Scotland of the eighteenth century, of Robert Burns and Sir Walter Scott coupled with the strong appeal that socialism made.

The Labour MP, James Barr, introduced yet another Government of Scotland Bill in 1927. When Barr's Bill was talked out, the National Party of Scotland was created. Scottish industrialists, alarmed by the party's manifesto, warned of the economic dangers of separation from England and in parliamentary elections the National Party made little impact.

In 1932, a small right-wing Scottish Party emerged out of the Cathcart Unionist Association in Glasgow. The group adopted a more moderate

Christopher Murray Grieve, 'Hugh MacDiarmid' (1892–1978), Scotland's most famous modern poet, and ardent nationalist. (*NPG*)

Sir Compton Mackenzie (1883–1973), author, born and educated in England but a staunch Scottish nationalist. (*SNPG*)

Dr Robert McIntyre (1913–).
(*SP*)

Wendy Wood, who died in 1981 at
the age of eighty-eight, publicly burned
emigration papers, raised the Scottish
flag at Stirling Castle and went on
hunger strike in the cause of Scottish
nationalism.   (*S*)

Home Rule programme and won the support of the Duke of Montrose and
Professor Dewar Gibb of Glasgow University. Within two years, the Scottish
Party, purged of its more extreme members, merged with the National Party
of Scotland to form the Scottish National Party. But politically the Nationalists were still weak. In the industrial heartland the voters had taken to the
Labour Party, who also had Home Rule in their manifesto and who were
considered more potent in practical terms. Then, as now, the Scottish
National Party was non-political, apart from their one main aim of Home
Rule. Right and left of the political spectrum were supposed to sacrifice their
views on all other issues until Scotland was free of the shackles of Westminster.

It was not until 1945 that the Scottish National Party scored an electoral
success. Dr Robert McIntyre won Motherwell in a by-election, only to be
booted out by Labour in the General Election three months later. During the
campaign McIntyre's opponent had made specific promises that the first
thing on the socialist agenda would be a Scottish parliament but in 1948 the
Labour government curtly rejected a demand for an inquiry into the case for
devolution of power. The Prime Minister, Clement Attlee, who had claimed
in 1936 that the economic reconstruction of the Scottish economy must be
worked out by the Scots themselves in power, felt there was no need for a
separate Scottish government in the new socialist Britain.

Disillusioned by Labour's reluctance to make their promise of Home
Rule a reality, John MacCormick, a young Glasgow solicitor, founded a
petition, the Scottish Covenant, which two-thirds of the Scottish electorate
signed. But the established Westminster parties scoffed at MacCormick's
success and accused the Covenanters, wrongly, of forgery.

As Britain became more prosperous in the 1950s, support for the
Nationalists waned. John MacCormick, however, continued to keep the
difference between Scotland and England in the headlines. The Queen was
Elizabeth II of England, but Elizabeth I of Scotland. In an attempt to outlaw
the title 'Queen Elizabeth II' in his native land, MacCormick took the issue
to court, along with Ian Hamilton who had been involved in the theft of the
Stone of Destiny. The judges found in favour of the Crown, declaring that
monarchs of Great Britain could call themselves what they liked. Many Scots
were genuinely upset by the arrogance of this exercise of Royal Prerogative.
Pillar boxes in Scotland bearing the insignia EIIR were tarred and blown up
by Wendy Wood's Scottish Patriots and others.

By 1962, the Scottish National Party had about 2000 members. Within
two years membership had risen to 20,000 and the Party could boast
branches throughout Scotland. In the General Election of March 1966,
SNP candidates made remarkable inroads when their popular vote more
than doubled. In three of Scotland's seventy-one parliamentary seats they
came second. The failure of Britain's politicians to solve Scotland's economic ills had given the movement new impetus. In November 1967, in a
by-election at Hamilton the SNP made a spectacular gain. Winnie Ewing
took a seat the Labour Party believed could be held by anyone they cared to
put up. The victory shocked the major political parties.

In 1968, Scottish Conservatives were told by their leader, Edward
Heath, that there should be a moderate devolution of power from Westminster. Two years later, the Scottish Conservative Conference voted nearly

Scottish Covenant

E 990 E

WE, the people of Scotland who subscribe this Engagement, declare our belief that reform in the constitution of our country is necessary to secure good government in accordance with our Scottish traditions and to promote the spiritual and economic welfare of our nation.

WE affirm that the desire for such reform is both deep and wide spread throughout the whole community, transcending all political differences and sectional interests, and we undertake to continue united in purpose for its achievement.

WITH that end in view we solemnly enter into this Covenant whereby we pledge ourselves, in all loyalty to the Crown and within the framework of the United Kingdom, to do everything in our power to secure for Scotland a Parliament with adequate legislative authority in Scottish affairs.

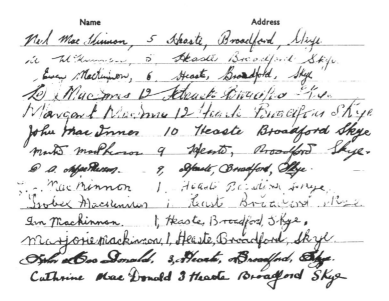

John MacCormick (1904–61) addressing a nationalist rally. The Scottish Covenant. (*SP*) (*NLS, left*)

Lord Kilbrandon (1906–).   (*STV*)

four to one in favour of a report by a Constitutional Committee, chaired by Sir Alec Douglas-Home, which advocated a third Scottish chamber of the United Kingdom Parliament, with 125 directly-elected members.

A Royal Commission, headed by Lord Kilbrandon, reported on the British Constitution in October 1973. The majority of his commission recommended a directly elected legislative assembly for Scotland and that Wales should have an executive assembly. But a minority report, headed by Lord Crowther Hunt, pointed out the inherent danger: would devolution, if put into practice in a meaningful way, be but a short step from the break up of the United Kingdom?

On 8 November 1973, the Scottish Nationalists made another spectacular gain in a by-election when Margo Macdonald took Glasgow Govan from Labour. The Conservatives regarded the victory as of no danger to themselves, believing the Nationalists were gaining ground at the expense of the

(*NLS*)

Labour Party. They were rudely shocked by the results of the General Election in February 1974, when the SNP won seven seats, mainly at the expense of Conservative candidates. The Nationalists polled over a fifth of the Scottish electorate: no political party at Westminster could feel safe.

The campaign had been brilliantly fought by the SNP. In the past the Party had consistently failed to convince the electorate that Scotland could stand alone in economic terms. But now the riches of the deep – oil and natural gas – seemed to answer the question once and for all.

The results of that year's October election shook both major parties. The SNP polled thirty per cent of the vote and won eleven seats. Labour became the largest party; but could only rule with the support of Nationalists, Welsh as well as Scots, and the Liberal Party. In November 1975 a Labour government White Paper offered the Scots a legislative assembly. Under the plan, the new assembly was to be given no major economic powers, but was to operate on a block grant from Westminster. The proposals had a mixed reception. The SNP argued that they did not go far enough and the majority of Labour MPs were either indifferent to the matter or opposed it. When a debate took place in the House of Commons in January 1976, it was obvious that opposition had hardened, and the Labour government went back to the drawing board.

It was not until November 1976 that a new Devolution Bill, thought by many to be no more than a propaganda exercise, was properly debated. The speeches reeked of vintage *Punch*, and both inside and outside the House the word 'devolution' became hated. When the Commons voted, on 22 February 1977, dissident Labour MPs and exasperated Liberals brought about the Bill's defeat. But in order to hold on to office, a pact was agreed between the Labour and Liberal parties which promised a third Devolution Bill.

Under the new Bill the people of Scotland and Wales were to vote on the proposals. When it came to the debate, an émigré Scot, George Cunninghame, MP for a London seat, proposed an amendment requiring the approval of forty per cent of the electorate. He was ably supported by the Labour Member for West Lothian, Tam Dalyell. For forty-seven days the great debate dragged on, parliamentary sessions lasting into the night.

The old Royal High School in Edinburgh, meanwhile, was renovated to house the new assembly at the cost of some £2 million. But on 1 March 1979 not enough Scots voted in favour to meet the required forty per cent. The fortunes of the Scottish National Party waned after the Referendum. In the General Election of May 1979, brought about by SNP MPs withdrawing their support from the Labour government, the Party lost nine of their eleven seats and popular support nearly halved as Scotland swung back to Labour. Now, given the economic recession of the 1980s, there seems a mood abroad in Scotland that Nationalism is an irrelevance. The future of Scotland is in the hands of those who determine the fate of the industrial Western world rather than the elected representatives of the Scottish people.

The Scot, at home, ceased long ago to be the master of his own fate. Since the First World War Scotland's economy has increasingly become a branch factory operation. By the 1930s, a large number of Scottish companies had moved their headquarters to England or become subsidiaries of English firms. The economies of Scotland and England became increasingly

George Cunningham (1931–), the Scots-born Labour MP for south-west Islington at the time of the Devolution Bill. (*STV*)

interdependent and English capital began to play the dominant role. By 1979 only four out of ten Scots in manufacturing industry were working for Scottish controlled companies and the majority of those were small firms employing, on average, seventy-five people.

In the 1950s the Americans moved into the whisky business. In 1950 Seagrams took over the Strathisla distillery and six years later Schenley Industries of New York bought out Seager Evans. Seemingly Scottish names hide foreign owners. Inver House Distillers is owned by Publicker Industries Inc. of Pennsylvania. Clyde Oil Extraction is owned by the East Asiatic Company of Copenhagen. John M. Henderson of Aberdeen is owned by Texan Gulf and Western Industries. Allart Jewellery of Glenrothes is the property of C. Ray Randall Manufacturing of Massachusetts. Scotland is one of the main producers of blue denim jeans. American-owned firms manufacture them. Levi Strauss have five Scottish factories. Blue Apparel have three.

The electronics industry in Scotland now employs more than 42,000 people in more than 270 companies. Today the country boasts the highest concentration of high technology manufacturing in the United Kingdom outside the London-to-Bristol corridor. The Scottish Development Agency, established to promote industrial development in 1975, claim that now more people are employed in electronics than in any two of the three traditional industries of coal, shipbuilding and steel. Since 1975 the industry has grown by eighty-eight per cent; but nearly four out of five Scots in the electronics industry work for American-owned companies, like NCR, IBM, Motorola, Burroughs and Honeywell. The remaining fifth work for English-owned companies like GEC. The new industrial Scotland has been nick-named Silicon Glen. The industry, however, is perilously in the hands of multinationals, who will manufacture their products elsewhere in the world if need be. The Glen may yet be cleared of factories, much as 200 years ago it was cleared of people.

By the 1970s, most of Scotland's proud and independent banks were under English control. In 1982, only government intervention saved the Royal Bank of Scotland from being taken over either by the Standard Chartered Bank or the Hong Kong and Shanghai Bank. The Monopolies and Mergers Commission's objections were illustrative of Scotland's economic problems:

> We accept that in certain cases the comparative economic difficulties of regions such as Scotland have been accentuated by the acquisition of locally-managed and controlled businesses by companies from outside, whether elsewhere in the United Kingdom or overseas. The development of a 'branch economy' creates the danger that it will be the operation in Scotland that is first to be closed or reduced in hard times, while the main business elsewhere is maintained. Further, a local operation, even while it flourishes, will generally be responsible for fewer and less important functions than if it were a wholly independent concern.
>
> We believe that an important factor in Scotland's economic difficulties has been the progressive loss of morale which the taking over of large companies has caused and we accept that this is damaging to Scotland. Entrepreneurial spirit and business leadership depend critically on self-confidence and, on balance we believe such self-confidence has been weakened.

The title page of the first ledger of the Royal Bank of Scotland, founded in 1727 as an offshoot of the company set up to manage the Equivalent.   (RBS)

Many of Scotland's blossoming new industries have already suffered. Nuclear Enterprises of Edinburgh had an outstanding reputation for advanced ultrasonic scanning equipment. EMI took them over and transferred some of the work south. When they ran into difficulty in developing their own scanners Nuclear Enterprises suffered. Now the US Fischer Corporation is attempting to rescue the once Scots firm.

The Glasgow-based Fibreglass Company Limited were taken over by Pilkington and the Scottish factory closed down in 1970. Within months Pilkington opened a big factory in the South with the help of government development grants. In 1951, Albion Motors of Glasgow were bought by Leyland Motors. Since then the Scottish factory has been downgraded to do no more than produce gearboxes and axles. In 1966, the Kilmarnock hydraulic engineers Glenfield and Kennedy were bought by the Crane Corporation of New York. The Scots company had a world-wide reputation for water-handling equipment. By 1977 virtually all orders had been diverted to America and Glenfield was in the hands of the receiver. In many respects the Scots have themselves to blame – they sold out.

Scottish institutions have also found their Scottishness and hence, some would say, their standing threatened by Westminster. Since the reorganization of local government in 1973, Edinburgh has been stripped of much of her status and prestige. The city's various Royal Charters were made defunct and her constitutional identity as a city was abolished. When the Prince of Wales was married in 1981, the Provost of Edinburgh was not invited to attend, as his city was no longer recognized as a capital.

The Kirk, bastion of Scots nationhood since the Union of 1707, has fallen on less religious times. It no longer holds sway over the nation, although it is still a forum for the way Scots think about issues such as nuclear disarmament. The Scottish education system, once the envy of the world, is no longer uniquely Scottish and some would say but a shadow of its former self. Although the able are still provided with opportunity, Scotland has one of the worst records in Europe for young people leaving school at the earliest possible moment with no qualifications whatsoever. In Scotland's universities, Scots professors are now probably outnumbered by English academics. The erosion has happened in a haphazard way rather than through any concerted attack by a Whitehall anxious to make Britain's educational system uniform. Perhaps, like the nation itself, Scotland's education system has lost its way: laurels have been rested upon too long and there is no focus within the country whereby the system can be examined as a whole. The Scots administer their system of education, but take few of the decisions that affect it: Scottish education has become a semi-detached entity within a larger United Kingdom structure.

The Scottish legal system is also under threat, from Whitehall, Brussels and the Hague. Scotland will lose disastrously if this system which grew up and developed quite naturally over hundreds of years and is part of Scottish life and Scottish tradition goes. Some of the worst culprits are MPs, who shout for the law of Scotland to be brought into line with that of England, assuming the sheer desirability of uniformity, which is not necessarily the case. Scotland is saddled in matters of industry and trade, for example, with large departments in Whitehall staffed almost entirely by English lawyers and it is a matter of the greatest difficulty to persuade them that the kind of

The Coat of Arms of the City of Edinburgh.   (CAC)

Since British membership of the EEC, the Scottish Development Agency has called upon community funds to restore some of Glasgow's old tenements.   (SDA)

proposals they put forward are not always suitable for Scotland and may be totally unworkable there.

Socially in Scotland, the spectre of the past is returning. To be fair, the quality of life has improved greatly this century. The grim miners' 'raws' have mostly disappeared and broken-down farm cottages are a thing of the past. Even in the Highlands you would be hard put to find a Black House, but housing remains a major Scottish problem. Despite Glasgow's gargantuan post-war building programme, the city still has slums. Now nobody starves, children have shoes to wear and the unemployed amuse themselves with video recorders purchased with redundancy money; but the deprivation of No Mean Street lives on in a new guise. In Pendeen Crescent in Glasgow, once officially declared the city's most deprived street, four out of five inhabitants able to work were found to be unemployed and over 200 tenants behind in their rent. Vandalism on the estate was costing the council a quarter of a million pounds a year.

Drink is still a curse. Despite the Licensing (Scotland) Act of 1976, which enabled public houses to open the hours they wanted and so cut down the concentrated drinking bouts associated with the old licensing hours, consumption remains high. Two per cent of Scotland's population over the age of fifteen have a serious drink problem and alcoholism is four times higher than in England. In recent years the young have taken to drugs and glue-sniffing: idle, worried minds, deprived of ambition, slowly killing themselves. Sorrow and boredom in search of solace.

East Kilbride in 1947 became Scotland's first 'New Town', an attempt to relieve the social pressures of Scotland's old industrial towns.   (*SDA*)

Health is a useful indicator to the real condition of a people's morale. Scotland still has the highest incidence in the world of death from lung cancer and coronary thrombosis causes more deaths than in any other country. Infant mortality, in a land that gave the world so much in medical knowledge and trained so many doctors, is higher than in England and Wales.

A proud patient is sick, despite comforting noises made at the bedside by government agencies and politicians. Invention was what Scotsmen were once world famous for; now they rely on imported expertise. The profitable oil industry employs a skilled labour force that sees Scotland as home only while oil is to be found there. In May 1981, the Queen officially opened the £1200 million oil terminal at Sullom Voe, the largest of its kind in Europe. Through the terminal upwards of a million and a half barrels a day of oil from the East Shetland basin are processed, half of Britain's needs and worth about £5 million a day to the country's balance of payments. But already there are signs that the oil boom is over. It has been estimated that by 1986 some 2000 people in Shetland could be unemployed.

Emigration, as in the past, is a cure. In 1980 over 2500 Scots emigrated to Canada, over 6000 leaving from Glasgow and Clydebank alone – emigrants to North America, Australia, New Zealand and South Africa who took skills with them and left the land of their birth the poorer. The loss is Britain's, not only Scotland's. Young people with few prospects join the army as their ancestors have done for centuries. The scenario in the twentieth century is the same, only the backdrop has changed.

In Scotland the recession of the 1980s has brought a deep sense of despair and frustration. Politicians have by and large shrugged off nationalism, but it is unlikely to go away. Political opinion now is divided on whether devolution is wise, but few argue it is not possible. Many Nationalists, and curiously some of them are English now living in Scotland, view their cause long-term. They argue that the history of the movement has been one of tides that have risen and fallen, but always left a tidemark a good deal further up the beach. Scotland's present depression might enflame heather that at present only smoulders. Nationalism may prove ultimately to be a moral rather than political issue. A greater degree of independence may be the only thing that can give the Scots back their self-respect and their dignity.

The Chamber of the Scottish Assembly is now used as a courtroom and occasionally hosts Scottish MPs when they come north to meet, the only concession Margaret Thatcher's government has made to Scottish national feeling. The ghosts of Scotland's past may yet conspire to help fill it with Scotland's own government. Scotland's future is uncertain in a way it has not been for many a century. Perhaps, given Scotland's story, the future seems bleak because her people are no longer quite so sure of themselves.

Illustration Acknowledgements

I have tried, wherever possible, to include pictures rarely published. I must thank, first and foremost, the Trustees of the National Galleries of Scotland and their staff who have helped provide nearly a third of the illustrations. I must also thank Harry Moulson and Paul Bonatti of Scottish Television who spent months in galleries and private homes throughout Scotland photographing hundreds of pictures, many of which have not been seen by the general public before. I would also like to thank Mr McNeish of the *Glasgow Herald* who was most helpful in finding illustrations to cover the latter chapters, as were the staff of the Glasgow Chamber of Commerce.

I list below those who have kindly allowed me to reproduce pictures in their care, together with the key used in the book to help the reader identify the source of the pictures used.

National Galleries of Scotland
  (SNPG: Scottish National Portrait Gallery,
  NGS: National Gallery of Scotland,
  HA: Hill-Adamson Collection at SNPG);
City of Edinburgh Museums and Art Galleries (CAC);
National Library of Scotland (NLS);
Peoples Palace (PP);
National Portrait Gallery, London (NPG);
National Museum of Antiquities of Scotland, Edinburgh
  (NMAS);
Glasgow Herald (GH);
Imperial War Museum, London (IWM);
Glasgow Chamber of Commerce (GCC);
British Library (BL);
National Maritime Museum, London (NMM);
National Trust for Scotland, Edinburgh (NTS);
Public Archives of Canada, Ottowa (PAC);
Scottish Gallery, Edinburgh (SG);
Scottish Television (STV);
His Grace the Duke of Atholl (A);
Aberdeen University Library (AU);
His Grace the Duke of Buccleuch and Queensberry
  (BQ);
Scottish Tourist Board, Edinburgh (STB);
Aberdeen Art Gallery (AAG);
Faculty of Advocates, Edinburgh (FA);
Quarrier Homes, Bridge of Weir (Q);
School of Scottish Studies, University of Edinburgh
  (SSS);
British Museum, London (BM);
Colonel Sir Donald Cameron of Lochiel (CL);
Glasgow Museums and Art Galleries (GAG);
Mitchell Library, Glasgow (M);
State Library of New South Wales, Sydney (NSWL);
Otago Early Settlers Association, Dunedin (OESA);

Royal College of Surgeons of Edinburgh (RCS);
Blair's College, Aberdeen (BCA);
Royal Bank of Scotland, Edinburgh (RBS);
Royal College of Physicians, Edinburgh (RCP);
Scottish Development Agency, Glasgow (SDA);
West Highland Museum, Fort William (WHM);
Cape Breton College, Sydney, Nova Scotia, Canada
  (CBC);
His Grace the Duke of Hamilton (H);
Hudson's Bay Company, Winnipeg, Canada (HBC);
Institute of Texan Cultures, San Antonio, Texas (ITC);
Manitoba Archives, Winnipeg, Canada (MA);
Mrs Patricia Maxwell-Scott (MS);
'Operation Drake', Scientific Exploration Society,
  Christopher Sainsbury, Ray Pringle-Scott (OD);
Palace of Westminster, London (PW);
The Scotsman, Edinburgh (S);
Scottish Experience, Edinburgh (SE);
Aberdeen Central Library (ACL);
British Aluminium Company (BA);
Central Press Photos, London (CPP);
Dundee Museums and Galleries (DCAG);
Dunfermline District Council (DDC);
His Grace the Duke of Norfolk (DN);
Fox Photos, London (FP);
Hunterian Art Gallery, University of Glasgow (HAG);
Hatfield House Library, Hertfordshire (HHL);
Hocken Library, Dunedin (HLD);
Jardine Matheson and Company (JM);
McDouall Stuart Museum, Dysart (KMAG);
Keystone Press Agency, London (KP);
The Earl of Elgin and Kincardine (LE);
Merchant Company, Edinburgh (MCE);
The Guardian (MG);
The Earl of Mar and Kellie (MK);

Richard Scollins (RS);
St Andrews University (SAU);
Scottish Development Department, Ancient
    Monuments, Edinburgh (SDD);
Scottish Labour History Society, Edinburgh (SLHS);
Mrs Aedrian Dundas-Bekker, Dr Robert McIntyre,

Mrs M. MacCormick, Mr Raymond Scott (SP);
Stirling Region Archives (SPL);
Scottish National War Memorial, Edinburgh (SWM);
Tate Gallery, London (TG);
Institute of Texas Studies (TS);
Wiggins Teape Group (WT)

Index